The Rural Settlements
of Medieval England

Maurice Beresford
(photograph taken by Philip Rahtz
at Wharram Percy, 1985)

John Hurst
(photograph taken by Philip Rahtz
at Wharram Percy, 1985)

The Rural Settlements of Medieval England

Studies dedicated to
Maurice Beresford and John Hurst

Edited by
Michael Aston, David Austin and
Christopher Dyer

Basil Blackwell

Copyright © Basil Blackwell Ltd 1989

First published 1989

Basil Blackwell Ltd
108 Cowley Road, Oxford, OX4 1JF, UK

Basil Blackwell Inc.
3 Cambridge Centre,
Cambridge, MA 02142, USA

British Library Cataloguing in Publication Data
A CIP catalogue for this book is available from
the British Library

Library of Congress Cataloging in Publication Data
The Rural settlements of medieval England: studies dedicated to M. W. Beresford and J. G. Hurst/edited by Michael Aston, David Austin, and Christopher Dyer.
    p. cm.
    Includes index.
    ISBN 0–631–15903–7
    1. Great Britain – History – Medieval period, 1066–1485. 2. England – Rural conditions. 3. England – Antiquities. 4. Land settlement – England – History.
5. Excavations (Archaeology) – England. 6. Landscape – England – History. 7. England – Historical geography. 8. Beresford, M. W. (Maurice Warwick), 1920– .
9. Hurst, John G., 1927– .
    I. Beresford, M. W. (Maurice Warwick), 1920– .   II. Hurst, John G., 1927– .
    III. Aston, Michael.   IV. Austin, David.   V. Dyer, Christopher, 1944– .
    DA176.R87 1989
    942.03–dc19   88–7622

Typeset in 11/13pt Caslon
by Hope Services, Abingdon
Printed in Great Britain
by Butler & Tanner Ltd, Frome

Contents

CONTENTS

CONTENTS

List of Plates

List of Figures

Abbreviations and Conventions

BAR   British Archaeological Reports
BL   British Library
CBA   Council for British Archaeology
CRO   County Record Office
DMV   Deserted Medieval Village
DMVRG   Deserted Medieval Village Research Group
MSRG   Medieval Settlement Research Group
MVRG   Medieval Village Research Group
OE   Old English
OS   Ordnance Survey
PRO   Public Record Office
RCHM   Royal Commission on Historical Monuments
RO   Record Office
VCH   *Victoria County History*

Note on County Names

Because of the preponderance in some chapters of evidence dating from before
the county re-organization of 1974, some contributors cite pre-1974 county
names, while others use post-1974 boundaries and names. Each is consistent
within its own chapter.

Introduction

Affection and awe are the twin feelings of the apprentice for his good master, and this book is offered in the spirit of those two emotions by some who learnt at least part of their craft in the company of Maurice Beresford and John Hurst. When they came together in the summer of 1952 at the deserted medieval village of Wharram Percy in Yorkshire, there could have been few who might have anticipated the enormous impact of their collaboration on the scholars and the scholarship of such an important part of rural history. Much of their intellectual lifetimes has been spent in studying the physical remains and documentary history of communities the length and breadth of England. Whether as teacher, administrator or coordinator of Wharram, both have also been involved in encouraging a generation to take on the study of settlements once thriving in the middle ages and now lying below green fields or the plough. It is a tribute to their collaboration in these fertile fields that we offer this book to them.

It is not, however, offered to them simply as a hollow crown. They are both, we know, concerned that their immense effort over nearly forty years to create and keep alive a research group interested in the subject of medieval settlement might be wasted, because their successors would not be committed enough to continue in a collaborative way. This book is also partly, therefore, an attempt to reassure them. In doing this, our intention has been to range across the multi-disciplinary subject they did so much to generate, and, by review and by demonstration of new methods and projects, to celebrate not just the past achievements, but also the bright future. So we would regard this work as following on in the tradition of joint and collaborative publication so often the hallmark of the research group John, Maurice and others founded. This book appears almost twenty years after they both edited the final draft of *Deserted Medieval Villages*. Of course, it is not so exhaustive nor so eclectic, but that in itself is the silent tribute to what they have achieved. In the time that has elapsed between one book and another so much has been written, so many archives raided, and so many holes dug and reported in the cause of medieval settlement that it would now take a volume three times the length to do as much as their book did when it finally appeared in 1971.

For those who follow, it might be easy to say that everything was simpler then, when starting a whole new area of enquiry, than it is for us now trying to define where we should go in the future. Looking back it all seems so obvious: all those acres of massive earthworks, all those maps, air photographs and documents which spoke of widespread desertion. Such a rich harvest it seems; how could anyone fail to see it? Yet it is also easy to forget what an effort it is to fight against the entrenched views and presuppositions with which old teachers burden each new generation of thought. Maurice Beresford and John Hurst may have reaped a fine crop, but they needed first to recognize its existence and how extensive it was before setting themselves to the painstaking task of bringing it in. There were at the time plenty of observers who were sceptical or belittled the importance of it all, but those of us who come later must thank them for opening the gate, because there is still much of the harvest to be gathered in.

Perhaps the early lives of both men prepared them well for the coming task. For both there was time in the countryside of the midlands which has proved the seed bed of so much intellectual speculation about the rural development of medieval and modern England. For Maurice these were the north Warwickshire landscapes near Rugby, first the study of ridge and furrow, then the discovery of village sites. His core fascination has been studying maps or mappable landscapes, which have led him to the topographical edge of economic history where there is so much possibility, indeed inevitability, of interface with other disciplines. There is a degree of irony in this because neither he nor John Hurst would admit to being able to draw or even sketch the plans of what they were seeing. If they had, we can suspect that they would not have found the time to see half so much as they did. It was perhaps John who should have had this skill since, after a more peripatetic childhood than Maurice in Cambridgeshire, Leicestershire and Sussex, he read for a degree in prehistoric archaeology from Cambridge in 1951. Practical training in field archaeology and survey, however, did not form part of the syllabus and John himself has recorded how he, and others, began to excavate the moated manor site of Northolt in Middlesex while still undergraduates at Cambridge, 'to train ourselves'.

John and Maurice met at Wharram Percy in 1952 and so began their long association with the site, and their productive study of deserted medieval villages. Maurice Beresford published his first full-length account of the desertion of villages in 1954, *The Lost Villages of England*. In 1971 together they produced *Deserted Medieval Villages*, which summed up the work of the Deserted Medieval Village Research Group in identifying and locating sites, and in analysing and excavating them. After 1971 work on the discovery and verifying of sites continued, which led to the publication of an updated distribution map in 1977. All of the information, arranged by site and county, is kept in the National Monuments Record, where it is now accessible through a computer. Also in the 1970s and 1980s the project at Wharram Percy reached maturity as the work generated a succession of interpretations of village origins and development.

All those who came into contact with Maurice and John felt the influence of their infectious enthusiasm. Naive school boys, amateur fieldworkers and fellow researchers were all welcomed into the new subject and would be encouraged in their work with advice and helpful references. The greatest privilege was to have 'your' site the subject of a 'visit' by one or both. Many of the contributors to this volume were introduced to the study of settlements through direct contact with them. John in his role as Inspector of Ancient Monuments enabled excavation work to be undertaken at a time when it was not particularly fashionable to dig medieval sites. He also ensured that the work of the Group was conducted in an international context through correspondence, lectures and visits. Maurice contributed to the international conference at Munich in 1965, subsequently published as *Villages Désertés et Histoire Economique*.

This is not a conventional *Festschrift*, because it does not include contributions by a full range of the friends and colleagues of the two scholars honoured. Had it done so, it would have run to many volumes. Our purpose in drawing up a list of contributors was to reflect the work of the succeeding generation. We therefore could not include perhaps the most obvious group of authors, that is the contemporaries of Maurice and John with whom they shared their research and ideas. Notable names include Mrs Le Patourel, Dr Thirsk, and Professors Barley, Darby, Jones, Rahtz and St Joseph. Their contribution to medieval settlement studies is reflected in the footnotes to these essays and by the appearance of their students and successors among the contributors. A younger group of scholars has also been excluded. They will have their chance in the next volume of essays to give an account of their contribution to the subject.

There is no uniformity of approach in these studies. We make no apology for this because we wish them to reflect the range of views that are informing research into rural settlements. Our contributors come from many academic backgrounds: archaeology, geography and history, though from different branches of those disciplines. Some contributors are generalizers and some are particularizers, though the difference is not as great as first appears, because even a study of a single village can be used to test a general theory. The authors differ in their chronology: some call the period 400–1066 the 'Anglo-Saxon' or 'Saxon' period and sub-divide it into 'early', 'middle' and 'late'. For them the middle ages extended from 1066 to 1500, divided between an 'early medieval' and 'late medieval' phase. Others regard the middle ages as the period between 400 and 1500, divided into 'early' and 'late' medieval in 1066.

The essays are grouped into three parts reflecting the main subdivisions of the subject: history and geography; fieldwork; and excavation. The last two parts are primarily archaeological in subject matter, reflecting the formidable contribution that archaeologists have made to the subject. The essays reflect recent trends in research methods, which can be summarized as follows:

1   A systematic approach to the collection of data has characterized archaeological work, partly because of the availability of public finance. Almost every county has its sites and monuments record, and many projects have been mounted in parishes and groups of parishes for the survey of earthworks and the collection of pottery and artefacts from ploughsoil. Perhaps this is best represented by work in Northamptonshire, notably at Raunds. Aerial photography, which has long been available as a source of information, has been refined and developed into a powerful research tool. Geographers have rigorously classified and interpreted village plans, exposing regular patterns and suggesting hitherto unsuspected lines of development. Documentary historians are publishing early charters in full and are beginning to make use of the voluminous manorial court rolls, including subjecting them to computer analysis.

2   Our disciplines have been influenced by other academic subjects. Both the social sciences (especially anthropology) and the natural sciences have affected archaeologists and geographers. They provide sophisticated ideas for explaining change in terms of structures, systems and processes, replacing the old simplistic explanations. Our authors can talk of sampling the evidence in a scientific way. Part of the subject has become a science in every sense because pollen and other environmental evidence is being used to reveal the ecological system in which medieval settlements functioned.

3   The combination of documentary and physical evidence, for example in the study of early field systems and late medieval peasant buildings, can give each source of information a new dimension of meaning.

4   Several papers show a concern for the greater preservation of the surviving field evidence in the wake of the great destruction consequent upon developments in modern agriculture.

The essays also reflect some of the new ideas in the interpretation of the settlement evidence:

1   Settlements are not seen in isolation but in their landscape setting, which embraces whole village territories, estates and even regions. Rural landscapes used to be divided simply into three or four types; now we are becoming sensitive to subtle local differences between the *pays*, each with its own pattern of settlement and land use.

2   Our period cannot be viewed in isolation, but in succession to the rural landscapes of the prehistoric and Roman periods and as a predecessor of the modern world. The middle ages thus appear as an episode in a continuous process of change. This has shifted our attention towards the problems of origins and development rather than just of desertion.

3   The former preoccupation with the nucleated village has now been replaced by an appreciation of the variety of settlements, with the result that research has begun to concentrate on isolated farms, hamlets and dispersed settlements. The majority of the medieval population, it should be remembered, did not live in villages, as these were confined to certain regions and in any case only came into existence at a relatively late date.

4   We now realize that simple determinism cannot explain the settlements and landscapes that we observe. Human choice played a major part in the ordering of settlements. Lords and peasant communities made decisions about creating and modifying the places in which they lived and worked.

How will the subject develop in the future? We cannot pretend that we have solved all of the problems; our efforts have done no more than scratch the surface. For example, the whole question of nucleation in the ninth to the twelfth centuries is still not resolved; the mechanics by which dispersed settlements were abandoned, peasant households were grouped at the centre of a territory, and then organized into a planned village, are not known. Still less are we sure why this happened.

So far true multidisciplinary cooperation has not been achieved fully on any research programme, although the Wharram project points in the right direction. The archaeologists have been drawn more towards the historical geographers than towards the historians, but in the long run documentary historians ought to be able to enter into dialogue in a way that has not proved fashionable in recent years. There is still more scope for the involvement of the environmental scientist in adding a new dimension to our undertanding of the changing countryside.

The recent historical research into the composition of the household and into ties of kinship and community, all contributing to our understanding of the demography of the peasantry, ought to be reflected in the study of the archaeological material and especially the house. Another aspect of anthropological perspectives on the medieval past comes from the theoretical archaeologists who stress the importance of interlinked systems, processes of change and such concepts as exchange mechanisms and their relationships to subsistence economies. None of our rural settlements were self-sufficient or existed in isolation – they were embedded in a complex social structure and extensive marketing network.

Our work tends still to be excessively Anglocentric. There is a real need for more awareness of the settlement history of Wales, Scotland and Ireland, which are important in their own right, and by comparison can extend an understanding of the English experience. The prolific work on the continent also needs to be more widely known and appreciated by English students of settlement.

Finally, we should conduct our research against a background of increasing public interest in all aspects of the past. It is important that as many sites as possible are preserved both for academic study and for potential display as monuments open to the public. We have a responsibility to make some sites accessible and to use them to explain the realities of medieval life. An ultimate aim must be to reconstruct a full-size medieval peasant settlement with its fields as a working model for the public to appreciate and as a laboratory to test many of our ideas.

The future development of the subject can only be possible because of the strong foundations laid by Maurice Beresford and John Hurst through their long years of discovery and research. One of the remarkable features of their collaboration has been their adaptability to new ideas. This is shown by the developing interpretation of Wharram Percy, and the gradual evolution of the Deserted Medieval Village Research Group into the Medieval Village Research Group and now the Medieval Settlement Research Group. This collection demonstrates that the work goes on.

Michael Aston
David Austin
Christopher Dyer

PART I

History and Geography

I

Early Medieval Estate and Settlement Patterns: The Documentary Evidence

DELLA HOOKE

INTRODUCTION

The documentary evidence available for the pre-Conquest period provides revealing details of the nature of the countryside and of the type of territorial organization then in force. Although contemporary narrative is not often of a descriptive character, and the law codes are somewhat ambiguous in their references to land units and their exploitation, there are numerous charters and associated documents which cast light upon the demarcation of minor estates and occasionally upon the land use practised within them. Added to this, place names offer a ubiquitous, if somewhat insubstantial, source of evidence which may help to give an initial insight into the nature of the landscape and further hints of settlement and administrative patterns.

ESTATE ORGANIZATION

The territorial divisions of early medieval England have long been the subject of discussion, much of it centring upon the perceived balance between continuity and change: whether patterns and institutions inherited from a Roman or pre-Roman past continued to influence units of government or whether the administrative arrangements of early medieval England were largely a response to measures introduced by the incoming Anglo-Saxons or their descendants. Obviously the balance may have varied across the country, yet the nature of, and the intercommunication between, early societies was such that certain similarities in their response to the exploitation of environmental resources are to be expected. It may, indeed, be queried whether the ethnic

I should like to thank Jean Dowling for retracing the maps. This work arises out of a project funded by the Economic and Social Research Council.

9

origin of the population had a great deal of influence upon the economic and settlement patterns of the countryside.

One common response to the exploitation of environmental resources resulted in the type of 'linked' territory which emerged in regions as far distant from each other as western Britain, the west midlands and Kent – vestiges of it may be detected in other regions as far apart as Wiltshire and Northumbria. Regions of high agricultural exploitation were linked administratively with other less developed regions characterized by much surviving woodland or moorland. Jones has envisaged this system as an ancient form of resource management which is reflected in the early Welsh law codes;[1] Ford and Hooke, examining the west midland evidence, have also suggested that this may have been a relict system which continued to be influential in the formation of Anglo-Saxon administrative units.[2] Ford stresses the possibility that such links perpetuated an initial system of actual transhumance, with stock being moved away from the more heavily cultivated regions to seasonal pastures in the woodland zones. More recently, Everitt has made a detailed study of the Kentish evidence, although apparently seeing the full development of the system as a phenomenon of the early medieval period.[3]

In Kent, Everitt notes the establishment of early 'Jutish' estates in the coastal foothills and the valley region of Holmesdale, and he traces the gradual colonization of the Downland and the Weald from these earliest estate centres. The charter evidence for the use of the *dens* of the Wealden woodlands as swine pastures is unequivocal and is recorded in numerous charters dating from the late seventh century, while droveways connecting the *dens* with their home estates can still be traced across the county. An early eighth-century charter[4] refers to the *Weowerawealde*, which seems to have been 'the wood of the men of Wye', and the *Limenwearawalde*, 'the wood of the men of the Lympne region', while the reference to *ðæm denbærum in limen wero wealdo, 7 in burgh waro uualdo*, 'the swine pastures in the wood of the men of the Lympne region and in the wood of Canterbury',[5] clearly indicates the use of these woodland tracts, most of which have now been identified.[6] In Warwickshire, a similar system linked the Feldon, the open cultivated zone in the south of the county, with the more heavily wooded Arden to the north-west, and although much transhumance

[1] G. R. J. Jones, 'Post-Roman Wales', in *The Agrarian History of England and Wales, A.D. 43–1042, Part II*, ed. H. P. R. Finberg (Cambridge, 1972), pp. 283–382.

[2] W. J. Ford, 'Settlement patterns in the central region of the Warwickshire Avon', in *Medieval Settlement: Continuity and Change*, ed. P. H. Sawyer (London, 1976), pp. 274–94; D. Hooke, 'Village development in the west midlands', in *Medieval Villages: A Review of Current Work*, ed. D. Hooke (Oxford University Committee for Archaeology, monography no. 5, Oxford, 1985), pp. 125–54.

[3] A. Everitt, *Continuity and Colonization: The Evolution of Kentish Settlement* (Leicester, 1986).

[4] P. H. Sawyer, *Anglo-Saxon Charters, an Annotated List and Bibliography* (London, 1968), S 1180; W. de Gray Birch, *Cartularium Saxonicum*, 3 vols and index (London, 1885–99), B 141.

[5] S 125, B 248.

[6] K. P. Witney, *The Jutish Forest: A Study of the Weald of Kent from 450 to 1380 A.D.* (London, 1976).

must have given way at an early stage to the establishment of granges and permanent settlement, the pattern of manorial linkages, ecclesiastical dependencies and hundred subdivisions remained for long a clear indication of an early interrelationship (figure 1.1).

Although such linked territories are less immediately recognizable in southern England, occasional administrative connections hint at a similar arrangement. For instance, two Wiltshire manors near the royal vill of Wilton, Washern and South Newnton, held rights in the woods of Melchet in 1086.[7] Wilton was the administrative centre of the county of Wiltshire and Washern and South Newnton had almost certainly formed part of the original royal holding here, but by 1086 had been granted to the church of Wilton, in whose lordship they then lay. Melchet lay some 25 km away in the south-east of the county and *silva Milcheti* occupied an area of heavy clayland, later to be declared royal forest.[8] If the lost *Frustfield* lay within the parish of Whiteparish, then this estate in Melchet Forest was grouped with South Newnton in a grant of King Edmund in 943.[9] Amesbury, another royal *tūn* situated to the north-east of Wilton in the valley of the river Avon, similarly held rights in the extensive Forest of Chute which lay to the east.[10]

The initial foci of such activities seem often to have been the royal vills, maintaining rights not only over their immediate territories but over these more distant lands. It was these vills which were frequently to emerge as the 'central places' of the Anglo-Saxon estate system.[11] It was at these vills, too, that early minsters were often established, serving their respective territories. For by the seventh century, at least, Anglo-Saxon power had been consolidated into definite kingdoms and within them a pattern of estates and estate-centres can readily be distinguished. In places, the latter may indeed have been established at centres of earlier importance but 'continuity' can rarely be proved – centres in regions of high resource potential may have continued to flourish because of their geographical advantages as much as for their political inheritance. It is at this stage that multiple estates embodying numerous dependent settlements subordinate to the capital centre become prominent. Pearce, examining areas in the south-west peninsula, follows Jones in suggesting that these may have developed from earlier antecedents in this area.[12]

Jones has discussed many such examples taken from various parts of the country. While not one displaying most strongly the features of multiple estate

[7] *Domesday Book* (Record Commission, London, 1783), fo. 68a, 68b.

[8] R. Grant, 'Royal forests', in *VCH Wiltshire*, vol. IV, pp. 391–460.

[9] S 492, B 782.

[10] *VCH Wiltshire*, vol. IV, pp. 424–7.

[11] D. Hooke, 'Territorial organisation in the Anglo-Saxon west midlands', in *Central Places, Archaeology and History*, ed. E. Grant (Sheffield, 1986), pp. 79–93.

[12] S. M. Pearce, 'The early church in the landscape: the evidence from north Devon', *Antiquaries Journal*, 142 (1985), pp. 225–75.

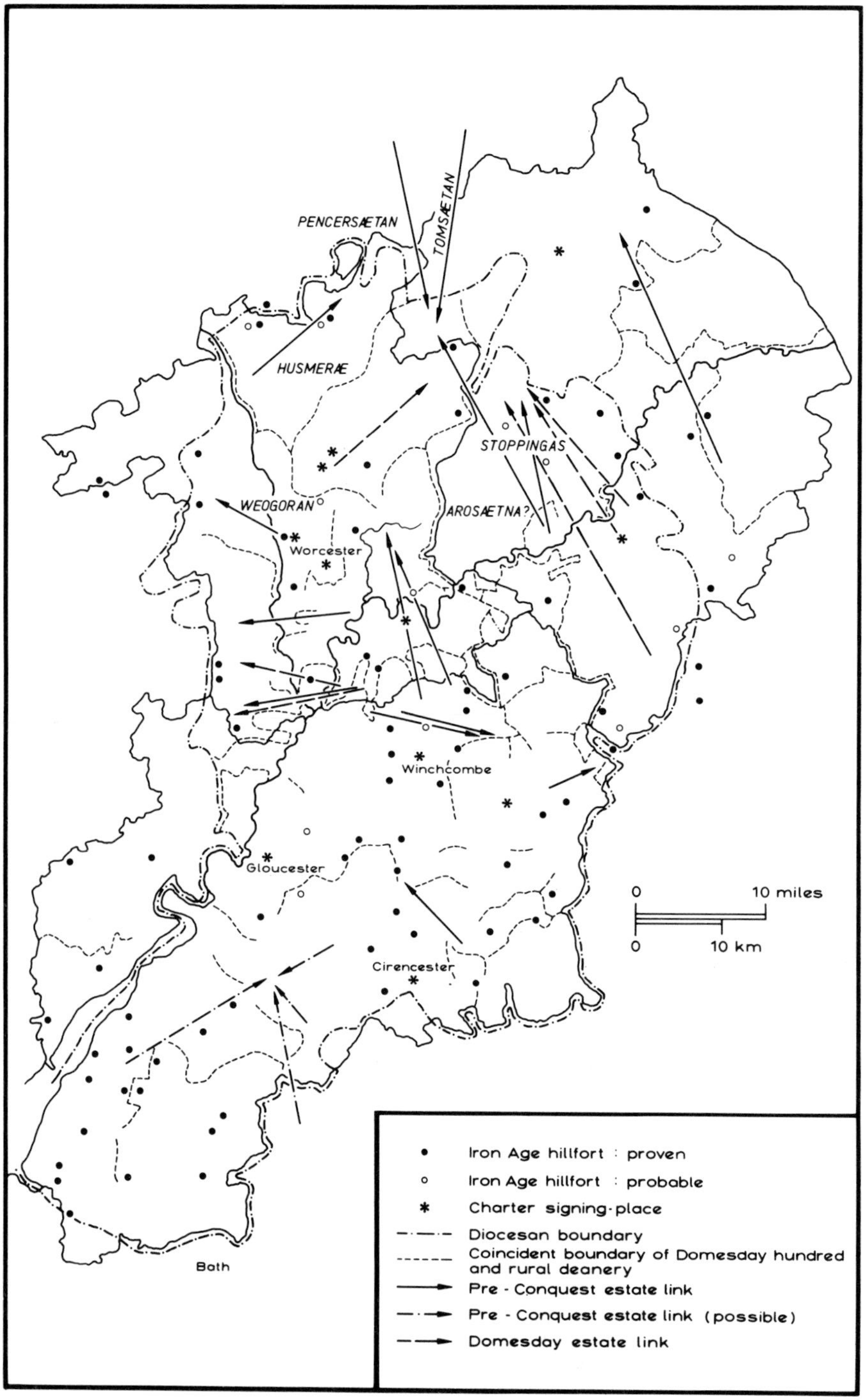
PENCERSÆTAN
TOMSÆTAN
HUSMERÆ
STOPPINGAS
WEOGORAN
AROSÆTNA?
Worcester
Winchcombe
Gloucester
Cirencester
Bath
0
10 miles
0
10 km
Iron Age hillfort : proven
Iron Age hillfort : probable
Charter signing-place
Diocesan boundary
Coincident boundary of Domesday hundred and rural deanery
Pre-Conquest estate link
Pre-Conquest estate link (possible)
Domesday estate link

FIGURE 1.1 *Linked territories in the west midlands in the Anglo-Saxon period.*

origin, Wrockwardine in Shropshire was, for instance, a royal manor in 1086 and the head of a multiple estate containing 7½ berewicks or outlying demesnes which intercommoned with other estates in an area of pastureland known as the Weald Moors. It lies to the north of the Wrekin and, in suggesting Wrockwardine to be the successor to the *Pengwern* of Welsh literary tradition, Jones is strongly arguing for a vestige of British territorial organization behind the administrative patterns of the Borderland estates. One other example, examined in detail by Jones, is Malling in Sussex where the multiple estate structure can be traced back through ninth-century charters.[13] This documentary source reveals similar estate patterns throughout southern and central England, wherever such evidence is available.

One of the constituent vills of Wrockwardine parish was Charlton, 'the *tūn* of the peasants (OE *ceorl*)'.[14] Finberg has noted the special relationship such settlements may have had with the royal estate centre.[15] Settlements with names containing OE *ceorl* (usually compounded with a habitative term) are regularly found within a few kilometres of such a centre and may have been responsible in some way for servicing the royal vill. Again such a relationship is found in the British *maerdref* settlements in which a particularly servile kind of tenure survived into the medieval period.[16] Other place names which suggest interrelationship between holdings, and perhaps a degree of interdependency, are those which refer to the production of a particular commodity or to a specialized function within a wider estate unit. Berewick estates, such as the two near Shrewsbury in Shropshire, incorporating OE *bere*, 'barley', with *wīc*, may have specialized in the production of barley, while the numerous Hardwicks, OE *heorde-wīc*, seem to refer to herding establishments, and another type of *wīc* settlement, giving rise to the name Cheswick, apparently specialized in the production of cheese. Other estates were concerned with the rearing of horses, such as Studley in the Arrow valley of Warwickshire. Mention should also be made of those place names which suggest physical relationships with a land unit. Thus in Shropshire, Aston, 'the east *tūn*', and Uppington, 'the upper *tūn*', appear to be so-named in relation to Wroxeter.[17] Such names are common, especially compounded with OE *tūn*, and Ford has noted that the relationship between Sutton and Brailes in the Warwickshire Feldon appears to be more ancient than the hundred divisions noted in 1086.[18]

---

[13] G. R. J. Jones, 'Continuity despite calamity: the heritage of Celtic territorial organization in England', *Journal of Celtic Studies*, 3 (1981), pp. 1–30; idem, 'Multiple estates and early settlement', in *Medieval Settlement*, ed. Sawyer, pp. 15–40.

[14] D. Hooke, *The Western Margins of Anglo-Saxon Mercia* (University of Birmingham Dept of Geography Occasional Paper, no. 22, 1986).

[15] H. P. R. Finberg, *Lucerna: Studies of some Problems in the Early History of England* (London, 1964), pp. 157–8; H. P. R. Finberg, 'Anglo-Saxon England to 1042', in *Agrarian History of England and Wales, Part II*, ed. Finberg, pp. 385–525, esp. pp. 453–4.

[16] Jones, 'Post-Roman Wales'.

[17] Hooke, *The Western Margins of Anglo-Saxon Mercia*.   [18] Ford, 'Settlement patterns'.

While Jones compares the multiple estates in England with the administrative arrangements noted in the early Welsh laws, he notes the arguments of other historians[19] who 'have cogently demonstrated that the institutions of the Celtic west and the Teutonic east stem from common Indo-European roots';[20] and the Frankish estates discussed by Nitz display many similarities with the English multiple estate of the mid to late Anglo-Saxon period, particularly with regard to the occurrence of functional place names.[21] In Upper Hesse and south Saxony such estates were established as part of a colonizing movement initiated by the Frankish rulers in the eighth and ninth centuries and around each fortified centre lay the various hamlets which served as studs, mill settlements and timber-producing centres.

The Anglo-Saxon period was, however, a period of both estate amalgamation and fragmentation. On the one hand, some estate centres continued to serve as the foci of hundred divisions, their minster churches served surrounding districts or *parochiae*, and some were to acquire additional prominence as fortified *burhs* and as market centres. A number were, indeed, to fulfil a sufficiently diverse number of functions as to become truly urban in character by the end of the pre-Conquest period.[22] Not all towns were to develop at old-established centres, however, for many were deliberately established for various reasons on new sites, while others grew at convenient places as a result of changing social or trading conditions.

In contrast, estate fragmentation appears to have gained momentum in the late Anglo-Saxon period.[23] While many of the land grants recorded in eighth- and ninth-century documents concern units of considerable size and often the major portions of multiple estates, later grants increasingly concern much smaller units of land, often the size of a later ecclesiastical parish or less. Such grants are recorded in a series of written charters, the production of which became necessary when lasting evidence was required of the transfer of rights and privileges.[24] The boundaries of the estates concerned are sometimes described in simple boundary clauses in the eighth century but in succeeding centuries these increase in complexity and in the amount of detail they include, offering a rich source of topographical data for a reconstruction of the late

---

[19] D. A. Binchy, *Celtic and Anglo-Saxon Kingship* (Oxford, 1970); T. M. Charles-Edwards, 'Kinship, status and the origins of the hide', *Past and Present*, 56 (1972), pp. 3–33.

[20] Jones, 'Continuity despite calamity'.

[21] H.-J. Nitz, 'Settlement structures and settlement systems of the Frankish central state in Carolingian and Ottonian times (8th to 10th centuries)', in *Anglo-Saxon Settlements*, ed. D. Hooke (Oxford, 1988), pp. 249–73.

[22] J. Haslam, 'The towns of Wiltshire', in *Anglo-Saxon Towns in Southern England*, ed. J. Haslam (Chichester, 1984), pp. 87–148; D. Hill, 'Towns as structures and functioning communities through time: the development of central places from 600 to 1066', in *Anglo-Saxon Settlements*, ed. Hooke, pp. 197–212.

[23] P. H. Sawyer, *From Roman Britain to Norman England* (London, 1978), pp. 155–6.

[24] F. M. Stenton, *The Latin Charters of the Anglo-Saxon Period* (Oxford, 1955); Sawyer, *From Roman Britain*, p. 175.

Anglo-Saxon landscape.[25] While initially all land rights seem to have been invested in the Crown, many of the earliest charters record privileges granted to the Church, which was soon to acquire vast estates which it began to regard as its own. Lesser men, too, appear to have been donated estates exempt from many of the more onerous duties and taxes and to have been free to bequeath them to their heirs. Such men are recognized in the law codes, their degrees of prosperity varying with their rank, the status of their lord and the size of their holdings.[26]

Estate demarcation coincided with the development of parishes in the Anglo-Saxon Church. As churches were established upon the estates of local lords, especially in the tenth and eleventh centuries, they began to appropriate some of the duties and benefits initially appendant to the mother church or minster of the locality. In terms of ecclesiastical territorial organization the minster *parochiae* became subdivided.[27] Consequently much of the estate pattern of early medieval England was to become fossilized in the boundaries of the ecclesiastical parishes as new churches were founded. Parish size was not uniform across the country and the minsters themselves often maintained nearby land endowments of considerable size under their own direct control. Conversely, parishes were also large in little developed regions, where presumably populations were small and resources were too limited to provide sufficient tithe to the church from limited areas (figure 1.2). Although many regions were well supplied with subsidiary churches by the time of the Conquest, many of which had become mother churches in their own right, the process of parish demarcation was not completed until the twelfth or thirteenth centuries in some more remote regions.

The parish was not, however, the smallest unit of administration in late Anglo-Saxon England, for most present-day parishes can be shown to have been made up of a number of individual townships, each regarded as a separate community in its own right. In many areas these units seem to have been in existence before the ecclesiastical parishes, as such, were firmly demarcated and in prosperous regions were themselves to constitute small parishes[28] (figure 1.2). Many of them can be identified as the estates which were the subject of charter grants in the ninth and succeeding centuries (a grant of one such unit, *Australis Heþfeld*, identified as the southern part of Hatfield in Norton juxta Kempsey, Worcestershire,[29] was already leased in 892 *cum antiquis terminibus,*

---

[25] D. Hooke, *Anglo-Saxon Landscapes of the West Midlands: The Charter Evidence* (BAR, British ser., 95, 1981); D. Hooke, *The Anglo-Saxon Landscape: The Kingdom of the Hwicce* (Manchester, 1985).

[26] F. Liebermann, *Die Gesetze der Angelsachsen* (Leipzig, 1903), vol. I, p. 456; F. M. Stenton, *Anglo-Saxon England*, 3rd edn (Oxford, 1971), pp. 488–91.

[27] J. Blair, 'Secular minster churches in Domesday Book', in *Domesday Book: A Reassessment*, ed. P. H. Sawyer (London, 1985), pp. 104–42.

[28] Hooke, *Anglo-Saxon Landscapes of the West Midlands*; idem, 'Pre-Conquest estates in the west midlands: preliminary thoughts', *Journal of Historical Geography*, 8 (1982), pp. 227–44.

[29] E. Ekwall, *The Concise Oxford Dictionary of English Place-Names*, 4th edn (Oxford, 1960), p. 224.

'with the ancient boundaries').[30] Central and southern England, at least, appears to have been an area in which the multi-township parish was to predominate. That they were already communities in the Anglo-Saxon period is shown by occasional reference to their inhabitants in charter grants. Thus, in Inkberrow (*Intanbeorgas*) in north Worcestershire (figure 1.2), the people of the sub-unit of Thorne (*Þordune*), the *þornhæma*, 'the people of Thorne', are recorded as holding twelve acres of land (probably arable) *on incsetena lande*, 'of the land of the people of Inkberrow', the main parish, in 963,[31] the terms *hæme* and *sæte* clearly referring to the inhabitants of each estate.

Much work remains to be done upon estate structure. In some regions a planned subdivision of land appears to have taken place by the tenth century – some would suggest as early as the seventh century.[32] Others have even postulated Romano-British estate divisions underlying later parish units.[33] It can be shown, however, that in parts of eastern and southern England, at least, parish boundaries bore little relation to field systems in use in the Roman period.[34] In many areas estate fragmentation seems to have been a late and more gradual process. If settlements within multiple estates had ever been involved with specialist functions, as their names sometimes suggest, then the trend towards fragmentation destroyed their interdependence. No longer could the 'barley farms', the 'rye farms' or the 'herding *wīcs*' concentrate upon their particular activities, and no longer could the *ceorl tūns* retain their special relationship with estate centres, for in late Anglo-Saxon England manors had come into being:[35] their individual lords were at pains to achieve economic returns from their estates, both to maintain their own needs, and to meet the demands of the Church and military organization; each land unit had to support its own lord and community, however large or small the latter might be. By the Norman Conquest the foundation of the medieval manorial system had already been established.

Place names may be considered in the light of estate composition. Gelling has drawn attention to the fact that many known estate centres bear names of topographical type, continuing an ancient naming tradition.[36] One of the

---

[30] S 1416, B 570.

[31] S 1305, B 1110.

[32] P. T. Unwin, 'Towards a model of Anglo-Scandinavian rural settlement in England', in *Anglo-Saxon Settlements*, ed. Hooke, pp. 77–98; A. Goodier, 'The formation of boundaries in Anglo-Saxon England, a statistical study', *Medieval Archaeology*, 28 (1984), pp. 1–21.

[33] C. C. Taylor, *Dorset* (London, 1970), pp. 41–83.

[34] P. T. H. Unwin, 'Townships and early fields in north Nottinghamshire', *Journal of Historical Geography*, 9 (1983), pp. 341–6; D. Hooke, 'Regional variation in southern and central England in the Anglo-Saxon period and its relationship to land units and settlement', in *Anglo-Saxon Settlements*, ed. Hooke, pp. 123–51.

[35] T. H. Aston, 'The origins of the manor in England', *Transactions of the Royal Historical Society*, 5th ser., 8 (1958), pp. 59–83; T. H. Aston, 'A postscript', in *Social Relations and Ideas: Essays in Honour of R. H. Hilton*, ed. T. H. Aston, P. R. Coss, C. Dyer and J. Thirsk (Cambridge, 1983), pp. 26–43.

[36] M. Gelling, *Signposts to the Past: Place-Names and the History of England* (London, 1978), pp. 122–5.

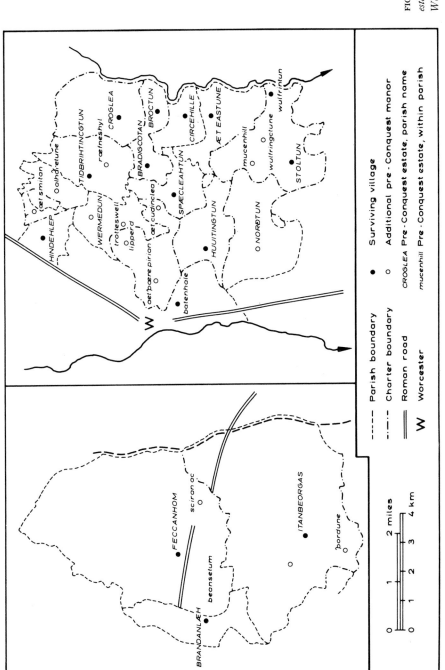

FIGURE 1.2 *Anglo-Saxon estates and parishes in Worcestershire.*

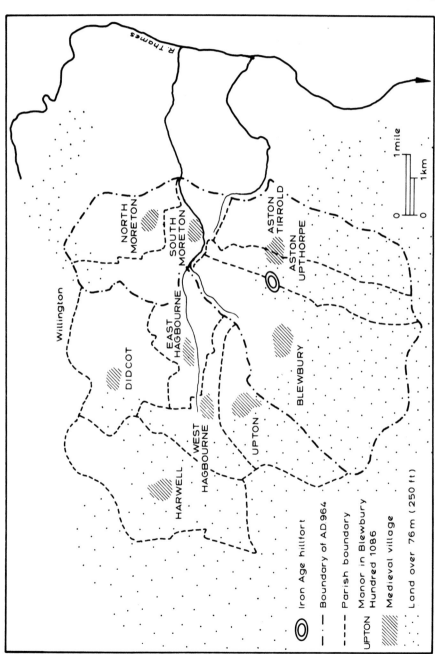

FIGURE 1.3 *The pre-Conquest estate of Blewbury, Berkshire.*

R Thames

WILLINGTON

DIDCOT

NORTH
MORETON

SOUTH
MORETON

EAST
HAGBOURNE

WEST
HAGBOURNE

HARWELL

UPTON

BLEWBURY

ASTON
TIRROLD

ASTON
UPTHORPE

Iron Age hillfort
Boundary of AD 964
Parish boundary
UPTON Manor in Blewbury Hundred 1086
Medieval village
Land over 76m (250 ft)

1 mile
1 km
0   0

examples cited is that of Blewbury, a great pre-Conquest estate in east Berkshire. This estate of 100 hides was granted by King Edmund to Bishop Ælfric of Ramsbury in 944[37] and its name is of the 'topographical-archaeological, type, referring to the iron age hillfort which lay centrally placed within it (figure 1.3). Divisions of the estate, however, included units bearing the parish names North Moreton, South Moreton, Aston Upthorpe and Aston Tirrold, in addition to that of Blewbury itself – all bearing names containing the habitative term *tūn*. Cox has shown how the *tūn* element came into more frequent use after the middle of the eighth century,[38] just as estate fragmentation was apparently taking place.[39] The term is often compounded with a personal name and studies[40] have shown how this was often related to estate ownership. Thus Tredington in Warwickshire seems to have taken the name of the thegn Tyrdda who held the estate prior to 757, while Woolstone, *Olvicestone*, in Oxfordshire, acquired the name of the lord Wulfric who only acquired the two adjacent estates of *Æscesbyrig* in 944 and 958 respectively.[41] Similar examples abound in which settlements bearing *tūn* names seem originally to have been only part of a once larger unit, and the numerous 'east', 'west', 'north' and 'south' *tūn*s (today's Astons, Westons, Nortons and Suttons), discussed earlier, provide additional examples.

One other small land unit appears in several charters and in place names – this is the *hīd*, 'the hide'. This has been interpreted as originally defining the amount of land necessary to support one free family with its dependents and it was an assessment of land (but not necessarily of area) in use in the earliest Anglo-Saxon documents.[42] Increasingly, the hide seems to have been regarded as the smallest viable unit for an individual holding (although some had become even further fragmented by 1086), referring by later Anglo-Saxon times to particular holdings which formed specific parts of larger estates, apparently held as compact units. The *ciric hide*, 'the church hide' (that is, 'the hide belonging to the church') of Wotton under Edge, Gloucestershire, occurs as a boundary landmark in a mid-tenth-century charter[43] which shows that it lay in the north-eastern sector of the parish, taking in the crest of the Cotswold escarpment. The term frequently occurs in late-recorded place names, often applied to holdings with such names as 'Hyde Farm', and occurs throughout southern England. A term *hiwisc* is found in the charters and place names of south-western England and is a derivative of *hiw-*, 'family', used in exactly the

---

[37] S 496, B 801.

[38] B. Cox, 'The place-names of the earliest English records', *Journal of the English Place-Name Society*, 8 (1975–6), pp. 12–66.

[39] Hooke, 'Village development', p. 134.

[40] Gelling, *Signposts*, pp. 177–8.

[41] S 503, B 796; S 575, B 902; Gelling, *Signposts*, pp. 180–1.

[42] For a discussion of the type of nuclear family suggested, see Charles-Edwards, 'Kinship, status and the origins of the hide'.

[43] S 467, B 764.

same sense as *hīd*. Upon the basis of later identified holdings, Costen suggests that the *hiwisc* was a self-contained unit of a 'pioneering' nature established in little-developed regions, the size of the *hiwisc* varying according to the quality of the land available, from *c*.80–90 hectares in areas of good quality soils to more than 500 hectares in Rodhuish in Carhampton, located at the foot of the Brendon Hills on the north-eastern fringes of Exmoor.[44]

PATTERNS OF FARMING AND SETTLEMENT

As changes took place in estate demarcation, more tangible changes occurred in many parts of England in farming practices and settlement patterns. An early form of open-field agriculture seems to have developed by the ninth and tenth centuries and to have been associated with increasing settlement nucleation. Open-field farming, in which villagers held unenclosed strips of arable scattered throughout a number of large fields surrounding the village settlement, probably did not reach its full development until the twelfth or thirteenth century.[45] Pasturage of domestic stock on the stubble, fallow and remaining common pasture was also strictly regulated, but regional variations in the system as practised across the country were marked. The strongest documentary evidence for the practice of open-field agriculture in the pre-Conquest period comes from the charters of southern and central England, but archaeological field evidence shows that strip farming was also widespread throughout eastern England where few charters have survived. Yet open fields did not become dominant throughout all these regions, developing only to their maximum extent in areas which were already cleared, with a substantial peasant population already engaged in cultivation.

The documentary evidence has been analysed by Finberg and others and it is largely tenth-century charters which refer to common arable lying in scattered strips.[46] Thus a charter of 963[47] shows that land of three hides at Avon in Wiltshire consisted of *singulis jugeribus mixtum in communi rure huc illacque dispersis*, 'single acres dispersed in a mixture here and there in common land', while the land at Ardington, Berkshire (now taken into Oxfordshire), in 961 lay *on ge mang oþran ge dal lande*, 'among other sharelands'.[48] The earliest

---

[44] M. Costen, '*Huish* and *worth*: Old English survivals in a later landscape', *Anglo-Saxon Studies in Archaeology and History*, ed. D. Brown, J. Campbell and S. Chadwick-Hawkes, no. 5 (Oxford, forthcoming).

[45] H. S. A. Fox, 'Approaches to the adoption of the Midland system', in *The Origins of Open-Field Agriculture*, ed. T. Rowley (London, 1981), pp. 64–111.

[46] Finberg, 'Anglo-Saxon England to 1042', pp. 483–506; and see, for example, D. Hooke, 'Open-field agriculture – the evidence from the pre-Conquest charters of the west midlands', in *The Origins of Open-Field Agriculture*, ed. Rowley, pp. 39–63.

[47] S 719, B 1120.

[48] S 691, B 1079.

reference to *gemænan lande*, 'common lands', occurs in a mid-ninth-century charter of Cofton Hackett in north Worcestershire, dating from 849,[49] but there is no proof that this directly referred to arable land, for the Ardington charter explicitly states that *feld læs gemane 7 mæda ge mane 7 yrþ land gemæne*, 'open pasture [is] common and meadowland [is] common and ploughland [is] common', and other west midland charters show that meadowland and woodland had been brought into the system, with rights in these other resources apparently proportional to shares in the arable.[50]

One should, however, perhaps distinguish between resources which were held in common by the members of one land unit and those which belonged to several townships. The charter of Thorne, the estate within Inkberrow parish in north Worcestershire, speaks of the shared arable land and by 811 meadowland in Tibberton, Worcestershire, was also held by the inhabitants of Bredicot, the adjacent estate to the south.[51] Such arrangements may on occasions have been made as fragmentation took place within a multiple estate,[52] but could, no doubt, be copied within the amalgamated estate holdings of the later Anglo-Saxon period if resources upon a particular estate were scarce or if financial benefit might accrue.

The open fields in the midlands and southern England seem to have developed in association with the individual township community. In many areas, the fields extended over only part of each township area, with pastureland, meadowland and woodland lying beyond. Thus, a study of the charter evidence available for the Wylye valley of Wiltshire and the vale of the White Horse in Oxfordshire shows that in both of these regions open fields had been established before the Conquest but extended only over the lower slopes of the chalk escarpment and over the fertile region on the edge of the clay vale below, where the chalk was intermixed with the clay. Above, the higher chalklands which had been cultivated in the preceding Roman period had been abandoned, left to revert either to pasture or, in the case of the Wylye valley, to pasture and woodland (figure 1.4).[53] In the Avon valley of Warwickshire, too, an area of intensive cultivation already in late iron age and Roman times, enclosed crofts seem to have lain near township margins beyond the open fields, as shown by the boundary clauses of Bishopton in Old Stratford and Longdon in Tredington,[54] suggesting that the latter had not reached their maximum extent by the time of the Conquest.[55]

---

[49] S 1272, B 455 (1).

[50] S 1373, K 680.

[51] S 1369, K 683.

[52] D. Hooke, 'Early forms of open-field agriculture in England', *Proceedings of the Stockholm Symposium of the Permanent European Conference for the Study of the Rural Landscape*, ed. U. Sporrong (Stockholm, forthcoming).

[53] Hooke, 'Regional variation'.

[54] S 1388, K 724; S 1321, B 1243.

[55] Hooke, 'Village development', p. 135.

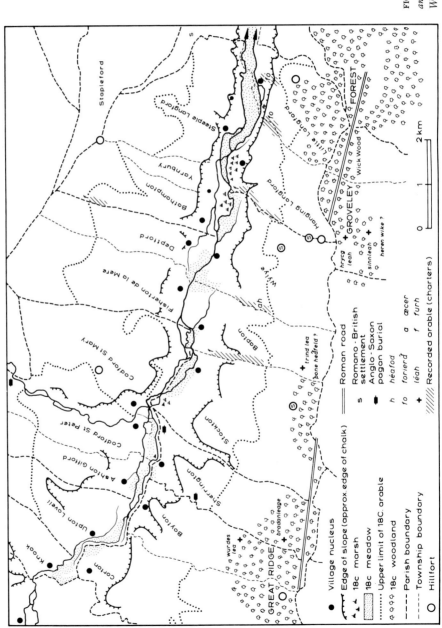

FIGURE 1.4 *Estate patterns and land use in the Wylye valley, Wiltshire.*

The layout of the open fields in many regions, although it cannot yet be dated, seems to have been a feature of late Anglo-Saxon times, for where early Anglo-Saxon settlements can be located from pottery scatters, as in eastern England, these seem to have been as dispersed as the Roman farmsteads before them.[56] Clustering may already have taken place at preferred locations, as in Roman times, but nucleation of settlement does not seem to have been an over-riding characteristic of the landscape at that stage. As the fields were laid out or re-organized, however, many outlying farmsteads seem to have been abandoned beneath them, their occupants presumably being drawn into a more centrally placed location. As an individual manorial centre developed under a local lord, with a church often being established near by, so the focal nature of the settlement was enhanced. The process was not, however, instant or final, and settlement in all areas remained prone to shift and relocation if circumstances altered.[57]

Although charter coverage is absent from many regions and limited in its nature for others, in some regions settlements beside boundaries are noted, with a tendency for these to increase in number westwards across the country. The vale of Evesham in south-east Worcestershire, for instance, one of the most intensively settled and cultivated zones of Roman Britain, was to remain a prominent corn-growing region at the time of the Domesday survey and throughout the medieval period. By later medieval times the region was characterized by strongly nucleated village settlement and regular midland open-field systems usually extending over most of each parish or township area. The Evesham boundary clauses, however, themselves of late compilation, refer to several settlements located near parish boundaries, none of which have survived. *Poticot*, alias *Potintun*, lay in the southern section of Bengeworth parish beside a Roman road known as the *fyrd stræt*, and *bunewyrðe*, 'Buna's ?farmstead', lay a short distance from the Roman Ryknield Street in South Littleton parish. Near the boundary of Elmley Castle, a little further to the west, *Byrdingcwīcan* (OE *wīc* with a personal name), was a dairying settlement on the slopes of Bredon Hill.[58] In the west midlands, many settlement sites can be shown by pottery scatters to have been occupied in Roman times and some of these minor settlements may represent surviving earlier farmsteads, although this has not yet been confirmed in any of the cases cited. In general, however, boundary settlement is a marked characteristic of more pastoral regions, regions in which open-field farming did not reach its full development.

Both charter and place-name evidence suggest that a scattered settlement pattern continued to be a characteristic of pastoral regions, as verified by the documentary and cartographic evidence of later periods. Individual settlements

---

[56] C. C. Taylor, *Village and Farmstead: A History of Rural Settlement in England* (London, 1983), pp. 109–24.

[57] Ibid.

[58] Hooke, 'Village development', pp. 135–6.

may have been small and numbers of them were usually included in any parish area. Many of them bore names containing the habitative term *worð*, such as the boundary settlement Lindsworth in King's Norton, *wynes wyrðe* in Tanworth, Warwickshire, or *cybles weorðiges* in Cofton Hackett, Worcestershire (table 1.1), while Cofton itself was described as a *hām-stall*, 'a homestead'. The Cofton charter[59] refers to two *ærn* settlements, possibly indicating functional buildings associated with some trade. In northern Hampshire the term *stede*, referred to in boundary locations in the wooded region to the north of the Meon valley estates, also seems to have referred to herding establishments.[60] *Worð* settlements noted in charters increase in number south-westwards and are a common feature of the counties of Somerset and Devon, where a dispersed settlement pattern remained characteristic of many regions in later centuries.

Outlying settlements bearing *wīc* place names seem to have been associated with dairying activities in areas rich in meadowland, some of them becoming township communities in their own right with their own field systems, such as Balking in the Ock valley of Oxfordshire, described in a tenth-century charter as a 'herding *wīc*' with its own meadowland and 'acres' of ploughland.[61]

Certain types of place name seem to have been consistently associated with minor settlement. No hard and fast rules can be implemented and there are always exceptions, but in general most *worð* settlements failed to become major parish centres. The term denotes 'enclosure' but Ine's law stating that *ceorles worðig sceal beon wintres 7 sumeres betyned*, 'a commoner's premises shall be fenced both winter and summer',[62] suggests that the *worð* enclosure was associated with a settlement or farmstead. The Worcestershire charters also show the term being used to denote actual farmsteads with their enclosed crofts and fields.[63] Because of the connection with enclosure, occasionally even major centres such as Tamworth, which was to become a royal centre of Mercia, bear such a name. In general the term seems to have come into widespread usage only after the mid-eighth century[64] and to have been common in woodland areas. As a west midland place name element, it is commonest in the wooded region of the Warwickshire Arden and along the Cotswold scarp and in the Severn valley region of Gloucestershire but occurs chiefly as a minor place name in charters in Worcestershire (table 1.1). A number of the Worcestershire *worð* boundary landmarks became later medieval farms or hamlets, as at Lindsworth in King's Norton and *wiððan worðing*, 'Wythall', but others such as *cinilde wyrðe/cynelde worþe* on the boundary of Cudley and

---

[59] S 1272, B 455 (1).
[60] K. I. Sandred, *English Place-Names in-stead* (Uppsala, 1963).
[61] S 713, B 1121.
[62] F. L. Attenborough, *The Laws of the Earliest English Kings* (Cambridge, 1922), p. 49; Ine c. 40.
[63] Hooke, 'Village development'.
[64] Cox, 'The place-names of the earliest English records'.

TABLE I.I *The incidence of* worð *and related terms as boundary landmarks in the pre-Conquest charters of central and southern England*

County	Feature	Sawyer no.[a]	Estate name
Warwickshire	wynes wyrðe	S 79	Oldberrow
Worcestershire	wiððan weorðing	S 1272	'Cofton'
	cybles weorðiges	S 1272	'Cofton'
	lindwyrðe	S 64	King's Norton
	cinilde wyrðe	S 1361	Whittington
	cynelde weorþe	S 1329	Cudley
	bunewyrðe	S 1599	Evesham lands
	cumbran weorðe	S 786	Chaceley
Gloucestershire	cumbre weorþan	S 1551	Deerhurst
	bydanwyrth	S 553	Pucklechurch
Berkshire	dunan wyrþe	S 542	Stanmore, Beedon
	baggan wurðe	S 614	Kennington
	beganwyrðe	S 605	'Abingdon'
	ryge wyrðæ	S 605	'Abingdon'
	ecgunes wyrðæ	S 605	'Abingdon'
	ecgunes wyrðe	S 567	'Abingdon'
	sunemannes wyrðige	S 713	Kingston Lisle
Wiltshire	witan wyrþe	S 229	'Downton'
	wytan wyrðe	S 891	'Downton'
	pytan wyrðe	S 540	'Downton'
	hiceles wyrþe	S 229	'Downton'
	hiceles wyrðe	S 540	'Downton'
	hiceles wyrðe	S 891	'Downton'
	hyceles wyrðe	S 275	'Downton'
	ða ealdan wyrðe	S 881	Fovant
	attenwrðe	S 899	Bradford-on-Avon
	chelewrthe	S 1577	'Brokenborough'
	chelworþe	S 1579	'Brokenborough'
	pleieswrthe	S 1577	'Brokenborough'
	hanan wurðe	S 364	Fovant
	wrthwelane	S 1579	Chelworth
	luddes worþe	S 1583	Grittenham
	wendenes wyrðe	S 1581	Downton
Hampshire	hremres wyrðe	S 412	Ecchinswell
	aeþeles wyrðe	S 412	Ecchinswell
	ealdan wyrðe	S 412	Ecchinswell
	worðige	S 376	Chilcomb
	wulfredes wyrð	S 1007	Hinton Ampner
	wulfreðes wyrðe	S 693	Kilmeston
Dorset	beteswirþe sled	S 419	Fontmell
	heldmannes wrthe	S 419	Fontmell
	ealdmannes wyrde /wyrþe	S 445	Orchard
	ealdmannes wrthe	S 710	Orchard
	ealdmannes wyerðe	S 656	Thornton, Marnhull
	wænecan wyrð	S 969	Hornton

[a] P. H. Sawyer, *Anglo-Saxon Charters, an Annotated List and Bibliography* (London, 1968).

Whittington near Worcester have left little trace. Of the Worcestershire charter *worð* settlements, five out of six lay in regions known to have been wooded in Anglo-Saxon times (*bunewyrðe* to the south of Evesham is the exception) and four out of five of those recorded in Berkshire. Of the latter, three lay in the wooded region which lay to the north of Abingdon, one at a site occupied in the Roman period.[65] The exception in the latter county is *sunemannes wyrðige* in Kingston Lisle (now in Oxfordshire), where the *worðig* may have been the early name for Kingston Lisle itself, a minor centre within a multi-township parish.[66] The distribution of this term suggests that its use inferred a particular type or size of settlement which was abundant in regions of scattered farmsteads. Costen finds *worð* names in Somerset to be widely distributed throughout the county, concluding that they represented survivals of an agricultural arrangement which was older than the open-field system.[67] While *wīc*, too, is not restricted to the more 'ancient' zones, it shows a close correlation with areas rich in pastureland and meadowland which was used for pastoral purposes, areas in which the open-field system of farming was a later or less influential development.

Another term which was rarely used for major settlements is *cot*, meaning 'cottage'. Although many settlements bearing *cot* names became township centres, the term was also commonly used for boundary settlements. It occurs in all types of countryside and in the west midlands has been found to be common in early-settled regions for small township communities.[68] Dyer has noted its presence near urban centres where cottars farming holdings smaller than those of most villeins presumably lived primarily by marketing and trade, and this is confirmed by the Worcestershire charter evidence.[69]

While place names are a valuable source of evidence, they are not a reliable guide to the form or location of individual settlements. Settlements can and do shift their locations with changing economic and environmental conditions[70] and accepted place names may move with them. Numerous ford place names, for instance, are now attached to villages sited at more elevated positions some way distant from an actual river crossing; this could arise from the attachment of an estate name to an actual settlement within that estate or to movement upwards from a low-lying position. Frequently, too, a district name will become attached to one or more settlements in the locality (the various Claydons in Leicestershire, discussed by Gelling,[71] could be reinterpreted in this way),

---

[65] Hooke, 'Regional variation'.

[66] D. Hooke, 'Anglo-Saxon estates in the Vale of the White Horse', *Oxoniensia*, 52 (1987), pp. 129–43.

[67] Costen, '*Huish* and *worth*'.

[68] Hooke, *Anglo-Saxon Landscapes of the West Midlands*.

[69] C. Dyer, 'Towns and cottages in eleventh-century England', in *Studies in Medieval History Presented to R. H. C. Davis*, ed. H. Mayr-Harting and R. I. Moore (London, 1985), pp. 91–106; Hooke, *Anglo-Saxon Landscapes of the West Midlands*, p. 293, fig. 3.39.

[70] Taylor, *Village and Farmstead*.

[71] M. Gelling, *Place-Names in the Landscape* (London, 1984).

so that the name of an individual settlement may ultimately bear little relationship to its immediate location. However, some habitation place names, in particular, definitely suggest actual buildings. OE *cot* means 'cottage' and *ærn* 'a building', while both OE *tūn* and *worð* indicate some form of enclosure,[72] but few can be directly offered as evidence of *village* settlement. Certainly the *tūn* of Daylesford, Gloucestershire, seems to have been a nucleated settlement, for the bounds run *be westan tūne*, 'to the west of the *tūn*', and later return *be Suðantūne*, 'to the south of the *tūn*',[73] close to the present village, and *tūn* became a popular name-forming element at the time settlement was becoming increasingly nucleated; but there is little early documentary evidence which helps with the recognition of settlement form.

There is an increasing amount of archaeological evidence, especially from eastern England, which suggests that a dispersed pattern was being supplanted by increasing nucleation in middle and later Anglo-Saxon times, but the process seems to have been far from complete by the time of the Norman Conquest. Aston quotes the 'Sevenhampton' names of Somerset as indicative of groups of dispersed farmsteads or hamlets, some of which cannot be identified today.[74] The incidence of boundary settlement, even in regions later characterized by a strongly nucleated pattern, has already been discussed, but the evidence of the Domesday survey may also be interpreted as an indication of incomplete nucleation.

THE EVIDENCE OF THE DOMESDAY SURVEY

The Domesday survey is not a reliable guide to settlement for it is quite clear that numerous individual settlements and farmsteads could be entered under the name of one vill. In Tredington, Warwickshire, for instance, the estates noted in pre-Conquest charters are not mentioned in the Domesday survey although they were clearly established by that date (figure 1.5). These include Armscote, Newbold and Talton, but only Longdon and Blackwell are noted independently in the survey.[75] There are many occasions, however, when the records seem to suggest the presence of more settlement foci than have survived to the present day. It is by no means certain that submanors necessarily gave rise to independent settlement foci, for tenurial units are an abstraction which need not necessarily be related to physical remains.[76] This seems sometimes, however, to

[72] A. H. Smith, *English Place-Name Elements, Parts 1 and 2* (English Place-Name Society, 25 and 26, 1956).

[73] S 1340, K 623; Hooke, 'Village development'.

[74] M. A. Aston, 'Rural settlement in Somerset: some preliminary thoughts', in *Medieval Villages*, ed. Hooke, pp. 81–100.

[75] Hooke, 'Village development in the west midlands'.

[76] F. W. Maitland, *Domesday Book and Beyond* (Cambridge, 1897), ch. 7.

have been the case and on many occasions the vills probably reflected individual settlement clusters, although these cannot all now be identified. Aston notes the large number of Domesday vills recorded in Somerset which cannot be matched by known villages and finds their incidence highest on estates not held by the Church or the Crown.[77] Assuming these to have been separate settlement foci, he suggests that such major landlords may already have instigated the processes which led to nucleation on their estates, a process which gave the opportunity for more organized settlement planning.

In Tredington, the manorial subdivisions lay in separate locations, but elsewhere later evidence suggests that different manors could form within a single settlement nucleus. One example quoted by Aston is Lopen in South Petherton, Somerset, where two of the Domesday manors can be identified as separate parts of the present village. Taylor, too, citing the case of Wollaston in Northamptonshire, discusses how manorial subdivision might give rise to the emergence of a polyfocal settlement.[78]

Wormleighton in Warwickshire may be quoted as an example of a present-day parish in which Domesday manors outnumbered surviving settlements (figure 1.5). This lies in the Feldon region of the county, an area of strongly nucleated villages with few outlying farmsteads recorded in medieval times. There are three separate entries for Wormleighton in the Domesday folios, all held by subtenants from their Norman lords.[79] The largest, of 3 hides, contained some twenty-one families and, in addition, two knights with their dependents who were holding just over one-third of the land – this holding before the Conquest had also belonged to three separate Saxon thegns. The second holding of 1½ hides was occupied by seventeen families, six slaves and a priest, and a third holding of ¾ hide was much smaller, occupied only by two bordars. In the medieval period there were two main settlements in Wormleighton, one of which, with a moated manorial centre, was finally abandoned in the sixteenth century. Thorpe, who made a detailed study of this parish, had regarded the surviving village of Wormleighton as a late replacement for the deserted vill,[80] but its church and evidence of some nearby desertion suggest that this was the centre of one of the other Domesday holdings, perhaps that of the Count of Meulan which possessed a priest. Of the third holding, and those of the knights, there is no field evidence.

Domesday entries are notoriously unreliable as evidence of settlement distribution, but when compared with references to estates in pre-Conquest charters it can be seen that the estates of numerous township communities were

[77] Aston, 'Rural settlement in Somerset'.

[78] ibid., pp. 88–9, citing *VCH Somerset*, vol. IV, p. 164; C. C. Taylor, 'Polyfocal settlement and the English village', *Medieval Archaeology*, 21 (1977), pp. 189–93.

[79] *Domesday Book*, fos 240c, 241d, 243c.

[80] H. Thorpe, 'The lord and the landscape illustrated through the changing fortunes of an English parish', in *Volume Jubilaire M. A. Lefèvre* (Louvain, 1964), pp. 71–126.

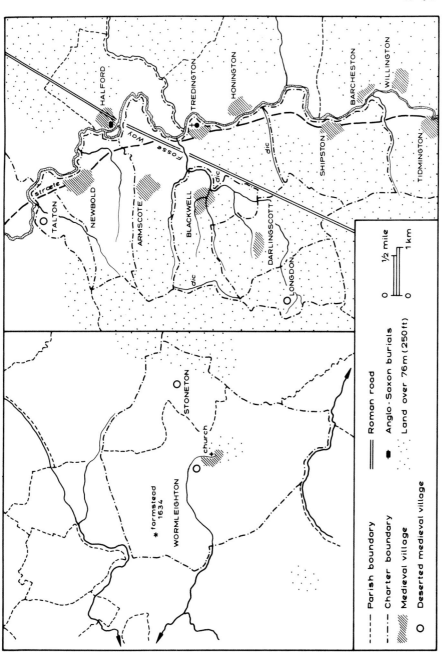

FIGURE 1.5 *Multi-township and multi-settlement parishes in Warwickshire.*

WORMLEIGHTON

* farmstead
1634

STONETON

church

HALFORD

TALTON

NEWBOLD

ARMSCOTE

BLACKWELL

DARLINGSCOTT

LONGDON

TREDINGTON

HONINGTON

SHIPSTON

BARCHESTON

WILLINGTON

TIDMINGTON

Fosse Way

street

dic

dic

dic

dic

--- Parish boundary
-·- Charter boundary
▨ Medieval village
○ Deserted medieval village

══ Roman road
● Anglo-Saxon burials
⋯ Land over 76m (250ft)

0   ½ mile
0   1 km

often subsumed within a recorded head-manor. Only rarely can this subsumption reflect actual settlement nucleation. One such instance of possible nucleation is, however, suggested by a Berkshire Domesday entry. In a region of intermittent woodland and arable cultivation which lies to the north of Newbury, thegns' halls had been noted on two of the manors in the parish of Peasemore. One of them, a 7-hide estate, had been held by Godwin and Herlwin before the Conquest, each possessing his own hall, but after 1086 the holdings were amalgamated and held by Richard, as subtenant of Gilbert of Bretteville. The survey notes '*Duae hallae fuerunt, modo una*', 'two halls, now one'.[81] On a second 8-hide Peasemore estate (amended to 3 hides) two thegns had owned two halls before the Conquest but no mention is made of their fate once the estate had passed into single ownership.[82] Such information does not occur in the records of all of the Domesday circuits and if *halla* may indeed be interpreted as 'a hall', it may be a valuable indication of settlement trends which probably went unrecorded in many other regions. It is interesting to note that the Berkshire region discussed above was again one of a semi-wooded environment where a dispersed settlement pattern seems to have only gradually given way to village development.

CONCLUSION

Great difficulties are encountered in linking documentary evidence with the physical remains of settlements. While the detailed reconstruction of settlement patterns can only be attempted at present for a very few places which may not be representative of others, even in their immediate locality, nevertheless some general trends have been identified in recent years and past assumptions have been more critically examined. Archaeological and field evidence has provided the largest amount of new evidence but it has been possible to relate this to known documentation to obtain an increasingly clear picture of the evolution of the English settlement pattern.

[81] *Domesday Book*, fo. 62a.
[82] *Domesday Book*, fo. 62d.

2

Initiative and Authority in Settlement Change

P. D. A. HARVEY

INTRODUCTION

Ever since Maurice Beresford first revealed the lost villages of England in 1954, work on medieval settlement has produced more and more evidence of change. Villages decayed and were deserted; but they were also created by simple planting or by bringing together existing villages or dispersed farms, they moved from one site to another, they were entirely rebuilt where they stood. They were endowed with churches – but not just once for all time, for the church might survive or decay, stay still or move, not necessarily in step with the rest of the settlement. The field system too need be neither a surviving relic of dark age colonization nor the product of gradual evolution: the fields, it is now agreed, might be reorganized as suddenly and as drastically as the settlement itself. Where once we saw underlying stability we now look for – and often find – flexibility and sudden change. Some of this change was the piecemeal work of many individual husbandmen, like much of the assarting of waste and reclamation from sea and fen that was achieved in the twelfth and thirteenth centuries.[1] Even a new town of the thirteenth century, Ravenserodd, could be held to have begun its mushroom growth in an enterprising individual's taking over a wrecked ship as a sort of wayside café for people sailing up or down the Humber.[2] But by their very nature many changes now discerned must have involved the cooperation, or the ordering, of whole communities of people. Where should we look for the initiative to plan these changes, the authority to put them into effect? Was it communal agreement that lay behind them or was it seignorial power?

We cannot yet give a definite answer. The sources of local initiative and

---

[1] For example, E. King, *Peterborough Abbey 1086–1310: A Study in the Land Market* (Cambridge, 1973), pp. 75–80, 83–7.

[2] *Calendar of Inquisitions Miscellaneous (Chancery)* (7 vols, 1916–68), vol. I, no. 1512.

authority varied over time, as we shall see. But they also varied from region to region and from place to place in ways not fully explored. In 1287 agreement was concluded over common pasture rights in Alvechurch and King's Norton, neighbouring places in Worcestershire; for Alvechurch the party to the agreement was the Bishop of Worcester, its manorial lord, but for King's Norton, a manor of royal demesne, it was twenty representatives of the community.[3] More work is needed on such differences in local executive authority. Here two points will be examined: the roles of custom and of lordship on the individual manor and the changing relationship between seignorial power and the local community throughout the middle ages. At best this will provide a background pattern against which we can set particular instances of settlement change.

LORDSHIP AND CUSTOM

The respective roles of manorial custom and manorial lordship have been seen as a problem.[4] Historians working on medieval rural communities have increasingly shown how local custom in practice restrained the lord's powers over his villein tenants. Under the common law, as it came to be defined in the late twelfth and thirteenth centuries, these powers were immense. The villein held his land and all his possessions entirely at the will of his lord, who could deprive him of any or all of them for any reason or for none; he had nothing he could call his own. His rents and services could be increased arbitrarily at any time, but he could not leave the manor. He had no right of inheritance, but having once acquired his holding he could not sell or sublet it and land he got from any other source passed automatically to his manorial lord. This was the law administered in the royal courts and any villein trying to bring a case there in defence of his rights or his holding would be sent away empty-handed: his goods and his lands lay wholly in his lord's jurisdiction, and it was only in his lord's manorial court that he could bring any case concerning them. But once in the manorial court an entirely different set of rules operated. The law administered there was local custom, the custom of the manor, and this allowed the villein all kinds of rights that the common law denied him. His rents and services were defined and fixed, he would inherit his holding by whatever rules applied in the manor, and would continue to hold it unless he voluntarily relinquished it or committed some offence for which custom decreed its forfeiture. There was an implicit assumption that his goods and his money were

[3] R. H. Hilton, *A Medieval Society: The West Midlands at the End of the Thirteenth Century* (London, 1966), p. 152.

[4] For example, E. King in *English Historical Review*, 101 (1986), p. 426 (review of *The Peasant Land Market in Medieval England*, ed. P. D. A. Harvey (Oxford, 1984)).

his own, and would pass to the lord only in accordance with customary rule, like the animal commonly taken as heriot on the villein's death. If he was mulcted ('amerced') in the court for a misdemeanour two of his fellow villagers, the affeerors, had at least a voice, even a decisive voice, in fixing the amount he had to pay. And although custom might place restrictions on his freedom of movement and of action he could usually buy his way out of them for a reasonable price: as John Hatcher has put it, 'Lords were concerned far less with controlling the lives of their villeins than with profiting from their right to do so'.[5]

The detailed customs varied from one manor to the next, but the rule of local custom in manorial courts was universal. This custom was defined and declared not by the manorial lord but by the villagers themselves who, as members of the court, were viewed as 'the guardians of custom, the collective memory of the neighborhood'.[6] Certainly the manorial lord had the right to disregard and override local custom and if he did he could rely on the full backing of the common law and the royal courts. But in practice this did not often happen. In the normal course of events the lord would respect the precedents embodied in local custom, partly, no doubt, because this enabled him to manage his property and his tenants harmoniously, and thus efficiently, but partly too because at his own level he would be as much a respecter of past precedent and declared custom as any of his tenants.[7] Breach of custom could lead to trouble, as at Broughton (Huntingdonshire) in 1291, when villeins doing harvest services went on strike for half a day, claiming that the loaves given them for lunch were smaller than usual.[8] When conflict arose between a manorial lord and his tenants, as from time to time it did, real or alleged breach of custom by one side or the other was often the cause.[9] Sometimes we see lords avoiding difficulties by what seems almost excessive respect for custom; in the early fourteenth century when Titchfield Abbey's tenants at Cadland (Hampshire) refused to elect a reeve, the abbot refrained from the obvious step of nominating someone himself, even though on many other manors such nomination by the lord was customary.[10] And the lord who wanted to alter manorial custom might feel he

[5] The position of the villein, in legal theory and in practice, is fully discussed by J. Hatcher, 'English serfdom and villeinage: towards a reassessment', *Past and Present*, 90 (1981), pp. 3–39; the quotation is from p. 10.

[6] J. S. Beckerman, 'Customary law in English manorial courts in the thirteenth and fourteenth centuries' (unpublished Ph.D. thesis, University of London, 1972), p. 12. I am grateful to Dr Beckerman for permission to cite this important unpublished work.

[7] Cf. Hatcher, 'English serfdom and villeinage', pp. 23–4.

[8] G. C. Homans, *English Villagers of the Thirteenth Century* (Cambridge, Mass., 1941), p. 262.

[9] Many examples are given in the works of R. H. Hilton, such as *The English Peasantry in the Later Middle Ages* (Oxford, 1975), pp. 58–69, or *Class Conflict and the Crisis of Feudalism: Essays in Medieval Social History* (London, 1985), pp. 108–13, 124–35; or, on one estate, by D. G. Watts, 'Peasant discontent on the manors of Titchfield Abbey, 1245–1405', *Proceedings of the Hampshire Field Club and Archaeological Society*, 39 (1983), pp. 121–35.

[10] Watts, 'Peasant discontent', pp. 126–7, cited by S. Reynolds, *Kingdoms and Communities in Western Europe, 900–1300* (Oxford, 1984), p. 133.

had to move with great circumspection. At Povington (Dorset), about 1230, harvest boon-workers, allowed a sheaf of corn at the end of the day's work, had been used to take enormous sheaves, four times larger than normal. However, their manorial lord, the Abbot of Bec, was so nervous of altering established custom that he cited scriptural authority to do so: 'as holy writ says that it is right to do away with evil usage and to change for the better what is evilly attempted', so, henceforth, the harvesters' sheaves should be of normal size.[11] This is not to say that manorial custom was usually static, though lords and tenants alike seem to have thought it ought to be and assumed that it was. D. G. Watts tells how at Titchfield 'The abbot did his utmost to distort custom in his own interest while at the same time regarding himself as bound by it.'[12] Everywhere it was, in R. H. Hilton's phrase, 'a shifting compromise', and it evolved gradually over the years.[13] Sometimes we can see this happening. In 1391 a 5s. fine was imposed when a villein's daughter of Oakington (Cambridgeshire) was unchaste, this being the custom of the manor according to the jurors – but they were wrong, for a hundred years earlier the amount had been 6d. or 1s.[14] This change was to the lord's advantage, but this was not always the case.[15] Despite the strength of their legal position, those thirteenth-century manorial lords who tried to prevent the growth and spread of a peasant land market had little success; where local demand arose among villeins to buy and sell land among themselves their lords seem to have been powerless to prevent them even from breaking up the standard customary holdings, the basis of the manor's tenurial structure.[16]

It is against this background that we must view the evidence for physical changes in the settlements of medieval England. Those who have discovered this evidence have mostly explained these changes as stemming from seignorial power: it was the manorial lords who moved or replanned villages, who reorganized field systems and so on. Often this is the only possible answer. It can only have been the manorial lord who in the twelfth century moved the village of Eaton Socon (Bedfordshire), church and all, so that he could build a

---

[11] M. Chibnall (ed.), *Select Documents of the English Lands of the Abbey of Bec* (Camden Society, 3rd ser., 73, 1951), p. 62. I owe this reference to the kindness of Dr A. C. Jones, whose articles on 'Harvest customs and labourers' perquisites in southern England, 1150–1350', *Agricultural History Review*, 25 (1977), pp. 14–22, 98–107, covering respectively the corn harvest and the hay harvest, give a valuable conspectus of an item of manorial custom that is often defined in surveys.

[12] Watts, 'Peasant discontent', p. 124.

[13] Hilton, *Class Conflict*, p. 126.

[14] F. M. Page, *The Estates of Crowland Abbey: A Study in Manorial Organisation* (Cambridge, 1934), pp. 334, 339, 416.

[15] Cf. the interesting comparison of a Teddington (Middlesex) virgater's rents and services in the early thirteenth century and the early fourteenth in B. Harvey, *Westminster Abbey and its Estates in the Middle Ages* (Oxford, 1977), pp. 219–22.

[16] P. D. A. Harvey (ed.), *Peasant Land Market*, pp. 344–9.

castle on its old site.[17] And in many more cases it seems, on the face of it, more likely that change came from the lord's initiative rather than from some communally agreed decision. So an odd situation has arisen. Historians, working on documents, often see the lord of the manor as moving gingerly, pussyfooted even, among the intricacies of his tenants' rights and privileges. On the other hand archaeologists and geographers, working in the field, see this same lord sweeping all before him, uprooting entire villages and replanning lands and settlements in the most arbitrary way.

This is less of a problem than it appears at first sight. Our knowledge of manorial custom comes partly from court rolls which record disagreements or statements on particular points, like the Oakington fine for unchastity in 1391, but more from custumals. These were surveys which recorded and defined the obligations between lord and tenant, largely so that the lord could counter with assurance any particularly optimistic recollections of custom that the villagers might produce in the future; thus the Abbot of Ramsey, confronted with his harvest workers' strike over the size of loaves, pointed to the custumal which said that a three-farthing loaf was to be shared between two workers. These records were not meant to be comprehensive codes of local custom, and we may reasonably see them as simply the visible tip of a mass of slowly evolving customs that affected every relationship of village life, not just between lord and tenant but between one villager and another, between bailiff and hired worker and so on. Very occasionally we get glimpses of this: at Wistow (Huntingdonshire) in 1294 the manorial court made Robert Juwel pay 1s. because 'by custom he ought to have given a meal to all the servants of the manor of Wistow on the day when he married his wife, and he did not do so'.[18] More often we get indirect evidence. Thus long after a manor had taken to measuring land by the rod and corn by the struck measure, piecework rates for hired workers might still be based on customary field acres for reaping and on heaped corn measures for threshing, despite the problems this created in accounting and auditing.[19] Within the community, in his dealings with its inhabitants, the lord of the manor was as much involved as anyone else in this close web of custom and precedent; but as its lord he had another role to play. There need be nothing inconsistent in a careful respect for local custom in the internal administration of the manor and the exercise of dictatorial powers in ordering its affairs overall. The lord's position might be summed up in a simple formula: local custom tended to be strongest in his relations with his

---

[17] P. V. Addyman, 'Late Saxon settlement in the St Neots area: I. The Saxon settlement and Norman castle at Eaton Socon, Bedfordshire', *Proceedings of the Cambridgeshire Antiquarian Society*, 58 (1965), pp. 48–50.

[18] Homans, *English Villagers*, p. 173.

[19] P. D. A. Harvey, *A Medieval Oxfordshire Village: Cuxham 1240–1400* (London, 1965), pp. 44, 55–6. In the case of the threshing, easily identified on manorial accounts, this can be paralleled on many other manors.

individual tenants, officers or employees, while lordship tended to be strongest in matters affecting the community as a whole.

This can only be hypothesis. No instance seems yet to have come to light of the same manorial lord acting in both roles – but given the scantiness of the evidence it would be an extraordinarily lucky chance if it had. All we can say is that it fits the facts as we know them and explains why historians, working on records of manorial administration, are most impressed by the strength of custom; archaeologists and geographers, working on material remains of settlements, by the strength of lordship. Moreover, it fits a much wider pattern. The form of organization that accepts arbitrary direction in external affairs while insisting on careful regulation of internal relationships is, in human terms, a very natural one. We see it in the modern factory. The owner can move it from one side of the town to the other or from one county to the next, changes that may seriously disrupt his employees' pattern of life, yet he is more likely to end up with a strike on his hands if he reduces the tea-break from ten minutes to five. Other analogies, past and present, are not hard to find.[20] But to draw for this purpose a sharp distinction between custom and lordship in the medieval community is misleading. The medieval villein, or the manorial lord, asked about the respective roles of custom and lordship in the community, would not understand the question. Custom and lordship were all one to him. It was custom that gave the villein a loaf of a certain size in return for his harvest work; but equally it was custom that entitled the lord, if he wished, to have the village pulled down and rebuilt on a new site. The exercise of lordship was merely custom as it applied to the lord of the manor. It is with lordship as an aspect of custom that we are concerned.

LORDSHIP AND THE COMMUNITY OF THE VILL

But custom, as we have seen, evolved and changed over the years; and lordship, as an aspect of custom, will have changed too. Nothing said so far has been meant to suggest that it was necessarily the manorial lord who initiated change in settlement, but only that seignorial power was a possible source of initiative: its seeming weakness in the face of local custom is not relevant to its role in settlement change. What was this role? Returning to our original question, was it the manorial lord or the local community that instigated these changes?

The local rural community, the vill – the word comprehends both nucleated village and dispersed settlement – has long been of interest to historians. They have increasingly come to see it as a body which must have had some sort of internal administrative organization, however rudimentary, and which could

---

[20] It is interesting, for instance, that one thing the British sovereign can do without reference to Parliament is to declare war.

take corporate action. The manor was the local unit of lordship and of estate organization, but royal administration used the vill as its smallest unit of government, never the manor. The vill was the unit of tax assessment and collection, the unit required to produce military levies, the unit represented, if need be, in the county court, the unit responsible for local law and order. It was the four neighbouring vills that testified to a coroner's inquest or, in a forest, to the forester's inquiry when a deer was found dead or wounded. Communal payments by vills are recorded from as early a date as we could expect to know of them. How these payments were divided among the villagers, how the tax collectors, soldiers, constables, representatives of the vill, were chosen is very uncertain; the methods used have left no written records.

But the vill did more than just respond to the demands of royal authority. In 1922 Joan Wake printed two documents, and referred to others, which showed the vill acting corporately in such things as repairing a bridge, holding land for public use, and reorganizing a field system.[21] Since then more evidence of the same sort has been brought together, notably by G. C. Homans in 1941, Helen Cam in 1950 and by W. O. Ault.[22] Ault's account of the vill in 1982 looked particularly at its obligations in royal administration, but earlier he had done much work on the by-laws entered on some manorial court rolls, seeing them as the products not of manorial administration but of the vill itself.[23] In 1985 C. C. Dyer argued cogently that from what we now know, or can deduce, about the organization and effective powers of the medieval vill we need not necessarily see seignorial authority as lying behind change in fields and settlements: it is possible, indeed likely, 'that villagers rather than lords were responsible for the planning of villages and field systems'.[24] Meanwhile, in 1984, Susan Reynolds published an important and penetrating study which sets what we know of the medieval vill in a new, revealing light. Looking at the period 900–1300, and at France, Germany and Italy as well as England, she argued that the vill could act collectively and was accepted as an entity for many purposes long before the idea of a legal corporate body had been worked out. In this it would be no different from other groups of people linked by similar geographical or institutional ties. In other words when we see the vill of the thirteenth, fourteenth or fifteenth century engaging in public works, organizing its fields, holding land, we are not seeing the first abortive fumblings towards legal corporate status that was never achieved, but the

[21] J. Wake, 'Communitas villae', *English Historical Review*, 37 (1922), pp. 406–13.

[22] Homans, *English Villagers*, especially pp. 328–38; H. M. Cam, 'The community of the vill', in *Mediaeval Studies Presented to Rose Graham*, ed. V. Ruffer and A. J. Taylor (Oxford, 1950), pp. 1–14.

[23] W. O. Ault, 'Open-field husbandry and the village community', *Transactions of the American Philosophical Society*, new ser., 55, part 7 (1965), which brings together much work from earlier articles; 'The vill in medieval England', *Proceedings of the American Philosophical Society*, 126 (1982), pp. 188–211.

[24] C. C. Dyer, 'Power and conflict in the medieval English village', in *Medieval Villages: A Review of Current Work*, ed. D. Hooke (Oxford University Committee for Archaeology, monograph no. 5, Oxford, 1985), pp. 27–32; the quotation is from p. 32.

natural, unselfconscious acts of a group long accustomed to acting collectively. This further strengthens Dyer's case: there is nothing inherently wrong in seeing the local community as responsible for planning changes and carrying them out.[25]

Yet some changes by their very nature can only have been the work of manorial lords. We have seen an example already from Eaton Socon; others that come at once to mind are the removals of villagers from properties given to Fountains and some other newly founded Cistercian abbeys in the twelfth century.[26] Mostly we can only guess where any particular change originated. At the same time some broad, long-term trends can be perceived which may at least guide our guessing. Within the vill some inhabitants, some groups, are bound to have carried more weight than others; there will always have been a village elite, even a village aristocracy, who will have had a fair measure of control over the rest.[27] Sometimes we get a glimpse of them, like the eighteen villagers of Pleshey (Essex) who in 1394 agreed to the removal and rebuilding of the parish church on a new site, 'with the assent of all our neighbours, the lesser as well as the greater'.[28] But the vill's most distinguished members would be missing from its counsels, for, as Dyer argues (and this, we shall see, is surely the key to what was happening), manorial lords took little interest in the internal organization of the vill, and were content to leave this to the inhabitants.[29] But if this was true of the absentee lords of great estates in the thirteenth and fourteenth centuries it is much less likely to have been true in the mid-eleventh century, when most local communities included one or more thegns living on the spot, thegns who can hardly have been uninterested in the affairs of the vill and who will presumably have expected to take the lead in ordering them. Taking this as our starting-point we could say, in broad, simple terms, that the period from the eleventh century to the fifteenth saw the gradual withdrawal of the seignorial class from the community of the vill, and that with its withdrawal the other elements in the community gained, perhaps in power and certainly in prominence in the written record.

This can be simply illustrated by four documents concerned with reorganizing lands, in each case lands both of tenants and of manorial demesnes. At Dry Drayton (Cambridgeshire) in the twelfth century lands were redistributed between five manorial lords; the charter recording this mentions the interest or participation of no one but the lords themselves. From Segenhoe (Bedfordshire) we have a record of a similar division of lands between two

---

[25] Reynolds, *Kingdoms and Communities*, esp. pp. 101–54; Dyer's article, originally a paper delivered in 1982, was written before this was published.

[26] D. Knowles, *The Monastic Order in England: A History of its Development From the Times of St Dunstan to the Fourth Lateran Council 940–1216*, 2nd edn (Cambridge, 1963), pp. 350–1.

[27] Hilton, *English Peasantry*, pp. 54–8; Dyer, 'Power and conflict', pp. 29–30.

[28] PRO, DL25/756.

[29] Dyer, 'Power and conflict', pp. 27–8.

lords, involving the displacement of some local tenants; later, perhaps in the late twelfth century, all their tenants by general agreement asked to have their lands redefined and redistributed, and after they had surrendered their lands to their two lords for the purpose this was done by six of the vill's older men.[30] At Marton (Yorkshire) in the fourteenth or early fifteenth century the vill's arable was divided into fields for a three-course rotation by nine men, three representing one of the two manorial lords, three representing the other and three representing the vill's freeholders.[31] And at Harlestone (Northamptonshire) in 1410 an adjustment to the vill's fields was recorded in a tripartite indenture of which two parts were held by the manorial lords, one part by the men of the vill, whose six representatives were named as one party to the deed; to supervise the scheme's operation nine men were named, seven for the manorial lords and two for the vill.[32] In these four documents we see the formal role of the manorial lord successively reduced and the formal role of the vill correspondingly enlarged. At the same time the formal roles are not necessarily a guide to the decision-making process or to the realities of power. At Dry Drayton, where the five lords seemingly acted without reference to the vill, are we to take the document at face value and see them simply as five individuals acting alone, or are we to see them as, jointly, the embodiment of the vill, or as its leaders or as its representatives? We cannot tell and at that time the question might well be meaningless; they were simply doing the job of manorial lords as custom allowed and required. But if we see the early medieval lord as an integral member of the community of the vill we need not assume that he (or his official) would join in the village assemblies postulated by historians to discuss the vill's affairs with his tenants, or even to lead their discussion;[33] it is just that without his assent the decisions reached by any group of villagers would be valueless if they in any way affected his interests. What changed in the course of time is what the lord saw as his interests; they seem to have become more and more narrowly conceived in simple economic terms. Just how they were – consciously or unconsciously – defined will of course have differed from lord to lord and from place to place. What the lord thought lay outside his interests at any particular time he was content to leave to the administration, the decision even, of the vill.

Occasionally we get a glimpse of the process of withdrawal, of the lord distancing himself from the vill in one or other detail. In 1424 Merton

---

[30] Page, *Estates of Crowland Abbey*, p. 162; P. Vinogradoff, *Villainage in England: Essays in English Mediaeval History* (London, 1892), pp. 457–8. Both are discussed by H. S. A. Fox, 'Approaches to the adoption of the Midland system', in *The Origins of Open-field Agriculture*, ed. T. Rowley (London, 1981), pp. 94–8.

[31] Homans, *English Villagers*, pp. 56, 421.

[32] Wake, 'Communitas villae', pp. 409–13.

[33] W. O. Ault, 'Village assemblies in medieval England', in *Album Helen Maud Cam* (Studies Presented to the International Commission for the History of Representative and Parliamentary Institutions, nos 23, 24, 2 vols, Louvain and Paris, 1960–1), vol. I, pp. 13–35.

College, Oxford, which had a manor at Gamlingay (Cambridgeshire), agreed to provide wood to repair a bridge there, but on condition that the vill did not claim in future that the college should contribute to its repair.[34] But it would not be difficult to find contrary instances, for the lords' disinvolvement was not the gradual, steady process that the four records of field reorganization might suggest: it proceeded fitfully, patchily, with backward turns and with much variation between one place and another. We have seen one example of this in the agreement of 1287 between the lord of the manor of Alvechurch and the men of the vill of King's Norton; we can rationalize the difference between the two places by saying that the Bishop of Worcester and the king held different views of their local interests as lords of Alvechurch and King's Norton respectively. Or again when, in 1241, the fen between Whaplode and Holbeach (Lincolnshire) was reclaimed, not just the manorial lords but everyone claiming a share in either vill participated in an agreement for its division; the £40 penalty for a breach of its conditions was to go not to the lords but to all those sharing the fen. Yet in Gloucestershire in 1313, two generations later, the tenants of Coaley and Frocester took no part in an agreement for intercommoning between the two manors; it was drawn up simply between the manorial lords.[35]

But however variable, however piecemeal, the process, we can see how certain broad developments encouraged it. The disappearance of the local thegns at the Norman Conquest and their replacement by mostly absentee lords must have opened a gap between lord and vill; however, subinfeudation will have reduced the effect of this, bringing many vills a resident knightly lord, and so will the farming of manors either by long-term leases that made the farmer little different from a resident lord, or by leases that gave the lord continuing local control. A subtler change was produced by twelfth-century legal developments; by giving new security to the free tenants they produced a class of local tenants with whom the lord would now deal, if not exactly as equals, at least apart from the rest of the vill. This probably divided the lord from the community as a whole far more than it divided the free tenants from their fellow inhabitants. The distinction thus created continued throughout the middle ages – we find, for instance, the lord of Moreton Pinkney (Northamptonshire) making an agreement about enclosure with his free tenants in the 1260s, and in the fifteenth century the free tenants of Lydd (Kent) had their own seal.[36] Lords' withdrawal from demesne farming, first, in the late thirteenth century, by giving increased responsibility to their local officials and latterly by a return to leasing, will again have tended to distance them from the

---

[34] Merton College muniments 2471.

[35] H. E. Hallam, *Settlement and Society: A Study of the Early Agrarian History of South Lincolnshire* (Cambridge, 1965), pp. 32, 226–7; Hilton, *English Peasantry*, p. 3.

[36] PRO, E326/11479; W. de G. Birch, *Catalogue of Seals in the Department of Manuscripts in the British Museum* (6 vols, London, 1887–1900), vol. II, no. 5145.

vill – as Dyer has said, its internal affairs were now of little interest to them. We can only guess at possible regional differences in the process of disengagement. At the local level it seems likely to have proceeded particularly rapidly on manors of royal demesne (as at King's Norton) and perhaps also at places where the demesne lands were leased to the manors' own tenants, and particularly slowly where the lord of the manor lived on the spot. It has been thought likely that vills of divided lordship had stronger, more developed communal organization than those where vill and manor coincided.[37] Certainly if neither the manorial lords nor their agents were resident in a vill of divided lordship liaison between them may have been difficult, but we should not suppose that lords will have found it harder than the combined body of their tenants to agree among themselves. Thus at Childrey (Berkshire) in the mid-fourteenth century the vill's hayward was appointed by each of the three manorial lords in turn,[38] and it would be interesting to know whether it was communal or seignorial initiative that gave us the terriers covering lands of more than one lordship that we have from some such vills in the fourteenth and fifteenth centuries.[39] The role of the manorial court is of interest here, and also of the parish; these were the two organizations that offered the local community an institutional framework.

The manorial court is first recorded in the early thirteenth century.[40] In the form it had then it is unlikely to have been of great antiquity: it has every appearance of being copied from the courts that twelfth-century lords of honours held for their tenants, adapting – aping even – their procedures to fit the needs of a single manor with its tenantry of peasants. We know of no Anglo-Saxon equivalent to the simple manorial court (the future court baron), though in some places private courts exercised locally certain aspects of royal jurisdiction (the future court leet). There must, though, have been some more or less formal way of settling disputes among the inhabitants of the pre-Conquest vill and this seems to have been taken over or superseded by the manorial court. But even where vill and manor coincided the manorial court practically never became the institutional embodiment of the community of the vill.[41] Certainly it played a part in agrarian regulation and in enforcing

---

[37] Thus Wake, 'Communitas villae', pp. 407–8; Cam, 'Community of the vill', p. 6; Dyer, 'Power and conflict', p. 29.

[38] *Calendar of Inquisitions Post Mortem* (16 vols, 1904–74), vol. VIII, no. 629.

[39] One such, for Portchester (Hampshire) in 1405, was drawn up by one of the two manorial lords in order to distinguish the two manors' lands: B. Cunliffe and J. Munby, *Excavations at Portchester Castle, vol. IV: Medieval, the Inner Bailey* (Society of Antiquaries of London, Research Report no. 43, London, 1985), p. 280.

[40] W. O. Ault, 'The earliest rolls of manor courts in England', *Studia Gratiana*, 15 (1972), pp. 511–18; P. D. A. Harvey, *Manorial Records* (British Records Association, Archives and the User no. 5, 1984), p. 42.

[41] This did happen at Kingsthorpe (Northamptonshire) but seems to have been most exceptional; interestingly, this was a manor of royal demesne leased to its own tenants (Ault, 'Village assemblies', pp. 26–7).

by-laws. But it did nothing to meet the demands that royal administration laid on the vill: it was not in the manorial court that the vill's constables or foot-soldiers or representatives at other courts were chosen, or that individual contributions to taxation or other communal payments were assessed or collected. Indeed, a manorial court sometimes even hindered the smooth operation of these processes by amercing villagers who in course of these duties were held to have damaged the lord or his tenants.[42] At first sight the manorial court might seem the outward expression both of the power of the lord and of his integration with the village community. In fact it was neither. It was used not as a vehicle for the widest powers of lordship – it is not, for instance, in manorial court records that we look for evidence of fifteenth-century lords' enclosures – but as a means of regulating local custom as between the lord and his individual tenants. In using the court in this way and in applying to local custom procedures borrowed from other courts the manorial lord may well have reduced the authority that custom allowed him, seeking from the court decisions that had once been his alone. And in formalizing these procedures, cutting them off from the vill's collective deliberations and obligations, the lord was taking another step in distancing himself from the community. We can even see the growth of new manors, new manorial courts, in the fifteenth century as evidence that other large freeholders were likewise separating themselves from the vill.

But if the community of the vill did not find its institutional home in the manorial court it had better luck in the parish. The embodiment of the vill in the parish organization was a slow process of great interest. Even its official aspect, the vill's replacement by the parish as the local unit of royal administration, took place gradually; already in 1377 the poll tax was collected by parishes, not vills, in two counties, Cornwall and Middlesex, and some sixteenth-century statutes giving parishes administrative functions provided for some sharing of power with the manorial courts.[43] This reflected still slower change at the local level. A mid-thirteenth-century charter giving land to maintain a light in Castle Donington (Leicestershire) church was placed on the altar 'in the presence of the parish'; but the distinction between vill and parish was not always maintained and already in 1296 we find, exceptionally, land described as lying not in the vill but in the parish of Langham (Essex).[44] The parish church was at first a useful recipient of any financial windfall that came the way of the vill, an object of common concern and obligation,[45] but by

---

[42] For example, Page, *Estates of Crowland Abbey*, pp. 386–7.

[43] J. C. Russell, *British Medieval Population* (Albuquerque, 1948), p. 123n; Harvey, *Manorial Records*, p. 56.

[44] PRO, DL25/1208, 1712.

[45] See, for example, *Manorial Records of Cuxham, Oxfordshire, circa 1200–1359*, ed. P. D. A. Harvey (Oxfordshire Record Society, 50; Historical Manuscripts Commission, Joint Publication no. 23, 1976), p. 648.

the fifteenth century it was not uncommon for fines for breaches of by-laws to be divided between manorial lord and parish church — an instance of the lord's withdrawal in favour of the vill, here replaced by the parish.[46] By the seventeenth century the parish, its statutory powers still increasing, had outside the northern counties entirely subsumed the vill as a collective body.

But without the manorial lord. In the parish organization that had been the community of the vill there was no place for the lord of the manor; his separation from the vill was now complete. As late as 1395 the manorial lord of Great Ryburgh (Norfolk) was referred to as lord not of the manor but of the vill;[47] two centuries later he would never have been called lord of the parish. But this is not to say that he had forfeited power, only that his perceived field of interest had narrowed. The lord might still in the fifteenth century act in concert with the vill, indeed as an integral part of it; thus the curious parish history of Barholm and Greatford (Lincolnshire), written in the fifteenth century, assumes that land will be bought and sold by the lord and the whole community of the vill acting together.[48] And when we consider the settlement changes of the fifteenth, sixteenth and seventeenth centuries – the evictions, the enclosures, the imparkings – we look to neither vill nor parish as the instigator but to the manorial lord or his local farmer, with or without the collaboration of the other freeholders. The position cannot have been different in earlier centuries.

CONCLUSION

The idea, the initiative, for change may have come from the community of the vill – mostly that is anyone's guess – and increasingly we see the vill, as a collective body, participating in the detailed working, the day-to-day administration, that change may have involved. But if what the manorial lord saw as his interests were affected by change the vill would be powerless to carry it out without his assent. Local custom and the law of property between them left no room for doubt where the authority for settlement change must always have lain.

[46] W. O. Ault, 'Manor court and parish church in fifteenth-century England: a study of village by-laws', *Speculum*, 42 (1967), pp. 53–67. At Shifford (Oxfordshire) in the late fifteenth century we see a halfway stage in the process: half of an amercement for poaching went to the lord, half to the local church, but of an amercement for neglecting to mend a path half went to the lord and half went towards repairing roads in the vill (*VCH Oxfordshire*, vol. II, p. 186n, citing PRO SC2/197/62, m.4r).

[47] BL, Additional Charter 60308.

[48] Edited and discussed by J. A. Cripps in *Local Maps and Plans from Medieval England*, ed. R. A. Skelton and P. D. A. Harvey (Oxford, 1986), pp. 266–88.

3

'The Retreat from Marginal Land': The Growth and Decline of Medieval Rural Settlements

CHRISTOPHER DYER

INTRODUCTION

Everyone who studies rural settlement, following the admirable example of the two scholars honoured by this book, needs to combine general ideas with detailed local studies. This essay examines a grand generalization that has long shaped our approach to settlement studies, in the light of recent research into agriculture, villages, hamlets and fields.

The theory to be tested is that there was a 'retreat from marginal land' in the later middle ages, which is widely believed to explain the contraction in cultivated land and in rural settlements.[1] Behind this idea lies the reasonable proposition that fluctuations in the population provided the impetus for changes in settlements. Numbers of people in England grew rapidly between 1086 and 1300, perhaps from about 2 to 5 or 6 million. Before 1086 demographic history is very uncertain, though the total for Roman Britain at its height is believed to have been nearer to the estimate for 1300 than that for 1086, so there must have been a great decline at some time between c.300 and 1000. Most historians, in view of the collapse of the commercial, industrial and urban economy of the Roman province, combined with the sixth-century plague epidemic, would be inclined to locate the population nadir, as on the continent, in about 600, and assume that recovery was going on from the seventh century. Many continental scholars believe that after a set-back in the ninth century a new wave of economic and demographic expansion was in full swing in the tenth and eleventh centuries, and it might be thought that England followed the same pattern, as it did after 1086. Everyone agrees that the population expansion ended at some time around 1300, but some advocate as early a date as c.1280, others a date after 1349, and the majority opt for some intermediate period, such as the time of the Great Famine of 1315–17. Numbers declined to

---

[1] M. M. Postan, *The Medieval Economy and Society* (London, 1972), pp. 15–26.

about 2 to 2½ million in the late fourteenth century and did not begin to recover until 1520 or later.[2]

EVIDENCE FOR THE RETREAT

The history of settlement before 1086 is especially controversial. Two historians considering evidence from Kent have arrived at very different conclusions, one stressing that settlements had been extensive for centuries before Domesday, while another argues for a long-term expansion of cultivation over the downs and the weald in the pre-Conquest period.[3] However, there is a general consensus for the whole country that Domesday depicts a well-settled countryside with as large an area as 7 or 8 million acres under the plough.[4] It is assumed that people for whom the cultivation of cereals provided the main source of foodstuffs would have selected the most fertile land by a process of trial and error. Therefore the further expansion of population led to the more intense exploitation of existing arable land, and the extension of cultivation over inferior 'marginal' lands. The frontier of cultivation was extended up the slopes of hills, into drained marshes and fens, and over former woodland. By about 1300 many of these newly acquired lands were producing poor cereal yields, and they were abandoned as not being worth further effort. This had repercussions on a society bearing a heavy weight of numbers, and therefore starvation and misery followed. The contraction of society continued through the fourteenth and much of the fifteenth century, hastened by the Black Death of 1348–9 and a series of subsequent epidemics. In this view of the sequence of events, the 'retreat from marginal land' was more than a signal of troubles ahead – it was the trigger for a chain reaction that transformed the historical process.

Both archaeological and documentary evidence support this view of the retreat from the margins. It seems to fit into a long-term sequence of the ebb and flow of settlement going back to the neolithic, indicated by the changing use of such upland areas as the chalk downs of southern England, which were once thought to be the centres of prehistoric cultures, and can now be regarded as fringe lands, utilized with varying intensity depending on the level of population in the more hospitable valleys. In the early medieval period abundant evidence for settlement and exploited resources is provided by the

[2] J. Hatcher, *Plague, Population and the English Economy 1348–1530* (London, 1977), pp. 68–73; P. Salway, *Roman Britain* (Oxford, 1981), pp. 542–52; R. Hodges and D. Whitehouse, *Mohammed, Charlemagne and the Origins of Europe* (London, 1983), pp. 52–3; R. Fossier, *Enfance de l'Europe* (Paris, 1982).

[3] P. H. Sawyer, *From Roman Britain to Norman England* (London, 1978), pp. 136–49; A. Everitt, *Continuity and Colonization. The Evolution of Kentish Settlement* (Leicester, 1986).

[4] H. C. Darby, *Domesday England* (Cambridge, 1977), pp. 129–32.

distribution of pagan cemeteries and the estates mentioned in pre-850 charters. Both are often concentrated in districts with high quality agricultural land, such as north-east Kent or the valley of the Warwickshire Avon. The choice of the best land in prehistory and the early middle ages is suggested by the excavation of gravel sites which show that these easily-worked soils have attracted settlement over thousands of years.[5] According to one interpretation of the Scandinavian invasion of the ninth century, any new settlements at that date had to be founded on inferior sites because the best land had already been taken into cultivation.[6] On Dartmoor arable farming arrived late and was abandoned after a short time. In the case of Holne Moor a large extension of cultivated fields in the thirteenth century reverted to grazing land in the fourteenth. Recent re-interpretations of the deserted hamlet of Houndtor based on pollen analysis suggest that the settlement was associated with an expansion of cereal cultivation in the early thirteenth century, and both settlement and arable farming retreated to lower slopes a century later.[7] Documents recording grain tithes in the Derbyshire Peak district, supported by archaeological evidence of relict medieval fields, show that in the early fourteenth century oats were being grown as high as 300 m above sea level, and that production began to decline in the 1340s.[8] Hamlet settlements at about 250 m have been located by a combination of documentary and archaeological research in Bilsdale in north Yorkshire. They seem to have grown up in the thirteenth century, and in the next century were either completely abandoned or reduced drastically in size.[9] The poor returns from recently settled lands are apparent from the documents. Much of the arable land in areas of colonization in the northern part of the west midlands are found to have been under oats, for example 62 per cent of the crops on the manor of Knowle (Warwickshire) in the 1290s, when land there was still being brought into cultivation.[10] Oats were the least valuable of all grains, their low price reflecting the fact that every eight bushels of grain yielded only two or three bushels of meal, whereas other grains lost only 20 per cent or less of their volume in the milling process. On the demesne lands of the bishopric of Winchester, which produced a wide variety of crops, the dozen

---

[5] D. Powlesland, 'Excavations at Heslerton, North Yorkshire 1978–82', *Archaeological Journal*, 143 (1986), pp. 53–173.

[6] The arguments are summarized in C. D. Morris, 'Aspects of Scandinavian settlement in northern England', *Northern History*, 20 (1984), pp. 1–22, esp. p. 13.

[7] A. Fleming and N. Ralph, 'Medieval settlement and land use on Holne Moor, Dartmoor: the landscape evidence', *Medieval Archaeology*, 26 (1982), pp. 101–37; D. Austin and M. J. C. Walker, 'A new landscape context for Houndtor, Devon', *Medieval Archaeology*, 29 (1985), pp. 147–52.

[8] I. S. W. Blanchard, 'Economic change in Derbyshire in the late middle ages' (unpublished Ph.D. thesis, University of London, 1967), pp. 50–1, 58, 64; W. E. Wightman, 'Open-field agriculture in the Peak District', *Derbyshire Archaeological Journal*, 81 (1961), pp. 111–25.

[9] J. McDonnell, 'Medieval assarting hamlets in Bilsdale, north-east Yorkshire', *Northern History*, 22 (1986), pp. 269–79.

[10] Westminster Abbey Muniments, 27694.

manors with some of the worst records of deteriorating yields in the late thirteenth and early fourteenth century were those which had seen the largest extension of cultivation by the assarting of woodland and the ploughing up of hill pastures.[11]

Contemporaries were only too aware of the problems, and at the end of the thirteenth century and especially in the first half of the fourteenth the documents contain a growing number of references to the stoney, sandy or infertile nature of land. Juries who supplied the information for the extents of Inquisitions Post Mortem, or assessors collecting taxes like the ninth of 1341, repeated these complaints. Estate managers commented on the sterile nature of demesne lands preparatory to the drastic step of leasing them out to tenants, leaving the peasants with the headache of obtaining a return from inferior soils.[12] When we observe the agrarian scene in about 1300 we can appreciate the logic of the pattern of settlement and cultivation. The remaining areas of dense woodland were often in places with steep slopes and thin soils, such as the Forest of Dean in Gloucestershire or parts of the Sussex Weald. In some cases colonization had been pushed to its limits, like the drainage schemes in eastern England or the Sussex levels, where already in the early fourteenth century the battle against flooding was being lost. Further strides in reclamation would not come until new techniques were introduced after 1500.[13]

DOUBTS AND OBJECTIONS TO THE 'RETREAT' IDEA

However, not all of our evidence supports the idea of a 'retreat from marginal land'. Firstly, there is the difficulty of defining which areas were 'marginal' and which were not. Most land in lowland England is capable of producing some crops, and judgements as to its quality depend on complex questions of chemistry, texture, environment, technology and economics. The views of modern soil scientists and farmers may not help us to decide the quality of a soil under medieval conditions. For example, lias clays in the west midlands have been described in a soil survey as 'marginal' for spring barley, yet we know that on this land barley yielded as well in the middle ages as on other soils.[14] The modern view is partly based on the difficulties of using heavy tractors on sticky clay, and in this respect at least the medieval ox-plough enjoyed an advantage. The character of a soil may have changed over the centuries. The modern

[11] J. Z. Titow, *Winchester Yields* (Cambridge, 1972), pp. 32–3.

[12] A. R. H. Baker, 'Evidence in the *Nonarum Inquisitiones* of contracting arable lands in England during the early fourteenth century', *Economic History Review*, 2nd ser., 19 (1966), pp. 518–32; C. Dyer, *Lords and Peasants in a Changing Society* (Cambridge, 1980), pp. 79–82.

[13] For example, P. Brandon, *The Sussex Landscape* (London, 1974), pp. 111–18.

[14] J. M. Bagg, *Soils and their Use in Midland and Western England* (Soil Survey of England and Wales, Bulletin no. 12, Harpenden, 1984), pp. 372–4.

moorlands, for example, have apparently deteriorated to their present unproductive state through mismanagement. Chalk downland may similarly have once been much more suited to cultivation.[15] Changes in climate, even a small shift in average temperatures, as has been shown in a study of the Lammermuir Hills in southern Scotland, could have made extensive corn growing risky and unprofitable, and led to the conversion of the land into rough pasture.[16] We must also remember that a medieval peasant producing grain mainly for his own use would have had a perception of land values that differed from that of a medieval demesne manager, or a modern capitalist farmer, both of whom would have been more aware of labour costs and market returns. 'Marginal' is a relative, not an absolute, term, and it is best applied comparatively.

Secondly, there seems to be no close correlation between the chronology of settlement and soil types. We find that settlements practising arable farming were being established at an early date in places where by any imaginable standard, either medieval or modern, extreme conditions made cultivation difficult and precarious. The houses excavated at Simy Folds in upper Teesdale at a height of 351 m have been dated to the eighth century, and a similar site at Gauber High Fell near Ribblehead is thought to belong to the ninth.[17] In East Anglia the fifth-century settlement of West Stow was established on the sandy soils of the Breckland, only to be abandoned after two hundred years.[18] It surely cannot be thought that at the early dates of these settlements, no better land was available than these bleak uplands or sandy heaths?

In the woodland areas of the midlands one notes puzzling differences in the settlement history of land of apparently similar quality. For example, in north Worcestershire, land at Cofton Hackett appears in a charter of 780 as a 5-hide estate, presumably supporting a peasant population. It contained a good deal of agriculture and settlement at the time of the writing of a charter boundary clause in 849, yet much comparable arable land in adjoining Alvechurch was not taken into cultivation until the thirteenth century.[19] In general, close examination of settlements in Feckenham Forest in Worcestershire or Wychwood in Oxfordshire shows that the soils that were subject to assarting from wood or pasture in the thirteenth century were not much different from those that had been used as arable over a much longer period.[20] Some of the

---

[15] M. Aston, *Interpreting the Landscape* (London, 1985), pp. 24–5.

[16] M. L. Parry, *Climatic Change, Agriculture and Settlement* (Folkestone, 1978), pp. 73–94.

[17] D. Coggins, K. J. Fairless and C. E. Batey, 'Simy Folds: an early medieval settlement site in upper Teesdale', *Medieval Archaeology*, 27 (1983), pp. 1–26; A. King, 'Gauber high pasture, Ribblehead – an interim report', in *Viking Age York and the North*, ed. R. A. Hall (CBA Research Report no. 27, 1978), pp. 21–5.

[18] S. E. West, 'The Anglo-Saxon village of West Stow: an interim report of the excavation, 1965–8', *Medieval Archaeology*, 13 (1969), pp. 1–20, esp. p. 3.

[19] Dyer, *Lords and Peasants*, pp. 22–3, 90–5.

[20] The Feckenham observation is based on the author's unpublished fieldwork. For Wychwood,

woodlands that were being cleared in the thirteenth century were not fragments of primeval forest, but former Romano-British cornfields, which had undergone a process of woodland regeneration in the early middle ages.[21]

It has become customary to divide lowland England into champion and woodland landscapes, that is between the areas of extensive arable cultivation in open fields attached to nucleated villages, and those with a mixture of arable, pasture and wood, organized in enclosed fields and characterized by dispersed settlements. The usual explanation of the difference was that the champion areas were 'old-settled' and the woodlands the product of colonization, largely in the twelfth and thirteenth centuries. Revisionism has now gone so far that one writer has suggested as alternative terms 'planned' and 'ancient' countrysides.[22] He means that the champion landscape is planned in the sense that it has gone through two radical reorganizations in the last 1200 years, firstly with the laying out of the furlongs and strips of the open fields in the early middle ages, the second with the enclosure movement of the eighteenth century. By contrast the hedge lines and sunken tracks of the woodlands often preserve remnants of pre-Conquest, Roman or late prehistoric boundaries and roads. This idea presents us forcefully with the stark truth that many woodlands have a much older settlement history than was once believed, but it takes the paradox too far because some at least of the woodland landscapes can be shown to have been the result of colonizing new land after 1100.

The third criticism of the 'retreat from marginal land' concerns the retreat itself. If the theory was to hold good, the deserted settlements should be found on the poor quality soils of late colonization, on the principle that the last settlement to be founded should be the first to be abandoned. In some parts of Europe, especially in eastern Germany, this seems often to have been the case. But the bulk of English deserted villages were in the champion districts. This means that the actual nucleated settlement may have been created as late as the eleventh or twelfth century, and no earlier than the ninth, but the land from which the inhabitants obtained their living had been under cultivation long before, and often its use extended back into prehistory. In the first phase of desertion before the Black Death, in the classic period of 'retreat', villages in areas such as north-east Gloucestershire and north Oxfordshire were declining and even disappearing. For example, Tusmore, reported as deserted after the first epidemic, was in severe difficulties in 1341, and the Black Death evidently gave it a final blow.[23] These places were far from colonizing settlements; the

B. Schumer, *The Evolution of Wychwood to 1400: Pioneers, Frontiers and Forests* (Leicester University Dept of English Local History, Occasional Papers, 3rd ser., 6, 1984).

[21] P. T. H. Unwin, 'The changing identity of the frontier in medieval Nottinghamshire and Derbyshire', in *Villages, Fields and Frontiers*, ed. B. K. Roberts and R. E. Glasscock (BAR International ser., 185, 1983), pp. 339–51.

[22] O. Rackham, *The History of the Countryside* (London, 1986).

[23] C. Dyer, 'Deserted medieval villages in the west midlands', *Economic History Review*, 2nd ser., 35 (1982), pp. 19–34, esp. p. 23.

majority were sited on lands which had supported populations in the iron age and in the Roman period.

Settlements were abandoned in the fourteenth and fifteenth centuries in woodlands and uplands also, some of them relatively new, some of them occupying old-cultivated land. The desertion of these hamlets and farmsteads has not attracted the same attention as desertions of whole villages. With a village went a complete field system, which was changed radically with conversion to pasture. The loss of a third or a half of the hamlets and farms in an area of dispersed settlement produced a patchwork effect on the landscape, which did not have the same impact either on contemporary observers or on modern historians. Without more research we cannot be sure of the scale of desertion of small settlements, but it is likely on the basis of present samples that the numbers of households affected by late medieval desertion were rather greater in the champion villages than in the woodland hamlets. Even if the numbers were approximately equal, only a proportion of the dispersed settlements can be regarded as the products of late colonization. At Hanbury (Worcestershire), for example, at least a dozen deserted farms lay near to land that had been cultivated before the Conquest and in Roman times, quite probably without any interruptions. Many settlements of twelfth- and thirteenth-century colonization survived until modern times, both in the woodlands of the midlands and the hills of west Yorkshire.[24] In other words, the retreat of settlement affected people living on old-cultivated lands rather more than those on recent assarts. Occasionally new settlements were founded in the fifteenth century in the woodland districts, mainly cottages on waste land, a process which emphasizes again that the champion landscapes bore the brunt of desertions.[25]

ALTERNATIVE APPROACHES

We have to take a number of varied influences into account in explaining the formation and decay of settlements. These were matters of choice by the people of the time, who were acting in response to a number of motives, not all of them based on economic rationality. Cistercian monks, for example, deliberately sought out 'deserts' in pursuit of an ascetic ideal, though they sometimes changed their initial site if it proved inhospitable.[26] The enforcement of forest law is another example of a non-economic influence on settlement. Royal

[24] M. L. Faull and S. A. Moorhouse, *West Yorkshire: An Archaeological Survey to A.D. 1500* (Wakefield, 1981), pp. 585–613.

[25] New houses were being built on the waste in *c.* 1470 at Ombersley, Worcestershire, and Sedgley, Staffordshire: Hereford and Worcester CRO, ref. 705:56, B.A. 3910/24; Staffordshire RO D 593/0/3/3.

[26] R. A. Donkin, *The Cistercians: Studies in the Geography of Medieval England and Wales* (Pontifical Institute of Mediaeval Studies, Studies and Texts, 38, Toronto, 1978), pp. 31–6.

officials collected fines in the forest from those who poached the deer or assarted the woods; their activities annoyed the inhabitants, but did not prevent the clearance of new land. However, the preservation of woods near royal hunting lodges, like those that survived into the seventeenth century around Feckenham in Worcestershire, suggests that royal interest in hunting had some inhibiting effect on assarting. The aristocratic parks that proliferated in the thirteenth and fourteenth century had irrational functions as pleasure grounds and status symbols. The modest profits from the venison and the use of the park for grazing cattle did not justify the loss of money deriving from the land's use as arable. Parks often contained land of cultivable quality, as is shown both by the inclusion within them of former arable, and the occasional record of lords ploughing up part of the land after the park had been enclosed.[27] The park could become a focus for settlement itself, as at Walsall (Staffordshire) in the early thirteenth century when the lord moved his manor house from the developing town to a site in the park which had previously been under cultivation.[28] In short, whether for reasons of ideology, status or pleasure, lords established settlements on poor land, or prevented the cultivation of potential arable.

Peasants could exercise some choices also, though within limits imposed on them by their lords, their village communities and their own lack of resources. There was no exact correlation between the legal status of peasants and the settlement pattern, but assarts and new lands of the twelfth and thirteenth centuries were often held by free tenure, and the highest proportion of customary or servile tenants is found in the nucleated villages of the champion. The free tenants were more tenacious in keeping their holdings in adverse circumstances, and they had good economic reasons to do so. A smallholding in customary tenure could pay rents and dues totalling 10d. to 12d. per acre, while a rent for an assart was often 2d. to 4d. per acre. The customary tenant was liable to extra dues, such as entry fines, while the freeholder owed only a modest relief. These burdens made the free land a more attractive asset, and its tenant may have been encouraged to continue cultivation even with poor yields. The market could exercise a considerable influence on settlement, in combination with other circumstances. Take, for example the Essex manor of Havering atte Bower, occupying a large area of poor land, London clay in the north and glacial gravels in the south, the one type difficult to work, the other easy, but neither especially fertile. Yields of wheat and oats from the demesne of Hornchurch (an enclave within Havering) were among the lowest recorded in medieval England. Yet the tenants of Havering enjoyed the privilege of free

---

[27] For example, at Beoley, Worcestershire, and Berkeley, Gloucestershire: BL, Egerton Rolls 8661; J. Smyth, *The Lives of the Berkeleys* (Gloucester, 1883), vol. II, pp. 14–16.

[28] S. and S. Wrathmell, 'Excavations at the moat site, Walsall, Staffordshire', *Transactions of the South Staffordshire Archaeological and Historical Society*, 16 (1974–5), pp. 19–53; 18 (1976–7), pp. 30–45.

tenure on a royal demesne manor, which gave them the benefits both of low rents and free disposal of their land. Havering lay near to the large London market, to which the tenants had easy access by road. The manor was extensively assarted in the thirteenth century, providing a classic example of land hunger pushing the frontier of colonization onto unrewarding soils. However, when the great contraction came, the settlements of Havering showed obstinate longevity. The numbers of tenants declined less than on many manors on more fertile soils, and they exhibited every sign of prosperity through the recession of the fourteenth and fifteenth centuries.[29] Closer to London a ring of villages occupying much land that was by no means of the highest quality, such as Stepney, Fulham and Lambeth, were stimulated by the closeness of the urban market to adopt horticulture as well as more conventional farming. Their records show few signs of the ruinous buildings and vacant holdings that appear so prominently in those of midland villages around 1400.[30]

Social circumstances could therefore improve the value of poor land, but human factors could also ruin potentially good land. The Gloucestershire Cotswold villages that were in evident decline by 1341 have already been mentioned. Their land had supported a rich Romano-British civilization, and arable cultivation was extensive by the tenth and eleventh centuries. Modern Cotswold farmers now grow abundant crops of cereals and vegetables. In the early fourteenth century hundreds of acres of arable lay uncultivated, and tenants were giving up their holdings and leaving their villages, complaining of poverty. The fertility of the soil in a two-course rotation depended on the combination of sheep and corn, the sheep being folded on the arable after feeding on the hill pastures, and treading their dung into the stoney soils. Any disturbance of the system could have had a disastrous effect on cereal yields, as can be shown from accounts of the demesne of Temple Guiting in 1327, where the temporary absence of the sheep reduced the grain yields to the point that the lord of the manor was making a loss on arable cultivation. We do not know the sequence of events that gave the peasants similar agricultural problems. Was it the slow drain on their resources of rent and tax demands? Or the shock of the sheep scab epidemics in the late thirteenth century? Or perhaps a combination of such setbacks reduced the size of the village flocks and 'marginalized' the land that had supported peasant populations for centuries?[31]

The English landscape is too complicated to allow us to think of a moving frontier of settlement, like that of north America in the last century. This analogy is bound to give us a conception of assarting as taking place on the edge

[29] M. K. McIntosh, *Autonomy and Community: The Royal Manor of Havering, 1200–1500* (Cambridge, 1986), esp. pp. 137–52.

[30] PRO, SC 2/188/65; 191/62; 205/12; 205/15.

[31] C. Dyer, 'The rise and fall of a medieval village: Little Aston (in Aston Blank), Gloucestershire', *Transactions of the Bristol and Gloucestershire Archaeological Society*, 105 (1987), pp. 165–81.

of a vast expanse of trees, through which a progressive wave of human conquerors reduced woodland to arable by vigorous use of axe and fire. It is often stated that this process was organized and directed by landlords, who either issued charters to the colonists and collected the profits in rents from the new land, or added land to their demesnes. Our documents tell a complex story. Assarting as a concept and an institution was an innovation of the twelfth century. Before that date new lands were incorporated into the field system and tenures of the village without being given a special status.[32] Twelfth- and thirteenth-century assarting was a piece-meal process, often initiated by local peasants, not by colonists from a distance, and lords tended to play a relatively passive role. The tenants of larger holdings were often prominent in the movement, intending either to add to their existing land, or to provide a holding for their younger son or daughter, who could not, under the rules of primogeniture, inherit any part of the main holding.[33] Assarting seems to have been a gradual process, as individual tenants took over and eventually brought under the plough parcels of former common land. It was sometimes a movement that created whole new settlements, but more often it involved shifts within a partially developed and settled agrarian landscape.

Long-term expansion and decline of settlements took place within distinctive agrarian systems of each region and district, which would be affected by changes in demography and the economy in different ways. It was once thought that each regional type reflected the ethnic composition of the population, but this is easily disproved because the agrarian regions do not coincide with the areas of supposed British, German or Scandinavian settlement. In its dying moments one protagonist of this approach had to invent a hitherto unknown ethnic group, the Friso-Jutes, to explain the peculiarities of eastern England.[34] Nor can we accept that regional differences represent different phases in an evolutionary development, with East Anglia having advanced through a champion system of nucleated villages and open fields, while in the west woodlands were changing into champion villages. Such evolutionary movements can rarely be traced in our evidence. For example, it was once believed that in the thirteenth century, influenced by population pressure, many villages working a two-field system changed over to three fields in order to increase the area under corn. In fact this happened infrequently. The peasants were evidently reluctant to risk more intensive cultivation which would have endangered the delicate balance between arable and pasture, and might have led to a reduction in manuring and to a decline in grain yields.[35]

[32] P. D. A. Harvey (ed.), *The Peasant Land Market in Medieval England* (Oxford, 1984), pp. 13–14.

[33] M. Stinson, 'Assarting and poverty in early fourteenth century western Yorkshire', *Landscape History*, 5 (1983), pp. 53–67.

[34] G. C. Homans, 'The rural sociology of medieval England', *Past and Present*, 4 (1953), pp. 32–43.

[35] H. S. A. Fox, 'The alleged transformation from two-field to three-field systems in medieval England', *Economic History Review*, 2nd ser., 39 (1986), pp. 526–48.

The effects of the periods of growth and decline on agrarian systems can best be appreciated by taking two concrete examples, both from the west midlands. One is the champion (Feldon) district of south Warwickshire and south-east Worcestershire, the other the wood/pasture district to the south of the modern city of Birmingham, in the middle ages in the Arden of Warwickshire and Feckenham Forest in Worcestershire.

The Feldon settlements at their peak of development in the thirteenth century were predominantly nucleated villages practising a two-course rotation in open fields.[36] They had limited resources of pasture and wood, and relied on long-distance contacts through estate links (see pp. 10–12) or the market for firewood and timber. The soils were mainly lias clay, with some alluvial gravels in the Avon valley. They maintained fertility by practising sheep and corn husbandry, and achieved the normal medieval grain yields of about three to four times the seed sown. A high proportion of the peasants held by customary tenure, for which their primary obligation was the payment of an annual cash 'rent of assize' which normally varied from 7s. to 21s. per yardland. Their ability to pay in cash indicates that they sold a good deal of their produce. The majority of holdings were assessed in terms of the standard yardland unit, mostly in halves and quarters; the yardland varied in size between 20 and 40 acres of arable land.

The area supported a large pre-medieval population, and was well settled in the pre-Conquest period. As the villages were already large by the time of Domesday, the expanding population of the subsequent two centuries put the inhabitants under considerable pressure. To some extent they intensified the use of land by subdividing holdings (if the lord consented), so that the numbers of complete yardland tenements diminished. They also used their fields more intensively by 'inhoking' or 'hiching', that is by taking part of the fallow field and planting it, thereby cultivating rather more than half of the arable each year. But there were limits beyond which they could not go. Excessive fragmentation of holdings would have impoverished them all. Impartible inheritance ensured that one heir would receive a viable holding. Younger sons might be able to marry a widow and then acquire her land, or buy a

---

[36] This last section is informed by such published works as R. H. Hilton, *A Medieval Society*, 2nd edn (Cambridge, 1983); idem, *The English Peasantry in the Later Middle Ages* (Oxford, 1975); J. B. Harley, 'Population trends and agricultural developments from the Warwickshire Hundred Rolls of 1279', *Economic History Review*, 2nd ser., 11 (1958–9), pp. 8–18; B. K. Roberts, 'A study of medieval colonisation in the Forest of Arden, Warwickshire', *Agricultural History Review*, 16 (1968), pp. 101–13; A. R. H. Baker and R. A. Butlin (eds), *Studies of Field Systems in the British Isles* (Cambridge, 1973), pp. 221–30, 345–63; C. Dyer, *Warwickshire Farming, 1349–c. 1520* (Dugdale Society Occasional Paper, 27, 1981); Z. Razi, *Life, Marriage and Death in a Medieval Parish* (Cambridge, 1980); T. R. Slater and P. J. Jarvis (eds), *Field and Forest: An Historical Geography of Warwickshire and Worcestershire* (Norwich, 1982).

small holding in the village, but as most holdings could support no more than a nuclear family, there was much emigration.

The system was therefore operating at high pressure in the thirteenth century, with each village developing a delicate balance in land holding and cultivation, having always to consider not just the needs of the villagers but also the surplus that had to be produced for the lords' rents and the State's taxes. The equilibrium was evidently upset in the early fourteenth century, probably by a combination of external demands and internal malfunctions of the agrarian system. After 1349, under the influence of both disease and migration, the villages had to adjust to new circumstances. The balance between tenants of holdings of different sizes was disturbed by the reduction in the numbers of smallholders and the rise of a few kulaks. The field systems had to be changed drastically so that labour-intensive cultivation could give way to an extension of grazing land. Villages which had grown up to serve a specific purpose – feeding large communities by extensive cereal cultivation – were neither large nor in need of so much grain. They faced catastrophe by the early fifteenth century, when a rump of peasants picked their way through weedy derelict fields to cultivate the remaining strips, and defended their crops from the expanding flocks of the village kulaks and intrusive neighbours. Landlords were faced with either restoring the village by combating migration and rebuilding derelict houses, or rationalizing their decaying assets by removing the remaining villagers and transforming the field system into an enclosed pasture. Some lords carried out this latter policy vigorously and speedily, but many delayed until the whole village had gone. So by the early sixteenth century a fifth of the villages had been deserted, and the remainder were much reduced in size. With varying degrees of success, the survivors adopted a system of mixed husbandry, with a reduced arable area cultivated on a four-field system.

In the woodlands the dispersed settlements in the thirteenth century cultivated some open fields of a complicated kind, and often held lands in severalty (enclosures). They relied a good deal on pasture, both in their closes and on large heaths and commons. The soil is predominantly red Triassic marl, which is not necessarily inferior to the lias of the Feldon, but which because of the higher ground of the Birmingham plateau suffers more from coldness and wetness. The peasants practised a combination of cereal cultivation (with some emphasis on oats) with a good deal of pastoral husbandry, especially cattle herding. The power of lords in the district was weaker than in the south: the Benedictine monasteries exercised less influence and there were more gentry landlords. Rents and obligations were correspondingly lower, and a high proportion of the tenants held by free tenure. There were more smallholders (measured in terms of arable land) than in the Feldon, but they were not necessarily poorer because they had access to extensive common pastures, and they were involved in crafts and industries, such as coal-mining, charcoal-burning and wood- and metal-working.

There is evidence of settlements in the woodlands of Arden and Feckenham from the bronze age onwards. Judging from the Domesday account of the area settlements were relatively thin. Charters of the ninth and tenth centuries suggest an agrarian landscape not unlike that of the thirteenth century, in which areas of woodland, pasture and marsh were interspersed with enclosures, patches of cultivation and isolated settlements. In the twelfth and thirteenth centuries the settlements became more numerous, and assarting extended the areas of cultivation and enclosure. A marked increase in the numbers of markets and small boroughs provided commercial outlets for pastoralists to sell their surplus of animals and animal products, and for the rural craftsmen. Their grain consumption was partially met by trade from the Feldon district. Extra people could be accommodated by adjusting but not transforming the system. There were signs of stress in the thirteenth century, when some communities resisted the enclosure of common pastures with violence. But although the peasants of Halesowen, the best documented manor in the district, suffered grievously in the famine of 1315–17, they were able to make up their numbers in the succeeding generation. The drop in population in the late fourteenth and fifteenth centuries was naturally accompanied by the abandonment of many settlements and a reversion of much arable to pasture. There may have been some small-scale regeneration of woodland, and areas were turned over entirely to grass. Enterprising lords specialized in large-scale meat production for the market, without destroying peasant communities, who were themselves profiting from small-scale pastoralism. The changes were not traumatic. They could be absorbed within the system, and indeed the profits of farming and industry meant that in 1524–5 the inhabitants of the 'underdeveloped' Arden of Warwickshire paid a larger share of their county's taxes than they had done two centuries earlier.

CONCLUSION

These case studies suggest three general conclusions. Firstly, that the retreat of the later middle ages affected settlement on all types of land, and that its most dramatic consequences were felt in the old-settled villages, not on the newly-colonized 'marginal soils'. Secondly, that the negative term 'retreat' derives from a deep-rooted prejudice that arable cultivation represents an advance towards civilization – yet the highly commercial wood/pasture economy brought many of the inhabitants of such districts considerable prosperity, and gave their settlements a vigorous and extended life. Thirdly, that we should not abandon such concepts as long-term growth and decline in the middle ages. To understand them more fully, and to know why and how they occurred, we must explore them in the context of local agrarian and social systems.

4

Nucleation and Dispersion: Distribution Maps as a Research Tool

BRIAN K. ROBERTS

INTRODUCTION

The Ordnance Survey 6″ to 1 mile maps (1:10,560) of the nineteenth century are one foundation for research in settlement history. Providing national coverage at a uniform scale and incorporating a standardized degree of detail, they record the more visible portions of cultural landscapes whose buried depths are now being revealed by archaeologists. Concealed within their detail is fundamental evidence concerning settlement and with this source it is feasible to map very large areas with speed and facility. The resulting distribution map can be both a way of organizing data and a powerful research tool, useful in the present state of understanding yet, perhaps more importantly, reinterpretable in the light of future discoveries and increased knowledge.

RURAL SETTLEMENTS IN TIME AND SPACE

Figure 4.1 has been devised to illustrate the problems underlying all such maps. Distribution maps will, as the time matrix shows, always conflate into one plane features from varied periods and separating these is a key research problem. The First Edition 6″ series themselves range in date between 1840 and 1889 and indeed will vary in date within a single county.[1] The single case isolated in the spatial-temporal matrix of figure 4.1 reveals a further problem. Any settlement can originate, expand, contract and even decay, perhaps to be refounded, wholly altered and grow again. There is never any guarantee that our evidence, in this case represented by dot symbols, will record the most critical phases. Nevertheless, these observations, when applied to distribution maps, raise questions concerning the varied degrees of continuity and change

---

[1] J. B. Harley, *The Historian's Guide to Ordnance Survey Maps* (London, 1964).

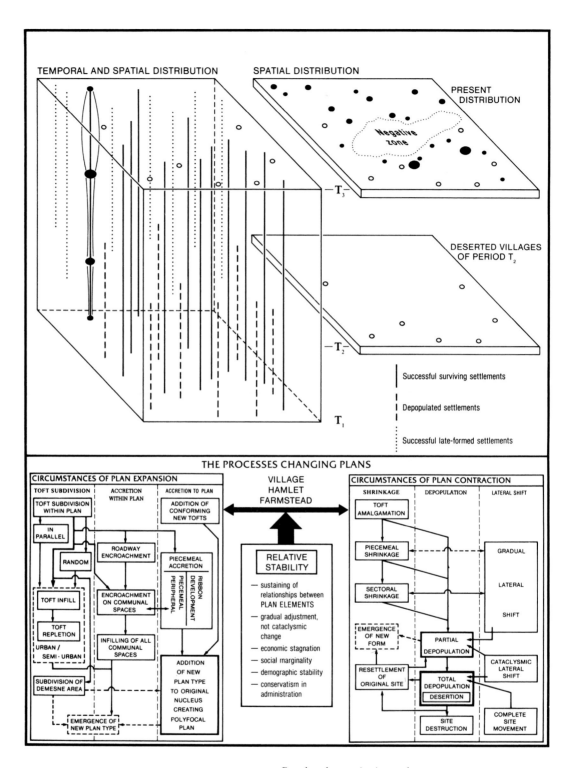

FIGURE 4.1 *Rural settlements in time and space*

underlying the visible forms and patterns. The lower diagrams of figure 4.1 summarize the varied processes which have, through time, acted upon established settlements. An attempt has also been made to suggest the qualities which inhibit change, creating a condition of stability. Paradoxically, this latter 'process', really involving gradual change, may well have been quantitatively more dominant in the through-time trajectories of most settlements than the more dramatic changes brought about by short phases of vigorous expansion or contraction. Relative 'stability', involving adaptation, continuity and maintenance, is remarkably difficult to grasp and evaluate, yet its importance is profound for it carries the past into the present.

This proposition has a bearing upon a more difficult question of the value of distribution maps based upon such late sources: if ancient village plans do survive centuries of occupation what does in fact survive? Most standing buildings will have been reconstructed or constructed during the last two or three centuries and occupy sites where generations of dwellings have shuffled, while the fabric of property boundaries and street lines will have undergone similar experiences. However, where a sequence of maps document essential stability we can see that the more recent morphology is normally conditioned (rather than wholly determined) by antecedent forms and substructural features. These reflect both the *in situ* succession of development on the site and any cultural or physical substructural features, pre-dating the settlement, which may be present.[2] These cultural elements are themselves reflections of the minutiae of land ownership and usage. In this succession of events the assemblage of plan elements within the earliest antecedent of the surviving morphology – conceptually the public, private and communal spaces,[3] but practically the toft compartments, church, demesne, greens and street areas – hold an important place.[4] To put this another way, the relationship between, say, a twelfth-century village plan and a mid-nineteenth-century plan can best be appreciated by using the idea of a 'skeuomorph'. An early railway coach was based upon a horse-drawn carriage and reflected this in its shape and decoration but was *not* in any sense a road carriage. This is equally true of village plans. Our problem concerns how much we can legitimately deduce about the road carriage from the railway carriage. Furthermore, it must be recognized that the form which eventually gives rise to the visible morphology of the nineteenth century need have no direct relationship with the chronology of settlement foundation. There is always the possibility of cataclysmic post-foundation changes.[5]

---

[2] B. K. Roberts, *The Making of the English Village* (London, 1987), figs 2.2, 10.5; C. Howell, *Land, Family and Inheritance in Transition* (Cambridge, 1983), pp. 114–46.

[3] Roberts, *Making of the English Village*, fig. 2.1.

[4] ibid., fig. 8.2.

[5] ibid., fig. 1.5; A. J. L. Winchester, *Landscape and Society in Medieval Cumbria* (Edinburgh, 1987), pp. 45–6, fig. 12.

CLASSIFICATION: THE MATRIX AND THE MAP KEY

To create a map from the 6″ topographical series each settlement must be coded by a symbol, and if this is to result in more than an array of disparate shapes then a system of logical classification is needed.[6] Such standardization is necessary so as to form the basis of rigorous comparison and a context for sustained discussion. This is essential to any academic discipline involving field study. Figure 4.2 summarizes one system. A perspective view has been used to emphasize that the six 'plates' are part of a conceptual three-dimensional matrix. In reality individual settlements lie upon two axes; within each individual plate are classificatory cells showing characteristic village plans. In practice, gradations of types can be found falling between each cell so that a mapping symbol always represents a subjective judgement. Errors will occur but these can be corrected. Of equal importance are the vertical axes, for the varied degrees of complexity found within settlements, ranging from the single cottage or farmstead in a dispersed pattern to the complexity of the town, are parts of a vertical gradation extending up the matrix. At any one time a settlement landscape will contain a mixture of these morphological types. These ideas can be extended in two ways: first, the relatively simple plan types of each cell can be combined to create 'polyfocal' or 'composite' plans. This aggregation can appear at any level of the matrix, giving complex villages and urban complexity at the upper end, and linked farmstead clusters and linked hamlet clusters at the lower end, that is, settlements where the simple elements of a pattern tending towards dispersal can nevertheless be shown to contain a measure of functional coherence. This extends the practical scope of the classification. The second extension is conceptual: when individual settlements are studied over a period of time they may be thought of as having a trajectory *through* the matrix, from farmstead to hamlet and village and in a few cases to town, while conversely a depopulated village may shrink and then finally decay to the status of an individual farmstead. This view introduces a dynamic aspect to morphological studies. Note that plan changes, that is, diagonal movements between successive plate cells, are as possible as are evolutionary changes where simple plans of a given type develop lineally upwards into more complex versions of the same type. Of course, when thinking of a single settlement's trajectory, each cell on each plate becomes a time phase map depicting an evolving form.

The application of this concept to the mapping of nucleated and dispersed settlements can be illustrated by reference to figure 4.3, the Eden valley. The basic map records the morphology of all nucleated settlements, from the towns to known and possible deserted villages, but only for a sample area have true

---

[6] A. J. L. Winchester, *Landscape and Society in Medieval Cumbria* (Edinburgh, 1987), pp. 2.3/4.

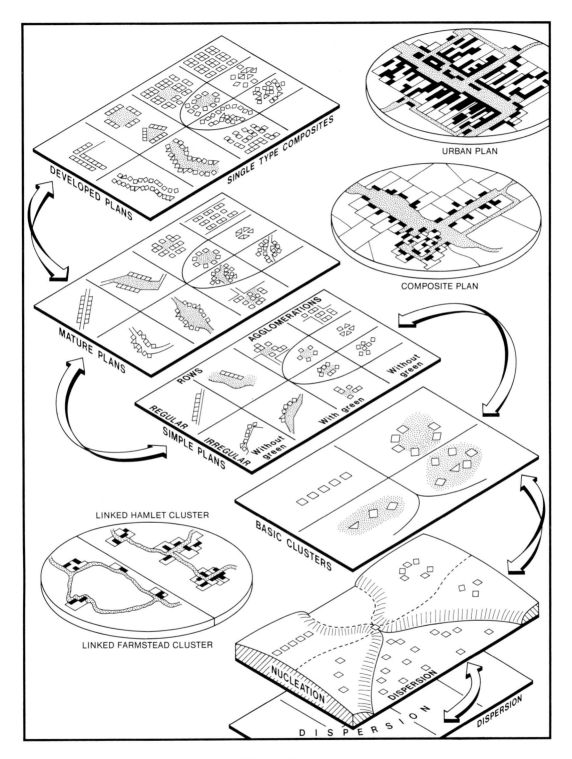

FIGURE 4.2 *Villages in time*

single farmsteads been included. The pattern of plans emerges as strikingly repetitious. However, what can this distribution map of late nineteenth-century village and hamlet forms add to our understanding of settlement evolution? The core of any analysis of settlement is chronology and the following simplified framework is needed to understand developments in the region:

1   A substratum of native British states, one powerful enough for its ruler, Urien of Reged, to be styled 'lord of Catraeth' (Catterick, a strategic location to the east of the Stainmore pass), was eventually made subject to English control.[7]

2   The initial Anglo-Saxon movements into the area took place 'during the first half of the seventh century'. These were important enough to ensure that the large majority of parish and township names *not* of Scandinavian origin are English.[8]

3   Scandinavian settlement during the first half of the tenth century led to the appearance of Danish and, later, Norse, place names.[9]

4   In 1092 William Rufus took Carlisle from the local ruler, Dolfin, garrisoned the castle, and then 'returned hither southwards, sending very many peasants thither with their wives and livestock to settle there and till the soil'. This was a sponsored colonization of a frontier region to enhance its security and the colonists could have been of very mixed origins, both English and Scandinavian. Presumably the establishment of military control and the planting of settlements went hand in hand, and may have taken place between 1092 and 1135, by which date Appleby and Brough castles were in place to guard the strategic Stainmore route. This frontier consolidation was not achieved without some reversals, notably the invasion by William the Lion in 1174.[10]

The difficulties of linking the physical aspects of settlement visible in figure 4.3 to the historical context are considerable. An entry in a *Curia Regis* roll of 1201 provides an initial step, citing a writ of Henry I by which he granted to Hildred of Carlisle and Odard his son *terram que fuit Gamel filii Bern et terram illam que fuit Glassam filii Brictrici drengorum meorum*. The subsequent history

[7] A. M. Armstrong, A. Mawer, F. M. Stenton and B. Dickens, *The Place-Names of Cumberland* (Cambridge, 1950), pp. xvii–xx; N. Higham, *The Northern Counties to AD 1000* (London, 1986).

[8] Armstrong et al., *Place-Names of Cumberland*, xxi–xxii; Higham, *Northern Counties*, pp. 256–74; idem, 'The Scandinavians in north Cumbria', in *The Scandinavians in Cumbria*, ed. J. R. Baldwin and I. D. Whyte (Scottish Society for Northern Studies, Edinburgh, 1985), pp. 37–51.

[9] G. Fellows Jensen, 'Scandinavian settlement in Cumbria and Dumfriesshire: the place-name evidence', in *Scandinavians in Cumbria*, ed. Baldwin and Whyte, pp. 43–8, 65–82; Higham, *Northern Counties*, pp. 322–35.

[10] J. Plummer and C. Plummer (eds), *Two of the Saxon Chronicles Parallel* (2 vols, Oxford, 1892, repr. 1965), vol. I, p. 227; G. N. Garmonsway, *The Anglo-Saxon Chronicle* (London, 1953), p. 227.

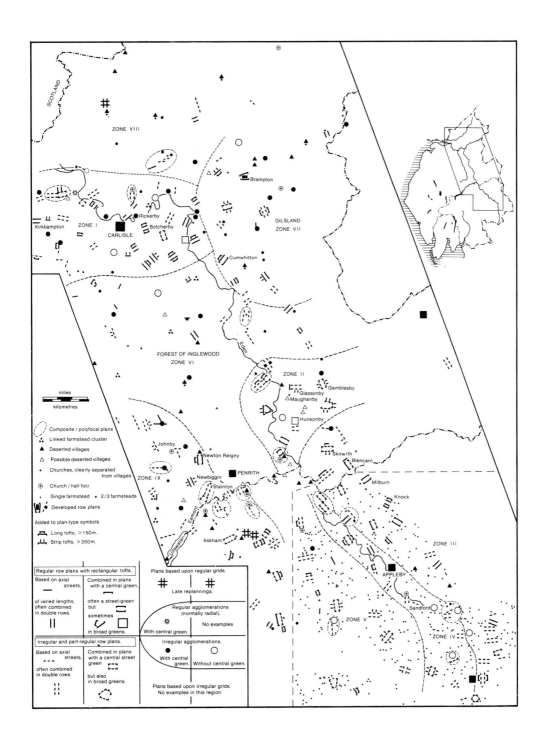

FIGURE 4.3 *Rural settlements in the Eden valley, Cumberland and Westmorland.*

of the estate shows that the villages of Gamblesby and Glassonby must derive their names from these individuals and allows two important inferences: firstly that place names in -bý were still being formed (or perhaps re-formed) in the period 1100–35, and secondly that such place names may give only a tenuous guide to the racial origins of their founders, for while Gamel is Old Norse and Bern possibly so, Glassan is Old Irish and yet his father possessed an Old English name.[11]

There are a number of -bý names in Cumberland with prefixes derived from non-Scandinavian personal names, which are Irish, French, Flemish and even Breton in origin.[12] When these are plotted (figure 4.4) they are seen to concentrate in two areas, first around Glassonby and Gamblesby with an outlying group of three on the eastern flanks of the Northern Fells of the Lake District (to follow A. Wainwright's nomenclature) and second quite literally in a ring around Carlisle. Not to associate these coherent groups with the consolidation of Norman power after 1092 would be stretching scepticism too far. Can these observations be used to throw light upon settlement history? Both Glassonby and Gamblesby are villages with distinctive plans, part-regular rather than wholly regular, a type common throughout the region, and one might infer that Gamel and Glassan were *locatores*, holding their lands by gift of the king and bringing in colonists in furtherance of royal policies. In the absence of hard evidence this can only be speculation but the case is a reasonable one. Within the township of Gamblesby the place name Addingham is probably 'one of the most ancient Anglian place names in Cumberland' and was the focus of a parish containing Unthank, Glassonby*, Maughanby*, Hunsonby, Farmanby*, Robberby*, Winskill and Little Salkeld, the asterisks denoting 'late' -bý names established within the older territory. Addingham lay close to the Eden and it and its medieval church have now been swept away. The township name of Hunsonby, 'dog keeper's -bý', hints at a link with drengage, a ministerial tenure of which an incident was often keeping dogs, and which could be contemporary with the drengages at Glassonby and Gamblesby noted above.[13] Thus there appear to be sound grounds for dating Gamblesby's rise as a parish centre, and probably its foundation, after 1092 and before 1135. The other settlements of this group fall into two classes: large successful villages; and what are, by the mid-nineteenth century, farmsteads as at Maughanby (figure 4.5). This distinction may reflect an element of choice, for land granted to a *locator* could either be stocked with men or retained in hand.[14] Of course, the broader vicissitudes of settlement history could lead to

---

[11] Armstrong et al., *Place-Names of Cumberland*, p. 192.

[12] ibid., pp. xxxi–xxxiii; G. Fellows Jensen, 'Place names and settlements: some problems of dating as exemplified by place names in -bý', *Nomina*, 8 (1984), pp. 29–39.

[13] D. Austin, *Boldon Book* (Chichester, 1982), p. 27; G. W. S. Barrow, *The Kingdom of the Scots* (London, 1973), pp. 15–16; J. E. A. Jolliffe, 'Northumbrian institutions', *English Historical Review*, 41 (1926), pp. 1–42.

[14] Roberts, *Making of the English Village*, fig. 10.4.

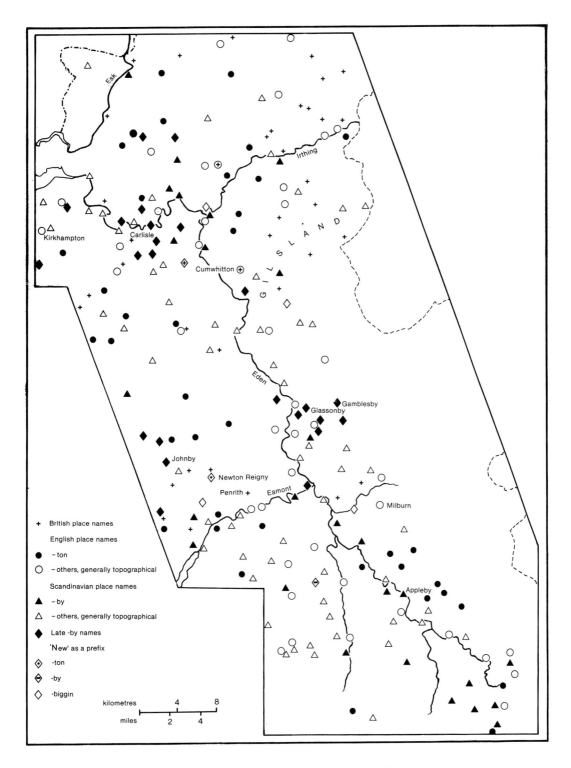

FIGURE 4.4   *Place names in the Eden valley, Cumberland and Westmorland.*

depopulation. At Maughanby ('Maffanby') earthworks of what could be a toft compartment seem to be present, while at Dolphenby five or six longhouses are visible as earthworks; field evidence suggests that Farmanby was never more than a single farmstead. This evidence for the presence of a distinctive block of colonizing activity north of the Eamont–Eden confluence poses a question. Why here? The answer must surely lie in military strategy.

Carlisle was the key regional fortress from which William Rufus dislodged Dolfin to gain control of the area. Gilsland, the north-eastern flank of the Eden valley, was not taken from the native ruler Gille until around 1156.[15] The castles at Appleby and Brough were present by 1130,[16] while north of the Eamont the main Roman road ran along the western flank of the Eden, through the wastes of Inglewood (shown on the Gough map of the early fourteenth century).[17] Men settled in the Gamblesby–Melmerby zone were ideally placed to become aware of the progress of raiders southwards via the Fell Edge lowlands east of the Eden and perhaps even via the upland green ways, where movement would be detected by shepherds. Were this the substance of the argument, then it would be tenuous indeed. However, Carlisle is ringed by a second group of late *bý* names: Botcherby and Rickerby, Etterby and Tarraby, Upperby and Aglionby, to which may be added Willow Holm, derived from Guerri the Fleming. Once again, on nineteenth-century maps some of these (Botcherby and Upperby – 'Hobricht's -*bý*') are regular villages, while others are not. Botcherby and Rickerby are significant, for both Bochard and Richard gave their names to streets within the city and to city gates. In fact Etard, and probably Richard, appear as personages in the Pipe Roll of 1130. Pipe Roll and place names combine to suggest quarters within the city where Bochard and Richard had control, and there were others, the *vicus hibernicorum*, *vicus francorum*, and somewhere a Fleming quarter.[18] Outside the town the associated rural settlements surely contained additional supportive agricultural populations, some of those peasants brought northwards, not only by William Rufus but by Henry I and those knights in possession of the newly conquered lands. The very mixture of languages and nationalities implied by this evidence shows the opportunities upon the frontier for those with ambition, horse, mail and lance, or a craft or trade (for the masons who worked upon the new cathedral were part of the movement). If there is a grain of truth in these arguments, then we may here be identifying the initial strategic footholds established between 1092 and 1130. However, to see all the strikingly repetitious village plans as of the same date would be incautious. Surely the

<hr>

[15] W. E. Kapelle, *The Norman Conquest of the North* (London, 1979), p. 200.

[16] J. Beeler, *Warfare in England 1066–1189* (New York, 1966), pp. 400, 418; D. Renn, *Norman Castles in Britain*, 2nd edn (London, 1973), pp. 90, 118–20.

[17] W. Rollinson, *A History of Man in the Lake District* (London, 1967).

[18] B. C. Jones, 'Note on the medieval topography of Carlisle', in *Archaeology in the North*, ed. P. A. G. Clack and P. Gosling (London, 1976), pp. 180–5.

Gospatric writ of 1041 × 1055 (or 1064) can be interpreted as an active encouragement to colonization, perhaps generating even earlier planted villages, while the subsequent troubled history of this border zone created opportunities for both replanning and refounding.[19] Furthermore, the time required for Norman and other adventurers after 1092 to secure possession and then found villages must have extended over thirty to forty years. These conclusions bring us face to face with a crucial problem: if we bring together the place names and other historical evidence with that of morphology, what is revealed concerning the likely course of settlement evolution?

SETTLEMENT LANDSCAPES

The Eden valley is dominated by settlements based upon rows (figure 4.3): the diagram in figure 4.5 identifies diagnostic features and classificatory trajectories by means of a flow diagram, while the lower section provides examples of four characteristic types. To meet the objection that only nineteenth-century maps have been used, some of the region's plans can be shown to have evolved from seventeenth-century antecedents possessing the same morphological character-istics,[20] and while changes have undoubtedly occurred, sufficient elements of earlier morphologies survive in nineteenth-century maps to be identified by the experienced eye. The process is analogous to architectural history. Where dating evidence is available, essentially giving a *terminus ante quem*, the varied plan types are all seen to be present before the mid-twelfth century. The pre-1150 church is set within the row at Kirkbampton in a village surely laid out over earlier field strips; the church in a toft of the planned row at Newton Reigny has a late twelfth-century aisle added to an earlier two-celled structure (the butt joint between nave and aisle is visible on the south-east external corner) and the late twelfth-century church at Cumwhitton was placed in the drift (cattle track between the settlement and the pastures) of an existing village.[21] One problem in using this method is the frequency of late and radical church restorations, but significantly Bouch concluded that nine out of ten of the older churches of the diocese were built or rebuilt during the twelfth century.[22] In essence the Victorians were replacing substantially decayed churches resulting from one major early building campaign. The presence of curvilinear churchyards are conceivably indicative of an earlier generation of churches.[23] Significantly, these are often wholly peripheral to the villages;

[19] C. R. Hart, *The Early Charters of Northern England and the North Midlands* (Leicester, 1975), p. 128.

[20] Roberts, *Making of the English Village*, fig. 3.12.

[21] ibid., fig. 3.12.

[22] N. Pevsner, *Cumberland and Westmorland* (London, 1967), p. 18; C. A. L. Bouch, *Prelates and People of the Lake Counties* (Kendal, 1948), p. 9.

[23] D. O'Sullivan, 'Cumbria before the Vikings: a review of some "Dark Age" problems in north-west England', in *Scandinavians in Cumbria*, ed. Baldwin and Whyte, pp. 31–2.

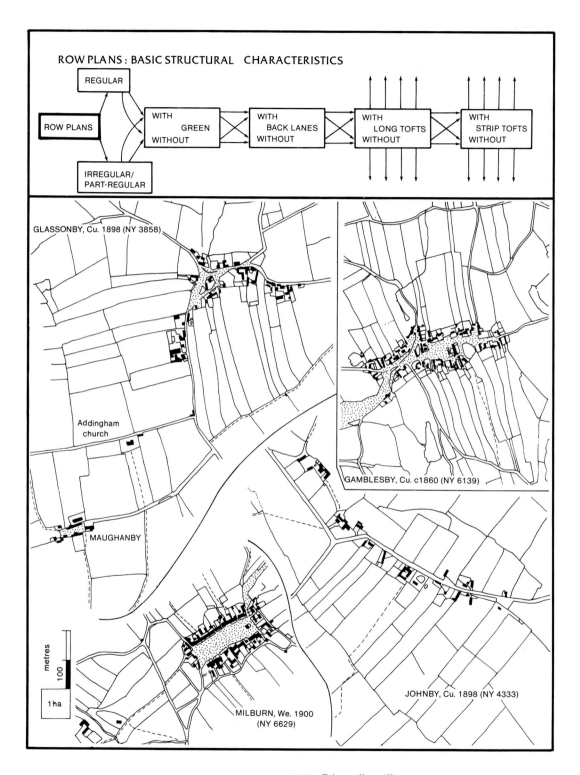

ROW PLANS : BASIC STRUCTURAL CHARACTERISTICS

REGULAR

ROW PLANS

IRREGULAR/
PART-REGULAR

WITH GREEN WITHOUT

WITH BACK LANES WITHOUT

WITH LONG TOFTS WITHOUT

WITH STRIP TOFTS WITHOUT

GLASSONBY, Cu. 1898 (NY 3858)

Addingham church

MAUGHANBY

GAMBLESBY, Cu. c1860 (NY 6139)

JOHNBY, Cu. 1898 (NY 4333)

MILBURN, We. 1900 (NY 6629)

metres
100
1 ha

FIGURE 4.5   *Eden valley villages.*

indeed, the separation of church and village is a regional characteristic, suggesting that the latter have been sited without close reference to an older pattern of church sites. At Long Marton a late Saxon or early Norman church is separated from a very regular village plan; at Milburn the planned village is some distance from the 'late Norman' church. Nevertheless, while these few indicators combine to point to the development of all types of row plans before the middle years of the twelfth century, they are clearly insufficient to distinguish a chronological typology between 1092 and 1150 or indeed before 1092.

If we build upon the preceding argument that there is a case for identifying villages planted between 1092 and 1130 in two zones (figure 4.3), around Carlisle (I) and north-east of Penrith (II), then it can be seen that each set of villages shows all of the morphological features noted in the flow diagram of figure 4.5, although all need not be present in an individual settlement. I usually err on the side of caution in identifying 'regularity', but as Glassonby shows (figure 4.5) there are grounds for a liberal use of the category to emphasize the repetitious qualities present, albeit adapted to local topographic circumstances: in the Eden valley most of the 'irregular' rows are in fact *part-regular*. Zone III is noteworthy for tightly regular plans associated with English names which are either topographic or have a topographic prefix and the suffix *tūn*. At this point it is worth digressing a little to ask what 'colonization' and 'plantation' meant in human terms. While the formal rigidity of some plans implies preparation by *locatores* (although there is no other evidence) the colonists must have come in bands, moving in family, kinship or neighbourly groups with their possessions. What attracted them, amongst other things, is clear from Gospatric's writ: 'whosoever dwells there shall be exempt from the geld'.[24] We must assume that colonization took place within the context of estates, with lords, or their officers, acting as agents. This brings the argument back to place names. One explanation of the toponymic pattern of the Upper Eden is that an English-speaking enclave was present along the Fell Edge (Zone III) where steep, often difficult, access from the Roman road and sour, sloping or peaty pastures had been less attractive to Viking land takers (figure 4.4, and see below). It could be that we are here seeing early twelfth-century 'English' colonists gravitating to an English-speaking region and using the existing earlier topographic specifics to name their villages. That the suffix *tūn* was used in the twelfth century is shown by examples from Pembrokeshire and the Upper Clyde valley, although in both of these areas the prefixes are personal names, surely those of the *locatores*?[25] Of course, viewed at the level of

[24] Hart, *Early Charters*, p. 134.
[25] I. W. Rowlands, 'The making of a March: aspects of Norman settlement in Dyfed', in *Proceedings of the Battle Abbey Conference in Anglo-Norman Studies 3*, ed. R. A. Brown (Woodbridge, 1980), pp. 142–225; Barrow, *Kingdom of the Scots*, pp. 288–90.

an individual village the *locator* was in a position to become the lord of the manor.

These arguments are in measure supported by the one village name in this area which is not English. Knock is in origin old Irish, a word meaning 'hillock', borrowed into Norse, but here a document of 1152–62 offers the explanation of a link between the name and settlement policy. It is a confirmation by Walter son of Ivo (de Greystoke?) to Edgar, son of Earl Gospatric and the grantor's sister, in frank marriage, of the land which Ivo and Agnes, his father and mother, gave them in frank marriage, namely ten manors (*maneria*): Ulnaby and Thornton Hall (*juxta Tese*, parish Coniscliffe, County Durham); in Westmorland, Knock-Salcock and Yanwath; in Cumberland, Blencow; in Coquetdale, Trewitt and Caistron, Great and Little Tosson and Flotterton; to hold by doing *utware* – forinsec service. Farrer casts some doubts on the authenticity of this document, but Kapelle seems to accept it.[26] In the 1120s Ivo's father, Forne son of Sigulf, a Yorkshire man, had become 'a trusted minister of the crown' in that county, being rewarded with an estate in Yorkshire and what became the barony of Greystoke in Cumberland.[27] In addition he also held Coquetdale in Northumberland, Coniscliffe in south Durham and probably large possessions in Upper Teesdale from the king. *Forni* is a well-evidenced Old Scandinavian name, as is *Sigolfr*. Ivo's Norman name is only to be expected. It is surely no accident that Knock, Yanwath, Blencow, Caistron and Trewitt have names including or likely to include Old Norse elements. This estate, severed from Forne's large holding and scattered across four counties, contains three elements which are English (Thornton, the Tossons and Flotterton), one element Danish (Ulnaby) and five Old Norse, surely a disproportionate balance of names if these are seen as a wholly random sample? Can we argue that the family's Scandinavian antecedents were affecting settlement nomenclature and that we see here the result of two factors: on the one hand, a tendency for colonists to move at the behest of lords within estates, so that the names in this estate may well reflect the pattern of land holding by a successful family of Norse-Irish origin rather than purely random activity; on the other hand, there may also have been a tendency for colonists to seek contacts with linguistically compatible groups. In this case, Knock (the affix 'salchild' or 'salcock' is possibly a family name – the *locator*?) must surely derive from the language of the inhabitants, enshrined in both everyday usage and documents, rather than adjacent English speakers?[28]

Viking name replacement in established English settlements is found along the varied and richer soils of the rolling valley lands (IV), with active

---

[26] W. Farrer, *Early Yorkshire Charters*, vol. II (Edinburgh, 1915), doc. 1241; see also footnote 505n; Kapelle, *Norman Conquest of the North*, p. 201.

[27] Kapelle, *Norman Conquest of the North*, p. 201.

[28] A. H. Smith, *The Place-Names of Westmorland* (2 vols, Cambridge, 1967), vol. II, p. 114.

Scandinavian colonization (figure 4.4) taking place amid the sweeter limestone pastures of the Lyvennet Uplands (V).[29] It is in these two regions that land quality was sufficient eventually to support accretive growth in established nucleii, giving the composite plans at Kirkby Thore and Warcop, new hamlets established from older centres at Little Ormside, Little Musgrave and Little Asby (by 1185), as well as new upland settlements, Rosgill and Sleagill, which had potential to support hamlet-sized populations. Many of these show signs of the most rigorous planning. In this region, whatsoever happened elsewhere, the Vikings took the best land, leaving English speakers as an enclave along the less attractive Fell Edge environment and in pockets along the valley.[30] At Sandford the loose irregular agglomeration around an informal green may represent a distinctive, perhaps Anglo-Saxon, plan tradition. The distinctive partly regular double row plans of zone V, arranged around a wide stream green used as meadowland, are an adaptation to the water-deficient limestone settlements. Their names are generally of Scandinavian topographic derivation, suggesting in these cases settlement replanning or primary development after initial name formation. The -bý names at the head of the valley, around the renamed Kirkby Stephen, may indeed be Scandinavian foundations rather than of twelfth-century date,[31] but their regular and part-regular plans are likely to be post-1092 creations.

Between zones II and III there is an interesting transition zone, with some villages comparable to zone II. Two of these bear British place names while Skirwith is a Scandinavian version of *Sherwood*, 'shire wood', both suggesting pre-1092 marginality. Ousby, in the same area, is a complex open-textured composite plan, made up of the planned hamlet of Hole, loose farm clusters at Row and Bradley (the latter surely being the Old English name?) and a possible planned row by Rayson Hall and the adjacent medieval church. At nearby Kirkland, the medieval church and hall are widely separated from what is now the main village – Blencarn – which in spite of a British name possesses a planned regular two-row street green plan. Its clear southern toft compartment, delimited by a back lane and with long tofts abutting, suggests an origin as a single row. In such settlements lacking complete nucleation we may be seeing resonances from an earlier pattern, perhaps of hamlet and church and hall scatters, which preceded the large villages. Similar traces possibly remain amid the settlement ambiguities of zone VIII in British settlement names *not* attached to historic villages (*Triermain* and *Couwhencatte*). In zone IX, the periphery of the Lake District, very distinctive large rather open planned villages (at Ellenby, Johnby and Lamonby) are associated with unambiguously late personal names, and are presumably of twelfth-century origin. Newbiggin super Stainton, now a regular row nearly 1.5 km long, is similar and was

[29] Fellows Jensen, 'Scandinavian settlement in Cumbria', pp. 75–81.
[30] ibid., fig. 5.2.
[31] ibid., p. 78.

named by 1200. Large plantations on or near earlier sites appear at Stainton and Askham but intermix with loose composites (Sockbridge and Tirril) and church and hall foci such as Barton with its round graveyard. In the Forest of Inglewood (zone VI), an area of mixed English and Scandinavian topographical names, nucleated settlements tend to be fewer in number, smaller and regular. Brougham lies at the southern end of the forest, a strategic location, where the late twelfth-century keep, like that at Brough, was sited on a Roman fort. As a settlement Penrith is a later arrival, yet bears a British name. Brougham is now a depopulated village and, as might be expected on this broad swathe of Grade 2 land, nucleations may once have existed in Nine Kirks, Hornby, Winderwath, Woodside and possibly Fremington. Gilsland (zone VII) was not taken from Gille son of Buet until around 1156. Here regular planned villages, again a mixture of types, lie along the western or lowland half of the territory and clearly overlie an older pattern with a mixture of British, English and Scandinavian names.

CONCLUSION

This attempt to link place-name studies and settlement morphology is an experiment. If the antecedent phases of the region's village plans are as old as this discussion suggests and a diversity of row types was already present before 1150, then one question emerges above all others: what causes plan variations? The limited evidence presented here may indeed conceal differences which result from variations in chronology. Local topography must play a part, but there is no simple correlation between the linguistic affiliations of the place names and plan types. One crucial factor was surely the extent and character of settlement existing before *villagisation* or *congregación*. However, three other factors must have had an influence: first, the estate context of each settlement, for even new foundations took place within well-established land-ownership frameworks; second, the element of choice exercized by *locatores*, noted above, and finally, the subsequent history of each settlement, the filter through which earlier forms must be discerned. Winchester points out that the region experienced destructive raids in the years 1316, 1322 and 1345, and his map of the devastation caused by the latter raid is, relatively speaking, as extensive as that in Yorkshire in 1069–70. If we accept that this represents real devastation, and not merely a claim to evade taxes, then this raises a fundamental point: what effect did these raids, and indeed the attrition of smaller incursions, have upon the morphology of the region's plans? It is possible, indeed probable, that devastation was followed by the reoccupation of some of the devastated tofts, accounting for a proportion of the visible earthworks, but death, kidnapping and military service undoubtedly caused a drain of manpower and initiated other economic changes at deeper levels. Thus, within the decline represented by the falling levels of rent income documented by Winchester lay the seeds of opportunity, by making land available.[32] That the visible morphology is indeed older than the raids is hinted by the evidence of the churches cited above, and the author's current view may be summarized as follows: the 'Milburn/Knock' type plans (figure 4.5) are largely the result of reorganizing viable settlements and farmlands, albeit introducing new colonists; the 'Gamblesby/Glassonby type' plans may arise where early twelfth-century organized landtaking was dominant; while the 'Johnby/Newbiggin' types represent a later phase of twelfth-century village plantation. If this basic model proves to be wrong (and work is only in the early stages), then it is argued that the approach demonstrated here is essential if we are to reveal and reconstruct settlement within a dynamic matrix and relate the survivors to their antecedents.

---

[32] Winchester, *Medieval Cumbria*, pp. 44–55.

5

The People of the Wolds in English Settlement History

H. S. A. FOX

INTRODUCTION

During thirty-five summers of excavation at Wharram Percy, Maurice Beresford and John Hurst must frequently have looked over towards the deserted or shrunken villages of Raisthorpe and Towthorpe, Thoralby and Mowthorpe to ask themselves about the special circumstances which rendered settlements prone to desertion in this corner of the Yorkshire wolds.

The argument tentatively presented in this essay is that the decline of so many villages in countrysides akin to the wolds of Yorkshire was closely related to the special character of their early settlement and exploitation; that in many places the history of desertion, and indeed post-desertion history, were stages in a long sequence of related developments, each one influencing the next. Historians have for long thought along these lines when writing of sequences of social development in 'woodland' regions: Hilton concluded that certain features of the social structure of Arden in the thirteenth century – numerous free tenants and smallholders, light labour services – owed something to the nature of the region's post-Conquest colonization; Birrell argued that those same features were in part responsible for the genesis of industrial by-employments in the medieval forest; Thirsk considered that the resilience of those same semi-industrial smallholdings to economic pressures in the seventeenth century meant that 'the stage was prepared for changes in the eighteenth century which wrought . . . an industrial revolution' in some former forests.[1] In the wolds, by contrast, the distinguishing marks of society were less

---

[1] R. H. Hilton, *The Social Structure of Rural Warwickshire in the Middle Ages* (Dugdale Society Occasional Paper, 9, 1950), pp. 11–12; J. Birrell, 'Peasant craftsmen in the medieval forest', *Agricultural*

I am grateful to Anne Tarver, Dr Richard Smith, Dr Peggy Smith and Dr Barrie Cox for practical assistance, to my colleagues Dr Ken Phillipps and Tony Brown for many useful conversations and to Jill Bourn, Stefan Brink, Professor K. Cameron, Dr Margaret Gelling, Dr Della Hooke and Dr Tim Unwin for providing advice over my queries.

blatantly drawn than in woodland regions. The links between each stage of development were perhaps more subtle, but they are there, I think, for the historian to grasp if he is patient enough with the evidence.

The evidence for this study is drawn largely from parts of Leicestershire, Northamptonshire, Nottinghamshire and Warwickshire. Illustrations are also occasionally taken from other areas within the Danelaw, though not from the Cotswolds, nor from Kent where Everitt's pioneering study first revealed the significance of the wold in that county's settlement history.[2] It is certainly not the intention here to delineate an historical model to which all settlements in the wolds of these midland counties conformed: differing combinations of character of lordship, character of tenure, age of settlement, specialization and siting could conspire to turn the societies even of nearby places in their own particular directions, and therein, in part, lies the fascination of local history. But there is a fascination too and an enhanced sense of understanding the past in the discovery of parallels and similarities in way of life among the groups of places which comprise a region and among regions as far apart as the Nottinghamshire–Leicestershire wolds and the Yorkshire wolds. The present study is a search in that direction.

In *c.*1130 the Leicestershire Survey refers to Old (that is, Wold) Dalby as *super Waldas*: this is the earliest known indication that the wolds of the Nottinghamshire–Leicestershire border were thought of as a distinct region, although there are several even older recordings of *wald* incorporated fully (that is, not as an affix) into the place names of the vicinity. Described by Lowe at the end of the eighteenth century as 'a range of high bleak country . . . [on] a cold clay', the region is differentiated from the vales which bound it by its undulating surface and, above all, by its deep, relentless covering of boulder clay.[3] Within the counties covered in this essay another wold region long regarded as distinctive is Bromswold, mentioned as early as the first quarter of the twelfth century in Richard of Ely's *Gesta Herewardi* which refers to the

History Review, 17 (1969), p. 105; J. Thirsk, 'Seventeenth-century agriculture and social change', in *Land, Church, and People: Essays presented to Professor H. P. R. Finberg*, ed. J. Thirsk (*Agricultural History Review*, 1970), p. 148.

  [2] A. Everitt, 'River and wold: reflections on the historical origins of regions and *pays*', *Journal of Historical Geography*, 3 (1977), pp. 1–19.

  [3] B. Cox, 'The Place-Names of Leicestershire and Rutland' (unpublished Ph.D. thesis, University of Nottingham, 1971), p. 281 and, for other early references to places 'on the Wolds' here, pp. 110, 196, 283, 332, and J. E. B. Gover, A. Mawer and F. M. Stenton, *The Place-Names of Nottinghamshire* (Cambridge, 1940), pp. 13, 238, 249, 258; R. Lowe, *General View of the Agriculture of the County of Nottingham* (London, 1798), p. 4. Early recorded place names containing the element *wald* here are Prestwold, *Seggeswald* (Cox, 'Place-Names', p. 301), Wymeswold, Waltham and possibly Walton (ibid., p. 332); there are also many late recorded names in 'wold'. Place names suggest that the limits of the wolds discussed in this essay were lower where the land surface of adjacent vales is low, higher where it is high, and for that reason a variety of contours has been used in the construction of figure 5.1, but the names are not numerous enough for the choices made here to be anything more than approximations.

outlaw's refuge in *Bruneswald* half a century earlier (figure 5.1). Place names suggest that Bromswold occupied all of the undulating, boulder clay strewn countryside between the Nene valley and the eastern boundary of Northamptonshire and extended also into adjacent counties.[4] Other regions with physical characteristics very similar to the features of these two wolds have never been described as such except in the faint language of early place names. Stretching eastwards from the flanks of the Soar valley is another undulating upland much dominated by boulder clay, the 'High Leicestershire' of the *Domesday Geographies*, the 'good and large sheepe pastures' of east Leicestershire according to William Burton in the seventeenth century.[5] Two ancient names in *wald*, Horninghold on the eastern edge of the region and *Brentingiswolde* towards its centre, probably recall a lost regional name.[6] In Northamptonshire, stretching in a great arc from the south-west of the county towards its centre near the village of 'Old or Wold' (so named on early editions of Ordnance Survey maps) is another similarly endowed region, 'High Northamptonshire',[7] which spills over into Leicestershire east of Lutterworth[8] and into the upland wolds which form the eastern fringe of Warwickshire. To

[4] *Gesta Herewardi*, included in T. D. Hardy and C. T. Martin (eds), *Lestorie des Engles* (2 vols, Rolls Series, London, 1888–9), vol. I, p. 392; C. Hart, 'Hereward "The Wake"', *Proceedings of the Cambridge Antiquarian Society*, 65 (1974), pp. 28–40. Early recorded names containing the element *wald* are *Bruneswald* itself, in the *Gesta*, and Harrold: A. Mawer and F. M. Stenton, *The Place-Names of Bedfordshire and Huntingdonshire* (Cambridge, 1926), p. 33. The limits of Bromswold as perceived in the early middle ages may be partially reconstructed from the names Newton Bromswold and Lutton (*on Brouneswold*, 1339) in Northamptonshire, Leighton Bromswold and Old Weston in Huntingdonshire, and Harrold and Wold in Odell in Bedfordshire, while the incorporation of the regional name into personal names in the twelfth century (ibid., p. 245) would seem to indicate a consciousness of Bromswold at that time.

[5] D. Holly, 'Leicestershire', in *The Domesday Geography of Midland England*, ed. H. C. Darby and I. B. Terrett, (Cambridge, 1954), p. 351; W. Burton, *The Description of Leicestershire* (London, 1622), p. 2.

[6] For *Brentingiswolde* see J. Nichols, *The History and Antiquities of the County of Leicester* (4 vols, London, 1795–1811), vol. II, appendix p. 87. This is an old name, for the personal name with which *wald* is compounded here was not current in the middle ages: it is not in P. H. Reaney, *A Dictionary of British Surnames* (London, 1958). Other, late recorded, names in 'wold' from this region are Old Hill in Billesdon (*le Wold*, 1404) and Barkby Holt in Barkby (formerly *Wolt* or *Wold*): Cox, 'Place-Names', p. 206; S. Postles, 'Barkby: the Anatomy of a Closed Township, 1535–1780' (unpublished M.A. thesis, University of Leicester, 1979), p. 123.

[7] Early recorded names in *wald* here are Old itself, the adjacent Walgrave and Longhold in Clipston: J. E. B. Gover, A. Mawer and F. M. Stenton, *The Place-Names of Northamptonshire* (Cambridge, 1933), pp. 128, 131, 111. Walton in King's Sutton is another possibility, although opinions vary: ibid., pp. 58–9; E. Ekwall, *The Concise Oxford Dictionary of English Place-Names*, 4th edn (Oxford, 1960), p. 495.

[8] Gilmorton had its *Old Field* (noticed for me by Tony Brown); one of the fields of Cotesbach was *Smallwold Field*: M. W. Beresford, 'Glebe terriers and open field Leicestershire', in *Studies in Leicestershire Agrarian History*, ed. W. G. Hoskins (Leicestershire Archaeological Society, 1949), p. 120. Dunton Bassett, Bruntingthorpe and Broughton Astley had fields called *Olte* (ibid., pp. 103, 105, and information supplied by John Goodacre), a name which may go back to 'wold', for *olte, holt, wolt* and 'wold' seem to have been used interchangeably in some areas: Postles, 'Barkby', p. 123; J. E. B. Gover, A. Mawer and F. M. Stenton, *The Place-Names of Warwickshire* (Cambridge, 1936), pp. 141, 146. But none of these names is recorded at a very early date. The best candidate for consideration as an early recorded *wald* name in this region is Walton, which generally has forms, without the medial e, indicating that the first element is probably *wald* not *walh* ('Welshman'). It is not, however, accepted as a *wald* name by Cox, nor by Cameron in his useful discussion of the Waltons of England: Cox, 'Place-Names', p. 451; K. Cameron, 'The meaning

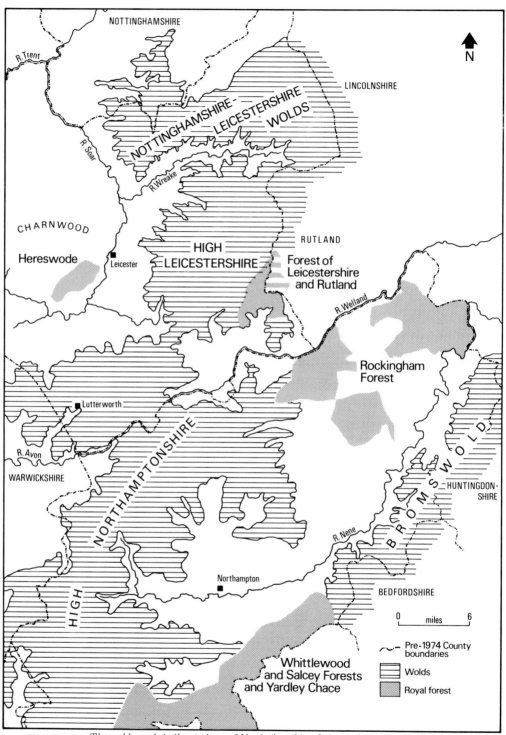

FIGURE 5.1 *The wolds, and similar regions, of Nottinghamshire, Leicestershire, Northamptonshire and Warwickshire.*

read of the wolds of Warwickshire may come as a surprise to historians accustomed to following Camden's division of the county 'into two parts, the Feldon and Woodland', but Camden's view of Warwickshire was, as he makes clear, a view *away from* this upland edge. Here we find the names *Kingemewolde*, probably recalling early conditions, and Coton, described in the hundred rolls of 1275 as *super Waldas apud Cotes*, revealing that the regional name was still alive during the thirteenth century. Dugdale, too, was aware of the distinction: 'these Hilly parts being then, and after called *Wouldes*, as many other of that kind are to this day in other Counties'.[9]

THE WOLDS PERCEIVED

The best guide to the nature of these landscapes in the early Anglo-Saxon period comes from the word *wald* itself. Its interpretation is not easy, for although the term is used in early written sources – the Anglo-Saxon Chronicle, for example, or Gospatric's writ – in contexts which clearly imply woodland, later usage equally clearly indicates that a wold (the middle and standard English form of *wald* within the area covered in this essay) was thought of as countryside *devoid* of wood. To Dr Johnson, for example, a wold was 'a plain open country . . . a place without wood'. The latest literary sources which use the word in its former sense come from the early thirteenth century, as do the first recorded uses of the later meaning.[10] Thus where the element occurs in names first recorded before about 1200, or in names for which there is good reason to suppose coinage before that date, we can be sure that a woodland context of some kind is implied. Such names are to be found in all of the regions surveyed in this essay;[11] in most there is more than one, lending weight to Gelling's interesting suggestion that *wald* was 'only considered appropriate to

and significance of Old English *walh* in English place-names', *English Place-Name Society Journal*, 12 (1979–80), p. 45.

[9] W. Camden, *Britannia* (London, 1610 edn), p. 561; Gover et al., *Place-Names of Warwickshire*, pp. 282, 104; W. Dugdale, *The Antiquities of Warwickshire* (London, 1656), p. 12. If *Kingemewolde* can be associated with nearby Kineton because both contain a first element meaning 'king', as suggested by the editors of *Place-Names of Warwickshire*, the name could possibly go back to a very early period. Apart from *Kingemewolde* the other early recorded name in *wald* is *Waldweie* in Southam: Gover et al., *Place-Names of Warwickshire*, p. 146. These, and many later recorded wold names here, make one wonder, again, about place names in the vicinity with modern forms in Wal-, Little Walton in Monks Kirby and Walcote in Grandborough, for both of which there is some, though not conclusive, evidence for a derivation from *wald*: ibid., pp. 114–15, 130–1.

[10] A. H. Smith, *English Place-Name Elements* (2 vols, Cambridge, 1956), vol. II, pp. 239–40; M. Gelling, *Place-Names in the Landscape* (London, 1984), p. 223; S. Johnson, *Dictionary of the English Language* (London, 1770), *s.v.* wold; *Oxford English Dictionary*, *s.v.* wold, citing *St Marherete* (*c.* 1225) for the former sense and some of the uses in the earliest version of Layamon's *Brut* (*c.* 1205) for the latter.

[11] See above, nn. 3–9, for the evidence. 'Wold' as an affix, as in Burton on the Wolds, is no evidence for *wald*.

districts', so that a name like Stixwold meant, to neighbouring peoples, 'Stigr's part of the region with the characteristics of a *wald*'.[12]

It is worth asking what those particular characteristics were, for the question may advance the interpretation of *wald* a little further. Ever since the date of the English Place-Name Society's first collection of *Chief Elements* it has usually been stated that the term was used for woodland that lay high, and high even became 'lofty' in one of A. H. Smith's translations.[13] Yet not all place names containing *wald* lie at high elevations. Southwold in Suffolk is situated in a very low coastal position; the site of Beverley – *in Deirewald* according to a late version of Bede – is low-lying in the extreme.[14] Then again, if the term signified high woodland one wonders why it was not used for some prominent wooded uplands whose regional names in fact incorporate the element *wudu* rather than *wald* – Charnwood, for example, or Wychwood or Needwood. Finally, the minor Cambridgeshire names *Waldelowe* (*wald* plus *hlāw*) and Woolden (*wald* plus *dūn*) may seem to us to be tautologies if *wald* does mean high woodland, although it must be remembered that OE topographical vocabulary was remarkably subtle, with different terms for physical features of only slightly differing forms.[15]

If we must remain doubtful that *wald* necessarily has an 'upland' implication, then what kind of woodland did it describe? An alternative meaning was suggested to me when consulting a list of medieval English royal forests and being struck by the fact that, of those with regional names, none contains the element *wald*. Where the regional name contains a word meaning wood, it is sometimes *holt* or *(ge)hæg*, but most often *wudu*: Stowood, Sherwood, Inglewood, Bernwood, Whittlewood, for example.[16] Now, with the exception of certain moorland forests in the north and the south-west, and with the exception of those whole counties which were royal forests for a short time before the disafforestations of Richard and John, the countrysides selected for imposition of forest law by Norman and Angevin kings tended to be well wooded. This certainly holds true for all forests with a regional name in *wudu*.

---

[12] Gelling, *Place-Names in the Landscape*, p. 227. In the counties surveyed here there are few isolated names in *wald* and, moreover, few isolated minor and late recorded names in 'wold'; 'wold' names, in general, tend to be found in the vicinity of names in *wald* which would suggest that in some cases they have an early origin.

[13] *The Chief Elements Used in English Place-Names*, ed. A. Mawer (Cambridge, 1924), p. 63; Smith, *Elements*, p. 239; A. H. Smith *The Place-Names of Gloucestershire* (4 vols, Cambridge, 1964–5), vol. I, p. 49.

[14] The *Deirewald* (earlier *Derauuda*) – in which the monastic site was situated – was probably not the Yorkshire wolds, for Beverley is on the flood plain of the river Hull; 'the wood of the men of Deira' is more likely to have been on the plain around Beverley itself, where there are several woodland place names – e.g. Westwood, Woodmansey, Pillwood, Platwoods – and a concentration of surviving woodland in 1086.

[15] P. H. Reaney, *The Place-Names of Cambridgeshire* (Cambridge, 1943), pp. 232, 240. It must be added that there are no really early forms for these names.

[16] N. Neilson, 'The forests', in *The English Government at Work, 1327–1336*, ed. J. F. Willard and W. A. Morris (3 vols, Cambridge, Mass., 1940–50), vol. I, pp. 448–67.

Wychwood, for example, still stood out as relatively densely wooded countryside according to the woodland entries in Domesday; so too did Selwood, seen in the eighth century as a significant line of demarcation between the two earliest dioceses of Wessex, presumably on account of its well-wooded and relatively sparsely inhabited nature.[17] The use of the term *wudu* in regional names to describe the *most densely* wooded tracts is nowhere better illustrated than in Nottinghamshire, Leicestershire and western Northamptonshire. Here Domesday Book reveals four relatively densely wooded tracts: Sherwood with many Domesday entries mentioning woodland several leagues in extent; Charnwood, the only part of Leicestershire with a concentration of extensive woods in 1086, and still well-wooded in later times; *Hereswode* (later Leicester Forest) to its east, measuring 4 leagues by 1 league; and Whittlewood. In regions of wold in these counties, by contrast, there were at the time of the Conquest merely small woods, often measured in acres or described as *spinetum*.[18] Such distinctions raise the possibility that in regional names *wudu* was applied to relatively densely wooded tracts of countryside while *wald* implied country which was more 'park-like', if one may be allowed the anachronism, distinguished by small isolated stands. And this tentative re-interpretation is supported by other evidence. First, in a number of sources *wald* glosses *saltus*, a word which was often used in a sense close to its classical meaning of 'forest pasture' or 'woodland pasture'.[19] Second, in passages written when *wald* still had its original meaning, the term was sometimes used in apposition to other words for wood – 'let us go into this *wald*, into the

---

[17] B. Schumer, *The Evolution of Wychwood to 1400: Pioneers, Frontiers and Forests* (Leicester University Dept of English Local History, Occasional Papers, 3rd ser., 6, 1984), p. 32; *The Anglo-Saxon Chronicle*, ed. D. Whitelock (London, 1961), p. 26; E. M. Jope and I. B. Terrett, 'Oxfordshire', in *The Domesday Geography of South-East England*, ed. H. C. Darby and E. M. J. Campbell (Cambridge, 1962), p. 215; R. Welldon Finn and P. Wheatley, 'Somerset', in *The Domesday Geography of South-West England*, ed. H. C. Darby and R. Welldon Finn (Cambridge, 1967), p. 176. There are, however, some examples of royal forests *adjacent* to regions of *wald*, where the *wald* seems to be the more open fringe of a relatively densely wooded area.

[18] I. B. Terrett, 'Nottinghamshire', in *The Domesday Geography of Northern England*, ed. H. C. Darby and I. S. Maxwell (Cambridge, 1962), p. 257; Holly, 'Leicestershire', p. 338; J. Leland, *Itinerary*, ed. L. T. Smith (5 vols, London, 1964 edn), vol. I, pp. 17–18; *VCH Leics.*, vol. I, p. 306; I. B. Terrett, 'Northamptonshire', in *Domesday Geography of Midland England*, ed. Darby and Terrett, p. 401. For the Cambridgeshire and Lincolnshire wolds see H. C. Darby, *The Domesday Geography of Eastern England* (Cambridge, 1971 edn), pp. 60, 297–9.

[19] Smith, *Elements*, vol. II, p. 239 for examples of this gloss. In this context it is also interesting to note that part of the *pays de Brie* (*Brigensis saltus*) in the Paris Basin is called Gault, from the Old French form of *wald*: *Paysages et villages neufs du moyen âge: recueil d'articles de Charles Higounet* (Fédération Historique du Sud-Ouest, Bordeaux, 1975), p. 45). *Saltus* occurs infrequently, compared to other Latin terms for wood, but where it is found it is often in the context of pasture or pannage in woodland: W. de G. Birch, *Cartularium Saxonicum* (3 vols, London, 1885–99), nos. 194, 260, 303; Du Cange, *Glossarium ad Scriptores Mediæ et Infirmæ Latinitatis* (Paris, 1885–7), *s.v. saltus*; T. Wright, *Anglo-Saxon and Old-English Vocabularies* (2 vols, London, 1883–4), vol. I, l. 718.17, where *saltus* is translated as 'lawnd', i.e. a pastoral glade in woodland, in a very late (fifteenth-century) vocabulary. Earlier vocabularies in this collection, including Ælfric's, give *holt* for *saltus*.

protection of this *holt*' – and we also have 'the wicked wood amidst a *wald*' These could well be references to isolated stands of wood in loosely wooded countryside, and the distinction made in the twelfth century between Bromswold and 'the *great* woods of Northampton[shire]' is also relevant here.[20]

In addition, very strong support for an interpretation of a *wald* as a tract of countryside characterized by isolated stands of wood, perhaps amidst pasture and some cultivated land, comes from other place name elements. In once densely wooded regions such as Arden or Sherwood the element *lēah* occurs in clusters of place names, the term probably being used here 'in a quasi-habitative sense . . . to denote sites . . . in forest clearings'.[21] At the other extreme, in the lower courses of the Trent, Soar, Welland and Nene which bound the wolds discussed in this essay, there is hardly a single ancient name in *lēah*.[22] Between these two extremes are the wolds themselves, where names terminating in *lēah* are scattered rather than clustered, a type of distribution suggesting to Gelling 'woods in open country'.[23] In High Northamptonshire, for example, *lēah* occurs in a moderate number of demonstrably old place names, but very rarely in adjacent parishes; Onley, now a deserted site, may mean 'the wood alone'. There are also scattered names in *hangra* ('wood on a slope', recalling the persistence of patches of woodland on steep land, a characteristic feature of the wolds), *grāf* and *lúndr* ('small wood').[24] In Bromswold too the presence, but not clustering, of woodland elements in place names is exactly what one would expect if, as suggested here, *wald* signified loosely wooded countryside in the perception of the peoples who gave these regions their names. The Weald of Kent, it must be added, stands out against these generalizations.

Whether or not the isolated stands which these names recall were ever parts of more continuous woodland is a question beyond the scope of this essay. The river Chater, which rises in High Leicestershire, is probably a Celtic name meaning 'woodland stream', and the Roman settlement astride the Foss on the Nottinghamshire–Leicestershire wolds was called *Vernemetum*, 'the great

[20] Smith, *Elements*, vol. II, pp. 239–40, the second reference being from the earlier version of the Brut where some of Layamon's uses of *wald* could possibly mean woodland despite the views of his amender; *Gesta Herewardi*, ed. Hardy and Martin, p. 392 (my italics). *On wuduwaldum*, glossing *in saltibus* (*Elements*, vol. II, p. 239), is also suggestive.

[21] Gover et al., *Place-Names of Warwickshire*, map in end pocket; M. Gelling, 'Some notes on Warwickshire place-names', *Transactions of the Birmingham and Warwickshire Archaeological Society*, 85 (1974), p. 64; Gover et al., *Place-Names of Nottinghamshire*, map in end pocket; Gelling, *Place-Names in the Landscape*, p. 199.

[22] This statement is based upon a map in H. S. A. Fox, 'La toponymie et les défrichements des anciennes forêts des Midlands', unpublished paper presented to Les Huitièmes Journées Internationales d'Histoire, Flaran, 1986.

[23] Gelling, *Place-Names in the Landscape*, p. 199.

[24] For example, Pytchley, Cransley, Mawsley, Walgrave and Loatland in the vicinity of Old. Gelling found exactly the same kind of distribution at the southern tip of the Yorkshire wolds: *Place-Names in the Landscape*, p. 225.

sacred grove'.[25] Both of these names suggest wooded environments in the first centuries after the birth of Christ. But there is no lack of Romano-British occupation sites on the wolds considered in this essay, and on wolds elsewhere in England, indicating that fragmentation of woodland had begun by then, if not considerably earlier.[26] At the end of the eleventh century, as the Domesday Book shows, relatively little woodland remained on the wolds. That the surviving woods were small remnants, often on manorial boundaries, is clear from both pre-Conquest and post-Conquest charters – such as that of 944 relating to Badby in High Northamptonshire, or a convention of 1236 between the abbot of Croxton Kerrial and a neighbour about a strip of *spinetum* along the bounds of Waltham on the Wolds.[27]

THE PASTORAL HERITAGE

Countrysides in which, between the arable lands, there were pastures supporting a scattering of trees, with larger stands here and there, made ideal, well-sheltered grazing grounds. Foliage within reach of browsing animals, the mast of beech and oak and the leaves of fallen trees provided sustenance for livestock; stands could be managed in such a way as to provide browse cut from trees and then spread out for feeding.[28] In the more densely wooded regions of England, traces of use for grazing in pre-Conquest times, and indeed much later, are not hard to find.[29] In the wolds, by contrast, which later underwent an arable revolution, the traces of a pastoral people are fainter, as we might expect.

[25] Cox, 'Place-Names', p. 94; A. L. F. Rivet and C. Smith, *The Place-Names of Roman Britain* (London, 1979), p. 495.

[26] This is not to contradict the suggestion later in this study about a relatively late *intensification* of settlement on the wolds, for the Romano-British sites were hardly full villages and could well have existed in a semi-wooded setting, while continuity of occupation after the fifth century has not been proven. For examples see P. Liddle, *Leicestershire Archaeology: The Present State of Knowledge* (2 vols, Leicester, 1982), vol. I, p. 28; RCHM *Northamptonshire*, vol. I, p. xxxii; vol. II, pp. xxxi–xxxvii; vol. III, pp. xxvi–xxxiv; vol IV, pp. xxviii–xxxii; M. L. Faull, 'Roman and Anglo-Saxon settlement patterns in Yorkshire: a computer-generated analysis', *Landscape History*, 5 (1983), p. 32; C. Hayfield, *An Archaeological Survey of the Parish of Wharram Percy, East Yorkshire*, vol. I, *The Evolution of the Roman Landscape* (BAR, British series, 172, Oxford, 1987). The system of single, double and sometimes triple dikes which divide up parts of the Yorkshire wolds, such as Argam Dikes, are thought to be even earlier than the Iron Age and are sometimes regarded as 'ranch' boundaries, an interesting hypothesis in the light of what is said later in this essay.

[27] A. E. Brown, T. R. Key and C. Orr, 'Some Anglo-Saxon estates and their boundaries in south-west Northamptonshire', *Northamptonshire Archaeology*, 12 (1977), p. 170; Nichols, *History and Antiquities*, vol. II, appendix p. 98.

[28] O. Rackham, *Ancient Woodland: Its History, Vegetation and Uses in England* (London, 1980), pp. 173–4, for wood-pasture systems.

[29] For example, W. J. Ford, 'Some settlement patterns in the central region of the Warwickshire Avon', in *Medieval Settlement: Continuity and Change*, ed. P. H. Sawyer (London, 1976), pp. 280–2; A. Everitt, *Continuity and Colonization: The Evolution of Kentish Settlement* (Leicester, 1986), pp. 121–7; C. Johansson, *Old English Place-Names and Field-Names containing Leah* (Stockholm, 1975), p. 25; Rackham, *Ancient Woodland*, pp. 175–202.

The results of a preliminary examination of the subject, for the Nottingham-shire–Leicestershire wolds and High Leicestershire, are very suggestive. In the parish of Shoby is a small area of wood and rough pasture called Shoby Scholes. The name is not recorded earlier than 1524, but there can be no doubt that it derives from the Scandinavian *skáli*. The term is most common in the north of England (although it occurs in two minor names as far south as Northamptonshire, both of them, significantly, in High Northamptonshire); cognate with 'sheiling', its meaning is 'temporary hut or shed'.[30] This very minor name takes us back to the seasonal use of these wood-pastures by livestock led up to them from the vales, probably not in this case from Shoby (which is less than a mile distant: the affix is no doubt modern) but from the Wreake valley. Other names pointing to exploitation of this kind are *Alestow*, Halstead and Somerby. The first, '*Áli*'s herding place', was no doubt associated with nearby Welby (*Alebi*, 1086) and, like Scholes, never became a permanent settlement.[31] Halstead is best rendered as 'sheltering place for animals'.[32]

After the excitement of discovery of a type of pastoral utilization long since vanished in these wold countrysides it comes as a disappointment to read, in most interpretations of the name Somerby, that it is 'the *bý* of *Sumarliði*' a Scandinavian personal name meaning 'summer warrior', one who seasonally left his homeland to seek gain elsewhere. Yet the latest discussion points out that early spellings of Somerby in High Leicestershire and of four identical names in Lincolnshire suggest, as a possible alternative origin, a Scandinavian word meaning 'summer slopes'.[33] This tentative reinterpretation is reinforced by the location of the Lincolnshire Somerbys: two are on the wolds and two in well-wooded countrysides which may well once have been used for summer grazing. Highly significant also is the fact that the township of Somerby in Leicestershire is a semi-detached part of the hundred of Framland, suggesting that when these units or their prototypes were established its territory was still considered to be an essential adjunct to the people of its mother settlement within the main body of the hundred.

---

[30] G. F. Farnham, *Leicestershire Medieval Village Notes* (6 vols, Leicester, 1929–33), vol. IV, p. 78; Cox, 'Place-Names', p. 296; A. H. Smith, *The Place-Names of the West Riding of Yorkshire* (8 vols, Cambridge, 1961–3), vol. VII, p. 282; A. M. Armstrong, A. Mawer, F. M. Stenton and B. Dickins, *The Place-Names of Cumberland* (3 vols, Cambridge, 1950–2), p. 503; Gover et al., *Place-Names of Northampton-shire*, pp. 260, 269; Smith, *Elements*, vol. II, p. 123. On the Yorkshire wolds (at the now deserted site of Argam, at the lost *Arras* in Warter, at Arram east of Hornsea and at Arras in Market Weighton) we find names in *erg* rather than *skáli*. For the possible connotations of this term see M. Higham, 'The "erg" place-names of northern England', *English Place-Name Society Journal*, 10 (1977–8), pp. 7–17.

[31] Cox, 'Place-Names', p. 273.

[32] Cox, 'Place-Names', pp. 327–8; K. I. Sandred, *English Place-Names in -stead* (Uppsala, 1963), p. 289; ibid., p. 174, and Everitt, *Continuity and Colonization*, pp. 171–2, for the pastoral connotations of *stede*.

[33] Ekwall, *Dictionary of English Place-Names*, p. 430; Smith, *Elements*, vol. II, pp. 167–8; Cox, 'Place-Names', p. 187; G. Fellows Jensen, *Scandinavian Settlement Names in the East Midlands* (Copenhagen, 1978), p. 70.

Names indicating seasonal occupation do not exhaust the evidence in place names for an earlier pastoral emphasis on the Nottinghamshire–Leicestershire wolds and in High Leicestershire. Gotham and Harby, two townships with land stretching up on to the scarp slope of the former region, recall goats and herds; here too is the lost *Goscote* in Wymeswold, the 'shelter for geese', a species which was certainly important in the economy of the open fields of the township in the thirteenth century and may well have foraged in the wood pastures in earlier times. *Netone*, 'the cattle *tūn*', was a Domesday manor, lost in later records, in High Leicestershire in the vicinity of Somerby.[34] Moreover, several townships in these regions contain lost names in *wīc*, *heorde-wīc* and *stoc*, all of which elements certainly or probably have pastoral connotations.[35] Some of the names discussed here may possibly tell of pastoral specialization *within* townships at a time when there was plenty of grazing land beyond the arable; later, as ploughland advanced, they necessarily became abandoned, leaving as their only traces a minor name submerged by the arable fields. Others, the names of townships themselves, such as Somerby, Gotham and Harby, may take us back to even earlier forms of pastoral organization when whole territories, later to become townships, within the wolds were used more exclusively, and perhaps seasonally, as grazing grounds.

The substratum of evidence for a once more pastoral orientation on the wolds of the Nottinghamshire–Leicestershire border and in High Leicestershire does not end there. The pattern of lanes on the western edge of the latter region is strikingly dominated by eastwards-running tracks which lead up from the Soar valley (figure 5.2b), some of them followed by parish boundaries, and although the physiography here may influence this dominant orientation it is tempting to regard them as droveways connecting vale and wold.[36] What Ford called 'linked settlements'[37] are not as common between vale and wold as they are between vale and woodland, perhaps because the links were more completely severed, and at an earlier date, leaving fewer traces in the topographical and written evidence; yet Gartree hundred has detached townships giving it an additional share of High Leicestershire, while Framland hundred, as already noticed, has a detached part in the vicinity of Somerby.[38] Furthermore, there are several examples of townships with small detached

[34] Gover et al., *Place-Names of Nottinghamshire*, p. 247; Cox, 'Place-Names', p. 156 for some doubts about this interpretation of Harby; ibid., p. 334 and Nichols, *History and Antiquities*, vol. II, appendix p. 98; Cox, 'Place-Names', p. 111.

[35] *Le stoc* in Great Dalby, *Stoch* in Croxton Kerrial, Hardwick in Shangton, *Herdwych* and *Stoc* in Kirby Bellars (Cox, 'Place-Names', pp. 153, 160, 251, 290).

[36] P. Russel, 'Roads', in *VCH Leicestershire*, vol. III, pp. 59–60.

[37] Ford, 'Some settlement patterns', p. 281.

[38] Framland also included the detached township of Withcote, three miles south of Somerby, while a lost *Franethorp* in Owston and Newbold may, on the basis of the personal name (which is the same as in Framland), recall another detached portion: Cox, 'Place-Names', pp. 137–8, 246. Cf. the contorted and inter-mixed wapentakes and hundreds of the wolds of Lincolnshire and Yorkshire and in Bromswold.

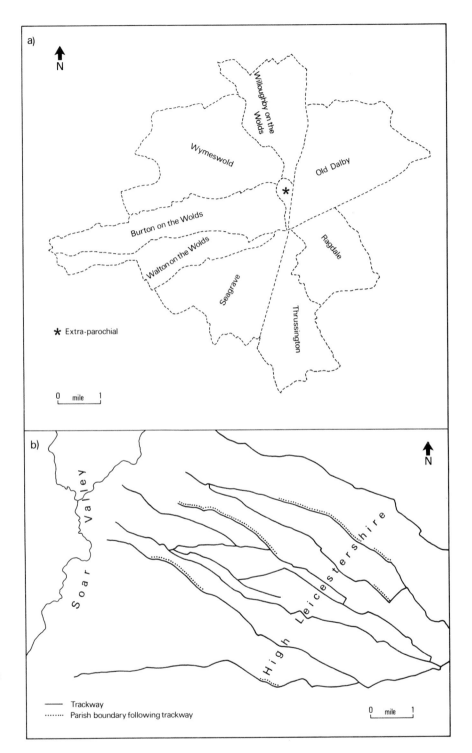

FIGURE 5.2 *(a) Boundaries on the Nottinghamshire–Leicestershire wolds; (b) Trackways from the Soar valley into High Leicestershire.*

portions amidst the land of their neighbours, indicating a partition of formerly intercommoned pasture.[39] Division of once intercommoned land is surely also indicated by the remarkable configuration of boundaries at the western edge of the Nottinghamshire–Leicestershire wolds where the limits of townships have been drawn in a spoke-like pattern which meets in a small area of extra-parochial land as its hub (figure 5.2a).[40]

THE LAST ADVANCE

By the twelfth century, the arable field systems of the wolds seem to have been not very different from those of many other parts of the midlands. A final concord for Preston Capes in High Northamptonshire, from the end of the twelfth century, refers to 44 acres of demesne arable and 6⅔ of meadow in North Field, 51 acres of arable and 2⅔ of meadow in South Field; one may envisage the fields of Preston stretching northwards and southwards from the village to the small meadow-bound streams which border the township. At Hothorpe, now a deserted village on the northern flank of High Northampton-shire, we can see the two arable fields as early as 1155, in a charter confirming a gift of all the men there of two acres from each virgate, one *ex una parte ville &* *aliam ex altera*, for the maintenance of a parochial chapel. From Croxton Kerrial on the Nottinghamshire–Leicestershire wolds, thirteenth-century charters refer to two arable fields as well as to a fringe of uncultivated wold (*brueria*, *vasta terra*) on the township's boundaries. But not all places have retained a reserve of wold, for by 1236 the cultivated *campi* of the adjacent vills of Stonesby and Freeby shared a common boundary, while when, in the twelfth century, the abbots of Whitby and Selby had a chance meeting on the Foss Way near Old Dalby, the encounter was *in campo qui Segesuuald dicitur* – the landscape is now dominated by arable fields, very different from the more pastoral and wooded landscape of earlier centuries.[41]

[39] Thus Syston and Barkby, South Croxton and Ashby Folville, Stockerston and Horninghold, Ingarsby and its neighbours: Postles, 'Barkby', p. 11, and Nichols, *History and Antiquities*, vol. III, p. 46; Ordnance Survey 1″ to 1 mile, index to the tithe survey; R. H. Hilton, 'Medieval agrarian history', in *VCH Leicestershire*, vol. II, pp. 180–1, 193. Cf. the intermixed pasture rights of some Bromswold townships: G. Foard, 'The administrative organization of Northamptonshire in the Saxon period', *Anglo-Saxon Studies in Archaeology and History*, 4 (1985), p. 194.

[40] For the extra-parochial hub, the boundaries of which are shown only approximately on figure 5.2, see F. and J. White, *Directory of the Town and County of the Town of Nottingham* (Sheffield, 1844), p. 405. For a similar pattern of boundaries resulting from division of pastures, see E. G. Fogwill, 'Pastoralism on Dartmoor', *Transactions of the Devonshire Association*, 86 (1954), p. 100.

[41] *Feet of Fines of the Tenth Year of the Reign of King Richard I* (Pipe Roll Society, 24, 1900), p. 151; *Documents Illustrative of the Social and Economic History of the Danelaw*, ed. F. M. Stenton (British Academy Records of Social and Economic History, 5, 1920), p. 342; Nichols, *History and Antiquities*, vol. II, appendix pp. 77, 98; J. T. Fowler (ed.), *The Coucher Book of Selby*, vol. I (Yorkshire Archaeological and Topographical Association, Record Series, 10, 1891), introductory pages, 21.

When the historian comes to ask about the timing of the transformation which brought almost the last of the old wood-pastures under the plough he is at once struck by the strength of Scandinavian influence on the place names of the wolds. The very high density of Scandinavian names, particularly those ending in *-by*, on the Lincolnshire wolds has often been remarked upon, as has the concentration of names in *-thorp* on the Yorkshire wolds.[42] The Nottinghamshire–Leicestershire wolds and High Leicestershire may be used as a statistical test case (figure 5.3). Within them are thirty-eight place names which are either purely Scandinavian formations, or are Scandinavianized OE names, or are hybrid names of the type Ashby, with an OE first element and a Scandinavian second element. Figure 5.3 has been drawn in such a way that it shows an identical area of wold and – south of the Trent and east of the Soar – of vale; 61 per cent of the total of names in these groups lies on the wolds and 39 per cent in the vales (24 per cent if the anomalous Wreake valley is excluded).[43] Few would doubt that, at the very least, such names testify to a strong Viking influence on land ownership and to the existence of a considerable body of people among whom the Scandinavian languages were spoken.

To go further and to suggest that some classes of Scandinavian names indicate the foundation of *new* settlements in the wolds is to fly in the face of recent re-interpretations: it is now being claimed that '*most* of the settlements with names in *-by* were taken over by the Vikings as going concerns rather than . . . [representing] the exploitation of vacant land.'[44] Re-interpretations which follow from exhaustive investigations must command much respect, but it is necessary also to ask if they are running ahead of what is known and what can be proven. Hybrid place names in *-by* of the type Ashby may, certainly, represent partial reshaping of pre-existing names.[45] Some purely Scandinavian names in

[42] P. H. Sawyer, *The Age of the Vikings* (London, 1962), p. 164; K. Cameron, 'Scandinavian settlement in the territory of the Five Boroughs: the place-name evidence', in *Place-Name Evidence for the Anglo-Saxon Invasion and Scandinavian Settlements*, ed. K. Cameron (English Place-Name Society, Nottingham, 1975), p. 125; G. Fellows Jensen, *Scandinavian Settlement Names in Yorkshire* (Copenhagen, 1972), p. 177.

[43] I have not included names in *-tūn* of the Grimston hybrid type, because in these cases there is little debate about the circumstances of their origin – as English villages named after a new Scandinavian owner: K. Cameron, 'Scandinavian settlement in the territory of the Five Boroughs: the place-name evidence, part III, the Grimston-hybrids', in *Place-Name Evidence*, ed. Cameron, p. 157 and the works there cited; Fellows Jensen, *East Midlands*, p. 285. As for names in *-thorpe*, I have not taken heed of the views of Lund – that these could represent OE *throp* – because of the simple fact that such names are so much more numerous in the Danelaw than to the west of Watling Street as to make that interpretation improbable: 'Thorp-names', in *Medieval Settlement*, ed. Sawyer, pp. 223–5. To be on the safe side I have, however, excluded names in *-thorp* which do not have a Scandinavian first element. The Wreake valley presents a rare example of a vale land dominated by Scandinavian place names; renaming is a distinct possibility here.

[44] G. Fellows Jensen, 'Place-names and settlements: some problems of dating as exemplified by place-names in *by*', *Nomina*, 8 (1984), p. 31 (my italics). See also Fellows Jensen, *East Midlands*, p. 369, and 'Place-names and the Scandinavian settlement in England', in *Collected Papers presented at the Permanent European Conference for the Study of the Rural Landscape*, ed. V. Hansen (Copenhagen, 1981), pp. 119–22.

[45] There is, of course, another possibility: that such names were entirely new formations among an Anglo-Scandinavian population for whom *by* had become a common word for a settlement, as is suggested by the

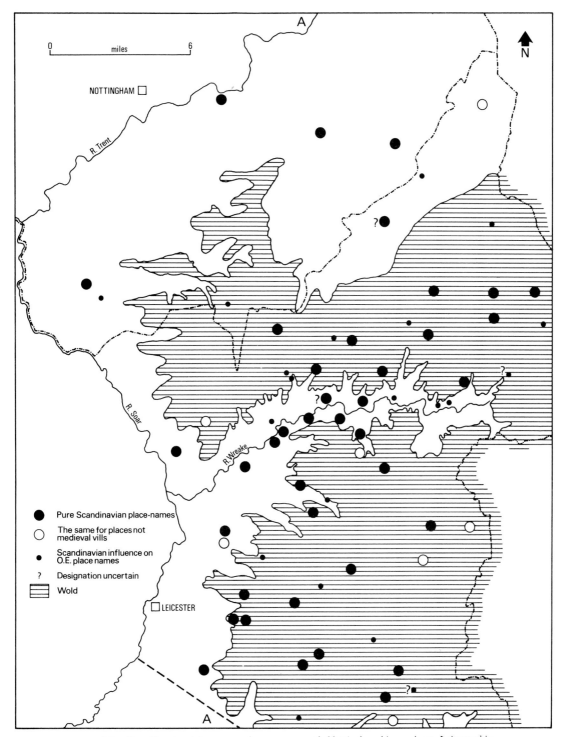

Legend:

● Pure Scandinavian place-names

○ The same for places not medieval vills

· Scandinavian influence on O.E. place names

? Designation uncertain

▤ Wold

NOTTINGHAM

LEICESTER

R. Trent

R. Soar

R. Wreake

FIGURE 5.3 *Scandinavian influence on place names, south Nottinghamshire and east Leicestershire (note that only names east of the Trent and Soar, line A-A, have been plotted).*

-*bý* may represent the total substitution of an Old English name for a Scandinavian one, although there is scarcely any evidence to demonstrate that this happened.[46] As for new theories about the mechanisms by which pre-existing settlements supposedly passed into Viking hands, we are told that 'most of the -*býs* result either from fragmentation of old estates . . . or from reclamation of land once occupied by the English but subsequently deserted.'[47] The latter argument is strange, for one is left wondering about the reasons, apart from some short-term abandonment following the activities of Viking armies, for the supposed desertion of settlements in the ninth and tenth centuries, generally thought of as periods of expansion rather than contraction. The former argument, representing names in -*bý* as the results of 'estate colonization', is interesting, yet because of the deficiencies of the sources there is hardly a scrap of direct evidence to support it.[48] A certain and universally applicable resolution of this problem will never be possible. Yet the now numerous case studies showing that places with Scandinavian names often occupy inferior sites – Payling's pioneering study, the researches of Cameron, on High Leicestershire and other areas, of Gelling on the Warwickshire–Leicestershire borderlands and of Fellows Jensen on Yorkshire and the east midlands – are suggestive here.[49] They suggest that with many, but not all, pure Scandinavian names we are in the presence of new settlements, for it

findings of B. Cox, 'The -*bý* / -*berie* variation in ten Leicestershire place-names', in Cox, 'Place-Names', pp. 74–7.

[46] The good examples of Derby and Whitby are cited with tedious repetition in the literature. It is sometimes stated that the relatively common place name Kirkby or the like must replace a pre-existing English name, on the grounds that settlements controlled by the Vikings are unlikely to have had churches, but this has always seemed to me to be a rather feeble argument in the light of their quite rapid conversion to Christianity. The ecclesiastical status of such places needs to be examined in detail, but could such names perhaps proclaim the first stages of the conversion? See also below, n. 48.

[47] Fellows Jensen, *East Midlands*, p. 369.

[48] It is quite reasonable to believe that *some* Scandinavian names, in certain settings and circumstances, arose in this way. Bleasby, a berewick of the estate of Southwell, was *Blisetune* in the tenth century but *Blesby* later; if we assume a pre-existing -*tūn* compounded with an OE first element, then we can see here a change, albeit in two stages and rather late in the day, to a purely Scandinavian name (Gover et al., *Place-Names of Nottinghamshire*, p. 155). The name of Tholthorpe, a sokeland of Helperby, and *Thurulfestune* in the tenth century, seems to have changed in the same way (A. H. Smith, *The Place-Names of the North Riding of Yorkshire*, Cambridge, 1928), p. 21; G. R. J. Jones, 'Early territorial organization in northern England and its bearing on the Scandinavian settlement', in *Fourth Viking Congress*, ed. A. Small (Edinburgh, 1965), p. 78; but see G. Fellows Jensen, *Yorkshire*, p. 130. For the possible origin of Ullesthorpe as an English-named *wīc* (a nice example in view of the pastoral connotations of this element) see C. V. Phythian-Adams, *Continuity, Fields and Fission: The Making of a Midland Parish* (Leicester University Dept of English Local History, Occasional Papers, 3rd ser., 4, 1978), pp. 20–1.

[49] L. W. H. Payling, 'Geology and place-names in Kesteven', *Leeds Studies in English*, 4 (1935), pp. 1–13; Cameron, 'Scandinavian settlement . . . the place-name evidence', pp. 115–38, and 'Scandinavian settlement in the territory of the Five Boroughs: the place-name evidence, part II, place-names in thorp', in *Place-Name Evidence*, ed. Cameron, pp. 139–56; M. Gelling, *Signposts to the Past: Place-Names and the History of England* (London, 1978), p. 235; Fellows Jensen, *Yorkshire*, p. 250 and *East Midlands*, pp. 299–328, where the inferiority of the sites of places with Scandinavian names is conclusively demonstrated for some areas, as on pp. 305, 313, 317, although in other areas the correlation does not seem to appear.

would be strange indeed if Scandinavian owners had so often been granted, or had appropriated or purchased inferior existing sites. If most of the *-thorp* names of Yorkshire and the *-bý* names of Lincolnshire really represent fragmentation of estates in the Viking age, why should that process have proceeded so much more fully in the wolds than elsewhere in those two counties; why was there apparently relatively less fission in the lowlands of south Nottinghamshire and east Leicestershire depicted on figure 5.3 than in the adjacent wolds?

What lends weight to the conclusion that many of the purely Scandinavian names of the wolds may represent new colonization between the end of the ninth century and the eleventh is the poor showing in these regions of the earliest strata of OE place name elements.[50] This is not to argue that these regions were ever an unused void but to suggest that they were relatively little favoured by early, seminal, settlement, leaving a good deal of land for later colonization.[51] In the several hundreds of square miles of countryside classified as wold in figure 5.1, the element *-ingahām* is not represented at all, and there is only one certain example of a name in *-ingas*, Peatling Parva, borrowed from that of its mother settlement on a tributary of the Soar, and therefore not necessarily of ancient coinage. Of the few places with names in *-hām*, two are Newnhams while the most characteristic site for the others is in a narrow tributary valley biting into the flanks of the wold; only Waltham (the *wald hām*) on the Leicestershire wolds and Cold Higham in High Northamptonshire occupy less peripheral positions.[52] The wolds do, however, contain many OE names, jostling their Scandinavian neighbours, with elements suggestive of colonization at a relatively late date and on land which was not of the best quality. To take High Leicestershire as an example, we find Cold *New*ton, *New*bold Folville and *New*bold in Owston, the first a daughter settlement of Lowesby, a pure Scandinavian name, suggesting the existence of some vacant land even after the

---

[50] For the relevant elements I have followed Gelling, *Signposts*, p. 112.

[51] This point must be emphasized. A poor showing of diagnostic early place names does not, of course, indicate complete lack of settlement. Gumley was 'well-known' (*in loco celebre*) in the eighth century as a royal residence and Brixworth in High Northamptonshire was chosen as an early minster of Peterborough (F. M. Stenton, 'Godmundeslaech', *English Historical Review*, 20, 1905, pp. 697–9); idem, 'Medeshamstede and its colonies', in *Historical Essays in Honour of James Tait*, ed. J. G. Edwards, V. H. Galbraith and E. F. Jacob (Manchester, 1933), p. 326. Likewise there is some archaeological evidence from the wolds of post-Roman, pre-Viking settlements, as for example near Salmonby in the Lincolnshire wolds and indeed within the Wharram parishes (P. Everson, 'An Anglo-Saxon site at Salmonby', *Lincolnshire History and Archaeology*, 8, 1973, pp. 61–72); J. G. Hurst, 'Wharram: Roman to medieval', in *Angles, Saxons and Jutes: Essays Presented to J. N. L. Myres*, ed. V. Evison (Oxford, 1981), pp. 245–7. For the wolds in the middle Saxon period, none of the evidence is inconsistent with a picture of scattered minor sites with a good deal of pasture and some wood in between them.

[52] All relevant information is usefully mapped in B. Cox, 'The significance of the distribution of English place-names in -hām in the Midlands and East Anglia', in *Place-Name Evidence*, ed. Cameron, pp. 88, 91, 92, 94. I have not included Bringhurst and Horninghold as *-ingas* settlement names, for they must at first have related to woodland belonging to the people of *Bryni* and to the *Horningas*, not to their original settlements.

initial Viking impact on the region;[53] several, scattered, names bearing 'woodland' elements of a type generally considered to relate to relatively late settlement;[54] and Hungarton, 'the *tūn* on barren soil', a name which finds an exact parallel in Gaulby, 'the *bý* on sterile soil', a few miles away and forming with its neighbour Frisby an island of Scandinavian settlement surrounded by a ring of names in *-tūn*. The final stages in the occupation of the region, we suggest, was an achievement of the ninth, tenth and eleventh centuries, by people of both Scandinavian and Anglian descent.[55]

This intensification of settlement on the wolds must have had important repercussions for the older settled adjoining vales. If, as an example, we consider the Lincolnshire place name Stixwold, what are the implications for the older settled lands of the acquisition of this pastoral *wald* by an owner of Scandinavian descent and not earlier than the late ninth century – which is what the name tells us – of its detachment from the 'river and wold' territory to which it presumably once belonged, and of its eventual transformation by 1086 into a vill of twenty-one recorded tenants and only 200 remaining acres of underwood and *silva pastilis*?[56] The answer must surely be that the people of vale settlements who had formerly used pastures at a remove on the wolds were thrown back upon their own resources and began to develop field systems in which they used their own ploughland for both arable *and* pasture; tracts of arable thus came to be called *feld* (a term which formerly had a more exclusively pastoral sense[57]) or field; the feldons of the vales began to assume many of the characteristics which they were to bear in the high middle ages. It can be no coincidence that during the ninth and tenth centuries, just at the time when the wolds were coming to be more fully and independently exploited, we find the first indications of the development of a mature common-field system in the vales, perhaps with its attendant community of the vill, and the associated development of nucleated villages.[58]

In the wolds themselves, the combination of a relatively late advance to full

[53] Nichols, *History and Antiquities*, vol. III, p. 348.

[54] Noseley, Baggrave, Launde, a number slightly less than is found on an equivalent area of the Nottinghamshire–Leicestershire wolds or in High Northamptonshire.

[55] The same conclusion was reached by Everitt for the Kentish Downland: 'River and wold', p. 15.

[56] C. W. Foster and T. Longley (eds), *The Lincolnshire Domesday and the Lindsey Survey* (Lincolnshire Record Society, 19, 1924), pp. 84, 126, 168.

[57] Gelling, *Place-Names in the Landscape*, p. 236 for the development of *feld. Feldon* as a regional name is as fascinating as *wald*. In early sources, some as early as the eleventh century, the term most usually occurs in the names of tracks leading from a feldon to a region with different characteristics, a woodland or a wold. Such names have a significant distribution at the boundaries of regions.

[58] H. S. A. Fox, 'Approaches to the adoption of the Midland system', in *The Origins of Open-Field Agriculture*, ed. T. Rowley (London, 1981), pp. 83–8; D. Hooke, 'Open-field agriculture: the evidence from the pre-Conquest charters of the west midlands', ibid., pp. 58–9; C. C. Dyer, 'Power and conflict in the medieval English village', in *Medieval Villages: A Review of Current Work*, ed. D. Hooke (Oxford University Committee for Archaeology, monograph no. 5, Oxford, 1985), p. 31; C. Taylor, *Village and Farmstead* (London, 1983), p. 130, although the band of dates given there for the origin of nucleated villages is a little later than would be accepted by many scholars.

occupation and an earlier pastoral heritage bequeathed certain enduring features of land utilization and settlement. Gray noted that the two-field system tended to be adopted in the 'bleak, . . . unfertile uplands' of midland England, many of which were wolds, and other scholars have noted the same thing; certainly in Northamptonshire over 90 per cent of two-field vills listed by Gray lay within the areas classified here as wold.[59] The quality of the land no doubt played a part, but another reason for this preference by the husbandmen of the wolds may well have been their pastoral traditions: two fields could support up to 50 per cent more livestock than three, the exact figure depending upon the rotations which were followed and availability or otherwise of small reserves of wold beyond the arable. This suggestion needs to be explored further through examination of demesne livestock accounts, but it is rendered plausible by the reported preference of wolds farmers in seventeenth-century Yorkshire for systems allowing as much fallow as possible: 'they sow no winter corn . . . theire designe being sheepe, the winter corns would straighten the herbage for them.'[60] A date for the origin of these two-field systems will probably always elude us, although it might reasonably be supposed that, because pastures diminished later and less completely on the wolds, common fields developed slightly later there than in feldon regions. The example of Dry Drayton (once *Waldretton*) shows that their formation might in exceptional cases have taken place as late as the twelfth century.[61]

The wolds were distinguished not only by two-field systems, whose presence no doubt contributed to low valuations of arable, but also by villages which tended to be small and by townships of small acreage; compared to feldon regions, density of population was low (as exemplified by Leicestershire: table 5.1).[62] The lay subsidy of 1334 reveals relatively lowly assessed vills in the wolds,[63] and although low assessment for taxation does not automatically imply a small population, it does so here in these regions with few opportunities for industrial by-employments – as the poll tax returns demonstrate. Of pre-village settlement in the wolds we know relatively little, although fieldwalking

[59] H. L. Gray, *English Field Systems* (Cambridge, Mass., 1915), p. 73; H. P. R. Finberg, *Gloucestershire: An Illustrated Essay on the History of the Landscape* (London, 1955), p. 40; F. M. Stenton (ed.), *Transcripts of Charters relating to the Gilbertine Houses of Sixle, Ormsby, Catley, Bullington and Alvingham* (Lincolnshire Record Society, 18, 1922), p. 20, for the prevalence of the system in Lindsey, which included the Lincolnshire wolds; H. S. A. Fox, 'Two- and three-field systems in England: medieval and early modern', unpublished paper presented to the 13th meeting of the Permanent European Conference for the Study of the Rural Landscape, Stockholm, 1987.

[60] O. Wilkinson, *The Agricultural Revolution in the East Riding of Yorkshire* (York, 1956), p. 3.

[61] Fox, 'Approaches', pp. 95–6.

[62] Table 5.1 aggregates surviving data from: (i) all vills in the Leicestershire wolds, High Leicestershire and the countryside east of Lutterworth, and (ii) all Leicestershire vills outside those regions and east of the Soar and north of the Welland. Townships whose areas span both vale and wold have been excluded from the analysis.

[63] For a remarkable correlation between the distribution of small vills and the Lincolnshire wolds see G. Platts, *Land and People in Medieval Lincolnshire* (History of Lincolnshire, Lincoln, 1985), p. 155.

TABLE 5.1 *Some differences between vills in the wolds and feldon of Leicestershire*

	(a) Mean value of arable per acre, Henry III–Edward III (in pence)	(b) Mean assessment for the fifteenth of 1334[a] (in shillings)	(c) Mean number of people per thousand acres assessed for the poll tax of 1377	(d) Mean acreage of townships (in acres)
Wolds	4.5	39	49	1425
Feldon	6.0	67	74	1687

[a] Figures for rural vills taxed at a tenth have been converted to the fifteenth; boroughs have been excluded.

Sources: (a) J. A. Raftis, *Assart Data and Land Values: Two Studies in the East Midlands, 1200–1350* (Toronto, 1974); (b) R. E. Glasscock (ed.), *The Lay Subsidy of 1334* (British Academy Records of Social and Economic History, new ser., 2, 1975); (c) Poll tax returns at PRO, E 179; (d) J. Curtis, *A Topographical History of the County of Leicester* (Ashby de la Zouch, 1831) and W. White, *History, Gazetteer and Directory of the Counties of Leicester and Rutland* (Sheffield, 1877).

at Brixworth in High Northamptonshire and in High Leicestershire, as well as John Hurst's discussion of the vicinity of Wharram Percy, point to a once considerably more dispersed pattern before the formation of villages; lost minor place names, often with pastoral connotations, tell us the same thing.[64] When villages were formed they tended to be, and to remain, small: the territories of some of them originated in the sharing out of common pastures, while the less productive two-field system may have inhibited growth to any great size. One might add, more speculatively, that a combination of relatively late colonization in some cases, a pastoral heritage, and perhaps an initial preference by Scandinavian settlers for small hamlets and single farmsteads, still left some faint marks on the villages of the wolds at the beginning of the fourteenth century.[65]

THE RETURN OF THE FLOCKS

The distinguishing marks of wolds villages were subtle not blatant ones, but they were real enough to bequeath some serious difficulties to these regions

[64] D. Hall and P. Martin, 'Brixworth, Northamptonshire: an intensive field survey', *Journal of the British Archaeological Association*, 132 (1979), pp. 1–6; information on High Leicestershire kindly supplied by Peter Liddle; Hurst, 'Wharram: Roman to medieval'; above, n. 35 for minor names to which could be added other examples, the 'lost names' of *Wistoft* and *Toft* on the Nottinghamshire–Leicestershire wolds, several quite vanished names in *-thorp* in Leicestershire, some of the lost names in *-stede* in Northamptonshire and perhaps the 'seven properties' which may possibly lie behind the enigmatic place name Sewstern in Leicestershire (Cox, 'Place-names', p. 319 and Gover et al., *Place-Names of Nottinghamshire*, p. 322; Cox, 'Place-Names', pp. 236, 246, 260; Gover et al., *Place-Names of Northamptonshire*, pp. 469–70; Cox, 'Place-Names', pp. 149–50).

[65] Some scholars have suggested that, in Scandinavia, a *by* was originally a single farmstead or hamlet: their views are summarized in Fellows Jensen, *East Midlands*, pp. 10–11, and Smith, *Elements*, vol. II, pp. 66–8. For the generally relatively lowly status of settlements with Scandinavian names see Fellows Jensen, *Yorkshire*, pp. 222–7, and *East Midlands*, pp. 332–41.

during the vicissitudes of the later middle ages. Maurice Beresford's discussion of regional contrast in intensity of desertion within the midlands was limited to perceptive comment on the way in which formerly heavily wooded regions and fenlands were largely immune from deliberate acts of depopulation, for a greater emphasis on pasture could be easily accommodated within existing structures of fields, settlement and society.[66] Now that the wolds have been identified as a distinct and distinctive class of region with its own special characteristics of settlement, we may ask how these regions fared in this respect during the fourteenth and fifteenth centuries. Figure 5.4 shows that in both Leicestershire and Northamptonshire later medieval depopulation, although by no means absent from the feldons, was a very marked feature of the wolds.[67] In Northamptonshire 73 per cent of all villages which were or may have been depopulated in this period are in regions classified here as wolds. In Leicestershire the figure is 50 per cent, despite the fact that less than half the area of the county is so classified, and rises to 62 per cent if depopulations of uncertain date are excluded.

It would be wrong to seek a single or too simple an explanation for these regional contrasts within the midlands, but at root the link would seem to be that concentrations of small vills resulted, eventually, in concentrations of deserted villages. It has long been recognized that the deserted village tended to have been a small village.[68] The connection is very simple: whether depopulation resulted from internal 'disintegration of the medieval village . . . as a coherent organism',[69] as was sometimes the case, or from seignorial eviction, or from a combination of both, the processes were bound to be swifter, to reach their climax earlier, to be more easily accomplished in the smaller settlements. Thus Cestersover, a deserted site on the wolds of Warwickshire, had only twelve messuages in 1385, suggesting that it had always been a small place, and had shrunk even further by the middle of the fifteenth century; at Steane in High Northamptonshire only four households were reported in 1428 and its old arable fields were soon to become 'Steane Grounds' on which a flock of 1,000 sheep was running in 1547. These are but

---

[66] M. W. Beresford, *The Lost Villages of England* (London, 1954), pp. 229–34.

[67] Information largely from K. J. Allison, M. W. Beresford and J. G. Hurst, *The Deserted Villages of Northamptonshire* (Leicester University Dept of English Local History, Occasional Papers, 1st ser., 18, 1966) and 'Provisional list of deserted medieval villages in Leicestershire', *Transactions of the Leicestershire Archaeological Society*, 39 (1963–4), pp. 24–33. Occasional help is provided by the standard eighteenth- and nineteenth-century county histories. Minor 'lost place names', such as those mentioned above n. 64, have naturally not been included on the map, though I have shown, with some reservations, Holt in Ab Kettleby (not in the first printed DMVRG list) (W. G. Hoskins, 'The deserted villages of Leicestershire', in his *Essays in Leicestershire History* (Liverpool, 1950), p. 72; Nichols, *History and Antiquities*, vol. II, p. 16). Bromswold is not well represented on figure 5.4 because many of the townships on the Northamptonshire side of the region are atypical, having a share of both vale and wold.

[68] For example, Beresford, *Lost Villages*, pp. 247–60; Allison et al., *Northamptonshire*, pp. 16–20.

[69] R. H. Hilton, 'A study in the pre-history of English enclosure in the fifteenth century', in his *The English Peasantry in the Later Middle Ages* (Oxford, 1975), p. 162.

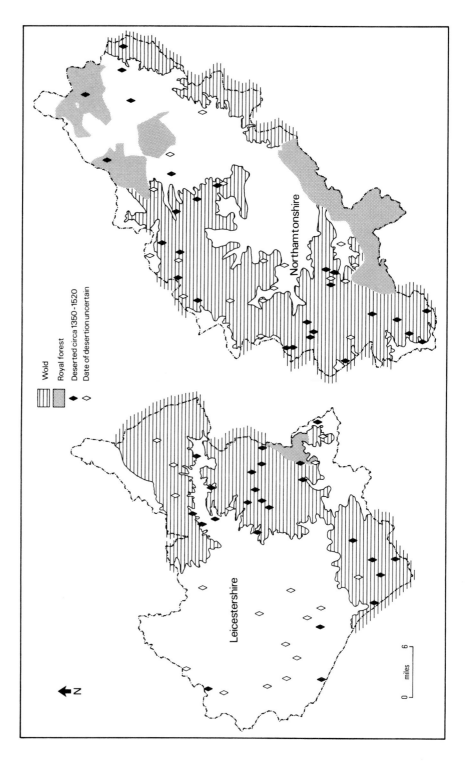

FIGURE 5.4 *Later medieval desertion of villages: Leicestershire and Northamptonshire.*

two examples of small villages in which internal disintegration would have had more damaging and lasting effects than in more sizeable places. The populations of small villages could dwindle to such an extent that it became difficult to maintain the common disciplines and routines of the open fields, as happened at Chapel Ascote, also on the wolds of Warwickshire, in the early fifteenth century; services like ale brewing and no doubt smithery would become no longer viable; promotion of cottagers to the ranks of occupiers of full holdings would seriously diminish labour supply. Under such circumstances emigration to larger and more attractive villages and a rapid turnover of the more transient and under-capitalized among potential tenants were added to local trends in mortality and fertility to hasten the weakly village's decline.[70] And deliberate seignorial depopulation was naturally more easily accomplished where villages were small and their integrity and viability weakened.[71]

Concentrations of small vills on the wolds, then, resulted in concentrations of deserted villages. But there were other reasons why husbandmen in these regions should have fared particularly badly in the later middle ages. One was that arable land on the wolds was not valued highly (as the figures in table 5.1 make clear), perhaps partly because the prevailing two-field system was less productive of grains than its three-field counterpart, but with not much less expenditure of labour (a factor likely to be crucial in a dwindling village); partly because the soils derived from boulder clay, where they prevailed, were difficult to work, requiring greater inputs of labour than did lighter lands. Under these circumstances, and with prices depressed, tenants were likely to vacate their holdings to take up better ones elsewhere – creating that general scarcity of 'tenants to occupie their landes' of which Sir Edward Belknap complained in his defence of the decay of Burton Dassett in south-east Warwickshire – and lords with vacant holdings on their hands to use them for flocks and herds rather than for cultivation.[72] Another reason must surely be that, at least as far as the wolds considered in this essay are concerned, the feldons had the advantage over them in terms of relative closeness to large urban markets. When demand for grain declined the people of the wolds, with less productive systems and further from markets, were the first to suffer. If they did so during the crises of the early fourteenth century – when they complained of the impotence of their holdings, the unprofitability of soils and the flight of their neighbours – it is to be expected that they suffered even more

---

[70] M. W. Beresford, 'The deserted villages of Warwickshire', *Transactions of the Birmingham and Midland Archaeological Society*, 66 (1945–6), p. 89; C. Dyer, 'Deserted medieval villages in the west midlands', *Economic History Review*, 2nd ser., 35 (1982), p. 25; Allison et al., *Northamptonshire*, pp. 10, 46; Dyer, 'Deserted medieval villages', pp. 31–3.

[71] Few of the depopulations after 1488 involved really large numbers: Beresford, *Lost Villages*, pp. 116–17, 257–8.

[72] N. W. Alcock, 'Enclosure and depopulation in Burton Dassett: a 16th-century view', *Warwickshire History*, 3 (1977), p. 182.

when demand for grain fell further during the course of the later middle ages.[73] And, certainly, the policy of Leicester Abbey towards its supply of grains, for its own kitchens and possibly also for the urban market, favoured feldon rather than wolds villages during this period.[74]

The return of the flocks – in some cases those of tenants themselves, as when deserted arable fields were taken over by a neighbouring vill, to produce arrangements similar but not exactly parallel to those of the distant days of the *wald*;[75] in some cases by lords, who could also develop their linked 'grazing towns' and 'home farms'[76] – by no means affected all of the villages of the wolds. Even some of the smallest survived: particular forms of tenure[77] may have saved some and lordship cannot but have been of some importance, for example in saving a village from the unwelcome attentions of those small gentry families who were such frequent depopulators.[78] But despite many survivals, at a regional level the wolds stand out as relatively heavily affected. Moreover, it was within these regions alone that, although Maurice Beresford was generally correct when he wrote that abandoned villages 'do not lie easily to the view like a shore where the sea has retreated',[79] one may in fact discern something of a shoreline of this kind: at the seven adjacent deserted sites around Lowesby in High Leicestershire, for example, the seven around Chapel Ascote on the wold edge of Warwickshire (countryside in which both Spencers and Catesbys had interests) – and, of course, in the neighbourhood of Wharram Percy.

[73] For the remarkable concentration on the Lincolnshire wolds of such complaints made before those who assessed Lindsey townships for the *Nonarum Inquisitiones* of 1342 see Platts, *Land and People*, p. 156. The husbandmen of the Cotswolds and of the Cambridgeshire wolds complained in the same way: A. R. H. Baker, 'Evidence in the "Nonarum Inquisitiones" of contracting arable lands in England during the early fourteenth century', *Economic History Review*, 2nd ser., 19 (1966), pp. 522, 526.

[74] R. H. Hilton, *The Economic Development of some Leicestershire Estates in the 14th and 15th Centuries* (London, 1947), p. 80.

[75] For example, Badsaddle in High Northamptonshire, Prestgrave in High Leicestershire and Hardwick on the high land of east Warwickshire (Allison et al., *Northamptonshire*, p. 35; Nichols, *History and Antiquities*, vol. II, p. 523; Dyer, 'Deserted medieval villages', p. 29).

[76] For example, Hilton, 'English enclosure', p. 163, for the Catesbys; H. Thorpe, 'The lord and the landscape', *Transactions of the Birmingham Archaeological Society*, 80 (1965), p. 57, for the Spencers. For later symbiosis between deserted and surviving townships see J. Goodacre, 'Lutterworth in the Sixteenth and Seventeenth Centuries' (unpublished Ph.D. thesis, University of Leicester, 1977), pp. 130–3.

[77] For speculations on the relationships between type of tenure and desertion see Beresford, *Lost Villages*, p. 258, and J. E. Martin, *Feudalism to Capitalism: Peasant and Landlord in English Agrarian Development* (London and Basingstoke, 1983), pp. 123–7.

[78] L. A. Parker, 'Enclosure in Leicestershire 1485–1607, (unpublished Ph.D. thesis, University of London, 1948), p. 194; Hoskins, 'Deserted villages of Leicestershire', pp. 99–100. Everitt has shown that the downs of Kent tended to be dominated by minor landlords (*Continuity and Colonization*, pp. 175–7), and it is interesting to speculate that the same may have been true of the wolds considered in this essay.

[79] Beresford, *Lost Villages*, p. 204.

CONCLUSION

Some historians still classify large parts of central England as the 'midland plain'. In this essay I have elaborated upon a *genre* of region which has always belied that notion. In the distant centuries with which it begins the distinctiveness of the type was perhaps at its most striking: hence the ancient generic regional name. It was in the early middle ages that distinctions between wold and feldon were at their least conspicuous, as intensification of land use and population brought about a convergence in their characteristics although latent differences still remained, as we have seen. During the later middle ages, when another turn was given to the kaleidoscopic pattern of English regions, a divergence in regional fortunes took place and there emerged some of those distinguishing characteristics which were to mark out the wolds in all subsequent centuries. Certainly, a traveller to the wolds two, three or four hundred years ago would have been aware that he was entering a special social landscape. He would have been aware, in places, of problems of vagrancy within groups of parishes by now churchless and with neither churchwardens nor overseers of the poor; aware too, at times, of feelings of despair among labourers and husbandmen who saw opportunities for work, secure tenures and grain supplies dwindling even further as a result of post-medieval enclosures – despair which erupted in the so-called 'midland' revolt of 1607.[80] Later, where the wolds once again came under the plough in the late eighteenth and early nineteenth centuries, the traveller would have encountered certain features of labouring life – long daily journeys to work, seasonal immigration of labour, gang organization, hiring on a yearly basis – which, though not confined to the wolds, were characteristic of them, arising from local deficiencies of labour in countrysides, always relatively thinly populated, which had witnessed a good deal of medieval depopulation.[81] And despite that second arable revolution, and other changes in the nineteenth century, the observant historian can still discern the distinctiveness of the wolds today.

[80] ibid., pp. 74–7, and Beresford, 'Deserted villages of Warwickshire', pp. 64, 94, for vagrancy; Martin, *Feudalism to Capitalism*, p. 165, for the revolt of the wolds in 1607; L. A. Parker, 'The agrarian revolution at Cotesbach, 1501–1612', in Hoskins, *Studies in Leicestershire Agrarian History*, pp. 41–76.

[81] 'The resident labourers are few, compared to the work to be done; especially in harvest; when numbers flock to it [the wolds region] from the surrounding country. In less busy seasons, the work is mostly done by yearly servants': W. Marshall, *The Rural Economy of Yorkshire* (2 vols, London, 1788), vol. II, p. 253. See also T. W. Beastall, *The Agricultural Revolution in Lincolnshire* (History of Lincolnshire, Lincoln, 1978), p. 116, for High Leicestershire and the Lincolnshire wolds; J. A. Sheppard, 'East Yorkshire's agricultural labour force in the mid-nineteenth century', *Agricultural History Review*, 9 (1961), pp. 43–54; M. W. Beresford, 'Documentary evidence for the history of Wharram Percy', in *Wharram: A Study of Settlement on the Yorkshire Wolds*, ed. J. G. Hurst (Society for Medieval Archaeology, Monograph Ser., 8, 1979), vol. I, pp. 14–16.

PART II

Fieldwork

6

A Regional Study of Deserted Settlements in the West of England

MICHAEL ASTON

INTRODUCTION

This chapter reviews what is presently known of settlement desertion in the historic counties of Gloucestershire, Somerset and Wiltshire. The first part considers how our knowledge of deserted medieval settlements developed, particularly after the inception of the DMVRG (1952) and the publication of Maurice Beresford's *The Lost Villages of England* in 1954. The sources of information indicating such sites are discussed, with some appraisal of their distribution and what is known about the circumstances of their abandonment. The second part considers the region's relationship to the national picture of settlement development and decline. The west country has as wide a variety of settlement types and forms as anywhere in the country and their origins are likely to be as complex, but as yet research has not advanced very far into such topics in the region.

THE CURRENT STATE OF KNOWLEDGE

Before 1954

The first antiquary to refer to a deserted settlement in the region was probably John Leland when he wrote of Deerhurst in Gloucestershire in the 1540s: 'The olde priory stode est from Severn a bow shotte, and north of the town. There remayne yet dyverse names of streates, as Fisschar streate, and other. But the buildinges of them be gone.'[1]

[1] L. Toulmin Smith (ed.), *Leland's Itinerary in England and Wales*, vol. IV (London, 1964), p. 134.

I am grateful to Linda Viner and John Chandler for assistance with sites in Gloucestershire and Wiltshire respectively. Dr Joseph Bettey and Michael Costen of the Extra-Mural Department at Bristol University have provided much stimulating discussion and innumerable examples from their wide knowledge of the west country. Tony Philpott and Gordon Kelsey and his colleagues prepared the photographic work.

Each of the three historic counties has been well served by county historians and earlier generations of local historians.[2] Not much attention, however, was paid by these or later authors to the existence of deserted medieval settlements. Rudder refers to the legendary explanation for Manless Town in Brimpsfield (Gloucestershire), and Beresford[3] points out that Collinson listed places which he knew (or thought – since he lists Minehead) had been abandoned. Among them is Earnshill (Curry Rivel) and Eastham (Crewkerne), described as 'depopulated'; Hardington (Hemington), 'almost depopulated'; Horseley (Brewham), a 'depopulated hamlet'; and Sock Dennis (Ilchester), 'an obliterated place'. He also remarks on 'divers other places of ancient note, but now nearly depopulated', including West Chilton, Beer and Salthay in Cannington and Petherham in Otterhampton. Hartrow in Stogumber is also described as 'a depopulated place, but in ancient times a considerable village, the ruins of the dwellings being frequently discovered in the gardens and the fields' with 'anciently a small chapel'.

1954 to 1971

From the beginning of modern research into medieval settlements until 1971, the publication date of Beresford and Hurst's *Deserted Medieval Villages*, fundamental research into the location, field identification and reasons for site desertion was undertaken in this region as elsewhere. In 1954, 15 sites were known in Gloucestershire, 16 in Somerset and 28 in Wiltshire, making 59 for the region altogether. By 1971 the numbers were 67 for Gloucestershire, 27 for Somerset and 104 for Wiltshire, making a grand total of 198. As these figures show, research into the identification and listing of sites was erratic and uneven between these three counties; this is also reflected in the other activities of the group such as the gathering of air photographs and the conducting of excavations.

The lists published in 1971 were compiled as a gazetteer in 1968. Interim stages can be seen in the lists for Gloucestershire of 28 sites in 1959 and 54 sites in 1962, and the 1961 list for Wiltshire with 104 sites.[4] A list was also compiled in 1960 for Wiltshire by David Algar, John Musty and others. In 1962 other sites were deleted as not being truly *deserted* settlements – three in Gloucestershire and one in Wiltshire.

Figure 6.1 shows the sites which had been identified and accepted as deserted medieval villages by 1971. Large numbers of the sites identified were visited

---

[2] Sir Robert Atkyns, *Ancient and Present State of Gloucestershire* (London, 1712); see also S. Rudder, *A New History of Gloucestershire* (Cirencester, 1779); John Collinson, *The History and Antiquities of the County of Somerset* (Bath, 1791); Sir Richard Colt Hoare, *Modern Wiltshire* (London, 1822).

[3] Rudder, *A New History*, p. 310; M. W. Beresford, *The Lost Villages of England* (London, 1954), p. 385.

[4] *DMVRG Annual Report*, 7 (1959), Appendix C: 'Gloucestershire'; *DMVRG Annual Report*, 10 (1962); *DMVRG Annual Report*, 9 (1961), Appendix B: 'Wiltshire'.

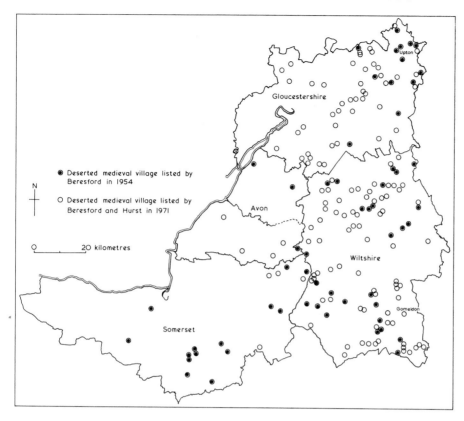

FIGURE 6.1 *The discovery of sites in the west country: sites recorded by 1954 and 1971.*

by John Hurst and/or Maurice Beresford during this time, as the record cards of the DMVRG make clear. Air photographs were taken by J. K. St Joseph and important excavations were conducted at Upton in Blockley, Gloucestershire, and Gomeldon in Idmiston, Wiltshire.[5] It is apparent from all these data that relatively little was achieved in Somerset over the same period. There was, for example, no excavation in the county to compare with Gomeldon or Upton, although smaller-scale excavations were undertaken at some places, mainly in north Somerset (now Avon).[6]

Since 1971

Nationally a great deal has happened in the study of deserted villages since 1971. The dropping of 'deserted' from the Group's name in that year

[5] Upton excavation reports: R. H. Hilton and P. A. Rahtz, 'Upton, Gloucestershire 1959–1964', *Transactions of the Bristol and Gloucestershire Archaeological Society*, 85 (1966), pp. 70–146; P. A. Rahtz, 'Upton, Gloucestershire 1964–1968: second report', ibid., 88 (1969), pp. 74–126; J. Musty and D. Algar, 'Excavations at the deserted medieval village of Gomeldon, near Salisbury', *Wiltshire Archaeological and Natural History Magazine*, 80 (1986), pp. 127–69.

[6] These are listed in M. W. Beresford and J. G. Hurst (eds), *Deserted Medieval Villages* (London, 1971), pp. 154, 162–3 and 165–6. To these should be added Long Ashton (now in Avon).

recognized the importance of surviving and shrunken settlements and increased attention was paid to the rest of the medieval settlement pattern. It also allowed a greater appreciation of desertions in the pre-medieval period, always of interest to the Group, and in post-medieval times. The study of hamlets and farmsteads gathered momentum.

With the cessation of the excavations at Upton and Gomeldon in 1968 it is possible to see the end of an era – the heyday of deserted village studies, particularly in Gloucestershire and Wiltshire, lasted for about a decade. Only in Somerset did research continue, particularly between 1974 and 1978, and then mainly to catch up with the state of knowledge in the neighbouring counties.[7] A revival of interest can then be detected generally in the 1980s, and Saville, in his survey of field monuments in the Avon and Gloucestershire Cotswolds in 1980, listed 43 sites.[8] Some of these had been recorded by Beresford in 1954 – 7 – and Beresford and Hurst in 1971 – 16 – but 19 were 'new' sites previously little recorded, or not at all. In 1981 and again in 1984 the Gloucestershire lists were revised.

A summary of the situation in Somerset was published in 1982,[9] and a detailed gazetteer of Wiltshire prepared for the Wiltshire Sites & Monuments Record by Lesley Marshman in 1980. The situation in Avon in 1986 was described as part of the archaeological survey of the new county formed in 1974.[10] Here a complete inventory of sites was made from all previous sources including parish surveys and local history material. An attempt was made to record shrunken villages, hamlets and deserted farmsteads as well as the 'platforms' on the Levels which probably indicate seasonal steadings. In many ways the map of Avon sites represents a truer reflection of settlement loss over the last 1500 years, or at least our knowledge of it, than any of the maps so far prepared for the other counties; it compares well with Bond's map of Oxfordshire settlements.[11] An earlier attempt, with rather less detail, was published for Somerset in 1985.[12]

It is now very difficult to produce meaningful distribution maps of sites in any county (although an attempt has been made here for Wiltshire, (figure 6.2), the only county not recently mapped), since it is clear that a great deal of

[7] See, for example, reports of research in *MVRG Annual Reports*, 22 (1974), p. 10; 23 (1975), pp. 14–15; 24 (1976), pp. 9–10; 25 (1977), pp. 14–16 (with a map of deserted farm sites in western Somerset); 26 (1978), p. 12; and 27 (1979), p. 9.

[8] A. Saville, *Archaeological Sites in the Avon and Gloucestershire Cotswolds* (Bristol, 1980), esp. pp. 19–21 and map 7.

[9] M. Aston, 'The medieval pattern 1000–1500 AD', in *The Archaeology of Somerset*, ed. M. Aston and I. Burrow (Taunton, 1982), esp. pp. 130–3 and fig. 13.11.

[10] M. Aston, 'Medieval settlements in Avon', in *The Archaeology of Avon*, ed. M. Aston and R. Iles (Bristol, 1987), pp. 95–106; see esp. fig. 8.1.

[11] C. J. Bond, 'Medieval Oxfordshire villages and their topography: a preliminary discussion', in *Medieval Villages*, ed. D. Hooke (Oxford, 1985), pp. 101–23, esp. fig. 9.4 on p. 108.

[12] M. Aston, 'Rural settlement in Somerset: some preliminary thoughts', in *Medieval Villages*, ed. Hooke, pp. 81–100.

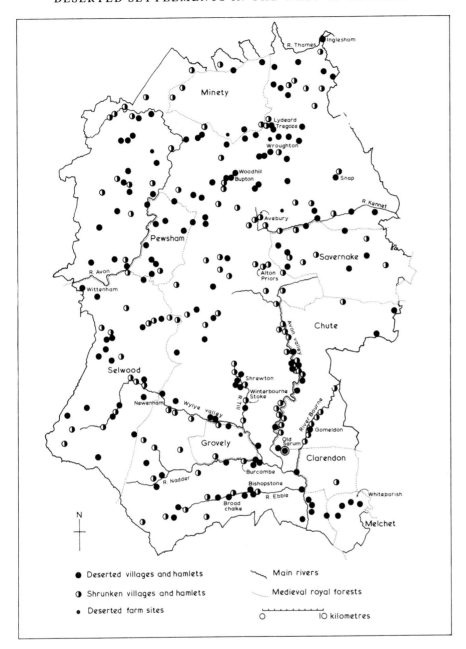

FIGURE 6.2 *Deserted medieval settlements in Wiltshire: sites located by the end of 1987.*

local research is needed into individual parishes and townships in order to understand in any detail the former extent of medieval settlements in them. Such detailed work is under way, particularly by the editors of the *Victoria County Histories*, which are in progress in all counties except Avon, and parish survey work elsewhere is providing detailed historical and topographical research for a selection of parishes.

Such research has demonstrated the great variety of settlement types and forms in this region and the varying fortunes to which they have been subjected. These studies enable us to see rather more clearly how deserted settlements fit into the overall settlement pattern of the area, what sort of remains we can expect to locate and why and when some settlements in the area disappeared. As Taylor has reminded us, with his study of Whiteparish in Wiltshire, such research needs to be constantly reviewed in the light of new ideas.[13]

THE EVIDENCE FOR DESERTION OF SETTLEMENT IN THE REGION

Documentary Evidence

Even more than in other regions of the country, there are very few direct documentary references to places being deserted in the west country, for many of them were not manorial centres or villages and therefore escaped the documentation of the larger estates. Some of the major sources used by Maurice Beresford in his initial work are not available for this region or have not been translated or published.[14] Nevertheless the prime sources such as the lay subsidies, poll taxes and so on all yield useful information. As in other counties, those areas examined in recent years by the *VCH* editors often show best which settlements were deserted and sometimes when and why; they also show how poor the references to such sites usually are. As yet not much more than half the region has been covered by *VCH* volumes, and much of the material therein was completed before settlement studies were regarded as of interest. Some editors still display a poorly developed topographical approach and do not appreciate that the places under study actually exist 'on the ground'.

A number of examples can be quoted, however, where research on a particular parish has filled in something of the history of a deserted site. In Wiltshire, for instance, the well-known site of Snap was studied as part of the parish of Aldbourne. The traditional explanation that this site was destroyed by a butcher/sheep dealer in the twentieth century is shown to be only partly correct. Although it was the 'smallest settlement in the parish in the 14th century', and 'one of the poorest in the county', there were still 19 poll tax payers in 1377; the real decline occurred in the nineteenth century, from 41 residents in 1851 to only 2 in 1909.[15] But in Somerset the few documentary

---

[13] C. C. Taylor, 'Whiteparish', *Wiltshire Archaeological Magazine*, 62 (1967), pp. 79–102.

[14] For example the 1377 poll tax for Somerset does not survive for the complete county and that which does is unpublished. I am grateful to M. W. Beresford and M. Midgley for the loan of a typescript on which to work.

[15] For Snap see C. C. Taylor, *Village and Farmstead: A History of Rural Settlement in England* (London, 1983), pp. 235, 239 and fig. 100; J. Freeman, 'Aldbourne', in *VCH Wiltshire*, vol. XII, p. 71; and M. Weaver Smith, 'Snap – a modern example of depopulation', *Wiltshire Archaeological Magazine*, 57 (1960), pp. 386–90.

references to Bineham in Long Sutton show just how difficult it is to trace the history of some of these sites even with the resources and expertise of the *VCH*. There is virtually no documentary reference to the settlement at all beyond the fact that it 'was still occupied in 1720, though it had probably been in decline from the 16th century'.[16]

Elsewhere, casual references to aspects of a settlement's history can enable us to see desertion taking place even if this is not directly stated. Thus for Little Marston in West Camel parish we are told, in different places, that there was formerly a separate vill, a manor house, a chapel, a mill and a separate field system of two open fields; by 1503 the arable fields had given place to pasture for sheep. Nowhere, however, are we told that Little Marston was a separate settlement and that it is now deserted.[17] At Speckington in Yeovilton parish rents were reduced from the fourteenth century onwards and in 1451 at least three 60-acre holdings complete with farmsteads were let at reduced rents 'until better tenants should come'. There are earthworks at the site, but since it is mainly covered by the perimeter fence of the Yeovilton Naval Air Station, it is unlikely that more information will be forthcoming.[18]

As these examples show, almost any medieval or post-medieval documentary source might have information about a particular site, but to search it all represents a monumental task and as yet this has not been undertaken methodically for the west country. Domesday Book has been used to locate some lost settlements; the few places to which it refers, but which cannot be located, have provided much food for thought. In Somerset Michael Costen has located several of these as part of his research into place names and Anglo-Saxon charters. Thus Ponteside probably lay west of Banwell (now in Avon) and Shepworth in West Lydford parish.[19]

There are few Cistercian monasteries in the region and none is definitely known to have depopulated any settlements, although Stanley Abbey in Wiltshire may have altered the status of several settlements which later appear as granges. However, the foundation of the first Carthusian house in England, at Witham in Somerset, now seems to have resulted in the removal of peasants. St Hugh is said to have arranged for 150 dispossessed people from the priory site in the Forest of Selwood to be resettled at Knapp in North Curry before the final establishment of the house in 1178–9.[20]

The location of lost and ruined churches, and to a lesser extent chapels, often

[16] For Bineham see R. H. Leech, 'Air reconnaissance over Somerset – some recent results', *Somerset Archaeology and Natural History*, 122 (1978), pp. 69–73 and plate 6; and R. W. Dunning, 'Long Sutton', in *VCH Somerset*, vol. III, p. 154.

[17] For Little Marston see R. W. Dunning, 'West Camel', in *VCH Somerset*, vol. III, pp. 72, 74–5 and 79.

[18] For Speckington see R. W. Dunning, 'Yeovilton', in *VCH Somerset*, vol. III, p. 171.

[19] I am grateful to Michael Costen for discussing his research with me and allowing me to quote examples in advance of his own publications.

[20] See D. H. Farmer, *St Hugh of Lincoln* (London, 1985), p. 17.

provides a useful indicator of former settlements, although in this region of predominantly dispersed hamlets and farmsteads some caution is necessary – it is possible to have an isolated church with little if any accompanying settlement, as at Raddington (Somerset) or Oldbury on Severn (Avon, formerly Gloucestershire). Nevertheless, the loss of Rowley or Wittenham church on the Wiltshire–Somerset border provided one of the earliest indicators of a deserted settlement in the region when the amalgamation of the living with Farleigh Hungerford was discussed by Jackson in 1879.[21] The recorded loss of churches at Woodwick (to Freshford, Avon, formerly Somerset) in 1444, Fairoak to Berkley (Somerset) in 1460, Standerwick to Beckington (Somerset) and Goose Bradon and Earnshill to Curry Rivel (Somerset) all indicate settlement loss. In Wiltshire the spectacular ruin of St Leonard's, Newenham, outside Sutton Veney, and the rebuilding of Farley on a new site in the seventeenth century, point to the same changes in settlement distribution. The loss of churches in Gloucestershire can be used in the same way. At Sezincote the church had been abandoned by 1638 following fifteenth-century desertion of the village; it was in ruins by 1751 and has now disappeared. Further research on the Pope Nicholas Taxation of 1291 and the bishops' registers (of Worcester for Gloucestershire, Bath and Wells for Somerset, and Salisbury for Wiltshire) would no doubt yield other significant missing churches.

Surviving churches can also be used as a clue to settlement change, particularly if they are redundant. There were 29 redundant churches in the region vested in the Redundant Churches Fund in 1984 and of these 10 are associated with deserted or shrunken villages and hamlets. Some, such as Cameley and Charfield (Avon), Ozleworth (Gloucestershire), Hardington Bampfylde and Stocklynch Ottersey (Somerset) and Alton Priors and Inglesham (Wiltshire) are very clear indicators of desertion.[22] The nineteenth-century social commentator William Cobbett provided an appraisal of the use of churches as indicators of abandoned settlements when, on one of his 'rural rides' to the Avon valley north of Amesbury in the 1820s, he wrote:

> It is manifest enough, that the population of this valley was, at one time, many times over what it is now; for, in the first place, what were the twenty-nine churches built for? The population of the 29 parishes is now but little more than one-half of that of the single parish of Kensington . . . What, then, should all these churches have been built for? And besides, where did the hands come from? And where did the money come from? . . .
> . . . Nothing can more clearly show, than this, that all, as far as buildings and population are concerned, has been long upon the decline and decay.

---

[21] For Rowley alias Wittenham see Rev. R. E. Jackson, *A Guide to Farleigh Hungerford* (London and Chippenham, 1879), pp. 73–87.

[22] See *Redundant Churches Fund Sixteenth Annual Report and Accounts* (1984), from which the list and figures are taken.

Dilapidation after dilapidation have, at last, almost effaced even the parsonage-houses . . . The land remains; and the crops and the sheep come as abundantly as ever; but they are now sent almost wholly away, instead of remaining as formerly, to be, in great part, consumed in these twenty-nine parishes.[23]

The pattern of early territorial boundaries is closely related to medieval settlement, as has been shown by Desmond Bonney, Christopher Taylor and others.[24] If, therefore, the earliest pattern of tithing, township, or manorial units can be established it can be used to define individual settlements and indicate potential lost sites where there are gaps. This method has been used extensively in Wiltshire (and Dorset) along the chalkland river valleys but its potential has hardly been tapped elsewhere. For instance, attention was drawn to Nether Adber (Somerset) partly by a tithing of that name with no settlement in it.

Where maps are available of tithing boundaries, as they are in the English Place-Name Society volumes for Wiltshire and Gloucestershire, the task of lost settlement location is made easier; the very existence of these place-name volumes for two of the three historic counties aids in the identification of deserted settlements.[25] The example of the parish of Wroughton in north Wiltshire is relevant, since the tithing boundaries are known from the eighteenth-century enclosure map. This is an area of particularly dense desertions and the existence of the tithings of Elicome and Overtown with little trace of settlement indicates more shrunken sites in the same area. Bishopstone and Broad Chalke in south Wiltshire have similar tithing divisions; here they are associated with a number of lost chapels.[26]

It is beyond the scope of this chapter to discuss all the available national documentation. The amount and its accessibility varies from county to county, although the 1334 lay subsidy is available for all.[27] Maurice Beresford published the main sources for Wiltshire, while for Somerset the 1284 Kirby's Quest, 1315 *Nomina Villarum* and the 1327 lay subsidy were published in the late nineteenth century.[28] A list of small places which were exempt from tax in 1428 exists for Wiltshire and includes a number of later casualties. The

[23] William Cobbett, *Rural Rides* (Harmondsworth, 1967), pp. 311–13.

[24] D. Bonney, 'Early boundaries and estates in southern England', in *English Medieval Settlement*, ed. P. H. Sawyer (London, 1979), pp. 41–51, esp. figs. 4.8, 4.9 and 4.10; see also C. C. Taylor, *Dorset* (London, 1970), esp. fig. 15.

[25] A. H. Smith, *The Place-Names of Gloucestershire* (4 vols, Cambridge, 1964–5); and J. E. B. Gover, A. Mawer and F. M. Stenton, *The Place-Names of Wiltshire* (Cambridge, 1939).

[26] See D. A. Crowley, 'Bishopstone', in *VCH Wiltshire*, vol. XI, pp. 3–19, and the map of the tithings on p. 4; for Broad Chalke see J. Freeman, 'Broad Chalke', in *VCH Wiltshire*, vol. XIII, pp. 37–52.

[27] R. Glasscock (ed.), *The Lay Subsidy of 1334* (London, 1975).

[28] For Wiltshire see M. W. Beresford, 'Fifteenths and tenths: quotas of 1334', 'Poll tax payers of 1377' and 'Poor parishes of 1428', in *VCH Wiltshire*, vol. IV, pp. 294–314; for Somerset see F. H. Dickinson (ed.), *Kirby's Quest for Somerset etc.* (Somerset Record Society, 3, 1889).

existence of surnames in the 1327 lay subsidy which refer to places still traceable on the tithe and modern maps has been used to demonstrate both the existence and the desertion of farms and hamlets up to the present day on Exmoor and in west Somerset.[29]

The Black Death (1348–9) cannot be shown to have permanently damaged any settlements in the region, or at least there is no documentary material which demonstrates this. Many places seem to disappear after the middle of the fourteenth century, such as Orchardleigh near Frome in Somerset, while others which may have been deserted at that time, like South Cadbury and Witcombe in Martock in the same county, were clearly resettled later on as they are still there. At Earnshill, however, there is a reasonably certain reference to the loss of a settlement at this time: in 1352 the curate petitions the bishop to have his church combined with the nearby church of Curry Rivel since there are no people there on account of the recent '*pestilenciam*'.[30]

Only for north Gloucestershire is there adequate documentation for the desertion of villages in the fourteenth and fifteenth centuries. In 1954 Maurice Beresford drew attention to the John Rous list of the 1480s which, though mainly concerned with Warwickshire, does include reference to Sezincote, Norton and Upper and Middle Ditchford in Gloucestershire as deserted by the end of the fifteenth century. This is the era of classic, but in this region rare, documentation referring to the eviction of peasants by rapacious landlords. At Dixton fifteen villagers were ousted and 190 acres enclosed, and at Didcot, also in Gloucestershire, thirty villagers were evicted by the Abbot of Tewkesbury in 1491.

More recent work, mainly by Dyer, has shown that often these evictions came at the end of a long period of decline reaching back to before the Black Death. Dyer suggests that the fourteenth century is perhaps even more significant, at least on the Cotswolds, for the abandonment of settlements,[31] although a number may have disappeared as a result of the plague itself – Chevenage/Ledgemore, Lowsmoor and Wontley. More typical of the evidence is the example of Sheldon near Chippenham in Wiltshire. The abundant documentation of the manor has enabled Gibbs to give a very full account of the history of the village. Even so the date of its desertion can only be narrowed down to the period 1475–1582 and the reasons for abandonment remain unclear.[32] At Snap in the same county the reasons for final desertion less than a hundred years ago are already confused and the subject of local folklore. How

---

[29] See M. Aston, 'Deserted farmsteads on Exmoor and the lay subsidy of 1327 in west Somerset', *Somerset Archaeology and Natural History*, 127 (1983), pp. 71–104.

[30] For Earnshill see T. Scott Holmes (ed.), *The Register of Ralph of Shrewsbury, Bishop of Bath and Wells 1329–1363* (Somerset Record Society, 10, 1896), pp. 731–2.

[31] C. Dyer, 'Deserted medieval villages in the west midlands', *Economic History Review*, 2nd ser., 35 (1982), pp. 19–34.

[32] E. Gibbs, *Sheldon Manor* (1982).

long will it be before the reasons for the abandonment of Imber, on Salisbury Plain, in 1943 as part of an expanded military training range, are forgotten?

When they are looked at in detail the reasons for the desertion of settlements in this region are many and varied. There are no 'obvious' or 'catastrophic' reasons and each case has to be examined on its merits – the obvious explanation of slow 'social and economic changes' covers all but tells us little.

Cartographic Evidence

There are few good early maps of any part of the west country which show deserted village sites in any detail – there is certainly nothing like those of the villages of Whatborough, Boarstall and Inclesmoor about which Beresford has written.[33] Most maps in the region date only from the eighteenth and nineteenth centuries; there are very few for the seventeenth century and even fewer for the sixteenth.

From the sixteenth century comes the most remarkable map in the region (figure 6.3), for not only is it the earliest map for Somerset but it shows the

FIGURE 6.3 *Hazlegrove in Queen Camel, Somerset: part of the map of 1573 showing the remnants of the village with its green, village cross and abandoned crofts.*

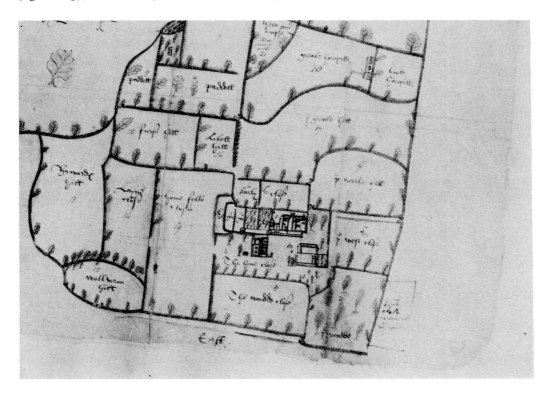

33 For Whatborough (Leicestershire), mapped by Thomas Clerk in 1586, see Beresford, *Lost Villages*, plate 5; for Inclesmoor see M. W. Beresford, in *Local Maps and Plans from Medieval England*, ed. R. A. Skelton and P. D. A. Harvey (Oxford, 1986), pp. 147–61.

location of two deserted villages. When it is realized that it only covers one small part of the average-sized parish of Queen Camel, the circumstances seem even more noteworthy.[34] By the date of the map, 1573, the hamlet of Padel has disappeared — perhaps, with its poorly drained fields, taken into the neighbouring park of Coages. The adjacent hamlet of Hazelgrove is still just about in existence; but it was to disappear in the next decade or so. What appears to be a rectangular village green with a few houses and a row of abandoned hedged crofts is shown together with the steps and stump of the village cross on the green. All this is now covered by an eighteenth-century house and its parkland estate, although the grounds and gardens of this follow the outlines of the earlier settlement. The later house was added to the manor house, shown on the map, which remains as the sixteenth-century rear wing of the mansion.

Nothing comparable to this exists as far as is known for anywhere in Wiltshire or Gloucestershire. There are, however, good seventeenth-century maps which incidentally show places now abandoned. The well-known map of the Forest of Dean in 1608 shows a row of cottages at High Meadow in Staunton where there is now only a field, and the map of Hill (Avon, formerly Gloucestershire) in 1659 shows the scattered wood and parkside hamlet of Woodend as an irregular row of cottages along a lane which still exists.

It is with the development of landscaped parkland in the eighteenth and nineteenth centuries that our best hopes lie of finding contemporary cartographic material showing earlier villages. The desertion of the village of St Audries or West Quantoxhead (Somerset) can be shown very clearly in a set of maps from 1761 to 1886.[35] In the same county the hamlet of Croft in Hinton St George is shown on several eighteenth- and nineteenth-century maps as it is eclipsed by the enlargement of Hinton Park.[36] In Gloucestershire, where there is a great density of large emparked estates, the effect on settlement was often drastic. Near Hatherop on the Cotswolds the settlements of Williamstrip, Overthrop and Netherton or Netheruppe have all gone, although the latter is shown on a map as late as 1848. The village then had a very regular plan with the main street densely built up with houses; a little later the site was incorporated into the park. The map of Stourton (Wiltshire) shows the most common evidence — small-scale clearance of cottages adjacent to a park — in this case the fine estate of Stourhead.[37] Many other places were not mapped early enough and earthworks of former settlement areas only infrequently

---

[34] Somerset RO DD/MI c/186. I am grateful to Derek Shorrocks, the County Archivist, for drawing my attention to this map and for allowing me to reproduce it here (figure 6.3).

[35] M. Aston, *Interpreting the Landscape* (London, 1985), fig. 23.

[36] R. W. Dunning, 'Hinton St George', in *VCH Somerset*, vol. IV, p. 39; and Somerset CRO maps DD/ PT GI N2S c/1756 map of 1796 and tithe map 1838 D/D/Rt 80.

[37] For Netherton, see map in Gloucester RO D 540/P4, date 1848; for Stourton see K. Woodbridge, *The Stourhead Landscape* (London, 1986). The maps of 1722 and 1785 show clearly that there were cottages near the church where there is now open space.

remain. At such places as Dyrham and Doddington (Avon, formerly Gloucestershire), Great Badminton and Sherborne (Gloucestershire) and Lydiard Tregoze (Wiltshire) the effects of emparking on neighbouring settlements must have been drastic; the settlements at Washerne, Standlynch and Barford (Wiltshire) are known to have been destroyed before park creation.[38]

Evidence from Air Photographs

Air photographs exist for all regions of Britain, mainly taken since the end of the Second World War. Most have been taken for administrative or planning purposes but there are also collections made specifically for archaeological research. Almost any air photograph is likely to be of some interest and many have been found to contain useful archaeological information. However, of the archaeological photographs there is little doubt that the collection built up at Cambridge by J. K. St Joseph and his successor D. R. Wilson is of paramount importance. The early involvement of St Joseph with the DMVRG ensured a steady supply of photographs showing both new sites located by his aerial camera and enhanced information for those already known.

In the west country, the counties of Gloucestershire and Wiltshire are rather better covered than Somerset for the reasons outlined above. The progress of data compilation for the region would be an interesting task but has not been attempted for this study. Some significant sites have been located from the air. Among very many examples that could have been chosen, St Joseph's air photograph of Nether Adber in Mudford parish, Somerset, taken in 1966, led to the location and study of that site.[39] More recently large numbers of new shrunken sites have been located by new aspiring aerial archaeologists. Roy Canham and Alison Borthwick have considerably supplemented the number of sites in the clay vales of north Wiltshire while much of the later location of sites in Somerset was achieved by the present writer using grants from various research funds.[40]

Of the non-archaeological air photograph collections there can be little doubt that those taken by the RAF between about 1944 and 1948 have proved to be the most useful. The majority were taken in low sunlight conditions in the winter and hence are particularly good for the location of earthwork sites. Such photographs indicate large numbers of shrunken and deserted sites in south Gloucestershire, in the area of the later Water Park, and in south-east

---

[38] J. H. Bettey, *Wessex from AD 1000* (London, 1986), pp. 110–15.

[39] M. Aston, 'Deserted settlements in Mudford parish, Yeovil', *Somerset Archaeology and Natural History*, 121 (1977), pp. 41–53.

[40] I am grateful to the Colt Fund of the Society for Medieval Archaeology, The Travel Fund of Bristol University and the Maltwood Trust (for Archaeological Research in Somerset) of the Royal Society of Arts for grants to carry out aerial reconnaissance work in the region.

Somerset. It is surprising that so little use has been made of these photographs in the past as an aid to the discovery of new sites. Nether Adber mentioned above, for example, is very clear on the 1947 vertical RAF picture of the area but its recognition and recording had to wait another thirty years.

Field Evidence

A very large number of sites in the west country are known only from the fact that there are earthworks remaining; sometimes their names are not known and often nothing of their history seems to exist. At Wraxall in Avon (formerly Somerset), for example, a very fine site remains with a wide holloway, earthwork platforms, prominent boundary bank and a fishpond. And yet there is still a village at Wraxall only one field away from the site, and the parish has a large number of other hamlets and farmsteads; the name of the deserted site remains a problem. A rather more impressive site was recently located by Rob Iles at Cromhall in Avon (formerly Gloucestershire) with standing walls and good earthworks.

An examination of the record cards of the Archaeology Division of the Ordnance Survey reveals that all through the post-war period surveyors out on the ground recorded deserted settlements and areas of shrunken village earthworks as part of their revision of archaeological material for OS maps. Sometimes they were working from references to known sites but very often they were the first to record a site and the record card is the first and only report of the existence of a previously unknown deserted settlement. In Somerset this is the case for the extensive earthworks of the deserted village of Horsey near Bridgwater and for the impressive site of Weston, in Combe St Nicholas parish, with its medieval chapel converted into a cottage.

Fieldwork is the best method of locating major areas of shrunken settlements and the smaller farmstead sites. Both of these are likely to be either poorly documented (particularly in the case of the latter) or not separately assessed at all (as in the case of the former), since the settlement is to all intents and purposes still there. My own fieldwork has largely been concerned with the location of such areas of settlement desertion, particularly in Somerset and to a lesser extent in Wiltshire, Avon and Gloucestershire. Some areas of shrinkage are far greater than the larger deserted village sites. At Hawling on the Cotswolds air photographic and field evidence shows that the present village is merely a small part of the area previously occupied; there are very clear earthworks of longhouses, cottages, farmyards and enclosures. Recent documentary research has demonstrated that a large part of the earthworks were actually part of the neighbouring settlement of Roel, also deserted (plate 6.1).[41]

Very large numbers of the villages in south-east Somerset can be seen to be

---

[41] *MSRG Annual Report*, 1 (1986), p. 25.

PLATE 6.1   *Hawling,*
Gloucestershire: this oblique air
photograph shows the shrunken
village earthworks of croft
boundaries and building plots.
(7 September 1986)

PLATE 6.2 *Bishopstone, Wiltshire: the oblique air photograph shows the shrunken village earthworks. Beyond the former village street lined with crofts there is an extensive area of post-medieval water meadows. (24 March 1982)*

shrunken to a greater or lesser extent. In a study of 38 medieval settlements in the area between Ilchester, Yeovil and South Cadbury, no less than 19 (50 per cent) were found to have shrunk from their maximum extent, or moved, as indicated by surrounding earthworks; 11 (*c.*28 per cent) had no evidence and 8 (*c.*22 per cent) were deserted. The claylands in north Gloucestershire show much the same degree of shrinkage and disappearance of settlements, Along with the well-known deserted villages of Didcot and Burnt Norton there are equally impressive shrunken settlement earthworks at the villages of Saintbury and Stanley Pontlarge. Another predominantly clayland area also has one of the densest areas of deserted settlement. Along the chalk escarpment near Wootton Bassett in Wiltshire there is a deserted or shrunken village site in almost every field – Highway, Clevancy, Corton, Bupton and Woodhill. Similar work in the Wiltshire valleys of the Avon, Bourne, Ebble, Till and Wylye shows that virtually every place marked on the modern 1:50,000 OS maps has shrunken village earthworks around it. Settlement must have been almost continuous in these valleys in earlier times. One really must question the gaps and ask why are there no (obvious) settlements in them.

There are deserted villages in these valleys as well, such as the well known Gomeldon, but the majority of sites are shrunken. They are mentioned in the documents, including Domesday Book, but little is known of the reasons for their contraction. New discoveries are easy in these valleys. Recently a large area of very prominent earthworks at Bishopstone, near Salisbury, was noted on an air photograph (plate 6.2). There are a church and a small village there, but the earthworks indicate a long village street lined with crofts on each side.

Those on the south side back on to extensive water meadows. Nothing seems to be known about this part of Bishopstone, though it is in a parish covered in one of the *VCH* volumes for Wiltshire.[42] Not far away a large shrunken site at Burcombe, west of Wilton, was first noted by the present writer in 1987: as well as a small group of cottages and an Anglo-Saxon church, there was formerly another village street and probably a mill.

Perhaps the greatest surprise comes from the recognition of earthworks at well-known sites. Thus at Avebury, in the heart of Wiltshire, substantial shrunken village earthworks have now been recognized both at Avebury itself, within the prehistoric circle, at Avebury Trusloe nearby and at Beckhampton a mile or so away – places usually of interest only to prehistorians. There is little in the records to indicate this shrinkage. Avebury and Avebury Trusloe, assessed as a single unit, had a high population in 1334 and there were still 134 poll tax payers in 1377. Again, the real fall in population seems to have come in the nineteenth century, from 590 in 1801 to 488 in 1841.[43]

Moated sites are not a particularly common feature in the region. Many of the clayland sites described below are surrounded by water-filled ditches but they cannot be described accurately as moated. Many of the upland farms on Exmoor are of the same date and had owners of the same status as the moated sites in the midlands, yet they were not moated, probably because of the difficult topographical and geological conditions. Very similar sorts of sites, farmsteads and small hamlets, are a characteristic feature of the west country landscape, but so far they have been little studied. Large numbers of deserted examples are now being recognized from their field remains; few are mentioned in early records, let alone adequately documented.

Apart from isolated examples, the first group to be recognized were those on the south-facing slope of the Mendip hills overlooking Wells and stretching along the slope at a general height of 230 m to Cheddar. These were recorded by the Evertons in the 1960s and have since been supplemented by the fieldwork of Hawkes and Russett. The names of most are known but little else. Yet the sites are impressive on the ground with low stone walls and clear outlines of longhouses, cottages and barns. The most impressive is Ramspits in Westbury sub Mendip parish, which consists of two separate farm units, each around a yard with adjacent paddocks and fields. Apart from the field name of the site on the tithe map, it is known only that two tofts were leased with pasture in 1463, a record which might suggest that it was already deserted by that date.[44]

---

[42] *VCH Wiltshire*, vol. XI, pp. 3–19.

[43] J. Freeman, 'Avebury', in *VCH Wiltshire*, vol. XII, pp. 86–105.

[44] A. and R. Everton, 'St Cuthbert Out', *Archaeological Review*, 6 (1971), p. 42 and fig. 3; see also H. C. Maxwell-Lyte and M. C. B. Dawes (eds), *The Register of Thomas Bekynton, Bishop of Bath and Wells 1443–1465*, Part 1 (Somerset Record Society, 1934), p. 406; V. Russett, 'Four deserted settlements in Cheddar', *Somerset Archaeology and Natural History*, forthcoming.

A very similar site exists on the south side of Dundry Hill, at Pickwick in Norton Malreward parish. This was excavated in the 1960s by Barton and seems to consist of three or four enclosures with the remains of a number of buildings, including several longhouses; it was abandoned in the nineteenth century when the farm was moved to a better location at Model Farm below.[45] Recently Williams has located other such sites in similar locations on Dundry Hill. All have slight platforms and enclosures, are associated with abandoned field banks and strip lynchets and usually have numerous springs nearby. We know their names – Crownhill, Cranwell, Sheppys, Chartlewell and Piscombe – but little else about them. As Williams's fieldwork progresses around the hill it is becoming clear that there is a farm site every 400 to 500 metres.[46]

The densest concentration of abandoned farm sites in the region, however, occurs in west Somerset where a great many remain as field monuments. Attention was first drawn to them by local people and since then Richard McDonnell has recorded many on the ground. Although some seem to be completely undocumented, like some of the Dartmoor sites, they have good earthworks of longhouses and enclosures – there is a particularly fine series of sites on North Hill near Minehead. Others, however, are 'documented', as indicated above, by reference to surnames contained in the 1327 lay subsidy. On the ground these sites vary from fine earthworks of longhouses, as at Twitchen in Oare and Holmoor in Exford, to sites where all trace has been recently removed along with the clearance of hedges in Exmoor National Park. The majority, because they have only been abandoned since the early nineteenth century, still have standing walls and ruined buildings as well as earthwork enclosures. Particularly fine examples can be seen at Mousehanger in Winsford parish, Clicket in Timberscombe and Hazery in Treborough.[47]

Along the clay belt near the coast in Somerset and Avon there is another group of sites which are only known from their earthwork remains. Typically these consist of slightly raised platforms, no more than a metre or so at the most above the surrounding Levels, roughly rectangular or rectilinear in shape, with vague areas of slight earthworks and nettle patches on top. All around there are invariably vast areas of drainage ditches or 'rhynes' although at some in north Somerset and north of Avonmouth in Avon they are associated with extensive areas of ridge and furrow.[48] Some are approached by wide raised causeways with deep side ditches from the nearest 'high' land. The largest of them are made up of a number of platforms and some can be associated with documented

[45] K. Barton, 'Pickwick Farm, Dundry, Somerset', *Proceedings of the University of Bristol Spelaeological Society*, 12 (1969), pp. 99–112.

[46] R. Williams's field reports in *Bristol and Avon Archaeology*, 3 (1984), pp. 59–61, and *Bristol and Avon Archaeology*, 4 (1985), pp. 58–60.

[47] M. Aston, 'Deserted farmsteads on Exmoor'.

[48] See R. Iles, 'The medieval rural landscape', in *The Archaeology of Avon*, ed. M. Aston and R. Iles (Bristol, 1987), pp. 109–21, esp. fig. 9.4.

places in the early middle ages. Outside Bridgwater on the west bank of the Parrett in the parish of Chilton Trinity there is a very extensive site along a holloway leading down to the river. The Parrett has probably changed its course here, as the tithe map shows part of the parish on the east bank of the river and there are a number of abandoned meanders. There is a lost Domesday vill with a church, called Pigness, somewhere in this area and it is likely that these earthworks represent the site. Robert Dunning has been able to show that one of the tithings of Chilton Trinity was called Pigness and this is the only known settlement within its area.[49] Not far away in the parish of Bawdrip another site is situated on one of the small knolls that occasionally occur in the Levels. It is approached from the east by a prominent causeway and has a number of well-defined platforms. The field names on the tithe map make it clear that this is the lost Domesday vill of Crook.

The rest of the sites are undocumented as far as is known. It is possible, however, to say something of when they came into existence and perhaps why. It is reasonably clear from the fieldwork of Nash in the Burnham on Sea area of Somerset that the Roman land surface is buried up to a metre below the present ground surface; similar circumstances seem to apply in the Avonmouth area. By the time documents for such estates as Glastonbury Abbey become available in the twelfth century there is no mention of drainage operations of the clay belt where these sites occur – they are not found further inland where the more low-lying and later drained peat levels and fens are situated. Williams, in his book on the draining of the Somerset Levels, says little of the clay belt since it had been drained before the documentation on which his study is based.[50] They are thus definitely post-Roman and probably pre-twelfth century in date. It is likely that the platforms represent the farmsteads of an undocumented phase of late Saxon land colonization, probably associated with episcopal and monastic estate management. They began perhaps as seasonal steadings but later some of them were permanently occupied as farmsteads. Only one site, at Otterhampton, has been excavated; this was not extensively examined and seems to have produced only rather undiagnostic, undatable, unglazed black pottery.

ORIGINS AND DEVELOPMENT

Finally, the origin and development of these medieval settlements needs to be considered against the background of settlement studies elsewhere in the country where in general rather more detailed work has been undertaken. It can now be argued that the settlement pattern of dispersed farmsteads and hamlets is rather older here, as elsewhere in the country, than that of nucleated villages. There have been few excavations to demonstrate this conclusively but at

---

[49] *VCH* volume in preparation.

[50] S. G. Nash, 'A deep water inlet at Highbridge', *Somerset Archaeology and Natural History*, 117 (1972–3), pp. 97–101. A longer report is deposited in the Local History Library at Taunton Castle; M. Williams, *The Draining of the Somerset Levels* (Cambridge, 1970).

Pickwick, already mentioned, the excavations revealed that the site was occupied in late prehistoric and Roman times as well as in the middle ages. Given that this conclusion is based on pottery it is highly likely that the site was occupied in the post-Roman and Anglo-Saxon periods as well, when that part of the region was largely aceramic.

A study of farmsteads in west Somerset suggested two possibilities. Firstly, the pattern of farmsteads was very old; it could be traced back to the fourteenth century relatively easily and in a few cases to the twelfth and thirteenth centuries. Excavations of the abandoned site at Hurscombe showed that the documented fourteenth-century farmstead had pottery of at least the twelfth century. Everett has argued from Domesday Book that much of the settlement pattern was established by 1086,[51] and I have suggested that the same areas of land were worked in the early middle ages as in the late prehistoric period.[52] At some sites there is a close association between ringworks or hill slope enclosures and later medieval farmsteads. None of the former have been dated but they are similar to the examples in nearby Devon and Cornwall, which have. In some cases, as at Spangate in Wootton Courtenay and Twitchen in Oare, the later farm actually sits within a ringwork while elsewhere they are adjacent to or very closely associated with them; examples include Sweetworthy and Bagley in Luccombe and Rode in Winsford.

The second possibility is that most of the places which appear as single farms had originally been small hamlets. This compares very well with the situation in Devon at sites such as Houndtor, Babeny and Lettaford on Dartmoor and with the interesting study by Fox of Hartland parish.[53] The parish where it can be demonstrated best in Somerset is Brompton Regis. From a survey of 1629 it can be shown that, of 46 recorded settlements, 30 were single farms at that date, 5 could be called large hamlets with over five holdings, including Brompton itself, while no less than 11 were hamlets of between two and four tenements.[54]

That some of the farmsteads in the west country originated in the medieval period is very likely, although increasingly it is difficult to show any large-scale colonization in the region. It is possible that some wooded areas still remained to be settled by 1100, although I doubt this, given the example of Witham Priory mentioned above; but as has been suggested the claylands may well have had farms established at this time. On the Mendips the destruction of the deserted farm of Dursdon produced only medieval pottery, suggesting that

[51] P. J. Leech, 'A deserted farm in the Brendon Hills', *Somerset Archaeology and Natural History*, 126 (1982), pp. 43–60; S. Everett, 'The Domesday geography of three Exmoor parishes', *Somerset Archaeology and Natural History*, 112 (1968), pp. 54–60.

[52] Aston, 'Deserted farmsteads on Exmoor'.

[53] See H. Fox, 'Contraction: desertion and dwindling of dispersed settlement in a Devon parish', *MVRG Report*, 31 (1983), pp. 40–2.

[54] M. Aston, 'Deserted farmsteads on Exmoor'.

colonization of the upper slopes occurred then, or a little earlier in the (aceramic) late Saxon period.

The clearest evidence for a pattern of predominantly dispersed settlements in the tenth and eleventh centuries has come from the study of early charters and place names; in Somerset this is being undertaken by Michael Costen, who has shown that such names as 'huish' or 'hewish', 'hyde' and 'worth' or 'worthy', which are widespread in the region, relate to single farm holdings of the period. In the case of Rimpton parish two charters clearly indicate the addition of a 'hide' onto a 'huish' on the edge of the parish before the whole estate is granted by Brihtric Grim in his will to the Old Minster at Winchester.[55]

It is not difficult to show that such habitative place names also exist only as field names in other parts of the region, suggesting perhaps abandonment of earlier sites as open fields were laid out associated with villages. Examples include Allington and Hollington in Barnsley and Hinton, Westwick and Dudworth in Lechlade (Gloucestershire). Some caution is necessary, however, when collecting such names from late sources; the names Reddington in Ampney Crucis (Gloucestershire) and Paddington in Minety (Wiltshire), both apparently indicating lost 'tuns', turn out on further examination to be 'denu' or valley names (*Radingeden* and *Padingden*).[56] Nevertheless the sheer volume of field names ending in 'wick', 'cote', 'worth' and 'ton', all probably originally indicating farm sites, suggests very strongly that the earlier settlement pattern in the region was predominantly a dispersed one.

If this evidence is taken together with 'innox' names (probably indicating a non-common-field arable field system) and the widespread occurrence of 'oldfield' and 'oldland' elements, which have been used elsewhere as indicators of pre-village settlement,[57] then the circumstantial evidence for a very different pattern of settlements and field systems in the pre-medieval period is very strong. As elsewhere in the country it begins to look as if the establishment of villages and their common fields is a rather special, relatively late and somewhat intermittent phenomenon. To this can be added the late appearance of village greens in some settlements in the region; at Stoke Gifford outside Bristol recent excavations have suggested considerable modifications to the village plan involving a shift in farm sites by the fourteenth century, probably associated with the creation of a large triangular green (figure 6.4).[58]

The place which shows these changes best in the region is Frocester in the

[55] M. D. Costen, 'Rimpton in Somerset – a late Saxon estate', *Southern History*, 7 (1985), pp. 13–24; and idem, 'Huish and worth: Old English survivals in a later landscape', in *Studies in Anglo-Saxon Archaeology and History*, ed. D. Brown, J. Campbell and S. Hawkes (Oxford, forthcoming).

[56] See n. 25.

[57] For 'Innox' see Gover et al., *Place-Names of Wiltshire*, p. 134; for the use of 'oldfield' see P. Allerston, 'English village development: findings from the Pickering district of north Yorkshire', *Institute of British Geographers Transactions*, 51 (1970), pp. 95–109.

[58] For Stoke Gifford see J. Russell in *MVRG Annual Report*, 33 (1985), pp. 17–19. I am grateful to John Hunt, James Russell and the Bristol and Avon Archaeological Research Group for permission to reproduce figure 6.4.

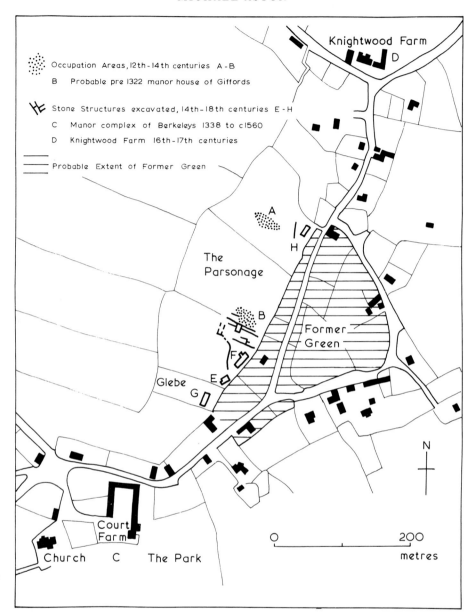

FIGURE 6.4 *Stoke Gifford, Avon: map of c.1840 with features excavated 1984–5.*

Vale of Gloucester.[59] Here local farmer Edward Price has established the succession of settlement from earliest prehistoric times to the post-medieval period. He has excavated an iron age farmstead which was succeeded by a Romano-British farmstead and a villa. There is at least one post-Roman

[59] The research on Frocester is being prepared for publication by E. Price. A map of the parish, with the distribution of deserted farmsteads, can be seen in Aston, *Interpreting the Landscape*, fig. 75, and pp. 122 and 124.

building on the site of this. A succession of plough ridges shows that narrow ridge and furrow was in use around the rubble mound of the ruined villa before wide prominent ridges were developed in the thirteenth century when the villa site was overploughed. This change in field system accompanied a major change in the settlement pattern of the parish. Fieldwork in the area of ridge and furrow earthworks which have been ploughed has shown that there were at least ten small farmsteads (to judge from the limited spread of the finds) in the area where there was later only the village of Frocester. The pottery found on these sites is all from the thirteenth century – there is nothing later. It thus looks as if a scatter of farmsteads associated with fields of narrow arable strips was replaced in the thirteenth century by a more nucleated settlement with common fields.

The Wiltshire village of Shrewton suggests another development where several small farmstead clusters have amalgamated into a single large village.[60] In this part of the Till valley, there were formerly up to eight separately named vills. Of these, Netton has disappeared completely both as a place and as a name, Elston, Abbaston, Homanton and Bourton are all deserted or severely shrunken places, and Rollestone is a shrunken village with a small redundant church. Only Shrewton and Maddington remain as substantial settlements, the latter with a redundant church. Each of these places has a very regular area of crofts suggesting a degree of planning, as did the area of Netton before modern housing encroached on the site.

All these places were called Winterbourne at the time of the Domesday survey, a name which remains only at the probable estate centre of Winterbourne Stoke. The place names are all good indicators of the ownership of the vills and perhaps give us some indication of how an early large estate was broken up and granted away by the king. Thus Shrewton was the sheriff's *tūn*, Maddington the maidens' (the nuns of Amesbury) *tūn* and Abbaston belonged to the Abbot of Winchester. Both Elston and Rollestone refer to the post-Conquest estate owners – Elias and Rolf. The names Netton and Bourton, meaning respectively cattle *tūn* and bower *tūn*, may refer to renders made by these places, of cattle and building or fortification works, to the estate *caput*. What had been several small hamlet or farmstead clusters seem to have grown together, perhaps with some regulation of plan and probably as a result of population increase, before later shrinkage produced the present varied pattern of survival. Shrewton nevertheless represents the supreme example of a 'polyfocal' settlement in the region.

To these examples of the survival of a dispersed settlement pattern in west Somerset and the changes from dispersed to agglomerated at Frocester and Shrewton we can add the example of a planned settlement at Shapwick in Somerset.[61] The estate there belonged to Glastonbury Abbey from pre-Conquest

[60] For Shrewton see Gover et al., *Place-Names of Wiltshire*, pp. 233–7.

[61] For Shapwick see N. Corcos, 'Early estates on the Poldens and the origin of settlement at Shapwick', *Somerset Archaeology and Natural History*, 127 (1983), pp. 47–54; and idem, 'Shapwick: The Enclosure of a

times to the sixteenth century. It is one of a number of villages on the north side of the Polden hills all of which belonged to the abbey and many of which have regular rectilinear plans. There are several eighteenth-century plans for both the village and the parish; at that time the village plan was rather more regular than today because the creation of the park around the manor house in the late eighteenth century involved the removal of many streets and a large number of houses.

Corcos has been able to show that in the middle ages the field system of strips in two large common fields was also regular. He also drew attention to a number of field names which seemed to suggest an earlier pattern of dispersed farmsteads – 'manycrofte', 'langenworthy', 'shortenworthy', 'shortgoldworth' and so on. From this evidence he ventured to suggest that Shapwick must have originated in its present form 'as a result of a deliberate and planned wholesale reorganisation'; elsewhere it is suggested that this happened in the tenth century. If this is the case then we have here in the south of England an example of the planning of settlements similar to that observed in the north. It remains to be seen whether further research will be able to demonstrate this adequately.

CONCLUSION

For the west country, as elsewhere, it can be shown that the recognition of deserted villages has led to a total reappraisal of the origins of rural settlement in the region. The painstaking recording of earthworks and the correlation of documentary, cartographic and field evidence, which was so much the hallmark of past work by members of the MSRG and which owes so much to the example set by Maurice Beresford and John Hurst, has provided a sound basis on which further settlement studies can be based. As this chapter has tried to show, it is perhaps with the detailed analysis of particular sites in their regional and historical setting that most progress will be made in the future. Such studies will hopefully provide a fitting tribute to the two men who have provided so much encouragement to others.

Somerset Parish 1515–1839' (unpublished M.A. thesis, University of Leicester, 1981–2), from which this quotation is taken.

7

Grassy Hummocks and Stone Foundations: Fieldwork and Deserted Medieval Settlements in the South-West Midlands, 1945–1985

C. J. BOND

INTRODUCTION

One of the great strengths of medieval settlement studies in England since the Second World War has been their multidisciplinary character, so admirably exemplified by the fruitful collaboration of Maurice Beresford and John Hurst over so many years. Archaeologists, documentary historians, historical geographers, historical ecologists, architectural historians and many others have come together to coordinate their efforts in a quite unprecedented way beneath the umbrella of the DMVRG, which Beresford, Hurst and a few others had founded back in 1952; and although our perception of research problems and our strategies for tackling them have evolved and changed almost beyond recognition since those early years, that close interdisciplinary cooperation still continues within the first group's modern successor, the MSRG. We have learned the lesson that no-one, archaeologist, historian or geographer, can any longer work effectively in isolation in this field.

The cornucopia of investigative methods now available has given us the ability to recover information of a range and quality which would have been unthinkable in the early years of the DMVRG. Unfortunately the application of those methods is inevitably hampered by practical limitations of finance. Consequently, it is now generally agreed that the best way forward is by means of a limited number of major research projects, meticulously planned and executed multidisciplinary investigations in which the whole battery of research techniques can be brought to bear upon a few carefully selected sites. The immense value of such projects is not to be denied. However, we run certain risks if we commit all of our eggs to this basket. Much of the empirical work which has taken place in the past has tended to emphasize the uniqueness of places, the individuality of their development and the differences between them. Attempts to project overall generalizations about settlement evolution from the evidence of a small number of intensively-researched sites may ultimately prove totally misleading. Moreover, settlement patterns need to be examined on a regional scale as well as a parochial one. Alongside the major, intensive projects, therefore, there is a continuing need for more broadly-based investigations.

The principal tools of the more extensive approach are field survey, documentary research and aerial photography. This chapter will review the contribution of fieldwork on the ground to the study of medieval rural settlement in the south and west midlands, concentrating particularly upon the ancient counties of Oxfordshire, Warwickshire and Worcestershire, but also drawing upon work in the neighbouring counties. The selection of this particular piece of countryside has not been dictated by any abstract geographical considerations, but is an arbitrary personal choice prompted merely by the fact that it happens to be the region most familiar to me and the scene of most of my own work. It embraces a wide range of physical terrain, from the sticky claylands of the Warwickshire Feldon to the arid sandy soils of Kinver Forest and the windswept brashy uplands of the Oxfordshire Cotswolds, and from the sodden marshland of Otmoor to the high peaks of the Malverns. It includes classic open-field landscapes, forest landscapes and a variety of hybrid and intermediate forms. It also spans the divide between the counties such as Oxfordshire and Warwickshire which figured early on in the literature on deserted villages and were held to be classic localities for their occurrence, and those more westerly counties originally thought to be almost devoid of such sites.[1]

Within this regional framework it is proposed to examine the evolving role of field survey over the past forty years, the changes in its aims and the developments in its organization; and then to explore more closely the purpose of mapping earthworks as an aid to the interpretation of the remains of deserted medieval settlements.

THE ORGANIZATION OF FIELD SURVEY

Compared with excavation, the essentially complementary approach of field survey has always tended to be under-valued and under-financed by the archaeological establishment. With the exception of the invaluable contributions of the RCHM and a few enlightened local authorities,[2] it has progressed largely through the voluntary efforts of university extra-mural classes, local archaeological groups and individuals beavering away within their own territories. As a

[1] A contrast still reflected in the maps in M. W. Beresford and J. G. Hurst (eds), *Deserted Medieval Villages* (London, 1971), figs. 5, 13.

[2] See, for example, R. F. Hartley, *The Medieval Earthworks of Rutland, a Survey* (Leicestershire Museums, Art Galleries and Records Service, Archaeology Report no. 7, 1983); and the series *Bedfordshire Parish Surveys: Historic Landscape and Archaeology* (Bedfordshire Planning Department, 1983 onwards).

result it has certain strengths, but also certain weaknesses. On the credit side, the individual or small group can put in much more concentrated effort within a limited area, building up a wealth of local knowledge and contacts which the museum- or unit-based professional, with responsibility for an entire district, county or larger region, cannot hope to emulate. On the other hand such work can sometimes become blinkered, over-parochial and unrelated to the general progress of academic research. The haphazard distribution of interested parties and the varying levels of their experience and competence makes any sort of regional synthesis difficult. Taken as a whole (and leaving aside the work of the Royal Commission whose published inventories have only impinged upon the margins of the region in question),[3] field survey still lacks any effective organizational structure and is bedevilled by uncertainty of direction and uneven standards.

On the other hand, a significant contribution towards the indexing and retrieval of the cumulative results of fieldwork has been made by the emergence of the local authority Sites & Monuments Records, pioneered by Don Benson's work in Oxfordshire in the 1960s. The Oxfordshire record currently contains details of some 148 deserted and 113 shrunken villages, in addition to indexing many other parameters of settlement and landscape of all periods.[4] Even after two decades, Sites & Monuments Records are still in their infancy, preoccupied with assimilating the enormous backlog of widely dispersed published information, keeping pace with incoming records and transforming their internal structure from manual punched-card to electronic retrieval systems, while all the time attempting to respond to the demands of their many users. The inevitably uneven pace and quality of input to such records has led one critic to express the memorable view that 'the majority of them contain data which more closely resemble the discoveries of Walpole's *Three Princes of Serendip* than those of a scientific enquiry.'[5] It would be difficult to deny that there still remains a considerable element of truth in this accusation, but this is essentially a transient problem; all Sites & Monuments Records should be under a continuous process of correction and enhancement as well as moving towards ever more sophisticated techniques of retrieval. They already represent a much more organized and comprehensive reservoir of archaeological information than is available from any other single source, and no future

[3] RCHM (England), *Buckinghamshire* (2 vols, London, 1912, 1913); *Herefordshire* (3 vols, 1931, 1932, 1934); *Northamptonshire* (6 vols, 1975, 1979, 1981, 1982, 1984, 1985, continuing).

[4] Descriptions of the Oxfordshire record system include D. Benson, 'A Sites and Monuments Record for the Oxford region', *Oxoniensia*, 37 (1972), pp. 226–37, and C. J. Bond and J. M. Campbell, 'Environmental Record Centres as a source for landscape historians: the case of Oxfordshire', in *Recording Historic Landscapes, Principles and Practice*, ed. P. Brandon and R. Millman (Polytechnic of North London Dept of Geography, Occasional Publication no. 2, 1980), pp. 24–9.

[5] D. Miles, 'Confusion in the countryside: some comments from the upper Thames region', in *The Romano-British Countryside. Studies in Rural Settlement and Economy*, ed. D. Miles (BAR, British ser., 103, 1982), pp. 53–79, esp. p. 62.

survey campaign, site evaluation programme or regional synthesis can afford to ignore them.

CHANGING PERSPECTIVES IN SETTLEMENT STUDIES

The difficulties in formulating and effecting a satisfactory programme of field survey have been compounded by profound changes in our own perspectives as our subject has developed. Beresford's pioneer work on deserted villages in Warwickshire and its subsequent extension over the rest of England represented the first nails in the coffin of the static, ethnic and deterministic models of settlement which had predominated until the 1950s.[6] Beresford's successful blending of documentary research with field investigation enabled him to demonstrate beyond question, and in defiance of the prevailing academic orthodoxy, that large numbers of settlements which existed in the middle ages were subsequently depopulated; and he put forward the view that evictions by Tudor landlords in order to enclose the arable strips of the dispossessed villagers for sheep farming were a potent cause of such desertions.[7] On the archaeological front, the initiation of large-scale open-area excavations, notably by Hurst at Wharram Percy, has demonstrated the potential for major internal changes in medieval village plans, especially within individual crofts; perhaps even more importantly, it has pointed to a lack of continuity between areas of early Saxon and medieval settlement, a point echoed by local work at Seacourt (Berkshire, now Oxfordshire) and more recently at Burton Dassett (Warwickshire).[8] At the same time more careful examination of Roman sites such as Shakenoak (Oxfordshire) and Barton Court (Berkshire, now Oxfordshire) showed that their occupation did not necessarily cease at the beginning of the fifth century, and that the critical break often came in the middle or even late Saxon period.[9] The early work of E. T. Leeds at Sutton Courtenay (Berkshire, now Oxfordshire), followed by more recent excavations at Eynsham, Radley and elsewhere, has revealed a pattern of early Saxon

[6] The influence of the traditional approach is still evident in the chapters covering settlement morphology and the Anglo-Saxon and medieval periods in the two post-war British Association handbooks covering the region: *Birmingham and its Regional Setting: A Scientific Survey*, ed. R. H. Kinvig and M. J. Wise (Birmingham, 1950); and *The Oxford Region: A Scientific and Historical Survey*, ed. A. F. Martin and R. W. Steel (London, 1954).

[7] M. W. Beresford, 'The deserted villages of Warwickshire', *Transactions of the Birmingham Archaeological Society*, 66 (1945–6), pp. 49–106; idem, *The Lost Villages of England* (London, 1954).

[8] M. Biddle, 'The deserted medieval village of Seacourt, Berkshire', *Oxoniensia*, 26/27 (1961–2), pp. 70–201, esp. pp. 117–20; I am grateful to Nicholas Palmer of the Warwickshire Museum Service for information on his current excavations at Burton Dassett.

[9] A. C. C. Brodribb, A. R. Hands and D. R. Walker, *Excavations at Shakenoak* (5 vols, Oxford, 1968–78); D. Miles (ed.), *Archaeology at Barton Court Farm, Abingdon, Oxon.* (Oxford Archaeological Unit Report 3/CBA Research Report no. 50, 1984).

settlement characterized by small, irregular and temporary hamlets or clachans, quite different from the pre-war model.[10]

Another important step forward has been the recognition that settlements cannot effectively be studied in isolation, but ought to be viewed in their overall economic and tenurial context. This has led to a greater emphasis on estates, field systems and the settlement hierarchy as a whole. Finberg's study of Withington (Gloucestershire) opened our eyes to the possibilities of continuity between Romano-British and medieval estates,[11] and there is now a general agreement on the likelihood of partial or complete transmission of estate boundaries, not just from the Saxon into the post-Conquest period, but even in some cases over a much longer time-span, reaching back into prehistory. This is not to deny that major changes in territorial organization can and do occur, especially the breakup of large multiple estates into smaller, more self-contained units in which there is a much more direct relationship between landowner and individual estate.[12] The generally dispersed pattern of shifting settlement which, according to our present understanding, seems to have been more or less the norm throughout the prehistoric, Roman and early Saxon period, evidently gave way in parts of the English midlands to a more stable pattern of larger nucleated villages. The reasons for this are not fully understood, but must include the rising pressure of population on agricultural resources, the emergence of the open-field system of farming with its emphasis on communal cooperation, the reorganization of the church into the parochial system, the breakup of the multiple estates, and the imposition of feudal authority after the Norman Conquest.[13] Given the admission of changing forms and processes of settlement before the Conquest, the widespread evidence for later medieval village depopulation, shrinkage, migration and replanning now seems less surprising. As the focus of research has turned more towards the overall evolution of settlement changes we are perhaps less obsessed now than we were in the 1950s and 1960s with determining the specific causes of village desertions at the end of the middle ages. This is still far from a dead issue, however, and while there has been a retreat from universal monocausal explanations, protracted decline over a period is held to be generally more

[10] E. T. Leeds, 'A Saxon village near Sutton Courtenay, Berkshire', *Archaeologia*, 73 (1923), pp. 147–92; (Second Report), *Archaeologia*, 76 (1927), pp. 59–79; (Third Report), *Archaeologia*, 92 (1947), pp. 79–93; S. C. Hawkes and M. Gray, 'Preliminary note on the early Anglo-Saxon settlement at New Wintles Farm, Eynsham', *Oxoniensia*, 34 (1969), pp. 1–4; R. Bradley, R. A. Chambers and C. E. Halpin, *Barrow Hills, Radley, 1983–4, Excavations: An Interim Report* (Oxford Archaeological Unit, 1984).

[11] H. P. R. Finberg, *Roman and Saxon Withington: A Study in Continuity* (Leicester University Dept of English Local History, Occasional Papers, 1st ser., no. 8, 1957).

[12] See, for example, D. Hooke, *The Anglo-Saxon Landscape: The Kingdom of the Hwicce* (Manchester, 1985), esp. pp. 75–116.

[13] C. J. Bond, 'Medieval Oxfordshire villages and their topography: a preliminary discussion', in *Medieval Villages: A Review of Current Work*, ed. D. Hooke (Oxford University Committee for Archaeology, monograph no. 5, 1985), pp. 101–23.

common than sudden cataclysmic destruction through plague or evictions, and historians such as Hilton, Dyer and Lloyd have stressed the importance of voluntary abandonment of their holdings by peasants, with enclosure being a result rather than a cause of depopulation.[14]

CHANGING AIMS AND APPROACHES IN FIELD SURVEY

As our understanding of rural settlement has evolved, so our perception of the purpose of field survey has changed with it. In the 1950s, in the wake of Beresford's initial discoveries, fieldwork was carried out on a superficial but extensive basis: our main concern was to locate deserted villages on the ground, by searching for earthworks in localities where the former presence of a village was suggested by basic topographical clues such as empty parishes or isolated churches, or by documentary evidence. This led to the production of county checklists, devices which achieved their most developed form in the Oxfordshire and Northamptonshire monographs published in the mid-1960s.[15] Gazetteers of this nature prompted new surveys in areas where previously little had been done, and as a result many new deserted settlements of a sort were also identified in counties like Shropshire, Staffordshire, Herefordshire and Worcestershire.[16]

Checklists provided a new basis for examining the distribution of deserted sites at both national and local level. At first the approach tended to be somewhat deterministic in character, attempting merely to relate high densities of sites to areas of physiographic adversity, such as high altitude, poor sandy soils or heavy clays. This itself reflected the contemporary and simplistic preoccupation with causes of desertion. Subsequently other factors contributing to settlement vulnerability have come under scrutiny. Basic propinquity

[14] R. H. Hilton, 'A study in the pre-history of English enclosure in the fifteenth century' (1957), repr. in R. H. Hilton, *The English Peasantry in the Later Middle Ages* (Oxford, 1975), pp. 161–73; C. C. Dyer, 'Population and agriculture on a Warwickshire manor in the later middle ages', *University of Birmingham Historical Journal*, 11 (1968), pp. 113–27; idem, *Lords and Peasants in a Changing Society* (Cambridge, 1980), esp. pp. 244–63; T. H. Lloyd, 'Some documentary sidelights on the deserted Oxfordshire village of Brookend', *Oxoniensia*, 29/30 (1964–5), pp. 116–28.

[15] K. J. Allison, M. W. Beresford and J. G. Hurst, *The Deserted Villages of Oxfordshire* (Leicester University Dept of English Local History, Occasional Papers, 1st ser., no. 17, 1965); K. J. Allison, M. W. Beresford and J. G. Hurst, *The Deserted Villages of Northamptonshire* (Leicester University Dept of English Local History, Occasional Papers, 1st ser., no. 18, 1966).

[16] A. Gaydon and R. T. Rowley, 'Deserted villages in Shropshire', *DMVRG Annual Report*, 12 (1964), Appendix E; P. V. Bate and D. M. Palliser, 'Suspected lost village sites in Staffordshire', *Transactions of the South Staffordshire Archaeological and Historical Society*, 12 (1970–1), pp. 31–6; R. Hickling, 'Deserted medieval villages' [in Herefordshire], *Transactions of the Woolhope Naturalists' Field Club*, 40 (1970–2), pp. 172–6, 400, 402; C. C. Dyer, 'D.M.V.s in Worcestershire: an interim report on work in the county and a classified list', *MVRG Annual Report*, 19 (1971), pp. 5–7; C. J. Bond, 'Deserted villages in Worcestershire', in *Worcester and its Region: Field Studies in the Former County of Worcestershire*, ed. B. Adlam (Geographical Association, Worcester Branch, 1974), pp. 35–45.

assessments have suggested that around 60 per cent of the deserted settlements in south Northamptonshire and south Warwickshire were 'crowded', in the sense that they lay in close proximity to other settlements, competing for limited land resources, whereas only about 40 per cent of the successful surviving settlements suffered from this problem.[17] Much more sophisticated statistical techniques have since been developed for analyses of this sort, but as yet they have seen little practical application. In the meantime the logical next step of examining each individual site within the context of its entire parish or township has placed resource assessment upon a much firmer base.

At county level the basic stage of site identification was followed up by efforts to define the quality and extent of each site. This process became essential with the establishment of the county Sites & Monuments Records, themselves a belated response to the urgent need to identify and define archaeological sites which were potentially or actually under threat from various forms of modern development. The utilization of Sites & Monuments Records within the local planning process prompted more elaborate attempts to evaluate sites for excavation or preservation priorities, taking into account quality of field evidence, documentation and other factors,[18] a process which had begun in some of the earlier county checklists.

At parish level the more detailed investigation of individual sites has tended to be dominated by documentary studies, but with a few exceptions, such as Dyer's examination of Woollashill (Worcestershire),[19] these were little concerned with the evidence on the ground. Of the small number of earthwork surveys published in the 1960s, a high proportion were sketch surveys, produced during reconnaissance visits by stop-gap methods intended to provide insurance against future destruction of the site without further record.[20] Such rapid surveys undeniably have considerable limitations, and were frowned upon by professional surveyors; nonetheless, many of the sites provisionally recorded in this way *have* since been destroyed with no opportunity for more accurate work, and so the compromise in standards was perhaps justified. In recent years the comparative stabilization of land use has permitted more time

---

[17] Beresford and Hurst, *Deserted Medieval Villages*, p. 29, fig. 4; C. J. Bond, 'Deserted medieval villages in Warwickshire and Worcestershire', in *Field and Forest: an Historical Geography of Warwickshire and Worcestershire*, ed. T. R. Slater and P. J. Jarvis (Norwich, 1982), pp. 147–71, esp. pp. 164–5.

[18] D. Benson and C. J. Bond, 'Problems and methods of evaluation', in *Planning and the Historic Environment*, ed. R. T. Rowley and M. Breakell (Oxford University Dept for External Studies/Oxford Polytechnic Dept of Town Planning, 1975), pp. 95–103, 124–7.

[19] C. C. Dyer, 'The deserted medieval village of Woollashill', *Transactions of the Worcestershire Archaeological Society*, 3rd ser., 1 (1965–7), pp. 55–61.

[20] C. J. Bond, 'Deserted medieval villages in Warwickshire: a review of the field evidence', *Transactions of the Birmingham and Warwickshire Archaeological Society*, 86 (1974), pp. 85–112; see also sketch plans of Worcestershire and Oxfordshire sites which appeared in *DMVRG Annual Report*, 18 (1970) and *MVRG Annual Reports*, 19 (1971)–24 (1976); for the methods used, see M. Aston and C. J. Bond, 'Sketch planning: an introduction', *CBA Group 9 Newsletter*, 3 (1973), pp. 8–12.

for the preparation of more accurate measured plans (figures 7.1–7.3). The use of earthwork surveys in interpretation will be discussed further below.

Since the 1960s field archaeology has played an increasingly independent role, as it came to be realized that, even in the middle ages, written sources do not reveal everything. Many further sites were discovered which were poorly documented, even wholly unrecorded; especially small deserted hamlets and farms which are less likely to figure in national taxation returns. Above all, we have seen the emergence of the so-called 'shrunken' village, to the point where it could be assessed as 'the commonest English earthwork of any type or period'.[21]

Fieldwork is never finished, and even in a county like Oxfordshire, which has been subjected to fairly thorough, if unsystematic, study over many years, new sites are still turning up. An example is Sugarswell, on the marlstone uplands of north Oxfordshire, where the only known documentation for a settlement was a casual reference to houses being burned down in 1318;[22] this led to a fruitless search in the immediate vicinity of the farm bearing that name, and only many years later was an extent of quite clear earthworks, including houses and crofts and a double-island moat, discovered almost on the county boundary some 500 m north of the farm.[23] While fully accepting, therefore, that the pattern is still incomplete, we can nonetheless now begin attempting to relate the distribution of deserted and shrunken settlements in Oxfordshire to the overall settlement pattern, in the expectation that, whatever further discoveries may be made at local level, they are unlikely to be on a scale sufficient to unbalance the present picture.[24]

It would be wrong to suggest that all the processes of basic recognition, definition and survey of deserted settlements, let alone the clarification of the causes of desertion, are yet approaching the end of their potential. However, in the 1980s the focus of attention has been drawn more towards shrunken and surviving villages. This was partly a result of non-academic factors, as it was realized that the threat of building and redevelopment in existing villages was as great or greater than the threat of ploughing and other forms of agricultural damage on deserted sites. This change of direction generated a range of implications reports, the most ambitious being Ann Ellison's survey in south-east Somerset,[25] which provided the model for a few individual village surveys in Oxfordshire and Gloucestershire during the same period.[26] Although

[21] Allison et al., *Deserted Villages of Northamptonshire*, p. 30.

[22] *Calendar of Patent Rolls*, 1317–21, pp. 100, 176.

[23] Discovered by Paul Gosling, Sarah Gosling and David Hall; *MVRG Report*, 25 (1977), p. 13.

[24] C. J. Bond, 'The Oxford region in the middle ages', in *The Archaeology of the Oxford Region*, ed. G. Briggs, J. Cook and R. T. Rowley (Oxford University Dept for External Studies, 1986), pp. 135–59, 184–9, esp. pp. 139–43, maps 14–15, pp. 185–6.

[25] A. Ellison, *Medieval Villages in South-East Somerset* (Western Archaeological Trust, Survey no. 6, 1983).

[26] Oxfordshire Village Surveys published in *CBA Group 9 Newsletter*: C. J. Bond, 'Stanton St John', in *Newsletter*, 8 (1978), pp. 76–87 and 'Bloxham', in *Newsletter*, 10 (1980), pp. 103–23; J. M. Steane,

planning needs and development pressures were the catalyst for this change, there were also academic justifications; for perhaps too long medieval rural settlement studies had been dominated by investigations of places which were atypical simply because they had failed, a perfectly understandable preoccupation while their recognition was still a novelty, but not altogether healthy or desirable in the longer term.

The re-examination of existing villages has been encouraged by further new approaches and techniques developed outside the world of local planning and in other regions of the country. The work of Brian Roberts has provided a much sounder methodology for the classification of settlement forms employing more strictly morphological principles.[27] Christopher Taylor's fieldwork for the Royal Commission, along with that of certain other workers such as Peter Wade-Martins and Jack Ravensdale, has opened up a much broader view of settlement dynamics, underlining not only the potential for fundamental changes in village forms during the middle ages, but also giving us a clearer impression of their antecedents.[28]

The morphology and dynamics of existing villages have become important themes in medieval rural settlement studies, but are too complex to be explored adequately here, and we shall now return to the field evidence for deserted settlements.

THE INTERPRETATION OF VILLAGE EARTHWORKS

Even the perception of earthworks, let alone their understanding, is an acquired ability; it cannot be taken for granted. Quite recently I took a group of American summer school students to visit some deserted village sites in Oxfordshire. Well primed by a couple of weeks of prior tuition and a heavy dosage of slides, they followed me across the fields to the first site, having some idea of what to expect. It happened that a guest had joined the party for the day, a young American girl who was a friend of two members of my class. She

'Charney Bassett', in *Newsletter*, 8 (1978), pp. 87–94, 'Great Tew', in *Newsletter*, 9 (1979), pp. 94–105, and 'Lewknor', in *Newsletter*, 10 (1980), pp. 124–33; D. H. Aldred, *Bishop's Cleeve: Archaeology and Planning* (Tewkesbury Borough Council, 1976).

[27] B. K. Roberts, 'Village patterns and forms: some models for discussion', in *Medieval Villages*, ed. Hooke, pp. 7–25, q.v. for references to other works by this author.

[28] RCHM (England), *Dorset* (5 vols, 1952, 1970, 1972, 1975); RCHM (England), *Cambridgeshire* (2 vols, 1968, 1972); RCHM (England), *Northamptonshire*, vol. I (1975), vol. II (1979), vol. III (1981), vol. IV (1982), vol. VI (1984); C. C. Taylor, 'Polyfocal settlement and the English village', *Medieval Archaeology*, 21 (1977), pp. 189–93; idem, 'Aspects of village mobility in medieval and later times', in *The Effect of Man on the Landscape: The Lowland Zone*, ed. S. Limbrey and J. G. Evans (CBA Research Report, no. 21, 1978), pp. 126–34; C. C. Taylor, *Village and Farmstead: A History of Rural Settlement in England* (London, 1983); P. Wade-Martins, 'The origins of rural settlement in East Anglia', in *Recent Work in Rural Archaeology*, ed. P. J. Fowler (Bradford on Avon, 1975), pp. 137–57; P. Wade-Martins, 'Village sites in Launditch hundred', *East Anglian Archaeology*, 10 (1980); J. R. Ravensdale, *Liable to Floods: Village Landscape on the Edge of the Fens, AD 450–1850* (Cambridge, 1974).

watched with increasing mystification and no little amusement as I gesticulated around the apparently empty field pointing out the village street, the boundary bank, the site of the chapel and the manor house, while her companions nodded sagely in agreement and earnestly made notes and sketches. She confided afterwards that she had been irresistibly reminded of the story of the emperor's new clothes. Unfamiliar with medieval earthworks, she was simply unable to appreciate the slight bumps in the grass which seemed so fascinating to the rest of the party – a chastening and salutary reminder that one needs to be attuned to the evidence even to see it, let alone to understand it.

It has to be admitted that the interpretation of earthworks without recourse to excavation is a hazardous occupation. It may be compared to trying to guess the contents of a parcel from its shape without unwrapping it. Our perception is limited to the top surface of the ground, and even at best this can only reflect the underlying archaeological features in a limited way, just as the wrapping muffles the contents of the parcel.

Most sites will always be difficult to understand. The spectacular earthworks usually illustrated in textbooks (including, indeed, the examples illustrating this article), where the entire plan of the village remains clearly visible under grass, are very much in a minority. It is estimated that in Oxfordshire, Warwickshire and Worcestershire, between 50 and 65 per cent of the recognized deserted village sites either consist of vague formless hummocks with no coherent plan, or have left no visible earthwork evidence whatsoever. Over much of the region, especially in south Worcestershire, south and east Warwickshire and central and south Oxfordshire, timber building remained general throughout the middle ages, and as a result, while the outline of the streets and of individual crofts may show up in the form of ditches and holloways, it is difficult to pick out the sites of buildings (figure 7.1). Not infrequently even the basic street layout is difficult to detect. Modern ploughing has damaged many formerly impressive sites, such as Bainton (Oxfordshire) and Chesterton Netherend (Warwickshire).

Even where the pattern of earthworks is clear, as we find on some sites on the Oxfordshire Cotswolds (Broadstone, Lower Chalford, Coat), this will only reflect the final phase of stone building on the site before it was abandoned and fell down to grass, and it will usually conceal a much longer and more complex earlier sequence of development. At Lower Chalford (figure 7.2), where the ground falls sharply away to the north, one could speculate whether the prominent bank continuing across the village street about half-way down the site, defining crofts on both its eastern and western sides, might be a relic of an earlier system of land boundaries of pre-medieval date; while the vague and indeterminate earthworks north of this line and west of the street, contrasting with the clearly-defined buildings elsewhere on the site, may hint at an area of earlier abandonment. The real situation will certainly be even more complicated.

The area occupied by each site needs to be defined for Sites & Monuments Record purposes, but the historical implications of its extent are more difficult to assess. As the scale of deserted medieval settlements ranges from single farms up to substantial market towns, so the amount of ground covered by one site may range from less than a hectare (Slape, Oxfordshire) to 40 hectares or more (Dassett Southend, Warwickshire); but the ratio of areal extent to population is not a constant one. Substantial areas within some settlements may be given over to paddocks and enclosures of various sorts not containing houses. How closely the population of a site at any given time is reflected in its extent depends upon the building density – the number of house sites within the village perimeter – and to what degree those houses were in simultaneous occupation. Our ability to recognize houses at all may be severely constrained in the claylands, and even in conditions of good visibility it takes an extremely fortunate combination of circumstances before we can prove contemporaneity or non-contemporaneity of habitation between different parts of the site.

In some cases the field evidence does seem to match up well with the documentary record. A survey of the earthworks at Somerford (Oxfordshire) identified seven small buildings fronting onto the main street, with space for perhaps one or two more houses, and this accords well with the seven cottars and one or two freehold tenants recorded there in the hundred rolls of 1279.[29] However, it would be over-optimistic to expect such close correspondences to occur very frequently. On many sites, for example Quarrendon (Buckinghamshire), the extent of earthworks and/or number of visible houses seems far in excess of the size of population implied by the documentary record. The question then arises, is this due simply to a large number of people slipping through the mesh of the medieval taxation net, or does it reflect changes in the village plan prior to the final desertion involving the abandonment of some areas and extension into others? The latter possibility is underlined by the classic case of Wawne (Yorkshire) and instances within the region such as Combe (Oxfordshire) and Cublington (Buckinghamshire), where the village appears to have been resettled on a new site after the Black Death and survives on that new site.[30]

Sometimes we find the opposite: at Coat (Oxfordshire) tax returns and rentals of the thirteenth and fourteenth centuries suggest that it contained about a dozen holdings, but a survey of the earthworks revealed no more than about half a dozen farmsteads (figure 7.3); there is no evidence of further habitation extending beyond the surveyed area, and it is difficult to see how the remaining holdings can have been accommodated within the perimeter of the

---

[29] 'South Midlands Archaeology', CBA Group 9 Newsletter, 13 (1983), pp. 65–7; the plan is also reproduced in MVRG Annual Report, 30 (1982), pp. 9–10.

[30] C. Hayfield, 'Wawne, East Riding of Yorkshire: A case study in settlement morphology', Landscape History, 6 (1984), pp. 41–67; C. S. Emden, Combe Church and Village (Oxford, 1951); M. Reed, The Buckinghamshire Landscape (London, 1979), pp. 150, 160.

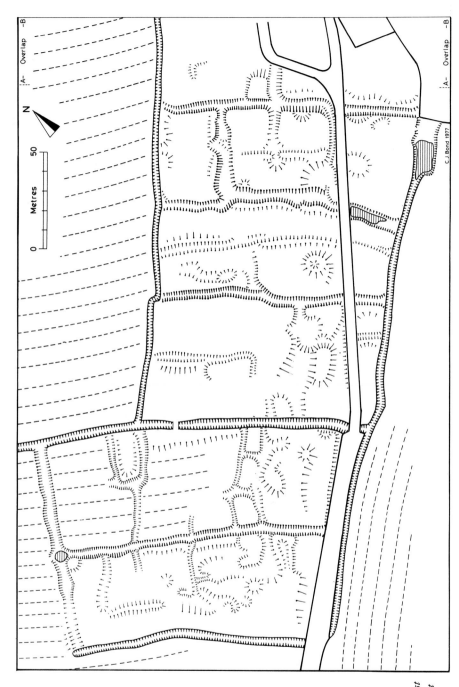

FIGURE 7.1 Settlement
earthworks at Wretchwick,
Oxfordshire (above, south-west
Wretchwick; below, north-east
Wretchwick).

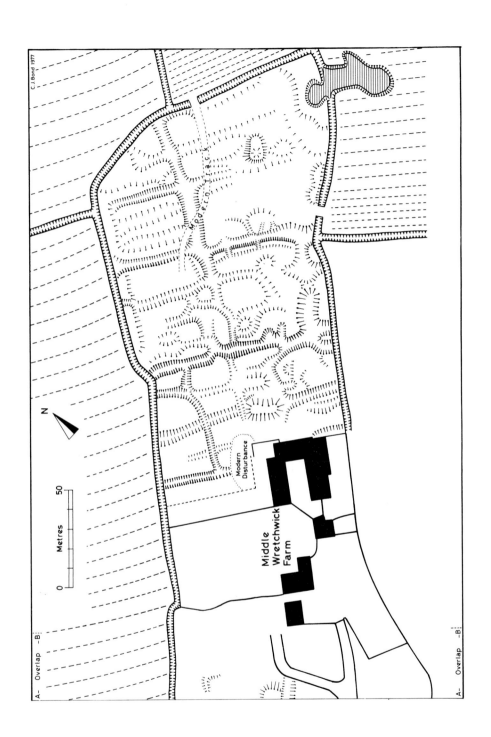

Modern Track

Modern
Disturbance

Middle
Wretchwick
Farm

N

Metres

0   50

A-   Overlap   -B

A-   Overlap   -B

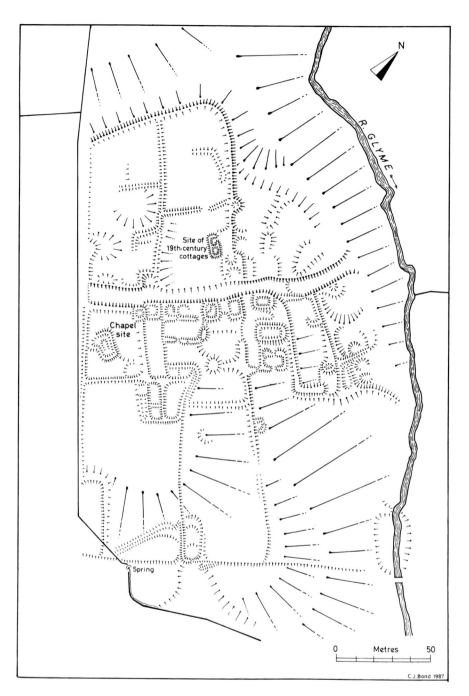

FIGURE 7.2 *Settlement earthworks at Lower Chalford, Oxfordshire.*

hamlet. Similarly at Chelmscote in Brailes (Warwickshire), the small extent of earthworks seems to represent very inadequate accommodation for the nine taxpayers recorded in 1327 and eight in 1332.[31] We should beware, however, of seeking too facile an equation between the tax records and the field evidence. There are important lessons to be learned here from David Aldred's work at Roel (Gloucestershire), where it now appears that ten of the thirteen people taxed at Roel in 1327 were actually living at Hawling, 2 km away to the south-west.[32]

Accepting that there are some fundamental difficulties which cannot always be overcome, there is nonetheless still much to be gained from careful study and surveys of earthwork sites. A considerable variety of building plans can be observed. The classic longhouse with cross-passage seems to be common on the Cotswolds, but there are also examples of long two-roomed buildings without a visible cross-passage at Brookhampton (Warwickshire) and Broadstone (Oxfordshire).[33] Farmyard complexes with domestic occupation physically separate from byres and barns are widespread, and from the evidence of examples at Coat (Oxfordshire) were well-established before the middle of the fourteenth century (figure 7.3); Eynsham Abbey failed to collect any rents from this hamlet in 1350, there is no documentary record of any subsequent occupation and the site has produced no pottery later than the mid-fourteenth century, so it can probably be added to the small list of Black Death de-populations. Some of the buildings observed at Somerford and Lower Chalford seem to be single-cell rectangular buildings, reminiscent of those excavated at Seacourt, if on average slightly larger in size.[34] Buildings of higher status can usually be identified by their enclosure within a precinct boundary; on clayland sites the manor house or some other part of the manorial compound was frequently moated, while on upland sites like Broadstone it may be surrounded by a substantial bank. Religious buildings can sometimes be recognized by their orientation; at Lower Chalford (Oxfordshire) a small two-cell building within a rectangular enclosure at the top of the village street is the only building in the settlement deliberately to seek out an east–west alignment (figure 7.2), and there can be little doubt that this is the chapel recorded in the mid-twelfth century.[35]

Comparison of earthworks on many different sites allows us to identify

[31] For a fuller account of Coat see *CBA Group 9 Newsletter*, 12 (1982), pp. 41–3; for a sketch plan of Chelmscote see Bond, 'Deserted medieval villages in Warwickshire', fig. 4, p. 98.

[32] *MSRG Annual Report*, 1 (1986), p. 25; I am grateful to David Aldred for further information on this site.

[33] For Brookhampton see Bond, 'Deserted medieval villages in Warwickshire', p. 96 and plate 3; for Broadstone see C. J. Reeves, 'A medieval village', *Oxoniensia*, 36 (1971), pp. 49–51.

[34] Biddle, 'Seacourt', esp. pp. 120–2, where the *internal* dimensions of the excavated buildings are quoted as averaging 7 × 4 m. The *overall* dimensions of house earthworks observed at Somerford were in the region of 12–15 m long × 8–10 m wide, and at Lower Chalford 10–15 m long × 8 m wide.

[35] J. Jordan, *A Parochial History of Enstone in the County of Oxford* (Oxford, 1857), p. 29.

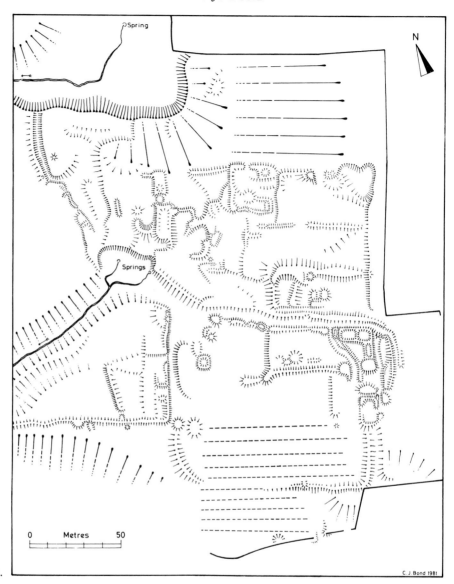

FIGURE 7.3 *Settlement earthworks at Coat, Oxfordshire.*

several recurrent features which imply changes in the layout of the village. On the large scale such changes can involve planned extensions to the settlement. There are a very considerable number of cases where part of the village consists of distinctively regular blocks of apparently planned crofts, contrasting with the more irregular layout of what is assumed to be the older part of the settlement: examples may be observed at Burston, Quarrendon and Littlecote (Buckinghamshire), and Wormleighton and Netherend in Chesterton Magna

144

(Warwickshire).[36] At Tusmore (Oxfordshire), a Black Death desertion, there are four such crofts at the south end of the village site.[37] At Wretchwick (Oxfordshire) the pattern of earthworks south-west of the modern farm is distinctly more regular and rectilinear than that of those to the north-east, and one of the crofts in the former area overlies ridge and furrow (figure 7.1). At the now-ploughed site of Cestersover (Warwickshire), aerial photographs reveal that the more regular crofts making up the southern half of the village overlay earlier ridge and furrow, quite clearly representing an extension of the settlement over its former open fields. The same phenomenon has also been recognized in several recent surveys, for example Abthorpe and Weston (Northamptonshire) and Somerford and Water Eaton (Oxfordshire).[38] At the shrunken village of Coughton (Warwickshire), Hooke has recorded regular crofts of about 4 poles in width, their dimensions clearly influenced by the ridge and furrow which they overlie.[39] At Dassett Southend (Warwickshire) current excavation of a block of regular enclosures between the modern road and the main holloway on the site points to this part of the site being occupied only in the thirteenth century.[40] Market charters were acquired for Cestersover in 1257 and for Dassett in 1267, but there is no reason to suppose that urban aspirations generally lay behind such village extensions.

The village boundary is worth careful examination. Do the re-entrants occurring in the course of the boundary banks at Broadstone (Oxfordshire), Willicote (Warwickshire) or Upton (Gloucestershire) imply additions to the village, or an adaptation to pre-existing land parcels? At Coat the boundary bank in the south-western part of the hamlet projects out from the general line to embrace half a dozen ridges, but because of their identical orientation it is difficult to ascertain their relative chronology. How do we interpret the small blocks of ridge and furrow which we sometimes find unambiguously inside the village boundary, such as the four 40 m-long ridges within a rectangular close at Abdon (Shropshire)? What is the significance of buildings which apparently lie just outside the boundary bank, such as we find at Norncott (Shropshire)?[41] Changes on a smaller scale can be seen where individual buildings seem to have

[36] For Burston and Quarrendon see M. W. Beresford and J. K. S. St Joseph, *Medieval England: An Aerial Survey* (2nd edn., Cambridge, 1979), pp. 122–4; for Wormleighton see Bond, 'Deserted medieval villages in Warwickshire', fig. 1 and p. 91; for Chesterton see Bond, in *Field and Forest*, ed. Slater and Jarvis, fig. 7.1 and pp. 155–7.

[37] D. Miles and R. T. Rowley, 'Tusmore deserted village', *Oxoniensia*, 41 (1976), pp. 309–15.

[38] Bond, 'Deserted medieval villages in Warwickshire', fig. 2 and pp. 93–4; RCHM (England), *Northamptonshire*, vol. IV, pp. 1–2, 164–5; *MVRG Annual Report*, 30 (1982), pp. 9–10; *MVRG Annual Report*, 31 (1983), p. 9.

[39] D. Hooke, 'Village development in the west midlands', in *Medieval Villages*, ed. Hooke, pp. 125–54, esp. p. 147 and fig. 16.

[40] N. Palmer, *Burton Dassett Excavations* (Interim report, Warwickshire Museum, 1987).

[41] For Abdon see R. T. Rowley, *The Shropshire Landscape* (London, 1972), fig. 9; for Norncott see *MVRG Annual Report*, 29 (1981), p. 10.

encroached out over their street frontage (Somerford) or have even caused the apparent diversion of a street (Coat).

The most potent sources of confusion on medieval settlement sites are the disturbances connected with post-depopulation land use. These include overploughing, such as occurred at Onley (Northamptonshire), where the narrow ridge and furrow overriding the crofts and houses contrasts with the broad ridge and furrow beyond the village boundary; comparatively narrow ridge and furrow overlies several other Northamptonshire sites, such as Kirby in Woodend, Sulby and Glassthorpe, but this phenomenon has not been observed further west or south.[42] Paddock enclosures, which may have been what John Rous had in mind when he described landlords who 'enclose the area of the village with mounds and surround them with ditches', occupy Chesterton Green and part of Wormleighton (Warwickshire). Drainage channels can be especially confusing where they become juxtaposed with medieval crofts; at Wretchwick each alternate croft ditch seems to have been dredged out and overdeepened after depopulation for drainage purposes, and a similar series of drainage gullies cuts across the green at Baulking (Berkshire, now Oxfordshire).[43] Small-scale stone robbing and clay digging are features of many sites; at Grafton Flyford and Upton Snodsbury (Worcestershire) clay digging has actually followed the line of the medieval holloways, presumably because there was less overburden there to be removed first. The creation of gardens and parks in the Tudor period and later may add new features; at Wormleighton it would be quite possible to accept the long string of fishponds as of medieval date, were it not for the fact that they directly overlie the main village street.[44] Short-lived post-medieval reoccupation is another hazard. At Abdon (Shropshire), although excavation by the churchyard in the higher part of the site revealed a thirteenth-century longhouse, one of the most prominent earthworks in the lower part of the site turned out to be an eighteenth-century building connected with industrial activity in the area.[45] At Lower Chalford stone was robbed from the foundations of the medieval buildings in the nineteenth century to build a couple of cottages,[46] now themselves collapsed but still identifiable as more sharply defined earthworks (figure 7.2).

The identification and survey of deserted nucleated settlements, despite all the difficulties, is a relatively finite task. By contrast, comparatively little work has been carried out on dispersed settlement in the region, though there were some early excavations such as Murray Threipland's examination of a medieval

[42] For Onley see Beresford and St Joseph, *Medieval England: An Aerial Survey*, pp. 38–9; RCHM (England), *Northamptonshire*, vol. IV, pp. 173–4; *MVRG Annual Report*, 28 (1980), cover.

[43] *MVRG Annual Report*, 23 (1975), pp. 6–7 and plan.

[44] Bond, in *Worcester and its Region*, ed. Adlam, includes a plan of Grafton Flyford, pp. 41–2 and 44. For Wormleighton see Bond, 'Deserted medieval villages in Warwickshire', fig. 1 and p. 103.

[45] Rowley, *Shropshire Landscape*, pp. 114–16.

[46] Jordan, *Enstone*, p. 27.

farmstead above Beckford on the southern slopes of Bredon Hill (Worcester-shire) in the 1930s and Taylor's discovery on the Clent Hills (Worcestershire) of several medieval huts associated with a kiln in 1952.[47] Some preliminary work has been carried out in Malvern Chase, where there is a considerable range of settlement forms.[48] The Forest of Arden is a classic area of dispersed settlement, and Hooke's work in parishes such as Oldberrow and Morton Bagot has identified a number of deserted hamlets and farmsteads.[49] Earthworks of small deserted settlements or assart farmsteads in woodland landscapes have also been located in the Chilterns and Wychwood Forest in Oxfordshire, where two examples have recently been excavated.[50] The most systematic survey of an area of dispersed settlement so far is that carried out by Dyer and Bassett in Hanbury in Feckenham Forest (Worcestershire), where nearly fifty abandoned medieval or post-medieval settlements ranging in size from a single house to half a dozen houses have been identified.[51]

CONCLUSION

The quality of information which can be gained from field survey is, by its very nature, limited. When we look at an earthwork, or even a ploughed site producing pottery scatters, our vision is blocked in the vertical dimension by the surface of the ground. We are, in effect, reduced to making educated guesses about the development of our village sites on the basis of a muffled view of their morphology, and in the full knowledge that excavation invariably demonstrates that medieval settlements are infinitely more complex than they first appear. Yet in its own way the information accessible from excavation is no less restricted, this time in the horizontal plane. No village site has yet been excavated in its entirety, and most will never be excavated at all. Fieldwork can at least provide some indications of the total number of settlements within a given area, it can define the size of each and, to some extent, their relative importance in the settlement hierarchy, and it can recognize certain aspects of

[47] L. Murray Threipland, 'Medieval farmstead on Bredon Hill', *Transactions of the Bristol and Gloucestershire Archaeological Society*, 67 (1946–8), pp. 415–18; G. S. Taylor, 'Walton Hill, Romsley, Worcestershire: excavation of a twelfth-century kiln and a twelfth–thirteenth-century hut site', *Transactions of the Birmingham Archaeological Society*, 72 (1954), pp. 10–13.

[48] C. J. Bond, 'The marshlands of Malvern Chase', in *The Evolution of Marshland Landscapes*, ed. R. T. Rowley (Oxford University Dept for External Studies, 1981), pp. 95–112, esp. pp. 100–3. Work on Pendock in this area is being continued by Christopher Dyer.

[49] D. Hooke and D. Marshall, *The Arrow Valley Project, 1: Morton Bagot, a Parish Survey, Part 1 – The Landscape, a Topographical Study* (University of Birmingham Dept of Geography, Occasional Publication no. 24, 1987).

[50] R. A. Chambers, 'A deserted medieval farmstead at Sadler's Wood, Lewknor (M40 Site 13)', *Oxoniensia*, 38 (1973), pp. 146–67; P. J. Fasham, 'The evaluation in 1971 and 1979 of an assart farmstead in Slape Copse, Glympton, Oxfordshire', *Oxoniensia*, 51 (1986), pp. 79–86.

[51] I am grateful to Christopher Dyer and Steven Bassett for progress reports of their work at Hanbury.

change, especially partial or total desertion, the presence of planned units within the settlement, and shifts in the position of the boundary between the village and its fields. The need for extensive survey and for basic recording of our ever-dwindling stock of earthwork sites is, therefore, as great as ever, and must proceed alongside the excavation programme. While systematic fieldwork forms a vital component in every ambitious multidisciplinary research project, there is no need for it to be restricted to such projects; indeed, there is a positive virtue in undertaking survey programmes not so tied, in order to provide some sort of balance.

Many lessons from the work of the last forty years are yet to be fully assimilated. Many problems remain unsolved. Many of our original questions are still only partly answered, and many new questions have arisen. Even our understanding of deserted villages, whose recognition first sparked off the modern resurgence of rural settlement studies, is still imperfect. Our knowledge of medieval hamlet and farm settlement remains woefully inadequate. Work on these subjects must be continued. Yet if we were to seek out the most outstanding problem of rural settlement evolution in the region, we would wish to know a great deal more about the processes by which the typical large midland nucleated villages began to emerge out of the generally scattered and mobile pattern of early Saxon settlement and its antecedents. In this context we should perhaps now be looking more closely at those rural settlements with minster churches which formed the centres of important early royal or episcopal estates; settlements which had served as focal or central places long before the Norman Conquest, without developing ultimately into towns. It is this category of villages, places like Benson (Oxfordshire), Tredington (Warwickshire) or Bredon (Worcestershire), which may well hold the key to a further expansion in our understanding of rural settlement evolution.

8

The Archaeology of Medieval Rural Settlement in East Anglia

PETER WADE-MARTINS

INTRODUCTION

The works of Maurice Beresford and John Hurst have provided untold inspiration for young archaeologists setting out on their careers in archaeology. As a discipline, 'landscape archaeology' was shaped most profoundly by their pioneering work in identifying the evidence for medieval settlement and land use in the countryside. The generation of medieval archaeologists and historians who dug and worked with them at Wharram and then carried on with their own research in every corner of England would be a fascinating study in itself.

East Anglia is the main grain-producing area of England. In parts a virtual prairie has been created by farm improvements where hardly a hedgerow or any other sign of the previous landscape survives. Since it has become recognized that the highly subsidized post-war farming system has now resulted in the over-production of cereals, beef and milk, as well as the excessive destruction of the landscape, some attempt has been made to halt the damage and make good. However, restoration schemes such as subsidized tree-planting seldom recreate or relate to the old landscape features which have been removed.

Most of the damage was done in the 1950s and 1960s when hedgerows were removed, earthworks were levelled and old meadow land ploughed up (plates 8.1 and 8.8) on a scale far greater than that seen in the preceding 'war effort'. Even now the damage continues. At a time when the words 'environment' and 'conservation' are tumbling off everyone's lips, the destruction goes on; sometimes it seems that the drainage and ploughing up of old grassland, mainly now in river valleys, will only come to an end when nothing is left. The much-publicized controversy over the ploughing of the Halvergate marshes in Broadland merely highlights a small part of a widespread practice affecting land in all parts of the region which were previously thought to be marginal to cereal cultivation. While it is true that a new scheme for designating

PLATE 8.1 *Little Livermere deserted village, Suffolk, shortly after the earthworks were destroyed in 1965. The light marks probably indicate the lines of buried boundary banks, and the rectangular light areas may indicate destroyed buildings: cf. plate 8.8. (3 January 1966)*

PLATE 8.2 *Pudding Norton deserted village, Norfolk, showing well-preserved earthworks. There is a regularity in the layout suggestive of village planning. (21 January 1967)*

PLATE 8.3 *Hockwold shrunken village, Hockwold cum Wilton, Norfolk. In addition to the very clear earthworks of the medieval village, there is also an associated pattern of narrow parallel fields in the foreground which overlie an irregular system of earthworks related to Romano-British fen-edge settlement. This fine photograph demonstrates the multi-period nature of settlement evidence often available to archaeologists. (1 June 1962)*

PLATE 8.4 *A remarkable snow-covered view of Roudham deserted village, Norfolk, on the eastern edge of Breckland. (5 January 1979)*

PLATE 8.5   *A part of Great Palgrave deserted village, Norfolk, where a row of tofts survives alongside an enclosed green. The deep ditch down the right-hand side of the tofts is the green edge and the two straight roads to the right are enclosure roads. (21 April 1960)*

Environmentally Sensitive Areas has taken the pressure off the Broads, it is too early to see what effect the designation of ESAs will have elsewhere.

TYPES OF EVIDENCE

In the 1950s and 1960s there were few archaeologists and historians who were more aware than John and Maurice of the importance of the evidence still to be seen around them. But, not many archaeologists had the time and the resources to record this vanishing scene. Today, when much of it has gone, we have to rely heavily on two exceptionally important sources. These are the 1946 National Air Photograph Survey consisting of vertical photographs, taken just before so much was lost, and the great collection of oblique aerial pictures taken from 1948 onwards by J. K. S. St Joseph, who could see from the air better than most what was happening on the ground. For East Anglian archaeologists these are vital sources of data which can occasionally be supplemented by pictures taken by a few private flyers. More recently, the Ordnance Survey and the Norfolk and Suffolk archaeological units have been adding to this record by their own flying programmes.

In the 1970s field archaeology became established as a profession, but even so it was much easier to obtain grants for rescue excavation than for survey work; digging has usually taken precedence over survey. As a result, thousands of post-holes have been minutely dissected and recorded but the number of earthworks which have received such detailed treatment is small indeed.

While the Historic Building and Monuments Commission's recent decision to finance the inter-county fenland fieldwalking survey (The Fenland Project) is a most welcome reversal of this trend, it is true that good quality published fieldwork is still limited, and overshadowed by the weight of published excavations. As a result, any current study of rural settlement in the region starts with a disadvantage.

Some earthwork sites do survive, but there are few which are sufficiently extensive to help us understand medieval settlement patterns. There are some seven well-preserved deserted village sites in Norfolk. In Suffolk there are none; Little Livermere was the last to go in 1965, when the soil-marks of the recently levelled earthworks were photographed by St Joseph (plate 8.1).

PLATE 8.6 *The well-known site of Godwick deserted village, Norfolk, now open to the public as a result of a management agreement, is interesting because as well as the earthworks of the village in the background, the foreground has a pattern of rectangular closes relating to the sixteenth-century manor house of Chief Justice Coke. (26 April 1960)*

PLATE 8.7 *Waterden deserted village, Norfolk, suffered badly in 1967 when most of the earthworks visible in the foreground of this photograph were levelled. The village street and a small green lay in the bottom of this valley and it was, no doubt, a fairly watery place to live. (27 April 1967)*

Even where settlement remains are severely eroded by cultivation, pottery scatters usually remain. East Anglia is fortunate in having well-fired middle and late Saxon pottery, as well as medieval wares; these make it possible to identify settlements from the seventh century onwards even though nothing else is visible on the surface.[1] Indeed, it was John Hurst with Stanley West who first described middle Saxon Ipswich ware in 1957.[2]

So in addition to excavation, the types of evidence available to the landscape historian in the region are:

[1] J. G. Hurst, 'Middle Saxon pottery', in G. C. Dunning, J. G. Hurst, J. N. L. Myres and F. Tischler, 'Anglo-Saxon pottery: a symposium', *Medieval Archaeology*, 3 (1959), pp. 12–13, esp. p. 12; S. Dunmore, V. Gray, T. Loader and K. Wade, 'The origin and development of Ipswich: an interim report', *East Anglian Archaeology*, 1 (1975), pp. 57–67, esp. pp. 59–60; J. G. Hurst, 'The pottery', in *The Archaeology of Anglo-Saxon England*, ed. D. M. Wilson (Cambridge, 1976), pp. 283–348, esp. p. 299.

[2] J. G. Hurst, 'Saxo-Norman pottery in East Anglia, Part II. Thetford ware with an account of middle Saxon Ipswich ware', *Proceedings of the Cambridgeshire Antiquarian Society*, 50 (1957), pp. 29–60.

1 A limited number of earthworks.
2 Air photographs of destroyed sites.
3 Anglo-Saxon and medieval pottery scatters.
4 Manuscript estate maps from the late sixteenth century onwards.
5 Enclosure and tithe maps of the nineteenth century.
6 Manorial and other documentary material.

Estate maps often show shrunken settlements which have since been deserted. Early editions of the large-scale Ordnance Survey maps can also be invaluable. Faden's 1797 map of Norfolk and Hodskinson's 1783 map of Suffolk are most useful, for these maps were surveyed just before the wholesale parliamentary enclosures of the commons began.[3] They show the framework of medieval greens and commons around which many of the medieval settlements grew.

[3] J. C. Barringer (ed.), *Faden's Map of Norfolk* (Norfolk Record Society, 42, 1975); D. P. Dymond (ed.), *The County of Suffolk Surveyed by Joseph Hodskinson* (Suffolk Record Society, 15, 1972).

PLATE 8.8 *Greynston (or Grenstein) deserted village, Norfolk, was levelled in 1959 just before this photograph was taken; this created a similar pattern of soil-marks to the one visible in plate 8.1. A triangular green with tofts on both sides can be seen. (26 November 1960)*

PLATE 8.9 *In 1984 after the main excavation of the Spong Hill Anglo-Saxon cemetery was over, the Norfolk Archaeological Unit returned to the site for one short season to investigate an area to the west of the cemetery where there is a remarkable juxtaposition of prehistoric, Roman and early Saxon domestic features. This photograph shows six sunken-featured buildings contemporary with the adjacent cemetery, with three cutting through the line of a Romano-British trackway. If it is ever possible to excavate in detail an extensive area of such features, the result would provide a remarkable insight into how a piece of landscape in the region has evolved over perhaps three thousand years. (4 February 1985)*

Whilst government funds for archaeological units are still mostly directed to 'rescue' work rather than wide surveys or works of synthesis, there is now a strong emphasis on survey work, especially fieldwalking, amongst amateurs and professionals alike in the region. Most of this work is still in progress, and is therefore not available for discussion here. It is clear now that landscape studies do need to be multi-period in their outlook, and the days when one searched an area only for the Anglo-Saxon and medieval settlement evidence have gone.[4] Rural settlement studies have to be multi-period, and after the remarkable work by Williamson on the boundary patterns around Dickleburgh discussed below, we have to accept that even the iron age has in places had just

[4] P. Wade-Martins, 'Fieldwork and excavation on village sites in Launditch hundred, Norfolk', *East Anglian Archaeology*, 10 (1980).

as much impact on the landscape as, say, the enclosure of the commons in the nineteenth century.[5]

Before looking back at published work, it is worth mentioning a number of current projects which should enhance our understanding of medieval rural settlements and the evolution of the East Anglian landscape. In the fens Bob Silvester for Norfolk and Mike Hardy for Suffolk are completing the detailed fieldwalking of all of the eastern fens. This is linked in with David Hall's work in Cambridgeshire and with an identical survey by Peter Hayes and Tom Lane in Lincolnshire. Publication of this work is proceeding, but any general review of settlement history of this unique area would be premature.[6] It is clear, however, that the Fenland Project, which combines extensive fieldwalking and documentary research, will provide us with a fresh view of the development of this unique area.

In the 'uplands' of west Norfolk, Andrew Rogerson is currently completing a detailed fieldwalking project of the parish of Barton Bendish allied to the documentary research by Alan Davison. In the flatter boulder claylands of central Norfolk, Rogerson is also conducting a minutely detailed fieldwalking exercise in Fransham and Wendling. Further research into the hedgerow patterns of south Norfolk is being conducted by Tom Williamson, Alan Davison and Kenneth Penn who are working together through the tithe maps and earlier maps for some 165 parishes between Wymondham and the east coast to ascertain the extent of the early boundary system identified around Dickleburgh. In south-east Norfolk Alan Davison and George and Alayne Fenner have just finished a very successful documentary and fieldwalking study of Hales, Loddon and Heckingham. A survey of most of the best-preserved deserted village sites was published in 1982;[7] a second volume covering other surviving sites and examples of those which are only known from air photographs or manuscript maps is now almost complete. These two reports should provide a fairly comprehensive assessment of field and documentary evidence for the deserted villages of Norfolk.

In Suffolk a detailed fieldwalking programme, a hedgerow survey and documentary research for ten parishes around the South Elmhams have been completed by Mike Hardy.[8] Other Suffolk surveys awaiting publication include the Mendham area (by Roy Colchester), Little Bradley (by the

[5] T. Williamson, 'Parish boundaries and early fields: continuity and discontinuity', *Journal of Historical Geography*, 12 (1986), pp. 241–8.

[6] R. J. Silvester, 'West Walton: the development of a siltland parish', *Norfolk Archaeology*, 39 (1985), pp. 101–17; D. Hall, 'The fenland project, no. 2: fenland landscapes and settlements between Peterborough and March', *East Anglian Archaeology*, 35 (1987).

[7] B. Cushion, A. Davison, G. Fenner, R. Goldsmith, J. Knight, N. Virgoe, K. Wade and P. Wade-Martins, 'Some deserted village sites in Norfolk', *East Anglian Archaeology*, 14 (1982), pp. 40–101.

[8] Unpublished, except for brief summaries in the following: M. J. Hardy, *Proceedings of the Suffolk Institute of Archaeology and History*, 36 (1985), p. 49; M. J. Hardy with E. A. Martin, *Proceedings of the Suffolk Institute of Archaeology and History*, 36 (1986), pp. 147–50.

Haverhill and District Archaeological Group) and Walsham le Willows. In south-east Suffolk the Suffolk Archaeological Unit has almost finished fieldwalking the sandy heathland around Sutton Hoo; the data from this work will provide useful information about the context of the Anglo-Saxon royal burial site.

It can be seen from the above that there is much important survey work in hand which should balance the previous emphasis on excavation. Most of it will be published in forthcoming volumes of *East Anglian Archaeology*, and readers familiar with this series will be able to keep up to date with developments over the next few years.

On the excavation side, Bob Carr's current work on the important middle Saxon settlement at Brandon in Suffolk will add substantially to our understanding of settlement sites of this period. Otherwise, there is currently no excavation on medieval rural settlements in progress.

THE DEVELOPMENT OF RESEARCH

Looking back, it is fair to say that medieval settlement research in East Anglia all began with Allison's study of the lost villages of Norfolk.[9] This work was a landmark, and in the region it transformed our perception of the evidence for medieval rural settlement. Inspired by Hoskins and Beresford,[10] he set out to collate all the data for deserted medieval villages in the county with the help of the late Rainbird Clarke who provided information from his Sites & Monuments Record. The starting point was a collection of references to deserted villages by Saltmarsh.[11] Allison attempted to analyse the possible reasons for rural depopulation and concluded that the Black Death caused few desertions and that depopulation of the countryside was a gradual process heightened where farming was difficult on marginal soils. He emphasized that landlord oppression in the sixteenth century was 'a potent force in village depopulation' as the wealthy consolidated their holdings at the expense of the peasants. Allison finished with a catalogue of 130 deserted villages which has been the starting point for many an enthusiast ever since.

Nobody has attempted to update Allison's list and probably now nobody ever will, simply because the more we understand the settlement history of East Anglia the more complex the subject becomes. We can now see that settlement patterns were never stable and that village centres were frequently shifting. To identify one particular spot as the site of a deserted settlement is over-

[9] K. J. Allison, 'The lost villages of Norfolk', *Norfolk Archaeology*, 31 (1955), pp. 116–62.

[10] W. Hoskins, *Essays in Leicestershire History* (Liverpool, 1950); M. W. Beresford, *The Lost Villages of England* (London, 1954).

[11] J. Saltmarsh, 'Plague and economic decline in England', *Cambridge Historical Journal*, 7 (1941–3), pp. 23–41.

simplifying an often complex story; a village may have had two, three or more different locations between the middle Saxon period and the present day. The gradual realization that settlement patterns have been constantly changing has been central to the development of research over the last thirty years.

The first area survey was carried out by a farmer, John Owles, at Witton in north-east Norfolk.[12] His careful collection of material over a period of nearly twenty years from 1960 produced a 'staggering range of artefacts ranging from mesolithic microliths to post-medieval porcelain sherds' from his 230-hectare farm. An early Saxon settlement was located and excavated to reveal a group of sunken-featured buildings on a slight hill. Ploughing on the hill had, however, already eroded the natural surface sufficiently to make adequate detection of post-hole buildings impossible. It is interesting that no contemporary cemetery was located, and it is indeed remarkable that so few early Saxon cemeteries have been recorded in this part of Norfolk.[13] This site was located 600 m to the north-east of the isolated church of Witton, and three other smaller contemporary settlement areas were also revealed by crop-marks, soil-marks and surface scatters of pottery; in this period the settlement pattern was certainly a scattered one.

For the middle and late Saxon periods Ipswich ware and Thetford ware pottery finds were mostly concentrated nearer the church. For the medieval period the archaeological evidence for the settlement pattern was inconclusive, probably because the evidence was largely limited to one farm. This survey was carried out in an area where no previous finds had been made, demonstrating for the first time in the region the value of intensive multi-period searching in relatively small areas.

The next study was my own 1967–70 survey of village sites in the Launditch hundred of central Norfolk.[14] The project was started well before it was possible to learn from the lessons of the Witton survey. It was a problem-oriented project aimed specifically at answering particular questions about medieval rural settlement patterns. The main questions were:

1   Why are so many churches isolated from their present settlements?
2   What were the origins of settlements around greens?
3   Were these greens the normal form of settlement in the Anglo-Saxon period?

[12] A. J. Lawson, 'The archaeology of Witton, near North Walsham, Norfolk', *East Anglian Archaeology*, 18 (1983).

[13] J. N. L. Myers and B. Green, *The Anglo-Saxon Cemeteries of Caistor-by-Norwich and Markshall, Norfolk* (Report of the Society of Antiquaries of London, no. 30, 1973), map 3.

[14] P. Wade-Martins, 'The development of the landscape and human settlement of west Norfolk from 350–1650 A.D., with particular reference to the Launditch hundred' (unpublished Ph.D. thesis, University of Leicester, 1971); idem, 'The origins of rural settlement in East Anglia', in *Recent Work in Rural Archaeology*, ed. P. J. Fowler (Bradford on Avon, 1975), pp. 137–57; idem, 'Fieldwork and excavation on village sites', pp. 3–9.

4 What proportion of villages were truly green villages in the middle ages?

5 Why were there so many moated sites in East Anglia and at what date were they created?

Similar questions were being posed at the time by David Dymond in a stimulating article on the Suffolk landscape.[15]

The archaeological information then available was not adequate to answer these questions and therefore the project was primarily a fieldwalking one, making use of estate maps from the sixteenth century onwards where they were available. The fieldwalking was deliberately restricted to the areas around isolated churches, around greens and in and around moated sites, with no systematic complete *area* survey. There was little attempt to relate the sites located to others in the vicinity; as a consequence, the results oversimplified the issues and it was not therefore possible to appreciate how scattered settlement could be, particularly in the middle Saxon period.

Nevertheless, the results were satisfactory in that they did show that in many cases churches were isolated because they were located on sites of abandoned middle and late Saxon settlements which had moved away to other places (as at Longham, Mileham, Horningtoft, the Weasenhams, Wellingham, Stanfield and others). A deserted village site in Breckland (Caldecote) was also examined for comparison, and a similar result showing settlement shift from a church to a green was achieved.

With regards to village greens, sufficient evidence was gathered to show clearly that settlement around greens before the twelfth century was very unusual, a view which has not been overturned by subsequent work elsewhere. The earliest pottery around greens was Early Medieval ware, dating from *c.*1100 onwards. This, of course, does not date the commons as areas of common grazing – only the settlements around them. The results showed that there was a great expansion of population and also movement of settlement to the commons in the twelfth and thirteenth centuries. This expansion reached a peak in the fourteenth century. Then, as the population subsequently declined, the remnants of these settlements became scattered hamlets by the seventeenth century. Where late sixteenth- and seventeenth-century maps are available this end-product of the settlement decline is clearly documented. The eventually fragmented pattern is visible on Faden's map of Norfolk of 1797. In Launditch not all villages were green villages, but there were about twice as many of these as there were villages along streets.

It is extraordinary how few churches are located on greens, with those at Old Buckenham and Mulbarton in Norfolk, and Mellis and South Elmham St Michael in Suffolk being examples of a relatively small number of villages where greens and churches occur together.

[15] D. P. Dymond, 'The Suffolk landscape' in *East Anglian Studies*, ed. L. Munby (Cambridge, 1968).

The origin of moated sites was an issue less easy to clarify. The limited evidence available supported the established view that they are not usually earlier than the thirteenth century.[16]

In 1976 and 1977 members of the Norfolk Archaeological Rescue Group surveyed the earthworks of the best-preserved deserted villages in Norfolk.[17] The plans of these sites were described and discussed along with the architecture of the churches and the documentary evidence for the villages and their desertion. As the report warned at the time, it would be dangerous to draw general conclusions about East Anglian village patterns from these alone; they can be viewed as a useful group, but each needs to be related to the other settlements around it. Some, such as Pudding Norton (plate 8.2), and indeed Weasenham St Peter in the Launditch survey, seem to show strong signs of deliberate planning. Others, such as Godwick, have complex later earthworks overlying them. Godwick (plate 8.6) and Pudding Norton (plate 8.2) ran along streets, while Waterden (plate 8.7) was centred on a small green. Roudham is a good example of a desertion caused in part by the landlord buying in property in the eighteenth century.

Other fieldwork studies on particular village sites which deserve mention here are Hurst's study of Babingley, Green's search for the lost vill of Ness on the coast and Davison's work on Harling, Cotes and Caldecote.[18] The Haverhill and District Archaeological Group has carried out a parish survey at Wixhoe, but with rather inconclusive results.[19] In north-east Norfolk Bert and Barbara Dollin are systematically recording moated sites.[20] The detailed plan showing the distribution of 1000 middle Saxon sherds from a site at Hay Green, Terrington St Clement, represents one of the larger middle Saxon settlements discovered recently in the fens.[21]

That we are dealing with a multi-period landscape is stressed in a recent book of aerial photographs of Norfolk; in particular there is an example at Hockwold (plate 8.3), where the earthworks of a Roman settlement and a medieval shrunken village and its fields are all interlinked.[22]

---

[16] H. E. J. Le Patourel and B. K. Roberts, 'The significance of moated sites', in *Medieval Moated Sites*, ed. F. A. Aberg (CBA Research Report no. 17, 1973), p. 51.

[17] Cushion et al., 'Some deserted village sites in Norfolk', pp. 40–101.

[18] J. G. Hurst, 'Seventeenth-century cottages at Babingley, Norfolk', *Norfolk Archaeology*, 32 (1961), pp. 332–42; C. Green, 'The lost vill of Ness', *Norfolk Archaeology*, 34 (1966), pp. 2–8; A. Davison, 'West Harling; a village and its disappearance', *Norfolk Archaeology*, 37 (1980), pp. 295–306; idem, 'The distribution of medieval settlements in West Harling', *Norfolk Archaeology*, 38 (1983), pp. 329–36; idem, 'Petygards and the medieval hamlet of Cotes', *East Anglian Archaeology*, 14 (1982), pp. 102–7; idem, 'The desertion of Caldecote: some further evidence', *Norfolk Archaeology*, 39 (1984), pp. 53–4.

[19] L. W. Taylor, 'Wixhoe parish survey 1975–82', *Journal of the Haverhill and District Archaeological Group*, 3 (1983), pp. 66–111.

[20] B. W. Dollin, 'Moated sites in north-east Norfolk', *Norfolk Archaeology*, 39 (1986), pp. 262–77.

[21] A. Rogerson and R. J. Silvester, 'Middle Saxon occupation at Hay Green, Terrington St Clement', *Norfolk Archaeology*, 39 (1986), pp. 320–2.

[22] P. Wade-Martins (ed.), *Norfolk from the Air* (Norfolk Museums Service, 1987), plate 42.

Of the excavated sites, West Stow is undoubtedly the 'type-site' for early Saxon settlements in East Anglia.[23] This Breckland hamlet on a sandhill near the river Lark was a difficult one to excavate because the sandy subsoil made the identification of post-hole patterns a difficult process. Nevertheless, the site was far less eroded than Witton. The settlement consisted of a mixture of 'halls' with sunken-featured buildings clustered around them, indicating perhaps some form of family grouping.[24] Stanley West, the excavator, argues persuasively that these sunken-featured buildings were floored over at ground level with the spaces below acting as cellars.

The other contemporary settlement to be excavated is at Spong Hill, North Elmham.[25] The site was excavated to recover the early Saxon cemetery consisting of over 2000 cremations and 57 inhumations; an unexpected bonus for the excavators was the discovery of settlement evidence on three sides of the cemetery (plate 8.9). The domestic structures were, as at West Stow, a mixture of post-hole halls and sunken-featured buildings.[26] As the research design for the project was to excavate and publish the cemetery, the study of the settlement evidence has had to take second place for the time being. If it is ever possible to extend the excavation to expose the settlement area extensively the results could well be remarkable; the settlement pattern could then be related both to the cemetery and to the underlying iron age and Romano-British landscapes which again have hardly been explored.

The archaeological units in Norfolk and Suffolk have been particularly active with the excavation and publication of early Saxon cemeteries. As well as Spong Hill, cemeteries at Bergh Apton[27] and Morning Thorpe in Norfolk and West Garth Gardens near Bury St Edmunds in Suffolk have produced a major corpus of material which is appearing in a series of catalogues in *East Anglian Archaeology*. Preparations are now in hand for a final discussion volume on all these sites.

For the middle and late Saxon periods the only rural settlement extensively excavated and published is in North Elmham village.[28] A series of middle Saxon timber houses with continuous foundation trenches was found together with two partly preserved timber-lined wells. One of the biggest puzzles of the excavation was the very small quantity of Ipswich ware found in the middle

[23] S. E. West, 'West Stow. The Anglo-Saxon village', *East Anglian Archaeology*, 24 (1985).

[24] ibid., figs. 300–2.

[25] C. Hills, 'The Anglo-Saxon cemetery at Spong Hill, North Elmham, part I', *East Anglian Archaeology*, 6 (1977); C. Hills and K. Penn, 'The Anglo-Saxon cemetery at Spong Hill, North Elmham, part II', *East Anglian Archaeology*, 11 (1981); C. Hills, K. Penn and R. Rickett, 'The Anglo-Saxon cemetery at Spong Hill, North Elmham, part III', *East Anglian Archaeology*, 21 (1984); C. Hills, K. Penn and R. Rickett, 'The Anglo-Saxon cemetery at Spong Hill, North Elmham, part IV', *East Anglian Archaeology*, 34 (1987).

[26] Hills *et al.*, 'The Anglo-Saxon cemetery at Spong Hill, part III', fig. 133.

[27] B. Green and A. Rogerson, 'The Anglo-Saxon cemetery at Bergh Apton', *East Anglian Archaeology*, 7 (1978).

[28] P. Wade-Martins, 'Excavations in North Elmham park', *East Anglian Archaeology*, 9 (1980).

Saxon features. By contrast, there was a great wealth of animal bone from refuse deposits; it can be said, for instance, that sheep were kept primarily for wool rather than for meat and that the ewes were horned with a liveweight of about 30 kg, larger than a Soay but smaller than modern breeds.

For the late Saxon period a gradual transition to post-hole buildings could be demonstrated, with the wall posts becoming fewer and being spaced further apart as the craft of timber framing developed. Part of a late Saxon cemetery was also discovered and excavated; this is still the only large group of pre-Conquest burials we have from a rural context. The average age of death for adults was thirty-seven, later than comparable urban groups, such as at Red Castle, Thetford, and Norwich.[29] There was a great frequency of osteoarthritis and osteophytosis in the population, with no less than 90 per cent having osteophytotic changes to the spine by their mid-twenties, indicating a life of heavy manual work. The apparent presence of a black female in the population has been the cause of much speculation.

Two deserted villages have been excavated: Thuxton in 1963–4 (unpublished) and Greynston or Grenstein in 1965–6.[30] Greynston was a green village on boulder clay, and the earthworks had been levelled and ploughed five years before excavation. This destruction had removed much of the evidence for the clay-built structures, although the overall plan of the village could be recorded from the resulting soil-marks (plate 8.8). One toft was completely stripped and the frontage of another was exposed. Despite bad weather, the complete plan of a late fourteenth- or fifteenth-century farm was revealed. There was a house centrally placed within the toft and two farmyards in front, each surrounded by outbuildings. This was quite an elaborate establishment on which horses were used. The buildings were all apparently constructed of 'clay lump' (sundried clay and straw blocks), a building technique retained in East Anglia until the present century. The yards were made up with flints, presumably from stone-picking in the fields. Although the results certainly justified the effort involved, it would be better next time to choose a site where the earthworks are still intact and the evidence therefore better preserved.

Two moated sites have been excavated on a sufficient scale to produce worthwhile results; one at Brome in Suffolk in 1967 and the other at Hempstead in Norfolk in 1976.[31] At Brome, West found a thirteenth-century three-bayed aisled house of two phases overlying a pre-moat phase dating from the eleventh and early twelfth centuries. Only the massive aisle post-holes could

[29] C. Wells, 'Report on the human skeletons from Red Castle, Thetford', in G. M. Knocker, 'Excavations at Red Castle, Thetford', *Norfolk Archaeology*, 34 (1967), pp. 155–86; A. Stirland, 'The human bone', in B. Ayers, 'Excavations within the north-east bailey of Norwich castle, 1979', *East Anglian Archaeology*, 28 (1985), pp. 49–58.

[30] Wade-Martins, 'Fieldwork and excavation on village sites', pp. 93–161.

[31] S. E. West, 'Brome, Suffolk. The excavation of a moated site, 1967', *Journal of the British Archaeological Association*, 33 (1970), pp. 89–121; A. Rogerson and N. Adams, 'A moated site at Hempstead', *East Anglian Archaeology*, 8 (1978), pp. 55–72.

be traced, and further research is needed to determine whether they really were aisle posts or indeed wall posts as suggested for similar structures at North Elmham.[32] Structurally there is little difference between a house with heavy wall posts and an aisled hall. At Hempstead Rogerson found a later building with a fine floor of medieval decorated glazed tiles. Little more, however, can be said about the structure or its significance.

So, we do not yet have an excavation in the region which can give us an adequate picture of a medieval manor or any detailed indication of how it functioned. The manor house stood within the moat, and the farm buildings and yards were outside the moat usually in subsidiary enclosures, as pictured on a map of Longham in *c*.1595. The next site chosen for excavation should be one where the moat and the outer associated enclosure can both be stripped in order to gather a complete overall view of a manor as a working farm. Ideally, documents and excavation need to be used together to build up a comprehensive picture of how medieval manors were laid out and how they functioned, but documents alone can at times be most useful, as Yaxley and Virgoe have shown.[33]

Three churches have been excavated and published in detail for Norfolk, and one for Suffolk at Iken.[34] Of the three Norfolk examples, Rogerson's complete excavation at All Saints', Barton Bendish, gives us the most comprehensive picture of how a church grew from a small three-celled stone structure with an apse in the eleventh or twelfth centuries to a much larger church in the mid-fourteenth century with a square-ended chancel and a western tower. The other three churches were only partially excavated but each makes a significant contribution to church studies in the region. Other published excavations of churches are in urban centres in Norwich and Thetford.

So far we have dealt with settlements and buildings, but these need to be seen in the context of the evolution of the landscape and its organization as a whole; the roads, the fields, the commons and the woodland all have their own stories to tell. Williamson's 1986 study of the hedgerow pattern of the Dickleburgh area of south Norfolk, already mentioned, has done more than any other publication recently to make us question the long-held assumption that the framework of roads and fields on pre-enclosure maps is basically medieval. Now he has shown that at least on some of the heavy clays of south Norfolk the boundary pattern is *older* than the main Roman road from Colchester to the regional capital at Caistor St Edmund. Williamson took as his starting point the hedge lines as depicted on the early nineteenth-century tithe maps. After removing those lines which he identified as being of recent origin,

---

[32] Wade-Martins, 'Excavations in North Elmham park', figs. 165, 168, 170 and 175.

[33] D. Yaxley and N. Virgoe, *The Manor House* (Ipswich, 1978).

[34] A. Rogerson, J. S. Ashley, P. Williams and A. Harris, 'Three Norman churches in Norfolk', *East Anglian Archaeology*, 32 (1987); S. E. West, 'Iken, St Botolph, and the coming of East Anglian Christianity', *Proceedings of the Suffolk Institute of Archaeology and History*, 35 (1984), pp. 279–301.

he was left with about 80 per cent of the total; these clearly form a rectilinear pattern running on a north-to-south axis. This axis, askew to the Roman road, has to be either very early Roman or perhaps more likely iron age. We can now see that even on these 'marginal' clay soils there was a degree of organization and exploitation which nobody had previously expected. In north Suffolk, on the opposite side of the Waveney valley, Rackham has followed Dymond in identifying another rectilinear pattern in the South Elmhams which may be of similar date.[35] Further afield similar patterns have also been clearly identified in Essex.[36]

Before Williamson started looking at the area, the late Silvia Addington had already been working on the boulder clays of south Norfolk around Tasburgh and Fritton. She, as a local farmer's wife, understood the land and the problems of farming it. With her knowledge of botany and documents and her enthusiasm for fieldwalking she was able to produce a remarkable study of five parishes combining hedge-counting, documentary research and selective fieldwalking.[37] She examined the distribution of dog's mercury in the undergrowth of hedgerows together with hornbeam, ash, oak, and hazel in the hedges themselves. These indicated the areas of early woodland on the heavy clay upland, but she was careful not to be too precise about the date woodland had been cleared. Her finds of Roman pottery showed that there were some incursions on to the heavy soils by the Roman period. She also found late Saxon pottery near churches and demonstrated that the main movement of settlement to the commons dated from the twelfth and thirteenth centuries. There was, however, some evidence of late Saxon settlement around commons in two places.

CONCLUSION

This round-up of completed work on medieval rural settlement in East Anglia has been written at a time when much interesting work is in hand. This work is likely to underline still further that much of the landscape as we know it is not medieval in origin but older; the middle ages were but one stage in a continuous process of change. While there has in some ways been some remarkable continuity and stability in landscape patterns, there has in others been enormous change. The need now is to identify which aspects are ancient and which do demonstrate constant change.

[35] O. Rackham, *The History of the Countryside* (London, 1986), p. 158; Dymond, 'Suffolk landscape', p. 37.

[36] W. Rodwell, 'Relict landscapes in Essex', in *Early Land Allotment*, ed. H. C. Bowen and P. J. Fowler (BAR, British ser., 48, 1978), pp. 89–98; P. J. Drury and W. Rodwell, 'Settlement in the later Iron Age and Roman periods', in *Archaeology in Essex*, ed. D. G. Buckley (CBA Research Report no. 34, 1980), pp. 59–75; Rackham, *History of the Countryside*, plate XIII.

[37] S. Addington, 'The hedgerows of Tasburgh', *Norfolk Archaeology*, 37 (1978), pp. 70–83; idem, 'Landscape and settlement in south Norfolk', *Norfolk Archaeology*, 38 (1982), pp. 97–139.

9

Medieval Settlement Remains and Historical Conservation

DAVID BAKER

INTRODUCTION

Nearly three decades separated the publication of Maurice Beresford's *Lost Villages of England* from the completion of a national network of local field units and county archaeological officers, promoted by John Hurst and others. The interval between the formation of the DMVRG (with its accumulating archives) and the establishment of county Sites & Monuments Records involved in the planning process was almost as long. It is uncertain whether a degree of nucleation is required before a dispersed pattern of academic interest can successfully organize concern about the survival of its evidence; however, there is no doubt that groups like the DMVRG, in recognizing the impact of mechanized farming upon relict medieval landscapes, helped to define the 'rescue crisis' of the late 1960s. From this came conservation archaeology, giving new impetus to the preservation of what was being discovered.

I first met *Lost Villages* in the mid-1950s through a fine history teacher, Philip Whitting (1903–88), always on the lookout for stimulating 'A' level topics. Interest was reinforced by W. G. Hoskins's lectures on Tudor and Stuart economic history, a daring new alternative to the Oxford School of Modern History's traditional paper on constitutional documents. Ten years later, the insights from this grounding helped argue the place of the historical dimension in the environmental planning of a shire county, its villages filling with commuters fascinated by their new roots.

This contribution was optimistically conceived as a general survey of how medieval settlement remains are being treated by the processes of historical conservation. In the event, other duties got in the way of the fieldwork, let alone the devising and pursuit of yet another unwelcome questionnaire. The approach therefore has to be from the other direction, taking the various stages of the conservation process, and looking at them in terms of the particular problems and opportunities provided by the topic of medieval settlement remains. The result doubtless skates around many central issues in medieval settlement studies, but may provide some insight into the conservation or administrative attitudes (as distinct from academic or research ones) which will be so important for the survival of evidence into the 1990s and beyond. Particular reference is made to examples from my own county of Bedfordshire, which has an unusual, if heavily eroded, medieval settlement pattern.

The process of historical conservation involves a series of stages through which all classes of survivals pass.[1]

1 *Definition* of the field of interest, and *identification* of what constitutes evidence for it.
2 *Investigation*: collecting data by fieldwork and documentary research.
3 The *storage of data* for later retrieval and amendment.
4 The formulation and execution of policies for *preservation* of survivals. As a last resort, this involves converting them into records through rescue fieldwork.
5 The *communication of survivals and data* through further research to increase understanding, and through various forms of presentation, for education, tourism and local people.

These five stages do not flow in an even sequence: some occur in parallel, and some feed back into others. A version of the whole set is repeated by each group of generations as it contemplates its inherited historic environment.

DEFINING AND IDENTIFYING

The transformation of 'deserted medieval villages' into 'medieval settlement remains' is a classic illustration of how the definition of a subject area can change as research proceeds, and with it the types of evidence identified as relevant. This makes several fundamental points: defining and identifying have to proceed in parallel, not in sequence, as bureaucratic logic might dictate; there must be scope for review in defining the categories of remains which merit protection by statutory or other means; the need for this flexibility must be communicated so that it has credibility with the wider public, including those whose land may be affected.

'Lost villages' were first widely recognized at a time when archaeology was more site-based than it is today. One decisive agent of discovery was aerial photography whose elevated perspective drew attention to their settings in landscapes; another was the policy of the Royal Commission on the Historical Monuments of England to look at the whole land of counties like Dorset, Cambridgeshire and Northamptonshire. Many hitherto unknown complexes of

---

[1] D. Baker, *Living with the Past – the Historic Environment* (Bedford, 1983).

earthworks demanded categorization, if not as DMVs then as something else. This stimulated a fruitful interaction between archaeology, geography and medieval history, fed by accumulating observations in field and Record Office, and driven on by the application of new techniques and perspectives. The terms 'shrunken medieval village' and the omnibus 'village earthworks' were steps along the road towards recognizing the diversity of surviving remains and the complexities of the multi-period settlement patterns they represented. All of this has been reflected in the evolution of DMVRG through MVRG to merge with the students of moats, another specific site-type in the medieval landscape, and to form the MSRG.

Now, in the late 1980s, the stamp-collecting phase of DMV-hunting should be mostly behind us, even in those areas of Britain less well covered by primary survey. Types of evidence for medieval settlement are being identified against a broad background. Serious fieldworkers embrace preceding and subsequent periods; every site has a landscape context, and every landscape articulates patterns of settlement. Cynics see the topic becoming as long as the proverbial piece of string. At one level of enquiry, Christopher Taylor covered Dorset and Northamptonshire in about a decade apiece; at another, he has shown at Whiteparish and Whittlesford how a parish can easily absorb a lifetime (see pp. 207–27 below). Arguably, the challenge for the 1990s is to ensure communication between various endeavours within a greatly expanded research topic so that their results may interact and efficiently advance the study of medieval rural Britain.

INVESTIGATING

It is possible to categorize fieldwork programmes administratively by broad primary aims into those mainly concerned with systematic data collection and those seeking the solution of a defined problem. This is not a helpful distinction: data collection cannot occur within a spatial and academic vacuum; problem solving has to involve collection of data that seem relevant to the task. Fieldwork results depend upon what is sought with what techniques, so stating objectives and methods should help to reduce the risk of repetitive work, and add weight to site evaluations made for planning and preservation purposes.

Medieval settlement remains have been widely investigated, through documents, aerial photography, fieldwalking and excavation. Some work has concentrated upon single classes of evidence for all places, and some upon a particular place through all classes of evidence relating to it. However, most research programmes use both approaches, and the present accumulated state of knowledge about medieval settlement is the product of the balance between them.

One of the most informative classes of evidence is the aerial photograph which identifies often transitory earthworks, crop-marks and soil-marks. The main national collections have been developed through planned sorties supplemented by pictures of other features seen on the way to and from areas of search. Locally based flyers are able to saturate their area more thoroughly, identifying all survivals that ground and light conditions reveal. However, a photograph is not a site, but only one means of trying to understand it. The same is true of research conducted by classes of document, such as the patient work of the late E. E. Dodd in the PRO. Equally, the local society or research group which spends its weekends and summer evenings recording groups of earthworks or picking up pottery from ploughed fields is making its contribution to a larger, not always easily perceived, whole.

The use of all classes of evidence relating to a given area, or to a particular problem without pre-set geographical boundaries, is more exacting. It requires the teamwork of several skills, or the attention of the few individuals who possess many of them. The exceptional work of the English Royal Commission has already been mentioned. The way in which the data collection of routine earthwork recording can be conducted within a problem-solving context has been shown by the work of Christopher Taylor and Tony Brown in Northamptonshire and neighbouring counties including Bedfordshire during the 1970s and 1980s. An annual course on fieldwork techniques based at Knuston Hall combined lectures with practical work; interesting unsurveyed sites were chosen for exercises in recording and analysis. The opportunity to secure proper surveys of Bedfordshire's relatively few earthwork sites was eagerly grasped by the County Council archaeologists. The stock of classic motte-and-baileys was soon exhausted, and more battered lower-status sites were then offered, with what turned out to be a needless hesitancy. Three groups of earthworks, Hobbs Green at Odell, Scald End at Thurleigh and Thrup End at Lidlington, were approached as small-scale local training and recording exercises. However, under the stimulus of expert puzzlement about the nature and development of the Bedfordshire medieval settlement pattern, and with the addition of detailed documentary research, these three isolated sites provided a working hypothesis for the development of a post-Norman pattern of dispersal with hamlet earthworks clearly laid over pre-existing ridge and furrow. This perspective allowed the same fieldworkers to look afresh at one of the county's few surviving DMV sites, Chellington, realize that the scheduled site was but one of a series of small dispersed settlements in the same parish, and raise important questions about the continuity of this pattern with pre-Norman settlement.[2]

What are the implications of different investigative strategies for the study and conservation of medieval settlement remains? Scarcity of resources is an obstacle to the systematic accumulation of data by trawling comprehensively

[2] A. Brown, *Fieldwork for Archaeologists and Local Historians* (London, 1987), pp. 83, 90, 127.

through archives and fields; even the available resources may be poorly used in such work if it is not informed by wider research questions which focus attention upon particular places and sources. There are limitations in the unimaginative systematic approach, and quasi-inspirational flitting from one isolated site to another, with insufficient regard for settlement context. Attempts to find all the 'deserted medieval villages' for a given area are bound to fail, as the best of the early gazetteers freely recognized: fixed printed lists have to be superseded by revisable record systems. In any case, many sites are not what they seem at first sight or from a rapid identification survey, as several recent manuals on fieldwork techniques vividly illustrate.[3]

Modern national and local data collectors, such as county Sites & Monuments Records, have mostly learnt to live with the difficulties of handling information on matters as complex and ill-defined as medieval settlement remains. They collect and store available material, and provide on request properly referenced data and interpretations which may even conflict with each other. They aim to be accurate and comprehensive, but not definitive.

Some of these points can be illustrated by the parish survey programme run by Bedfordshire County Council from the mid-1970s, initiated by myself and Angela Simco who developed and managed it with the assistance of several able surveyors, latterly Stephen Coleman and John Wood. The survey was devised as an element in the basic development of the Sites & Monuments Record. Most existing published data had been collected during the previous three years. These needed checking; also, biases of location, period and site-type needed correcting by achieving a consistent county-wide coverage. The general objective was awareness of all reasonably knowable sites in the context of environmental planning; to this end a specified list of sources was systematically covered parish by parish in order to reduce uncertainties about who had looked at what, when and why. A full survey of the county's 128 historic parishes was felt to be practicable despite the funding uncertainties, provided that careful choices were made and discipline exercised. It is those choices and the results they produced, inevitably dominated by the medieval landscape, which concern us here.

Desk-based research concentrated upon secondary written sources together with aerial photographic coverage. Primary historical research was restricted mainly to map evidence and calendars or catalogues in an excellently organized County Record Office: looking at original documents was avoided unless there was clear justification for the extra expenditure of time. Similarly, fieldwork consisted of verifying the existence or survival of sites previously noted through the documentary work, and the checking of blank areas which it suggested were sensitive. The fieldwork was deliberately 'identification' survey; more detailed

[3] ibid.; C. C. Taylor, *Fieldwork in Medieval Archaeology* (London, 1974); M. Aston and T. Rowley, *Landscape Archaeology* (Newton Abbot, 1974).

analytical recording was recognized as a potentially fatal brake on progress and deferred until later required for casework purposes.

Each parish survey had three main products. Firstly, the Sites & Monuments Record, with its information sheets, record maps, retrieval system and other blocks of data, was developed. Secondly, each surveyor had to produce a short essay dealing with a standard series of non-site-specific topics, including medieval settlement. Thirdly, historic maps were transcribed onto an Ordnance Survey base: the value of this exercise for understanding the complexities of medieval settlement lay as much in what it showed of the historic landscape as in the identification of specific medieval habitation sites. All this material can be consulted at either the Planning Department or the County Record Office. Also, seven of the later surveys, done in the 1980s when the techniques of landscape history had more fully developed, have been published in packages containing a lengthy essay and a set of transcribed and redrawn maps.

The Bedfordshire parish survey was mainly concerned with the development of the Sites & Monuments Record. It neither hunted exclusively for medieval settlement remains, nor intensively studied a restricted area of them as a potential model for the wider county. Such work properly belongs to a further stage of work, refining and developing understanding by following up opportunities for research noted in passing: an example is the work by Taylor and Brown already described. Nonetheless, it did provide the opportunity for a preliminary integrated study of medieval settlement on the parish level, as a system which formed a landscape, only some of whose surviving traces have been located and recorded.

STORING AND RETRIEVING THE DATA

Survey produces data which have to be organized for storage and retrieval. Information is usually held in local and national record systems on a site-specific basis because they have to deal with physically identifiable survivals. Yet defining location and ascribing identity may be difficult if the evidence to be stored is uncertain or incompletely understood. This has implications for the study and conservation of any historical survival, and medieval settlement remains present many of the basic problems in an acute form.

The usual route out of the quagmire which surrounds attempts to define a site, calling it the location of past human activity, is not very helpful in this case. At one extreme the whole area covered by a local records system might be regarded as a unit of settlement; at the other extreme, a small block of isolated ridge and furrow entirely surrounded by modern arable might be defined as a site. In general, the larger and more complex the entity represented by the accumulated data, the more analysis and interpretation is required to identify it for the purposes of indexing and retrieval.

One approach to this problem is to describe physical survivals in terms that are as neutral and value-free as possible, relying upon location as the key: the retriever must then select and may have to verify or undertake further fieldwork before synthesizing. Thus there are 'earthworks' rather than 'village earthworks', and 'settlement remains' rather than DMVs. Another approach builds in more interpretation, allowing direct retrieval of interpreted features in the medieval landscape, like 'holloway', 'toft and croft', and 'house platform'; these elements can then be recombined or renamed. Systems with keyword hierarchies based on simple names and thesauruses try to provide the best of both worlds. General experience of this problem suggests that achieving a common national terminology is less important than knowing what other systems mean by their own terms and ensuring that each system practises internal consistency. Attempts to make retrieval systems effectively decide on whether earthworks or crop/soil-marks represent a village that is deserted, shrunken, moved, rolled over, etc., risk conflating two distinct stages of interpretation.

A related issue is the extent to which, for retrieval purposes, adjacent features should be combined as single items or split into components on a record system. Medieval settlement remains can be awkward in this respect: as understanding of their landscape context grows, so previously discrete features can be combined into single items, and the retrieval system must be amended in parallel. Also, settlement remains generate data that are not entirely site-specific. One answer to this problem is to treat each medieval parish as a single item in the Sites & Monuments Record as a reference point for generalized or non-site-specific information. The same treatment might be applied to each identifiable settlement within the parish. Cultivation remains could be recorded on a separate sub-system of specialized record maps rather than dispersed throughout the Sites & Monuments Record as a series of individual open fields or pre-enclosure field names. Such maps could be annotated to show at a glance what ridge and furrow is known to have existed from all sources, which blocks have been recorded by aerial photography or fieldwork, and which actually still survived at the time of the last field inspection.

PRESERVING

The priority in historical conservation has to be preservation of the physical survivals themselves, with preservation of a substitute record as the fall-back position. In pursuing these priorities, account must also be taken of the nature, rarity and quality of the survivals, the importance of the rival land uses which could result in their destruction, and the resources required to achieve physical preservation or preservation of a record. Applying such smooth cultural managerial generalizations to medieval settlement remains invokes familiar difficulties on a terrifying yet challenging scale.

The main problem is the breadth of the subject: it can range from whole relict medieval landscapes to quite small topographical features, yet in a variety of environments, from uplands with or without pressures of agricultural change, to lowlands densely occupied then and now. Just the combination of these two factors will give a wide range of values for local, regional and national comparisons. Moreover, the means of preservation, at least by law, are strictly limited; persuasion is a more widely applicable instrument, and one whose viability varies greatly according to local conditions. The importance of management of land usage as an instrument of preservation will also vary according to the size of what is being preserved.

The preservation of discrete landscapes or of the medieval settlement pattern is the most difficult task. The Monuments Protection Programme may embrace outstanding examples of the former, but mostly those already surviving through their compatibility with non-arable uses; here, continuity can be ensured through relatively inexpensive management agreements. In other cases, especially where uses are more varied, there needs to be an alliance of conservation interests. 'Background' value can be ascribed to a region containing large-scale medieval settlement survivals through designation as an Area of Outstanding Natural Beauty, or, more recently, as an Environmentally Sensitive Area. There is talk in government Green Papers of devising a Rural Conservation Area: though apparently primarily concerned with 'natural' landscape and wildlife aspects, these need not exclude historic landscapes and landscape features. Indeed, an accumulation of important natural and historical features usually allows one interest to reinforce the other, providing any direct conflicts can be resolved. The full implications of ordinary Conservation Areas ('*areas* of special historic or architectural interest') designated in towns and villages since the mid-1960s should be recognized: their boundaries should be expanded in cases where there are good adjacent village earthworks even though no specific controls would be obtained thereby.

The most battered and buried survivals of the medieval settlement pattern will have been repeatedly overlain by later development and land uses; preservation must seek to minimize the impact of further changes. New development could be arranged to respect existing survivals by retaining them in public open space; contact could be retained with mostly destroyed earlier settlement forms, known from documentary and map evidence, by ensuring that village expansion (or 'new' villages) resembled their predecessors in location and layout. The wider changes to the rural landscape expected as a result of 'set-aside' and 'extensification' should be used to give land with historical survivals uses which are compatible with their retention.

The preservation of the major discrete sites is a clearer task. The first problem is to decide which ones deserve the legal protection of scheduling as ancient monuments. The MVRG tackled this by using its archives and informed membership to compile a list of the best sites in the country, using a range of criteria including completeness, documentation and other factors. However, only a limited number of recommendations were implemented, not least due to an official reluctance to expand the schedule during the 1980s in advance of a wider revision.

That review is now about to take place (1988), and ought to be able to provide a more systematic base for selection. The Monuments Protection Programme's three main categories of individual monuments, groups of monuments and urban areas can embrace all realistically protectable medieval settlement remains. It will draw upon the material in Sites & Monuments Records whose development over more than a decade should have provided at least a minimum consistent level of local intelligence, based upon aerial photography and fieldwork. A system is being evolved for scoring sites so that comparisons can be made and a consistent approach adopted to the identification of those that appear to be of national importance. The main challenge here will be ensuring that the intrinsic importance of each site (as it is perceived now) receives full weight. The major opportunity for preservation provided by the process comes from its comprehensive approach: all sites recorded in this way will be evaluated through the scoring system; those that do not quite achieve the status of national importance will have any clear regional or local significance identified automatically, thereby making the basis of an argument for appropriate local action. Also, new information from further research can be used to revise initial scorings. At the time of writing, pilot studies for the Monuments Protection Programme have not yet advanced sufficiently to see how they will apply in detail to medieval settlement remains, but the broad approach gives grounds for optimism.

Preservation is not achieved by designation alone: management has to follow. Some of it mainly involves monitoring the effects of existing farming practices. Repetitive ploughing to the customary depth is permitted without the need for scheduled monument consent, but the freshly turned soil needs inspection to ensure that archaeological deposits are not being further eroded. On earthworks, sheep grazing regimes may be the best for keeping vegetation down, but they can cause severe localized erosion, or wear paths if temporary fencing is not moved around occasionally. Cattle can intensify the effect.

The County Farming and Wildlife Advisory Groups are beginning to work with their county archaeological colleagues in assisting farmers to identify natural and historical features on their land. Their protection can be incorporated into Farm Plans which will take on an increasing importance as the predicted 'extensification' of farming proceeds, and arable reverts to pasture or is planted up for woodland.

When preservation *in situ* cannot be achieved, the fall-back position is preservation by means of a record made in advance of destruction. The process is very expensive, especially for extensive sites like medieval settlement remains. In present circumstances the destructive agent or developer cannot always be expected to fund it totally, and national or local funds for such work have many other calls upon them. Priorities have therefore to be set. Any site scheduled as an ancient monument must be considered for such recording in (what should be) the rare cases where the strong presumption in favour of preservation is overridden by some socially essential development. The same ought to happen for other sites of regional or county importance, though this will often depend as much upon local personnel and resources as on national academic priorities.

Rescuing a medieval landscape from the myriad pressures of modern cultivation and development presents even greater difficulties. In most cases, threats will impinge piecemeal upon small parts at a time, and usually in situations where there is little realistic chance of preservation. A reasoned reaction to such threats has to start from some overall understanding of the medieval settlement pattern, following systematic survey. Without that general awareness it will be difficult to define the areas of sensitivity for the planning officers' constraints maps, and decide how to react to planning applications for car ports near medieval churches, small estates off village High Streets or large barns at outlying farms. Even then, decisions will have to be made about the effective use of scarce 'watching brief' resources. The returns will be piecemeal and incremental compared with the large amount of data produced by a set rescue excavation; much of the evidence recovered may be valuable for being negative, or as a contribution to local ceramic studies. Publicizing the results and justifying the activity to a lay discovery-orientated audience will need careful management.

COMMUNICATING

Historical conservation seeks to preserve medieval settlement remains and their records as a valuable cultural resource. Bequeathing the heritage to the future is a function of the process so far described; communication about it in the present is the subject of this final section. A range of interests has to be served, from research through education at various levels to casual local curiosity.

Communication between record systems and researchers ought to take place as a matter of routine: whether it does, and if not, why not, is beyond the scope of this paper. However, other barriers can come between research results and a wider audience. The results of some projects, rawly presenting documentary references and employing morphological jargon, lack user-friendliness. With a little effort spent on translation and presentation, they could more easily satisfy an often burning wish to know about the history of a particular place. The generalization and simplification required in the interpretation and presentation of results can also force challenging re-examinations of detailed research.

One approach which tried to come to terms with some of the problems was developed in the series 'Bedfordshire Historic Landscape and Archaeology',[4] arising from the parish survey programme described above. The historic map transcripts and summary essays had originally been conceived as appendages to the main task of enhancing the Sites & Monuments Record. However, the need was felt to provide a more direct return for the investment of public money in the project. Accordingly, some of the later parish surveys, done over five years from the commencement of the programme, were taken through to publication. Each parish packet includes a set of maps and a long illustrated booklet. The maps are transcripts on an Ordnance Survey base, usually including the pre-enclosure landscape with as much of the medieval pattern as can be reconstructed, the landscape created by enclosure, and a record of subsequent changes up to the present day. The booklet is a chronological history of the parish, before and after its definition. The two elements are designed to be used together.

Booklet and maps provide different opportunities for different people. The booklet is written in chronological order and much of it is inevitably concerned with the origins, development and disintegration of the medieval settlement pattern. The chosen parish is the primary focus of attention, but what appears to have happened there is also presented in the context of wider general trends, to meet the interest of both local/landscape historian and 'intelligent layman'. Most of what is written about topography in the booklet can be seen illustrated on the maps, but only some of the detail on them can be discussed in the booklet. The maps can stand alone individually, and the features they record can be related to the modern landscape; they can also be compared directly one with another to show changes through time (see figure 9.1). Together, booklet and maps are valuable source material for teaching purposes: perhaps only advanced 'A' level project students could use them directly, but careful selection and adaptation can bring them to various levels of age and ability. In particular, teachers grappling with the new history and geography GCSE syllabuses find them relevant to the skills these are intended to develop, for their provision of questions as well as answers.

During the 1970s, village studies tended to be done rapidly and cheaply, mainly with rescue needs in mind: they sought to provide the rural equivalent of the urban 'implications of development' studies. It was difficult for most of them to go further than identifying sensitive areas and threats to them. Department of the Environment/Heritage Commission funding avoided long-term survey commitments of the Bedfordshire type (support was withdrawn halfway through the programme); instead, national resources were concentrated

[4] Available from County Planning Department, County Hall, Bedford, MK42 9AP.

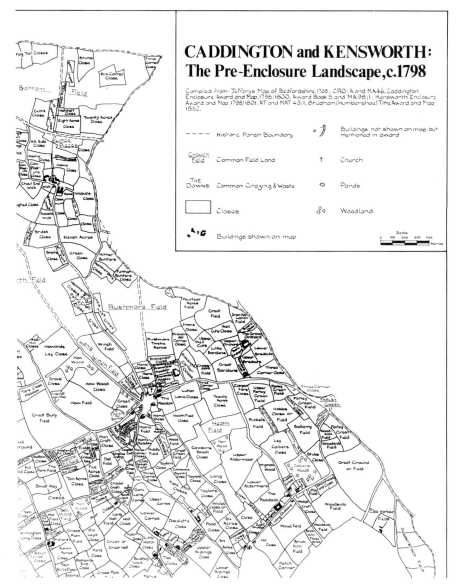

FIGURE 9.1 *Extract from an historic map transcript in Bedfordshire parish survey publication for Caddington and Kensworth.*

upon making Sites & Monuments Records a consistent source for the projected Monuments Protection Programme. Provision of up-to-date information about the medieval landscape has therefore not kept pace with the general growth of interest in the 'heritage'. Any vacuum can too easily be filled by work which is not aware of recent advances in landscape history, and perpetuates discredited myths and models of Black Death desertions and village plan types. It is essential to understand how far a teacher has to simplify often complex evidence in order to make it usable in the modern educational context, and it is not clear how far recent work on the medieval landscape is filtering through into materials for schools.

Beyond academics and teachers there is a far larger consumer of a conserved historic environment, namely the public which likes to spend some of its leisure time with the relics of the past. Concern for presentation and interpretation is at unprecedented levels. For the medieval period, however, the emphasis still seems to be mainly on the high-status sites, with castles, jousting and banquets reinforcing rather than demythologizing fundamentally Hollywood-derived images. The medieval village is scarcely visible in the background, unless pillaged by wicked nobles.

Of course, castles and abbeys were excitingly different from everyday life then and now, and their remains were able to survive much more substantially than those of the rural settlement pattern. Individual houses, or even small groups of them, may have been reconstructed in open-air museums, but the presentation is unavoidably that of complex artefacts rather than settlements or communities. The actual sites do exist, but even the best preserved tend to have little more than a church and manor house (which may be ruined), surrounded by grassy mounds and hollows. This may be enough for those who take 'pleasure in ruins' and find intricate explanation tedious, but there are other potential customers. Earthworks are forbidding obstacles to the curious but unacclimatized mind: it is difficult enough for experts to agree on what their surface indications suggest, and Wharram Percy has clearly shown how these can mask something quite unexpected.

The problems revolve around two issues, perception and reconstruction. Many casual visitors want to grasp basic concept and layout immediately so that they can then wander around and look at details within the overall scheme. This requires the careful selection of an initial ground level viewpoint where a similarly orientated aerial photograph can be correlated with it. There is also a strong case for a reconstruction drawing of how the place may have looked in its heyday from the same viewpoint, and for repeating both types of item at more than one position. Reconstructions should not be spurned because there is no detailed evidence: it is better to feed the public imagination with a suitably qualified expert guess than leave it face-to-face with uncompromising house platforms.

The next step in this line of argument is the 'living' reconstruction, either on a scientific basis as at Butser for the iron age, or on a more spectator and participatory basis as in places like Colonial Williamsburg. The difficulties should not be minimized: the fourteenth century presents greater problems of reconstruction and role-play than the eighteenth. Perhaps a medieval project like Butser should be started as soon as possible, before sponsorship for such serious studies is mopped up or they are upstaged by Hollywood-type versions in the burgeoning theme park and heritage reconstruction industries. Such a project might gain credibility and resources if geared partly to educational requirements through providing the medieval equivalent of the 'day in the life of a country house' participatory session.

The amount of on-site interpretation will depend greatly upon the extent to which the site can be staffed: the commercial calculation that has to be made will include accessibility to tourist routes and other attractions as well as the intrinsic importance of the site in question. In cases where little more can be provided than a couple of signposts and a few display boards, the Norfolk Archaeological Unit's low-cost approach to Godwick in Tittleshall parish can be commended (plate 9.1). Where more resources for display are available, there may be a need to reconcile the requirements of preservation and presentation. Even at a site which is in guardianship, an apparently typical house platform could be excavated, and the physical remains consolidated or represented in materials credible to the lay eye; a section of ridge and furrow with headlands, furlong boundaries, and perhaps even a visible relationship to village closes, might be delineated and explained. What cannot be easily demonstrated by remains on site, such as ploughing practices, could be explained through video in an interpretative centre. Much ought to be possible along these lines without risking the long-term conservation of a finite historic resource in the name of the short term consumer-orientated pleasures.

PLATE 9.1 *On-site interpretation at Godwick, Norfolk.*

CONCLUSION

The problems of how to display and interpret medieval settlement remains for a wider public merit a paper by themselves, but are fitting issues for the conclusion of this offering. The work of Maurice Beresford, John Hurst and the MSRG has established awareness of the presence and significance of medieval settlement remains in the English landscape; others, notably Christopher Taylor, Tony Brown and Richard Muir, have, with them, brought the fascination of the subject to a much wider audience. The impetus of the Monuments Protection Programme may extend formal protection over the best survivals. But their conservation through effective management, taking advantage of whatever opportunities are provided by changing policies on the use of farmland, is going to need a measure of public resources and willing consent from landowners, both of which should be facilitated by English Heritage's initiative in management, and their scheme of survey grants for landowners.[5] These will come the more easily if there is an awareness of what is important and why, learnt from a range of statements aimed at different levels of interest in the community: the development of these is one of the major tasks of the next forty years.

[5] T. Darvill, *Ancient Monuments in the Countryside – An Archaeological Management Review* (English Heritage Archaeological Report no. 5, London, 1987).

10

Alterations to Ridge and Furrow: Some Examples Illustrated

D. R. WILSON

INTRODUCTION

Medieval ridge and furrow was an early (and lasting) interest of Maurice Beresford's, so it is pleasant to be able to offer some further comments on its evolution. The ridge and furrow of former open fields used to be the commonest visible remnant of the medieval landscape over a large part of England, extending from the midlands south into Wessex and northwards as far as Lancashire and Northumberland. Perhaps it is still so in relative terms, but the extent and frequency of surviving fragments have been significantly diminished by the programme of intensive arable farming fostered in the 1960s and 1970s. This process is strikingly illustrated in plate 10.1 showing fields near Titchmarsh, Northamptonshire where three zones of survival or non-survival are readily distinguished. In the foreground, ridge and furrow is well preserved in three fields that have long been in permanent pasture, though there is evidence for a limited episode of post-medieval ploughing to be seen in the left-hand field, in the narrow ridges superimposed on its central portion. Beyond this zone of preservation is a group of two fields (formerly three) in which the pattern of ridge and furrow is continued in terms of soil-marks. These fields have been brought back into cultivation fairly recently, and although the surface has been virtually levelled, colour differences in the soil still show the essential layout of the medieval ridges. Any nuances in their surface relief have, of course, been lost. Outside these two zones of obvious archaeological interest extends an almost featureless expanse, in which ploughing over the years has obliterated all but the slightest traces. These, however, although unreadable in detail, are sufficient to show that the original system of ridge and furrow did indeed cover a wider area.

Despite the losses exemplified in plate 10.1, the abundance of the surviving remains has effectively inhibited any general overall survey of medieval ridge and furrow. The typical features have nevertheless often been described, and so

PLATE 10.1 *Ridge and furrow, south of Titchmarsh, Northamptonshire, looking north-north-east. (28 November 1972)*

PLATE 10.2 *Ridge and furrow, south of Watford, Northamptonshire, looking east. (15 November 1967)*

PLATE 10.3 *Ridge and furrow and deserted settlement, Othorpe House, near Slawston, Leicestershire, looking west. (13 May 1966)*

too has the correspondence between actual ridges and the individual strips into which the open fields are known to have been divided.[1] It is this correspondence that justifies description of these features as medieval, but it should not obscure the fact that a given system of 'medieval' ridge and furrow might have been in active use and management for at least 600 years, say from the twelfth to the eighteenth centuries.

During such a period considerable development and modification is only to be expected. The typical patchwork effect of interlocking furlongs is partly related to local topography and the need for unimpeded drainage down the furrows, but in part it can also be seen as the result of successive assarts. In this way the layout of ridge and furrow can itself furnish evidence for its own development. We should not be deceived by the complexity of the resulting pattern, however, nor indeed by the apparent solidity of the individual ridged strips, into thinking that either need have been a permanency, once established. The very same processes that brought ridge and furrow into being in the first place could equally have been applied to creating new layouts in place of the old.

Such wholesale rearrangements can hardly be expected to have left much physical trace, though some can be surmised from circumstantial evidence in

[1] M. W. Beresford and J. K. S. St Joseph, *Medieval England: An Aerial Survey* (Cambridge, 1st edn 1958, 2nd edn 1979); C. Taylor, *Fields in the English Landscape* (London, 1975); D. Hall, *Medieval Fields* (Aylesbury, 1982).

the form of land holdings, estate boundaries and so forth. Less drastic alterations, on the other hand, were undertaken piecemeal and these are much more readily detectable. Their traces, which are not uncommon, may be studied on the ground but are best appreciated from the air, which allows the broad view that is so often needed to make sense of puzzling features. These minor alterations are of more than passing interest, since they show us the open fields in operation as a going concern, requiring adjustments of layout to adapt

PLATE 10.4 *Ridge and furrow, east of Smeeton Westerby, Leicestershire, looking south-east. (28 November 1972)*

186

PLATE 10.5 *Ridge and furrow, south-west of Eyton, Herefordshire, looking south. (24 November 1972)*

to changing circumstances, and it is with them that the remainder of this paper is concerned (plates 10.2–10.5).

A CHANGING PATTERN

These alterations show up as irregularities or variations in the normal pattern of ridge and furrow. It is evident that, to have survived for us to recognize and study, most such anomalies cannot have been long ploughed over, or they would have been smoothed away. In some instances this is a result of the alteration itself: a piece of former arable was converted to permanent grass and this has ensured the survival of the evidence. Elsewhere, however, we are led to conclude that the modifications were made at a very late stage in the life of the open fields, not many years before a large part was turned over to pasture.

When we look at actual examples, the features seen can be interpreted with varying degrees of confidence. Perhaps least enigmatic are places where the ends of a number of ridges have been taken out of cultivation to provide more space, either for access or for some purpose such as a rick-place. On plate 10.2, at Watford (Northamptonshire), there is near the upper left corner a triangular area between three furlongs, whose shape is emphasized by the incised lines of two well-worn tracks. This triangular space was at some time enlarged by taking in the heads of the ridges on both its long sides, and the same was done to the ridges of the furlong on the right where it extends towards the viewer on the near side of a transverse hedge. The relict heads were not levelled off, but became somewhat smoothed in subsequent use, the limit of this smoother area being marked by lines of low humps where continued ploughing created new heads on the ridges.[2] A similar process can be inferred on plate 10.3 at Othorpe (Leicestershire) where a triangular space has been created beside a small moat just to left of centre; here the ends of the ridges have been more definitely flattened and their traces are only just visible.

We may usefully compare these two examples with the creation of a new lane across the middle of an existing furlong, as seen at the centre of plate 10.2. There can be no doubt that the lane is secondary: not only does it slice through a distinctive block of six half-size ridges, but we can see subdued traces of the other ridges actually passing underneath. A serious attempt has been made to provide a level track for carts and wagons, presumably by means of hand-digging, which produced the heaps of spoil on either side. These heaps coincide with the new heads of the truncated ridges, but they appear too substantial to be the result of ploughing alone. Other factors may be at work here, however, since the remains are in fact more complicated than has been so far noted. Careful examination shows that there is one more ridge on the near side of the lane than there is beyond it. This suggests that to the right of the narrow strips the lane had been following the line of a former headland; this headland had already been suppressed by the time that the lane was laid out, but it could have contributed indirectly to the spoil heaps, in a manner now to be explained.

When two furlongs abutted end to end, they could be run together by digging through the common headland to achieve continuous furrows, allowing the two halves to be ploughed as one. More often than not, the remade ridges change direction or wriggle as they cross the former headland, either because the two sets were not in perfect alignment, or because they featured the standard 'reversed–S' curve. Spoil from the digging operation would be piled between the furrows in a line of heaps that effectively marked the site of the former headland. Spoil heaps of this kind could therefore have been present already along part of the lane described in the previous paragraph, for there is undoubtedly a change of direction in the ridges along the relevant sector.[3] Further down the picture, in the same furlong, another line of heaps is seen, marking a former headland. These heaps are of complex form because some of the ridges on one side are of only half the normal width. Interpretation as a former headland is consistent with the presence of a very short ridge, just beyond the furthest heap, that comes to an end on the very same line.

The existence of ridges of varied width can be of much value in assessing features such as those just described. If the ridges on one side show a distinctive

---

[2] This explanation differs from that of Beresford and St Joseph, *Medieval England: An Aerial Survey*, 2nd edn, p. 30.

[3] A helpful view of the same site, looking directly along the ridges, appears in ibid., fig. 9.

pattern including some that are broader or narrower than the rest, and this is exactly repeated on the other side, it is clear that both were originally parts of the same furlong. Conversely, if the pattern differs from one side to the other, it implies that the ridges were originally in different furlongs, whatever their more recent history.

What remains uncertain is why some ridges, and only these, were made broader or narrower than their neighbours, and whether this treatment is an original or early feature or if it is a late development. Sometimes a broad ridge can be seen to have been enlarged at the expense of others, but this is rare. On plate 10.3, for instance, a broad ridge just to right of centre overrides the heads of five ridges running at right angles to it. There is no sign of new heads being formed, as if these five ridges had dropped out of cultivation at this time, and the broad ridge itself does not appear to have been ploughed in its present form, as if it were intended as a green balk, for access or as a ley. A similar broad ridge in the lower left quarter of plate 10.4 has likewise encroached on an adjoining furlong.

It is tolerably certain that unusually broad or narrow ridges have not resulted simply from changes in land tenure, with ridges remodelled to reflect the amalgamation or subdivision of individual holdings. In the first place, the broad ridges in most cases do not attain even a full double width, let alone the larger groupings of strips that are known from documentary sources. They generally appear integrated in their furlongs and could hardly have been created by a strictly local modification like that described above. Nor does the width of ridges conform to any modular scheme that would allow them to be rated as 'double', 'single' or 'half' in terms of some standard unit. Examination of plate 10.3 shows ridges in a variety of widths within the same furlong. Some narrow ridges are indeed half-size, but others are larger. Furthermore, the narrow ridges do not occur solely in pairs, so have not always been formed by simple subdivision. Singletons can be found on plate 10.3, and elsewhere – for example, Hothorpe, Northamptonshire – may be seen occurring after every second or third ridge of normal size. Like the broad ridges, these single narrow ridges appear integrated in their furlongs, and if their purpose were better understood, it might furnish a clue as to when their furlongs were last completely remodelled.

However they should be dated, the non-standard ridges are unlikely to have been introduced for other than good practical reasons. It seems fair to claim that their form was different because their agricultural treatment was different. The broad ridges may have been leys, while the narrow ridges may also have been taken out of the normal rotation in order to grow some specialized crop by more horticultural methods. The narrow ridges at least were not being ploughed in the traditional manner, and despite the existence of singletons, as already noted, most such ridges were in fact pairs that had pretty obviously been converted at some stage from ridges of normal width (plates 10.2, 10.4). This could have been quite a late development. The pattern of narrow ridges on plate 10.4, near Smeeton Westerby (Leicestershire), shows a much more complex and less apparently rational layout than those on plate 10.2. This may reflect the preferences of individual farmers and it reminds us of the flexibility of operation afforded by strip cultivation even in the changing agricultural scene of the seventeenth and eighteenth centuries.

The final illustration (plate 10.5), near Eyton (Herefordshire), is included to show that some alterations to ridge and furrow were peculiar indeed. A well-preserved block of ridge and furrow survives within a more or less trapezoidal field at the centre of the picture. The ridges are widely spaced – that is, an unusually broad space is occupied by the intervening furrows – presumably because of the low-lying and therefore damp situation beside the river Lugg. To fill the broader (southern) end of the field short ridges have been inserted here and there which taper away to nothing half-way down the field. If we assume that a pair of narrower ridges are a late modification, there were originally four of these shorter ridges, which are a standard device for coping with awkward spaces. Thus far, all is normal, but when we look at the right-hand half of this field, we see that five of the main ridges have been broken in half and then reconnected to the next ridge along. The unusual breadth of the furrows makes this a particularly perverse exercise, requiring a substantial construction to link one ridge to another. It is hardly credible to suppose that this was done through simple misunderstanding, despite the notorious example of the bungled modern rehabilitation of ridge and furrow at Kirby Bellars, near Frisby (Leicestershire).[4] We may nevertheless suppose that this remarkable result was not achieved in a single phase: there are hints that this part of the furlong was divided into two halves, perhaps at the time that the narrower ridges were created, and that the reconnection (for whatever reason) took place only later. Documentary research might possibly reveal what body was responsible and at how late a stage it all was done.

CONCLUSION

The remains of ridge and furrow seen today, although originating in medieval times, are the product of a long period of development, sometimes continuing into the eighteenth century. Traces of alterations in layout are not uncommon. These are likely often to have been made at a fairly late stage and so may reflect the changing needs and practices of post-medieval agriculture.

[4] D. R. Wilson, *Photo Interpretation for Archaeologists* (London, 1982), fig. 73.

II

Field Systems and Township Structure

DAVID HALL

INTRODUCTION

Reading Maurice Beresford's *History on the Ground*, shortly after publication, was the catalyst that initiated serious fieldwork for me.[1] Having the good fortune to live in an archaeologically rich countryside, and a few years previously having made a copy of an eighteenth-century enclosure map, conditions were fertile for a scholarly introduction to the historical geography of a local landscape. *History on the Ground* is a major work that indicates techniques successfully used to make many important discoveries by combining evidence from archaeological fieldwork and historical sources. This chapter selects one aspect of such studies, field systems, and uses the evidence as an approach to unravel the complexities of settlements.

The full potential of field-system studies has only been realized over the last thirty years or so. Fields are particularly suited for landscape studies; there are physical remains surviving on the ground that can be mapped, and there are large quantities of relevant written records. Since the wealth of medieval England was largely derived from land, it is natural that the management and transfer of property, both on the small and large scale, should leave a copious record. A township, that is a working field system independent of its neighbours, is likely to be the oldest unity in the landscape, predating the parish and possibly even predating the settlement site. Study of such units therefore provides a means of discovering information about land division in the Saxon period.

---

[1] M. W. Beresford, *History on the Ground: Six Studies in Maps and Landscapes* (London, 1957).

PREVIOUS STUDIES

The literature on pre-enclosure fields, especially the Midland type, is immense. Farms divided into strips of about a quarter of an acre, scattered throughout a township, and intermixed with the land of other men, have attracted the attention of historians and economists. As well as describing the layout and operation of subdivided fields, writers have sought to explain their origin and development. The early studies of Seebohm, Vinogradoff, Maitland, Gray, Bishop and the Orwins are well known and provide a background of data and theories.[2] Since 1964 contributions by Thirsk, Titow, Dodgshon, and volumes of edited papers published in 1973 and 1981 have brought theories up to date and presented more regional data.[3] The proceedings of several recent international conferences have put the British studies in a European context; more detail of some of the recent work is discussed below.[4]

Evidence from the work of Gray and other regional studies has shown the variety and complexity of British field systems, and Gray's classification into types has been modified and extended. However, the many types that exist can be considered to fall into only two major groups, the Midland and the remainder. The Midland system, as recently discussed by Fox, is characterized by having a large proportion of the available area under cultivation, which necessitates the use of fallow for communal grazing by the animals of the whole township.[5] Such use of the fallow further requires that it must lie in a compact block and that the strips of every landholder need to be uniformly distributed throughout a township to ensure that there should always be plots available for cultivation, no matter which part was fallow in a particular year. Nearly all other types of field system have a plentiful supply of rough pasture for animals and never developed an intensive fallow grazing arrangement. There was no need to equalize the distribution of strips throughout the township, they could lie in a more limited area; and such examples can be found in East Anglia and Kent.[6]

[2] F. Seebohm, *The English Village Community* (London, 1890); P. Vinogradoff, *Villainage in England* (Oxford, 1892); F. W. Maitland, 'The survival of archaic communities', in *The Collected Papers of Frederick William Maitland*, ed. H. A. L. Fisher (London, 1911), vol. II, pp. 313–65; H. L. Gray, *English Field Systems* (Cambridge, Mass., 1915); T. A. M. Bishop, 'Assarting and the growth of the open fields', *Economic History Review*, 6 (1935), pp. 26–40; C. S. and C. S. Orwin, *The Open Fields* (Oxford, 1938).

[3] J. Thirsk, 'The common fields', *Past and Present*, 29 (1964), pp. 3–29; J. Z. Titow, 'Medieval England and the open-field system', *Past and Present*, 32 (1965), pp. 86–102; R. A. Dodgshon, *The Origin of British Field Systems: An Interpretation* (London, 1980); A. R. H. Baker and R. A. Butlin (eds), *Studies of Field Systems in the British Isles* (Cambridge, 1973); T. Rowley (ed.), *The Origins of Open-Field Agriculture* (London, 1981).

[4] K. Biddick (ed.), *Archaeological Approaches to Medieval Europe* (Kalamazoo, Mich., 1984); D. Hooke, (ed.), *Medieval Villages: A Review of Current Work* (Oxford University Committee for Archaeology, monograph no. 5, Oxford, 1985); B. K. Roberts and R. E. Glasscock (eds), *Villages, Fields and Frontiers* (BAR, International ser. 185, 1983).

[5] H. S. A. Fox, 'Approaches to the adoption of the Midland system', in *Origins of Open-Field Agriculture*, ed. Rowley, pp. 64–111, esp. pp. 65–8.

[6] *Studies of Field Systems*, ed. Baker and Butlin, pp. 308–13 and 384–419.

There was more scope for variation ranging from an order similar to the Midland type to holdings in severalty, with any intermediate form to suit local requirements, making for an infinite variety of types.

FIELDWORK RESULTS

Considerable advances in the study of field systems were made in 1961 with the development of techniques for the reconstruction of complete township plans, which was made possible by the recognition of earthworks that had formed at the edges of medieval fields.[7] In many parts of the country strip ploughing was so extensive and was in operation for such a long time, lasting into the eighteenth and nineteenth centuries, that very clear evidence survives in the modern landscape. The ridging of individual strips and the accumulation of soil at the ends, where ploughs turned round, slowly caused earthworks to form. In this way every furlong came to have a linear bank of earth along its boundaries; these have in many cases survived modern agricultural practices and, when mapped, a complete furlong plan can be reconstructed for a township. The availability of a plan improves the scope of research because many places without a map have comprehensive written records. In Northamptonshire 145 parishes have now been fieldwalked for archaeological finds and earthwork remains, and detailed studies of historical sources have been made for individual villages. All the fenland of Cambridgeshire has been mapped along with parts of Bedfordshire, Buckinghamshire, Huntingdonshire, Leicestershire, Oxfordshire and the Yorkshire wolds, so making available a large quantity of plans from an area in excess of 700,000 acres.[8] Archaeological discoveries are relevant to studies of subdivided fields, because it has been found that there are many small and deserted middle Saxon settlement sites over which the strips run. This finding immediately helped to establish a reliable chronology, it now being clear that subdivided fields can be no earlier than the middle Saxon phase, perhaps created in the eighth or ninth century.[9]

When the above fieldwork techniques were applied to other areas, regional variations of field patterns emerged; the checkerboard type of the midlands is extensive, but simpler patterns with much longer strips up to a mile in length

[7] D. N. Hall, 'Modern surveys of medieval field systems', *Bedfordshire Archaeological Journal*, 7 (1972), pp. 53–66; idem, *Medieval Fields* (Aylesbury, 1982), pp. 25–8.

[8] The Fenland results are currently (1987) being published as a monograph series in *East Anglian Archaeology*.

[9] Saxon sites are found in many parts of Northamptonshire; for Brixworth see D. N. Hall and P. W. Martin, 'Brixworth, Northamptonshire: an intensive field survey', *Journal of the British Archaeological Association*, 132 (1979), pp. 1–6; for Saxon sites in the Peterborough region see D. N. Hall, 'The late Saxon countryside – villages and their fields', in *Anglo-Saxon Settlements*, ed. D. Hooke (Oxford, 1988), pp. 101–3.

are found in areas as disparate as the silt fens and the Yorkshire wolds.[10] The strips of the wolds are similar to the Holderness examples described by Harvey, but such systems are not the only type found in Yorkshire;[11] on the plain around York there are normal 'Midland' checkerboard fields. Close examination of Midland fields has shown that they too once consisted of much larger blocks, and that the rectangular patterns of later times were achieved by subdivision and re-orientation of long strips, as at Hardingstone and Raunds (Northamptonshire) and elsewhere.[12] This implies that fields were laid out in a planned operation.

The following section summarizes the chief results for Northamptonshire, which typifies the whole of the midland region. A wide variety of information is obtainable from an analysis of each parish, once the furlongs have been identified from historical sources using the reconstructed plans.[13] Spatial distribution of individual estates can be studied by plotting a single yardland, the standard farming unit. This establishes the basic structure of the system by identifying the great fields and the meadows.

THE NORTHAMPTONSHIRE RESULTS

Townships that have complete surveys of all their strips can be examined for land use at the time of the survey, as at Ashby St Ledgers.[14] Regional differences are apparent: townships with poor soil have much reversion to grass (leys) in the post-medieval period, but the more fertile soils of the Nene valley remained completely arable. Land use and topography can be extracted from the furlong names themselves, sometimes reaching back to late Saxon times, identifying former scrub or woodland (as in the Huxlow hundred, Clopton, Raunds and elsewhere).[15] The demesne, the home farm of the manor, occurs in two types, either distributed throughout the furlongs in the same manner as peasant holdings (see East Haddon), or more or less in a single block near to the village (as at Wollaston).[16] When a manor was split into two, the demesne was also divided, and so a vill with two manors having demesne lying side by side throughout the fields is likely once to have been a single manor. Several

[10] D. Hall, 'The changing landscape of the Cambridgeshire silt fens', *Landscape History*, 3 (1981), pp. 37–49; Hall, *Medieval Fields*, p. 52.

[11] M. Harvey, 'The origin of planned field systems in Holderness, Yorkshire', in *Origins of Open Field Agriculture*, ed. Rowley, pp. 184–201.

[12] Hall, *Medieval Fields*, pp. 48–50.

[13] Identification of furlongs is explained in Hall, *Medieval Fields*, pp. 29–31.

[14] ibid., pp. 31–2.

[15] D. Hall, 'Fieldwork and the documentary evidence for the layout and organization of early medieval estates in the English midlands', in *Archaeological Approaches*, ed. Biddick, pp. 49 and 58.

[16] Hall, *Medieval Fields*, p. 34; idem, 'Fieldwork and field books: studies in early layout', in *Villages, Fields and Frontiers*, ed. Roberts and Glasscock, pp. 117–19.

examples have been discovered, some already split in the eleventh century, as for instance at Kislingbury.[17]

Many vills have been found to be more complex than they appeared at first sight. A single nucleated settlement placed in the middle of its fields turns out to be double, consisting of two vills lying adjacent, each with an independent field system (examples occur at East Haddon and Hardingstone).[18] In other cases there is evidence of a smaller, otherwise lost estate, having been absorbed (as with Buscott in Higham Ferrers).[19]

The single holding, a yardland or virgate, can be related to the ground evidence. Normally one such holding will consist of a single ridge in every furlong throughout the system, or if the furlongs are very large, then two or three ridges, but spaced out. A holding of two or three yardlands will commonly consist of groups of two or three adjacent ridges similarly spaced out. Most field systems had a regular order of tenants holding strips, so if there were 32 yardlands, as at Hardingstone, there would be cycles of 32 tenants having a ridge each in a given furlong, the same neighbours always being adjacent. The number of lands in a furlong is frequently a multiple of the yardland rating for the vill: thus Hardingstone furlongs contain 32, 64, 96 lands, and so on.[20] Hence the field-system structure is intimately related to the fiscal assessment of the vill (taxes and rates being charged on the yardland from the thirteenth to the eighteenth centuries). Regular layouts of this type have been discussed by Göransson; the Northamptonshire evidence suggests that every township once had a regular ordering: for Ecton and Muscott the repetitive cycle has been demonstrated to be medieval.[21]

The number of yardlands at which a vill was assessed does not change over the centuries; it is a fixed value and in many places the total is a round figure, most frequently a multiple of 10 or 12. Further, this value can commonly be directly related to the Domesday assessment of 1086. For Northamptonshire the assessment was in hides, and typically a vill later found to consist of 48 yardlands will be found to have 4 hides in 1086 (Great Billing).[22] Harvey found cases in Yorkshire where there is a connection between the Domesday fiscal assessment and the later oxgang size of townships.[23] Not all vills have a

[17] Hall, 'Fieldwork and the documentary evidence', pp. 50 and 62, shows a plan of the total demesne without distinguishing the two manors.

[18] D. N. Hall, 'Hardingstone parish survey 1972', *Northamptonshire Archaeology*, 15 (1980), pp. 119–32.

[19] Hall, 'Late Saxon countryside'.

[20] Hall, 'Hardingstone'.

[21] S. Göransson, 'Regular open-field pattern in England and the Scandinavian solskifte', *Geografiska Annaler*, 43 (1961), pp. 79–105; Hall, 'Fieldwork and field books', pp. 121 and 125; Hall, 'Fieldwork and the documentary evidence', pp. 52–3 and 64.

[22] ibid., pp. 124–8.

[23] M. Harvey 'Planned field systems in eastern Yorkshire, some thoughts on their origin', *Agricultural History Review*, 31 (1983), pp. 91–103, esp. p. 101.

round figure for their fiscal units; Clipston, a vill of 84 yardlands, was assessed at 16 yardlands to the hide, so making a total of 5¼ hides. In the twelfth century a component estate of 57 yardlands in this vill relates precisely to its Domesday size of 3½ hides and ¼ of a virgate (4 Domesday virgates equal 1 hide).[24] In other words, the Domesday assessments relate directly to the holding size and therefore to the field systems. It is surprising to find that many vills have a round-figure yardland size related intimately to their field-system structure. The conclusion is that the round figure must have been given to a vill and township at the time the fields were first created, and that the whole process was a planned operation.

The above findings allow comment on some of the statements and theories of previous historians. Since the archaeological evidence has shown that Saxon sites underlie subdivided fields, it is clear that strip systems cannot be of Roman origin or brought from the Saxon homeland in north Germany, as Seebohm and Gray believed. The highly ordered layout of field systems, the existence of long strips and the physical relationships between fields and early fiscal ratings point, unexpectedly, to a single planned operation in the creation of each township. This does not mean that there is no place for assarting as a factor contributing to subdivided fields in some areas.[25] When a township was subdivided strips would be formed in the area then under cultivation, which often would be most of the ploughable area in the case of Nene valley townships. Other villages would still possess rough pasture or woodland, later to become incorporated in the fields. At Clopton the former woodland can easily be observed as a discontinuity in the furlong pattern, whereas at Raunds it is only observable partly from furlong names and mainly from subtle differences in the way that the assarts were divided and allotted between owners and tenants.[26] The amount of waste left when a township was laid out is reflected in the number of acres in a yardland; small sizes of 15–25 acres tell of an open landscape (as in the valley townships of Ecton and Wollaston), and large yardlands of 40–80 acres are found where there was former wood (occurring in the clayland vills of Raunds and Bozeat).[27]

WATFORD, NORTHAMPTONSHIRE, A CASE-STUDY

Watford is known to many for traffic chaos on the M1, but few travellers ever stop to see the village. It is a small shrunken settlement retaining many trees in

---

[24] D. Hall, in A. Williams and R. Erskine (eds), *The Domesday Book of Northamptonshire* (London, 1988).

[25] Seebohm, *English Village Community*, pp. 373, 410–17; Gray, *English Field Systems*, pp. 41 ff; Bishop, 'Assarting', pp. 26–40.

[26] Hall, 'Late Saxon countryside'.

[27] Hall, 'Fieldwork and field books', pp. 128–9; unpublished work shows that Raunds, Bozeat and Ravensthorpe had yardlands of 40, 64 and 60 acres.

the parkland of the manor house, Watford Court, demolished in about 1972. There is still much grassland with steep ridge and furrow (plate 11.1), some of it illustrated by Beresford and St Joseph.[28] The Seventh Series 1" to 1 mile Ordnance Survey map (Sheet 133, SP 60 69) shows that the parish of Watford contains part of a hamlet called Murcott and a farm bearing the name Silsworth Lodge. Further interest is roused by the county historian, John Bridges, writing in c. 1720; he noted: 'to Watford belong Catesby an inclosed manor with no house; Cumberford a depopulated village in an enclosed manor, now reduced to one house; five houses in Murcott; [and] Silsworth a depopulated hamlet consisting at present of one house . . .'[29]

PLATE 11.1 *Ridge and furrow in Watford Park, Northamptonshire (SP 604 695). This was formerly part of the demesne and was enclosed in 1595.*

Before the present study the only recent work was a small excavation made in the earthworks identified as Silsworth (which produced medieval sherds and, more interestingly, a sherd of middle Saxon Ipswich ware pottery),[30] and a report by the Royal Commission on Historical Monuments which sought to claim an 'unidentified, unlocated vill' in the tongue of the parish that crosses the Roman Watling Street.[31] In 1978, I undertook a fieldwork and historical research programme to elucidate the settlement and township structure of the parish of Watford. The usual fieldwork techniques were applied, visiting each field under winter conditions. Arable fields were searched for flints and pottery

[28] M. W. Beresford and J. K. S. St Joseph, *Medieval England; an Aerial Survey*, 2nd edn (Cambridge, 1979), pp. 37–8.
[29] J. Bridges, *The History and Antiquities of Northamptonshire* (2 vols, Oxford, 1791), vol. I, p. 585.
[30] *Northamptonshire Archaeology*, 8 (1973), p. 19.
[31] RCHM (England), *Northamptonshire* (London, 1981), vol. IV, p. 189.

sherds, and pasture fields were mapped for ridge and furrow. The whole system of medieval fields was easily reconstructed by mapping the linear banks of soil lying along furlong boundaries, referred to above.

The results were drawn up on the 1:10560 scale as shown on figure 11.1. Two Roman sites and one middle Saxon site were discovered – showing, typically for the east midlands, that there had been early settlement of the landscape in a form different from that of the middle ages. There proved to be

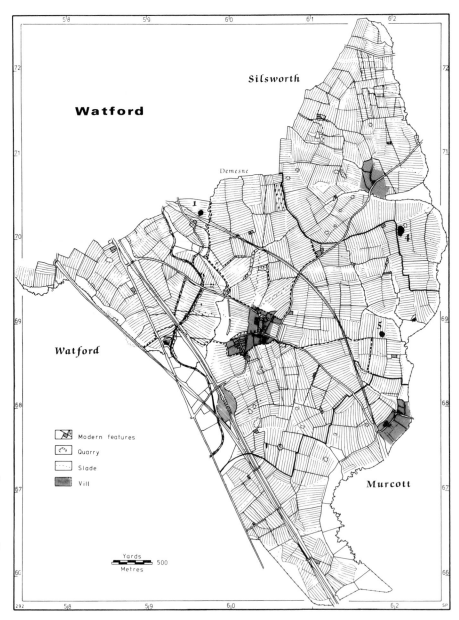

FIGURE 11.1 *Watford parish, showing the vills and townships of Murcott and Silsworth, Northamptonshire. Watford township had two fields and a separate demesne. The numbered sites show pre-medieval settlement, numbers 1 and 4 being Roman, and number 5 early/middle Saxon.*

three medieval settlements and no more, each clearly identifiable with earthworks and presumably to be associated with the vill names most frequently encountered in the documents: Watford, Murcott and Silsworth. The remaining area was completely filled by open-field strips, save for rather small parcels of meadow alongside brooks. No separate physical identity could be discovered for settlements that might be associated with the Catesby manor or Cumberford depopulated village mentioned by Bridges.

Next, all documents relating to the parish were studied for manorial, open-field, and topographical information. Estate maps and deeds were used to collect 'modern' field names; these names were needed to establish the enclosure history, locate furlongs, and to identify different townships, should they prove to exist.[32] The township structure was elucidated fairly easily. At the north-west of Watford is a curved line, consisting of a hedge placed on furlong boundaries, that looks like an ancient township boundary, since the furlongs either side of it do not relate. Silsworth was enclosed early, and from surveys of its hedged fields made in 1678 it was possible to confirm that the curve was part of the boundary and to identify the remainder on the north-east.[33] Murcott was enclosed in 1771 with Watford and there is a map distinguishing the territories of each township.[34] (Murcott is complicated by being partly in Watford parish and partly in the parish of neighbouring Long Buckby, which will be explained later.) Studies of the spacial distribution of the furlongs that belonged to the open fields showed that the ancient township division of Watford and Murcott was as indicated on the 1771 map.[35] The parish of Watford is thus shown to contain three townships, each with its own nucleated vill (figure 11.1).

From charter evidence the field-system structure of the townships was as follows. For Murcott, no medieval data survive for the field arrangements. A terrier of 1686 describes three fields, but there is also an area called Upper and Lower Ryehill.[36] At enclosure in 1771 it was stated that the arable was cropped three years and left fallow the fourth and that the rye hills were cropped one year and fallow the next.[37] These appear to be post-medieval modifications of cropping systems. For Silsworth, a charter of 1315 lists various furlongs distributed between three fields named West, North and South Fields.[38] Other charters give isolated names but few of the furlongs can be identified because

[32] Northamptonshire RO, maps 3159 (1760); 3158 (1771); 3162 (c. 1820); T41 (1847); 1932 Field-names.

[33] Northamptonshire RO, ZA 800; Northingworth Close, in the north-east angle with Silsworth, is stated to be part of Silsworth township in this document, but in error, which arises because it was grouped with neighbouring Vicars Field; the latter and Cooks Field are stated to be in Silsworth in 1626 (BHK 144).

[34] Northamptonshire RO, map 834.

[35] Worked out from the field names referred to in n. 32 and the terriers in nn. 36 and 40; space does not allow publication of the names.

[36] Northamptonshire RO, L56.

[37] Northamptonshire RO, map 834.

[38] Northamptonshire RO, OK 274.

almost no names have survived in the present-day fields, enclosure being so early. There is no information about the whereabouts of the demesne which was 14 yardlands in 1276, but there is an 'inland' furlong, suggesting that some of it lay in a block.[39]

Watford fields and furlongs mentioned in several charters dating from the mid-thirteenth century onwards show that there was a two-field system.[40] A complication arises with the demesne, which is fully described in 1276 and consisted of a limited number of whole furlongs whose names do not occur in the charters that relate to peasant holdings. The implication is that the demesne was a discrete area of the township and not intermixed with the tenants' land. This is confirmed by a detailed description of the manor called Cumberford, belonging to Richard, Lord Spencer, in 1595: the manor was a quarter of the original medieval manor of Watford (split off in 1276: see below); its demesne was intermixed with the other three-quarters belonging to Richard Burneby, and the purpose of the survey was to arrange an exchange of lands, because the whole had recently been enclosed by Burneby.[41] This action had caused the newly formed pasture closes to contain small blocks of Spencer's lands, clearly not very convenient. The Cumberford lands were described and marked out by witnesses, enabling the whole original undivided demesne to be identified as a large single block next to the vill and manor house on the north (figure 11.1). The presence of the demesne probably prevented the usual transition to a three-field arrangement, it being impossible to have three contiguous blocks (essential for fallow grazing) if one part of the total was in a fixed position. There were still two fields in 1627, but by 1632 a four-field arrangement was in use; court orders and regulations survive for this period.[42] Each yardland was allowed 40 sheep and 8 large beasts.[43] After partial enclosure in 1644 there was re-arrangement of the surviving half-township into four fields again, which lasted until parliamentary enclosure in 1771.[44]

The structure of the parish and townships can be further studied by the remarkable survey of 1276.[45] A strongly feudal manor is indicated by 19 yardlands in demesne worked by the holders of 35½ villein yardlands; there were 5⅛ cottar yardlands and 36½ belonging to freemen. However, as 25 of these free yardlands were the demesnes of Silsworth and Murcott, the real figure for freemen was 12 yardlands and the total demesne of 46 shows a dominant seignorial presence. Eustace de Watford, lord of the manor, had died in 1275 leaving four daughters; until then the manor had descended as a single

---

[39] ibid.; see n. 47 for the 1276 survey.

[40] Northamptonshire RO, OK 151 (c.1250); OK 140 (1320); OK 204 (c.1400); OK 32 (1627).

[41] Northamptonshire RO, OK 354.

[42] Northamptonshire RO, OK 32; OK 176.

[43] Northamptonshire RO, OK 186.

[44] Bridges, *History and Antiquities*, vol. II, p. 585; Northamptonshire RO, map 834.

[45] *Calendar of Close Rolls*, 4 Edward I, pp. 326–31.

entity since 1066, but in 1276 it was to be split equally between the four daughters, Atheline wife of William de Bray, Sarah the wife of John de Burneby, Joan the wife of William Parles, and Elena who was unmarried. The demesne and the villein holdings were split exactly equally between the four; the manor house was physically partitioned into three for the married daughters; the Burnebys had the overlordship of Silsworth, held by Edmund de Watford, and Joan and William Parles had the overlordship of Murcott, held by John, son of Philip de Daventry of Murcott. The total of yardlands for Watford parish was 96⅝, which was presumably meant to be 96. This includes the other two hamlets, Murcott being mentioned by name, and a freehold of 14 yardlands belonged to Edmund de Watford, whose family are known to be possessors of Silsworth. The assignment of yardlands to each township can be deduced as follows.

Murcott is stated to be 24 yardlands in 1705 and 24½ in 1771, the earlier figure probably being more accurate.[46] A continuity of holdings with previous centuries is clear from the 11-yardland freehold of John de Daventry in 1276, which is the same size as the chief holding belonging to the Spencers in 1771; presumably it was the demesne of this township since the Spencers had manorial rights over the fields.[47] Watford was also 24 yardlands in 1705 and 1771; at this date the figure refers only to the open-field land, the northern half being enclosed. Thus the size of Watford was originally 48 yardlands, and by deduction Silsworth was 24. The 96 yardlands are clearly related to the assessment of Watford parish as 4 hides in c.1124,[48] each hide being taken as 24 yardlands, and so Watford township was 2 hides, and Silsworth and Murcott were 1 hide each. At the time of the Domesday Survey in 1086, Watford was assessed at 2 hides,[49] the disparity between this and the 1124 value long being a puzzle to historians. An interpretation is now possible: the Domesday assessors gave the figure for Watford township only, missing out the two dependent vills and townships. The numerical analysis also implies that they existed in 1124, which was not previously known (apart from the archaeological finds at Silsworth).

The information given by Bridges can be explained from the above evidence and the subsequent manorial descent, of which the relevant items are as follows. Eustace de Burneby, son of John and Sarah, inherited his own quarter of the estate and acquired two more quarters from Elena de Watford and the de Brays. This three-quarters descended as the main Watford manor through the Burnebys until Sir Richard Burneby sold it to Sir George Clarke in 1623. Joan and William Parles's quarter passed to their descendants until heiress Joan Parles (born in 1448) married John Cumberford — hence the name

[46] Northamptonshire RO, Glebe terrier 1705; map 834.

[47] *Calendar of Close Rolls*, Edward I, 1272–9, p. 329; Northamptonshire RO, map 834.

[48] *VCH Northamptonshire*, vol. I, p. 387.

[49] F. Thorn and C. Thorn, *Domesday Book, Northamptonshire* (London, 1979), pp. 57–62.

Cumberford's manor for this quarter. It passed to the Spencer family in *c*.1590, and always had Murcott with it.[50]

The Cumberford manor, one of the quarters descending from a married daughter of Eustace de Watford, in 1276 had one-third of the original single manor house of the de Watfords. This is confirmed in 1620 when Cumberford's farm was stated to be in 'Watford towne' and that Sir George Clarke, the grantor, was unable to assign a gallery or garret on top of his manor house or a right of way through Cumberford's farm (because they did not belong to him);[51] in 1640 William Spencer owned the site of the manor of Cumberford 'adjacent to the courtyard and nere the capital messuage of Sir George Clarke'.[52] It is clear, therefore, from the established locations of the house and the demesne that Cumberford manor was really part of Watford main manor in origin, and that it is represented by the earthworks of Watford and that no other separate site need be sought elsewhere in the parish.

Silsworth, although a dependency of Watford manor, had separate ownership and descent. From a branch of the de Watford family in 1276 (and assigned to Sarah and John de Burneby of Watford), it descended to heiress Margaret Watford in the late fourteenth century; she married Robert de Cranford, lord of neighbouring Ashby St Ledgers. From that time Silsworth and Ashby were linked, coming through Robert's daughter Emma to the Catesby family. Hence the name Catesby's Manor at Watford refers primarily to Silsworth, although there was some land in Watford as well.[53] Hence, Bridges's statements about the manors and vills are explained.

Watford and Murcott villages are small and shrunken but Silsworth is quite deserted and has been for many centuries. As usual no precise date can be obtained for the desertion; an inquisition of 1429 refers to a messuage with a yardland and appurtenances, but that is the last indication suggesting that a normal village community existed.[54] By 1495 the township's fields are referred to as 490 acres of pasture and 300 acres of arable.[55] In 1590 the whole township was pasture and belonged to Richard Burneby.[56] The Catesby family, the owners in the fifteenth century, were not noted for being enclosers; their main possession, Ashby St Ledgers, remained open until 1764.[57] However, there was probably more interaction than normal between the two townships because of the common lordship. It is possible that after the fourteenth-century decline of population known to have occurred throughout the country, Silsworth,

---

[50] Bridges, *History and Antiquities*, vol. II, pp. 586–7.

[51] Northamptonshire RO, OK 27.

[52] Northamptonshire RO, OK 48.

[53] Bridges, *History and Antiquities*, vol. II, pp. 587–8.

[54] Northamptonshire RO, ASL 57.

[55] Bridges, *History and Antiquities*, vol. II, p. 588; Silsworth sounds empty in a 1487 grant of 'meadow, leys, pasture and crofts' (Northamptonshire RO, OK 77).

[56] Northamptonshire RO, XYZ 70 and 74.

[57] Northamptonshire RO, ASL 420 and 880.

already small, became smaller and that there was some drift of population to Ashby St Ledgers or the Watford townships, leaving Silsworth empty, and ripe for enclosure (an alternative method of obtaining income from its lands, there being too few people resident to plough them). A specific 'catastrophic' event causing its desertion probably did not occur and need not be sought.

The enclosure history of Murcott and Silsworth has already been touched upon, Murcott being a 1771 parliamentary enclosure.[58] At that time all of its open fields were, in terms of tithes, part of Long Buckby parish, except for 11 yardlands in the hands of the Spencers, which belonged to Watford. This holding, the same size as held as the freehold in 1276, and in 1648, is almost certainly the manorial demesne of the village, unchanged over the centuries.[59] At some time the remainder of the tithes had been given to the church of neighbouring Long Buckby. Until enclosure all the lands of both churches were intermixed, but afterwards one of the new allotments and the old enclosure that went with it, belonging to the Spencers, was defined as Watford parish. Thus a parish boundary was created between Long Buckby and Watford, dividing up the township of Murcott into two. Previous to 1771 open-field holdings in Murcott spread either side of this line. This example illustrates the danger of accepting, without confirmation, modern or eighteenth-century boundaries as being medieval.

The enclosure history of Watford is complex, as already indicated. Apart from very small encroachments on the open fields adding to the village tofts (three lands and a balk between the Daventry road and Grotencroft furlong were walled in so that Emma de Watford could enlarge her garden and vineyard in 1303), there was no enclosure until most of the demesne was enclosed in 1595 (a few furlongs lay away from the main block and were not enclosed).[60] The next event was the enclosure of one of the two fields, the north field. The reason seems to have been the desire to create a park around the manor house. An avenue of trees aligned westwards at right-angles from the front of the building was set by Sir George Clarke,[61] but the enclosed demesne did not quite lie in the necessary direction and so further land was required. Several exchanges of property show that he had consolidation of lands in mind; in 1628 William Rogers was granted a yardland 'in the Nether End Field and not elsewhere', and in 1632 Gifford Naseby exchanged land.[62] The Spencers had leased Cumberford manor to Sir George Clarke and finally sold the Watford, but not the Murcott, part to him in 1640, and the park is first mentioned in the same year.[63] The date of enclosure was 1644; no more open-

[58] Northamptonshire RO, maps 834 and 3158.
[59] Northamptonshire RO, BHK 248; AhI.6.
[60] Northamptonshire RO, OK 155.
[61] Northamptonshire RO, map 3161 (1740).
[62] Northamptonshire RO, OK 40; OK 176.
[63] Northamptonshire RO, OK 113 and 338; BHK 237.

field lands are described in the north after then and several of the closes formed are named in 1648.[64] The remaining half of the township survived until parliamentary enclosure along with Murcott in 1771.

To summarize the findings from Watford, the parish consisted of three settlements, each with its own independent field system, two of them being three-field and the other two-field. The two hamlets were subordinate to Watford manorially. The total number of peasant holdings was a round figure relating precisely to the Domesday and other early assessments. The demesne of Watford township lay mostly in a block next to the manor house. Silsworth was deserted early and enclosed in the fifteenth century; Watford was enclosed in three stages in 1595, 1644 and 1771, the seventeenth-century partial enclosure relating to emparkment. Murcott was a parliamentary enclosure of 1771, although the tithe history meant that part of it lay in neighbouring Long Buckby parish. The township boundary of Murcott follows the furlongs whereas most of Silsworth is a smooth line that predates them. This last township would therefore seem to be the older of the two. Both townships must be older than Domesday, confirmed in the case of Silsworth by pottery discoveries.

Watford and its townships illustrate findings now frequently being made that parishes, villages and townships are often more complex than they seem. Whether Murcott and Silsworth are to be seen as dependent hamlets split away from Watford at a date after its own foundation, or whether they are two quite independent vills that have been taken over administratively by Watford, is open to conjecture. The evidence points to the latter argument; the two hamlets are undoubtedly pre-Conquest, and perhaps settlement in the parish should be seen as consisting of four middle Saxon vills initially, one of them being deserted and one, Watford, later absorbing the remaining two administratively by the middle ages. The whole process of vill settlement and manorial consolidation to form a medieval 'parish' has to be considered in parallel with the evidence for township formation by breakdown of multiple Saxon estates. The two mechanisms are opposed and doubtless the balance varied from area to area, giving the wide range of types found in the English countryside.

CONCLUSION

The case of Watford shows how field-system studies, using both ground and historical evidence, can contribute to an understanding of settlement, and demonstrates the importance of field systems in attempting to understand estate and manorial history. Fields are so much more than just something that happen to lie around a vill; their intimate connection with manors, demesne and fiscal

---

[64] Bridges, *History and Antiquities*, vol. II, p. 585; Northamptonshire RO, AhI.6 and BHK 248.

assessments means that they are a valuable complement to excavation and other techniques used to study rural settlement in England. More detailed work of this type in different regions of the country will lead to a better understanding of the middle ages. It is essential to have a large sample such as ten adjacent townships or preferably a large part of a county. Although fieldwork on a moderately large scale has become accepted by rescue archaeology as a method of assessing the pre-Saxon periods, it has yet to be recognized (by funding survey projects) that there is a threat to medieval remains. A visit to Strixton after fifteen years showed that its furlong boundaries had been seriously eroded by recent agriculture, and they will not survive indefinitely. For the future a massive survey is required so that the whole country is recorded. We can then use historical material to form theories about the real data.

12

Whittlesford: The Study of a River-edge Village

C. C. TAYLOR

INTRODUCTION (FIGURE 12.1)

In 1967 I published an article on the village of Whiteparish, Wiltshire, which was an attempt to summarize the development of a village and its land through time.[1] This work was made possible by two important factors. The first was that I had lived in the village for five years, and as a result it was possible to appreciate all the minutiae of its landscape far better than if it had been merely a place visited regularly. The second, and much more important, factor was that in those days I was a young man, educated in traditional, not to say old-fashioned, historical and geographical theories of landscape development which had gradually evolved over fifty years and which had culminated in the publication of perhaps the most seminal work ever written on the English landscape.[2] As a result I was able to produce a neat and convincing story which purported to show how the village of Whiteparish had changed over a period of some 2000 years.

For the last twenty years I have lived in the village of Whittlesford, Cambridgeshire, and it has been possible to examine the landscape of that parish in even greater detail than at Whiteparish. More vital, I have been subjected to the ferment of modern scholarship in a variety of disciplines which has changed most if not all of the traditional ideas of the development of the English landscape. It has long been a hope that one day it would be possible to repeat the original paper, but taking as its subject Whittlesford. This has, alas, proved impossible, not because of any lack of enthusiasm, time or energy, but because of other less obvious but more pertinent reasons. The purpose of this paper is to explain this failure. In doing so, as will become clear, the paper is

---

[1] C. C. Taylor, 'Whiteparish, a study of the development of a forest edge parish', *Wiltshire Archaeological Magazine*, 62 (1967), pp. 79–102.
[2] W. G. Hoskins, *The Making of the English Landscape* (London, 1955).

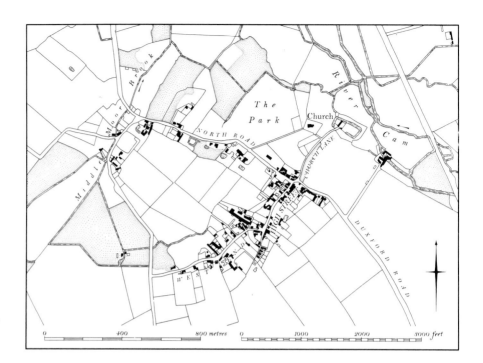

FIGURE 12.1 *Whittlesford, Cambridgeshire, in the early nineteenth century.*

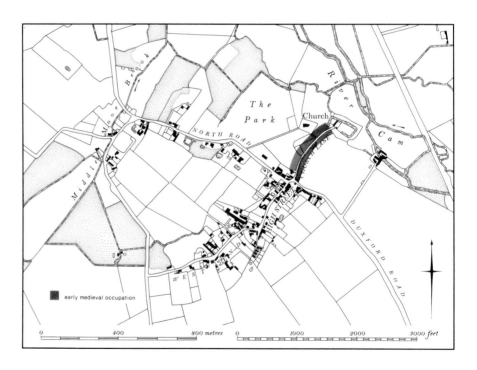

FIGURE 12.2 *Whittlesford: early medieval occupation.*

not so much the study of the development of a village, but more the development of a mind.

The village of Whittlesford lies 10 km south of Cambridge on the west side of the river Cam. According to the existing geological maps, almost the whole of the south-western part of the village is situated on Lower Chalk at the foot of a very low and degraded north-west-facing scarp formed by an outcrop of the Melbourne Rock, a hard band of chalk rock within the Lower Chalk. Thus this part of the village is on a spring-line. All the surrounding land is mapped as Lower Chalk or as river gravel.

If the building development of the last 150 years is ignored the village has a relatively simple form. It consists of a single main street lying at the foot of the Melbourne Rock scarp, extending in a south-west to north-east direction and with four marked changes of alignment. The south-west part is known as West End, the north-east as High Street. At its north end this street is crossed by another road running south-east to north-west, generally following the line of the river Cam. The actual junction of this road (known as North Road and Duxford Road to the north-west and south-east respectively) with the High Street is oddly staggered. Beyond this junction, the line of High Street continues north-east and is here called Church Lane. It crosses an almost flat area mapped as river gravel and leading to the isolated parish church and a moated site, both situated above the flood plain of the Cam. Beyond the village there is nothing of special note except for a scatter of cottages and farm houses and another abandoned moated site, all strung out along North Road and the Middle Moor Brook.

THE FIRST STAGE (FIGURE 12.2)

My initial view of Whittlesford in the late 1960s was tinged with disappointment. Unlike Whiteparish, there were no interesting problems connected with the exploitation of a forested environment. There was only a simple, nucleated village sited with due regard for all the obvious physical determinants, surrounded until the early nineteenth century by its common fields and all little changed since early Saxon times. A rapid check of the easily available historical sources revealed a dearth of information, reflecting no doubt the utter normality of the place. No local historian had, it seemed, ever looked at it, no major landlord or institution had ever owned it and even its pre-Saxon past was unknown except for vague and unverified reports of 'tumuli' said to be of iron age date in the extreme west of the parish destroyed in the nineteenth century.[3]

Whittlesford seemed a poor candidate for research, especially at a time when

[3] C. Fox, *The Archaeology of the Cambridge Region* (Cambridge, 1923).

the writer was engaged on unravelling the topographical histories of much more complex villages in north-east Cambridgeshire.[4] Nevertheless the first interpretation of the village was taken. The name of Whittlesford is simple. It is the ford of a man called Wit(t)el,[5] and thus the village was presumably named from a ford which crossed the Cam and, though no ford now exists, it was clear that there must have been one, presumably near the church, situated at the point where the projected alignment of Church Lane met the river.

The shape of the village was therefore easy to explain. The line of West End, High Street and Church Lane was that of an old track which once ran down to the Cam, crossing it at a ford. Whittlesford must have grown up along this track, its morphology conditioned entirely by the winding nature of the track and thus developing into a single-street settlement duly sited on a spring-line. The church would have then been established above the ford and next to the site of the major manor house, the latter represented by the later moated site.

The only real problem was to explain why the church and the moated site were now detached from the rest of the village. To a fieldworker who had only recently completed surveys of large numbers of shrunken villages in Dorset,[6] this was easily solved. There must once have been occupation all along Church Lane which, perhaps as a result of a decline in population, had been abandoned. No earthworks indicative of settlement existed there partly because of modern housing and partly because of later eighteenth-century landscaping. Nevertheless, with the permission and forebearance of a growing number of friends in the village, careful examination of gardens and shrubberies produced enough pottery of thirteenth- and fourteenth-century date to confirm that the area had been occupied in medieval times. The origin and growth of Whittlesford seemed obvious.

CONSOLIDATION (FIGURE 12.3)

The ease by which the layout of Whittlesford had been explained by traditional methods and ideas encouraged me to look at the villages in the surrounding area. Whittlesford is one of thirteen villages which lie along the river Cam south of Cambridge. Of these, eight have names which end with 'ford' and all but two have one or more main streets which trend generally south-west to north-east as at Whittlesford. The same is true of all the villages further north-east in the valley of the Linton branch of the Cam. In effect, almost every village along two adjacent river valleys had a superficially similar morphology.

This seemed to indicate a common factor at work and the only one which

[4] RCHM (England), *North-East Cambridgeshire* (London, 1972).
[5] P. H. Reaney, *The Place Names of Cambridgeshire* (Cambridge, 1943), p. 98.
[6] RCHM (England), *Dorset*, vols I-V (London, 1970–5).

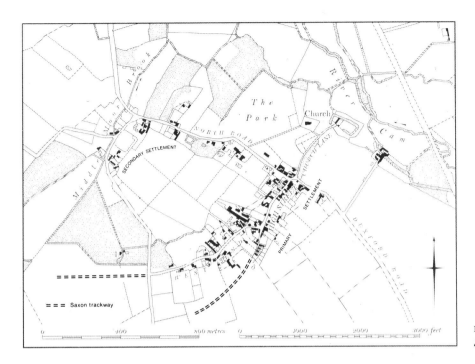

FIGURE 12.3 *Whittlesford: the Saxon trackway.*

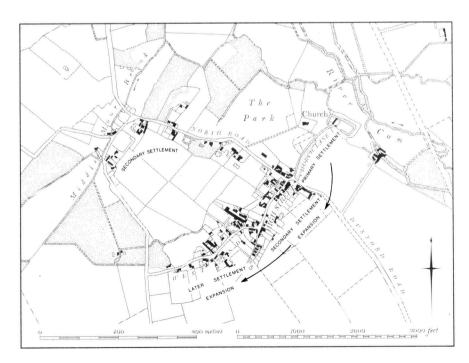

FIGURE 12.4 *Whittlesford: medieval expansion.*

provided a satisfactory explanation was communication. Today there is but one major route across the area from south-west to north-east, the present A505–A11 trunk road. All other main roads run south-east to north-west towards Cambridge along the river valleys. Yet where these latter roads intersect the village streets a curious pheonomenon is visible. At Duxford and Ickleton, to the south of Whittlesford, the valley-edge road turns into the main streets, following their full length and then turns equally sharply back again onto its original direction. Even at Whittlesford the staggered junction where the North Road–Duxford Road crosses the High Street–Church Lane line is a miniature version of this same discontinuity of the river-edge road system.

The only explanation for this seemed to be that when these villages were established, they were related to a broad communications system which lay across the valleys of the Cam in a south-west to north-east direction. The prime candidate for such a system was the Icknield Way which was alleged to have traversed the open chalk downlands of south Cambridgeshire in prehistoric and Roman times. It was thus possible to suggest that the real Icknield Way was not a single track, but a broad zone of communication perhaps 10–12 km wide and made up of numerous individual trackways. When these trackways reached the two branches of the Cam, they converged and crossed by means of fords.

Thus, when Whittlesford and its neighbours were established, these 'Icknield Way' tracks were still in existence and the villages were aligned along them and acquired their long 'street' form. The present north-west to south-east river-edge routes along the valley either did not then exist or, more likely, were much less significant. Only later, when the importance of the Icknield Way declined and the major movement of traffic tended to be in a north-west to south-east direction, did the riverside routes develop. Eventually the multiple tracks of the Icknield Way were reduced to a single main road (the A505–A11) and the remnants left as green lanes or field roads. Only in the main street of the villages did the original alignments survive.

This theory, later published,[7] gave support to the explanation for the growth of Whittlesford in a number of ways. The High Street–Church Lane line could now be seen as one of the routes of the Icknield Way running down to a ford across the river near the church. The theory also explained the marked bend at the junction of High Street and West End; for though West End turns sharply west at the end of High Street, the line of the latter is continued south-west for a short distance by a lane now called Orchard Terrace. This lane, now cul-de-sac, must have once have run on as another track. Thus it seemed that Whittlesford lay just north-east of where two of the old Icknield Way tracks converged and ran down to the ford as a single route. With the decline of the Icknield Way the southern track was abandoned as a through road while the north branch, West

[7] C. C. Taylor, *Roads and Tracks of Britain* (London, 1979), pp. 106–8.

End, survived as a field road and the way to the next village, Thriplow, to the west.

This concept of the Icknield Way also explained the scattered dwellings and the moated site lying along North Road and the Middle Moor Brook. Most of them lay on or near the river-edge road leading to Cambridge which could thus be seen as a secondary route. This somewhat dispersed settlement, therefore, set as it was on rather wet and unsuitable terrain could be interpreted as a secondary phase of settlement expansion in an area of poor land, along the road which was developing in importance.

At this stage, therefore, the origins and development of Whittlesford seemed even clearer, not the least because they appeared to fit into a wider local pattern.

THE FIRST PROBLEMS (FIGURE 12.4)

So far the interpretation of the development of Whittlesford village had been based on obvious topographical considerations. A start was then made on the written record.

It was decided to begin by attempting to ascertain how large Whittlesford had been in the past in terms of population. Without this information it seemed impossible to prove that the suggested secondary expansion and the Church Lane shrinkage had taken place at all. Whittlesford proved to have a reasonably good set of population statistics.[8]

The first indication of its size is in Domesday Book. There the recorded population totals thirty-three. Following the normally accepted theory that the individuals listed probably represented heads of households, the total population of Whittlesford was perhaps between 130 and 165. The next record is the hundred rolls for 1279 where 105 tenants are listed. Again, this may mean that the population in the late thirteenth century was between 420 and 525, a massive increase on the 1086 figure.

In 1327 only 33 people in Whittlesford paid the lay subsidy but R. E. Glasscock then suggested in discussion that this probably indicated a population of around 300 or perhaps a little more. The 142 people over the age of fourteen who paid the poll tax of 1377 probably indicate an actual population of around 200. This apparent fall in population levelled off in the fifteenth century, according to the evidence of a tithing roll for 1477 which gives a figure of 75 men over the age of twelve, suggesting a population of around 200. Nearly a century later, in 1563, there were 49 families in the parish, perhaps between 190 and 250 people. These figures point to Whittlesford being relatively small in the eleventh century, growing rapidly in the following 200 years and then declining.

---

[8] *VCH Cambridgeshire*, vol. VI, p. 263.

The post-medieval population records were also examined. The hearth tax returns of 1664 and 1674 suggest that the village had around 300 people, indicating an increase from the late sixteenth century, though a local census in 1728 gave a population of 260 to 280 people. During the late eighteenth century there is no doubt that Whittlesford increased in size for the 1801 census records 416 people in the parish. This rapid increase continued and in 1841 there were 579 people, and in 1891 there were 875.

The next task was to attempt to relate these figures to the landscape of the village itself, a difficult and perhaps dangerous exercise. Using the 1817 enclosure map it was possible to relate the size of Whittlesford then to the 1801 population. At that time the 400 or so people occupied about eighty dwellings of which fifteen lay outside the village proper, along North Road and in the Middle Moor area. In 1728 there were only sixty-three families in the parish and, even allowing for multiple occupancy of houses, the village may have been physically perhaps one-quarter smaller then than it was by 1817.

Moving back to the sixteenth century, the forty-nine families of 1563 suggest a village only two-thirds the size of the 1817 village and the same may be true of the period 1377 and 1477. All these figures, unreliable though they may be, indicate that from the late fourteenth century to the mid-eighteenth century Whittlesford was unlikely to have been the large compact village that is depicted on the enclosure map. If the dwellings occupied the same area as in in 1817, then there must have been many open spaces within its boundaries. Otherwise it must have been relatively small and occupied an area far less extensive than in 1817.

The 1279 figure, if the estimate of 420–525 is correct, gives a very different picture, for Whittlesford then had a higher population than it was to have until well into the nineteenth century. It seemed possible that in the late thirteenth century the village, in terms of its physical size and shape, may well have been close to the 1817 situation.

Here the evidence of contraction, discovered earlier along Church Lane, seemed important. The pottery discovered there extended to no later in date than the fourteenth century. It was likely that the large late thirteenth-century population could have been occupying the area of both the early nineteenth-century village and along both sides of Church Lane. If this assumption was correct, then the thirteenth-century village occupied a larger area than the nineteenth century one yet with roughly the same population. It therefore may have been far less nucleated or compact then than it was in more recent times.

The postulation of these theories occurred at a time when I was beginning work on the villages of Northamptonshire and being thus involved in the problems of interpretation of large areas of abandoned settlement earthworks around existing villages. Though normally said to be the result of 'shrinkage', it was soon apparent that in Northamptonshire at least many of these remains could not be explained by simple shrinkage, not least because there was no evidence of a decline in population which could have led to the abandonment of such extensive areas. As a result the concept of village mobility was conceived, whereby it was argued that villages moved about and thus areas of abandoned settlement could often be better explained as the product of displacement and movement of villages rather than massive decline.[9]

Applying this concept to Whittlesford, a new possibility emerged: this was that the eleventh-century village had occupied only the Church Lane area. The increasing size of the village in the twelfth century took the form of an extension west along High Street as far as the West End–Orchard Terrace junction. The presumed later expansion along West End could then have been accompanied by an abandonment of the Church Lane area perhaps in the thirteenth or fourteenth centuries. Why this should have taken place was unknown, but both the possibility of the expansion of demesne land around the moated manor house with the consequent removal of the Church Lane dwellings, together with the decline of the through road across the ancient ford, were considered.

Despite these complications, the story of Whittlesford appeared to be emerging. It looked as if there had been a small Saxon village, established on an ancient track-way at a river crossing. This village expanded rapidly after the eleventh century and involved both the extension south-west along the old track and perhaps the growth of a small secondary settlement at Middle Moor consequent upon the change in the communication pattern. Towards the end of this period of expansion there may have been further movement south-west along one of the tracks of the former Icknield Way with the simultaneous abandonment of the original village site. In the later fourteenth century, with a reduction in population, the village became less nucleated but covered the same area. Thereafter it remained fairly stable until the population increase in the eighteenth century, when there was a tendency for it to become rather more compact again.

NEW IDEAS AND FAILURE (FIGURE 12.5)

This neat explanation soon began to fall apart, partly as a result of new information on the village itself and partly because of my work elsewhere. The latter was perhaps the most important, for it involved the concept of polyfocal villages. The original idea was developed by an extra-mural class which I ran, and was based on the village of Great Shelford, only 4 km away to the north.[10]

---

[9] C. C. Taylor, 'Aspects of village mobility in medieval and later times', in *The Effect of Man on the Landscape: The Lowland Zone*, ed. S. Limbrey and J. G. Evans (CBA Research Report 21, 1979), pp. 126–34; RCHM (England), *Northamptonshire*, vols I–IV (London, 1975–82).

[10] C. C. Taylor (ed.), *Domesday to Dormitory* (Cambridge, 1971).

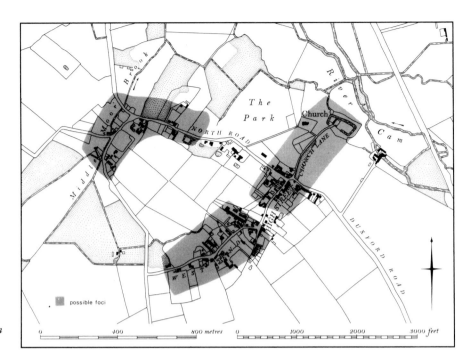

FIGURE 12.5 *Whittlesford: a polyfocal village?*

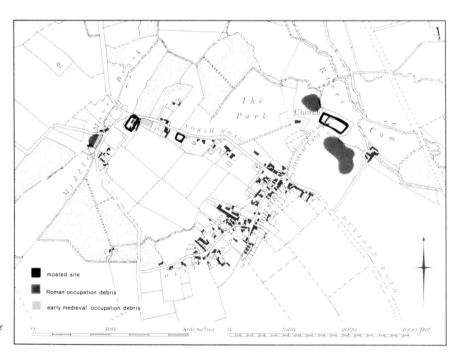

FIGURE 12.6 *Whittlesford: the evidence from fieldwalking.*

This theory was that apparently nucleated villages could have evolved, not by steady growth from one place, but by the coalescence of a number of separate centres which might have Roman or Saxon origins or which could have been the result of deliberately planned additions to an existing centre.

One way of identifying such original foci was the fact that they sometimes represented separate manors occasionally identifiable as early as 1086. This theory certainly worked at Great Shelford and was tested in other places, notably in Northamptonshire.[11] All the villages in south Cambridgeshire were also examined and many, including Whittlesford's near neighbour at Duxford, seemed to be of possible polyfocal origin.[12] It was therefore natural that Whittlesford should be considered as a possibility. What was needed was to identify possible foci and to compile a full account of the manorial descent of the village.

Topographical examination now suggested two possible foci in Whittlesford, one of the main village itself, and the other the scattered detached group of dwellings at Middle Moor. It also seemed just possible that West End might represent a separate focus detached from High Street, for not only was there the difference in alignment in the two streets, but also the slight indications on the enclosure map that a gap had existed between the two blocks in 1817, later filled by a nineteenth-century factory.

This somewhat tenuous evidence for separate foci was dashed by the arrival of the *VCH* account of the history of the village which appeared at that time.[13] There the manorial descent of Whittlesford was clearly laid out and there was no doubt that the village had always been a single manor from the late eleventh century onwards, though with some minor subinfeudation. There thus seemed no chance of explaining the possible foci in tenurial terms and the previous simpler interpretation seemed to be the most logical.

MORE DATA (FIGURE 12.6)

At this stage both world events and local contacts led to major new discoveries. The oil crisis, increasing relative poverty and the drive for self-sufficiency forced me to ask for the use of a village allotment. The parish council granted the request and an allotment was acquired, situated on a patch of gravel close to the Middle Moor Brook. The first season's digging immediately produced not only large quanities of thirteenth- and fourteenth century pottery, but also a little Roman material. Close examination of the adjacent allotments confirmed

---

[11] C. C. Taylor, 'Polyfocal settlement and the English village', *Medieval Archaeology*, 21 (1977), pp. 189–93.

[12] A. E. Brown and C. C. Taylor, 'Cambridgeshire earthwork surveys III', *Proceedings Cambridgeshire Antiquarian Society*, 68 (1978), pp. 69–71.

[13] *VCH Cambridgeshire*, vol. VI, pp. 263–8.

that there was extensive medieval occupation in the area as well as a smaller Roman settlement, probably of the third to fourth century.

Coincidental with these discoveries were others, made as a result of increasing contacts with parishioners. These contacts produced two different kinds of information. One concerned details of the village and its topography in the recent past which could not be gained through maps, the other resulted from access to land which hitherto had been impossible to walk over.

At Rayner's Farm, a fifteenth-century structure in Middle Moor, there is an L-shaped ditch, partly filled, behind the farm buildings. One of the elderly inhabitants of the village, then in his eighties, not only remembered this having a third side, but was confident that this had always been known as a moat. This was confirmed later on when a drawing by a nineteenth-century antiquary was discovered in the County Record Office which indicated that the moat had once surrounded the farm. It now seemed that the hamlet of Middle Moor had had two moated sites, not one, and that perhaps the present dispersed appearance was not the reflection of its past form.

The discovery of medieval and Roman pottery at Middle Moor led to thoughts of more organized fieldwalking to recover information about settlements over the whole parish. The fact that I now knew most of the farmers in the parish made this feasible and all willingly gave permission to walk over their land.

The results of fieldwalking were instructive. Much mesolithic material was discovered, together with evidence for Iron Age and Roman occupation, including a large villa, and at least three other Roman sites, all some distance from the village. More relevant to the story of the development of the village itself was the discovery of Roman pottery in the area east of the church, near the river. At first this latter material did not indicate a very large site, for the area available for examination was only one small arable field. However, the construction of a new village school, some old people's bungalows and an extension to the estate of council houses in the area south-east of the church made possible a find of large amounts of Roman pottery indicating settlement which covered 5 hectares at least.

Another place, which because it was permanently arable allowed fieldwalking to take place, was a small area in Middle Moor adjacent to Rayner's Farm. Here, not only were two house platforms still visible in the ploughland, but both contained quantities of medieval and later pottery. From this it was clear that occupation had existed at this point from the thirteenth to the eighteenth century.

NEW EXPLANATIONS AND FURTHER DIFFICULTIES (FIGURE 12.7)

The evidence from fieldwalking suggested that, in the Roman period at least, the parish was occupied by a number of settlements scattered all across its area.

These included two settlements where the two parts of the medieval village lay. This was a situation already discovered elsewhere in the east midlands.[14] However, nothing had been found to indicate any Saxon settlement within, near or beyond the village. It had, though, shown that the Middle Moor hamlet had, in the thirteenth and fourteenth centuries, been much larger than it was in later times, possibly a fully nucleated settlement rather than a dispersed one. The obvious question was therefore whether the post eleventh-century rise in population the documentary records suggested was actually accommodated at Middle Moor rather than in the main village and whether Middle Moor was thus a late secondary development as a result of that population explosion. However, if that was the case, then it was becoming difficult to see how the presumed population of 420–525 in 1279 could have occupied both parts of the village without assuming that the main High Street–Church Lane section was very thinly occupied. In simple terms, there was an apparent area of occupation in the thirteenth century twice as large as the early nineteenth-century village but with the same population.

The two separate moated sites now known in Middle Moor did, at least, fit into this interpretation. On the assumption that they dated from the twelfth or thirteenth century as seemed likely, they must have been built during this period of maximum population. For whom were they built? Certainly the manorial descent indicated an increase in subinfeudation at this time. A small sub-manor belonging to Barnwell Priory, Cambridge, was certainly leased out in the early thirteenth century to the Cheney family who in turn divided the land amongst a number of under-tenants. One of these moats could have been the home of the Cheney family while the other might have been the home of Baldwin de Freville, a major under-tenant of the Cheneys from sometime before 1333 until sometime after 1350.

Once again, however, new information came to light which led to further doubts and difficulties. In early 1978 the County Council Highways Department decided to improve the rather tight bend in the North Road running north from the main village to Middle Moor. The work involved the re-alignment of the existing road to the west for a distance of 200 m, thus cutting across the south-west edge of the field to its north-west. This field was ancient pasture known as The Park. Naturally the road-works were examined with results which, by now, should have been expected. It became clear that all along the north side of the old road there had been, in the twelfth to fourteenth centuries, a continuous line of occupation. Some of the individual structures there had apparently remained much longer, some until the eighteenth century to judge from finds in two places. This evidence of settlement effectively linked Middle Moor to the outskirts of the main village and greatly increased the

---

[14] RCHM (England), *Northamptonshire*, vols I-IV; C. C. Taylor, 'Roman settlements in the Nene valley', in *Recent Work in Rural Archaeology*, ed. P. J. Fowler (Bradford on Avon, 1975), pp. 107–19.

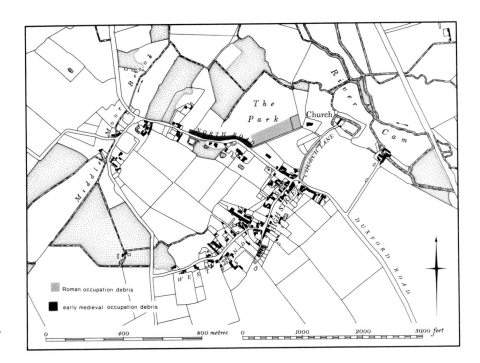

FIGURE 12.7 *Whittlesford: further settlement evidence.*

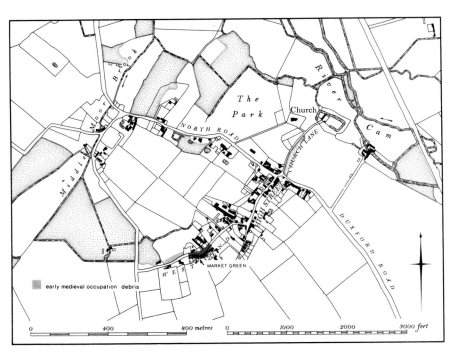

FIGURE 12.8 *Whittlesford: the Market Green.*

apparent size of the thirteenth-century village again. Other material found in the road works included some of Roman date. This indicated that there had been yet another Roman settlement here, but there was still no Saxon material to link it to the twelfth-century occupation.

More archaeological material soon appeared close by. The old Park, pasture for at least two-and-a-half centuries, passed into the hands of new owners who turned it over to arable. Fieldwalking on this land showed that, although the medieval occupation area was still confined to the edge of the old road, the Roman material extended east as far as the church. This indicated that the material, together with that found further to the east and to the south-east of the church, was perhaps all one settlement, covering as much as 10 hectares, partly under the site of the presumed Saxon village but orientated on a different axis.

The new medieval occupation material, disconcerting though it was, could be interpreted. Opposite, on the other side of the road, lay the southernmost of the Middle Moor moats. Was this the sub-manorial centre for the group of the contemporary houses opposite? If so, then the moat at Rayner's Farm might have been the sub-manorial centre to the northern part of Middle Moor, thus forming what in strict terms might be identifiable as two separate settlement areas. It appeared as if the polyfocal idea had some validity after all, this time with an older main focus, the village itself, and two other separate foci developed to the north of it as a result of population expansion and subinfeudation. The wheel of explanation had turned full circle. But had it stopped?

MORE EXPLANATIONS (FIGURE 12.8)

Once again my view of Whittlesford was changed by research elsewhere. At this time I was working on village morphology in Northamptonshire and was puzzled by the existence of greens or open spaces which appeared to have been attached to existing villages as secondary features. Gradually the idea was developed that many of these were perhaps to be associated with the granting of markets in the thirteenth and early fourteenth centuries. That is, these market grants, though they were usually abortive in strict commercial terms, had led to the deliberate establishment of a green or market place where the actual or hoped-for market was to be held. Numerous examples of this process were identified in Northamptonshire and more were noted in Cambridgeshire.[15] It was therefore inevitable that Whittlesford should be examined for this phenomenon. Baldwin de Tony, lord of the manor of Whittlesford in the early fourteenth century, had been granted a weekly market there in 1306 and this

[15] C. C. Taylor, 'Medieval market grants and village morphology', *Landscape History*, 4 (1982), pp. 21–8.

was renewed in 1367. The market was worth nothing by 1460 but at that date rents were still due from some tenements on the 'market green'.[16] It was therefore possible that Whittlesford too had had a new green added to it for a market and that this might have influenced the shape of the village. Where was this green? There seemed no doubt about this, for halfway along West End the street widens to form a small triangular area. Though no longer recognized as a green, at least three of the older inhabitants were quite sure that it had been known as The Green and one, without any prompting, claimed that it was once called The Market Green. Further, from the evidence of the enclosure map it was clear that this green had once been much larger and that the existing seventeenth century buildings, at least on its south-west side, were later encroachments.[17] At once the theory of the market grant seemed confirmed, and it then appeared possible that in fact much of West End could have been developed as a result of the establishment of a market place on the outskirts of the village. Thus, West End, separated as it seemed to have once been from High Street and centred on the Market Green, could have been the result of early fourteenth-century expansion following the establishment of the market. This theory seemed acceptable, though the continuing problem of an increasing area of occupation into which the presumed medieval population had to be fitted, remained. It was made even worse by new fieldwork evidence.

Certainly in the early nineteenth century, according to the enclosure map, the built-up area of West End stopped at the Market Green. Beyond, only two cottages existed, both of which survive, and which are of eighteenth-century date. Up to now it had been assumed that these cottages represented late development beyond the main village. But now new material came to light. During this time I had become involved in assisting with research into a geomorphological process which, in late glacial times, produced what are known as ground ice hollows.[18] One of the reasons behind the research project was that south Cambridgeshire, and the Whittlesford area in particular, has very large areas of this geomorphological phenomenon. It is best developed in low-lying areas of poor drainage and thus all the valleys of small streams as well as the edges of the river Cam have well-marked hummocky ground. On the north side of West End, beyond the Market Green, the existing pasture field had evidence of this and the area had always been ignored as a place of former settlement. Now, however, it was looked at more carefully with the result that a number of slight house platforms were identified close to the road. The fact that they were situated on the hummocky ground which appeared largely undisturbed and with no traces of closes or gardens behind them suggested that

[16] VCH Cambridgeshire, vol. VI, p. 270.

[17] J. Allen, 'The sad tale of Samual Richard', Whither Whittlesford? (Whittlesford Society Magazine, no. 28, 1982).

[18] A. G. Taylor, 'Late Devensian ground-ice hollows in southern Cambridgeshire' (unpublished Ph. D. thesis, CNAA, 1981).

these house sites, whatever their date, represented buildings which had a comparatively short life. The area was subsequently ploughed up and produced small quantities of fourteenth-century pottery. The opposite side of West End is now built over but examination of some of the gardens there produced no real evidence of early settlement and only the occasional medieval sherd was discovered.

This geomorphological research also indicated that, though the presumed original centre of the village lay on glacial sands and gravels, not river terraces as previously mapped, the present main part of the village of High Street and West End is actually situated in what must have been extremely wet and boggy land, immediately below the outcrop of the Melbourne Rock. Again local information supported this by identifying the course of the 'Village Ditch', now long since altered and culverted, which extended along part of the village street. This seems to have been a not entirely successful attempt to drain the village at some time. Indeed, flooding of parts of the village, as a result of poor drainage, was a recurrent feature even in recent times and has only been solved by modern drainage works.

All this new evidence suggested that the physical siting of Whittlesford was by no means as ideal as it had hitherto appeared, and not for the first time I was led to doubt the simplistic role of geographical determinism.

GROWING DOUBTS (FIGURE 12.9)

By now I had doubts as to whether I could any longer explain the development of the village. Long hours were spent in perusing the village landscape and re-examining documents but no clear picture emerged. Then, one evening while looking at the enclosure map yet again, a new and hitherto totally unnoticed feature came to light which changed the interpretation of Whittlesford yet again.

The main village public house stands a little to the north-west of the central cross-roads. In front of it is a large and convenient car park. It is a village tradition that the squire of Whittlesford, who owns the public house, had at some time in the past 'stolen' a piece of land from the village to provide this car park. The enclosure map had always made it clear that this 'event' had taken place in 1817 in the lifetime of the squire's great-great-great-grandfather who, on enclosure, had been quite legally allotted a rectangular piece of common land on the side of the street and in front of what was then a farm – so much for local tradition! This small enclosure had been obvious from the beginning of the study but its significance was not appreciated. Indeed, even when the idea of the existence of a market place following the 1306 market grant was being followed up this space was seriously considered as a possible site for it. It was

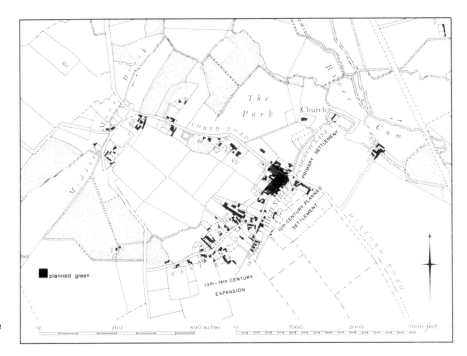

FIGURE 12.9 *Whittlesford: a planned green?*

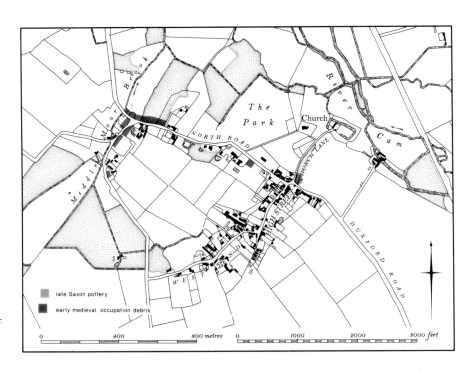

FIGURE 12.10 *Whittlesford: the evidence from Rayner's Grove and Church Lane.*

only rejected when what seemed to be a better market green was discovered in West End.

The evidence from the enclosure map was related to this open space in front of the public house. For, indistinctly shown on the enclosure map, there appeared to be a very narrow lane extending from the south corner of the open space, south-west, parallel to and 50 m from the High Street. This lane was only 75 m long and at its south-west end appeared to turn through 90° and run into High Street at a point where the latter changed direction slightly. This lane does not exist today. Its line was subsequently cut by the construction of access to the late nineteenth-century village school and by the erection of nineteenth-century cottages within and across older plots. Yet renewed and careful investigation on the ground revealed that traces of the lane did indeed survive, partly in a few old property boundaries and partly in the building line of a row of eighteenth-century cottages.

This at once suggested that the area between the High Street and the lost lane might once have been an open space or rectangular 'green' which, because at its north corner it met the former open space in front of the public house, might have originally been a much larger L-shaped green. If this was so then the original centre of the village must have had a remarkably rectangular, even planned, appearance. Did this mean that the original 'Saxon' village, for which there was still no evidence, was confined only to the area of Church Lane on the old Icknield Way track just before it reached the ford and that the north-east end of High Street was a later planned addition with a green perhaps of the twelfth century? This certainly fitted in with the writer's then current interest in planned villages.[19] This very large planned green must then have been mainly built over or encroached upon so that a new market green was necessary by the early fourteenth century.

CONFUSION (FIGURE 12.10)

The accumulating evidence was now outrunning my ability to assimilate it into a coherent form. Yet worse was to come. In 1981 the new farming enterprise which had already ploughed The Park turned its attention to the large area of woodland opposite Rayner's Farm known as Rayner's Grove. The trees of this ancient woodland were clear-felled and the area drained prior to replanting. A continuous area of twelfth- to fourteenth-century pottery, associated with slight house platforms, was discovered extending from just opposite Rayner's Farm for a distance of 250 m until it reached the area of The Park. As in West End, these house sites were situated on well-preserved hummocky ground, indicating that occupation was not only relatively short-lived but had been on extremely

---

[19] C. C. Taylor, *Village and Farmstead: A History of Rural Settlement in England* (London, 1983).

wet and water-logged land. In effect this evidence meant that there was continuous occupation debris from the south-west corner of the Middle Moor settlement, stretching in a broad arc all the way to the main village centre, except where modern houses obscured the ground. Further fieldwork even filled in these gaps for pottery, and slight house sites in a small paddock, were also soon discovered. Indeed, though now built over, the land immediately north-east of the road junction at Middle Moor also seemed to have been occupied. Though no houses existed there between 1817 and 1958, both the enclosure map and later Ordnance Survey maps showed three small, empty hedge plots there, suggestive of abandoned house sites. These, lying as they do at this road junction, which actually forms a small triangular green, indicated not only that Middle Moor was even larger than had previously been thought but was relatively compact.

This new evidence suggested that at some time, probably in the thirteenth century, the actual area of Whittlesford village was perhaps nearly three times that of the village in 1800, and indeed not far short of its area today when it has a population of 1500, three times that of 1279.

Early in 1983 one more piece of evidence was produced from the village. Planning permission was given for the building of two new houses on one of the empty plots on the south side of Church Lane in the area apparently devoid of settlement since the fourteenth century. The opportunity was taken to examine the foundation trenches for this site was within the presumed 'Saxon' village area, alongside the track to the original ford. The results were useful but somewhat disappointing. The ubiquitous thirteenth- and fourteenth century sherds appeared in abundance, but also, for the first time, a few sherds of twelfth-century and earlier pottery. This included one piece of developed Stamford ware and three sherds of early St Neots ware. These discoveries at least suggested that the occupation of this area was earlier than previous finds had indicated, but the lack of early or mid-Saxon occupation debris remained a problem.

Recently yet more evidence has appeared. There are now indications that there was once another moated site, opposite the Market Green in West End. If this is correct then the presumed early fourteenth-century expansion on this area may have been earlier and not, after all, associated with the Market Green.

This is the stage that research into Whittlesford has reached at present. No clear picture of the origin or development of the village has emerged and indeed from the heady days when all seemed obvious, little has been achieved except a slow descent into confusion. There is evidence of extensive Roman occupation yet nothing which is datable to the years between the fourth and the tenth centuries. The Saxon origins of the village remain quite unknown. The later history seems to be marked by expansion, contraction, movement and planning, yet no order emerges from the fact. I could summarize the results and suggest a possible sequence of development, but it is probably not worth doing so for too many unknowns remain.

CONCLUSION

What then may be concluded from this story of a research project into the origin and development of one undistinguished English village?

There are a number of possibilities. First, that I am past my best and should take up less demanding activities. Second, that no topographical historian should spent more than five years on a project such as this; to continue any longer only confuses the result. Third, that the study of Whittlesford, as with many aspects of modern archaeological, geographical and historical research, is being overwhelmed by data. Fourth, that, again as elsewhere, Whittlesford illustrates that we are in a period of conceptual flux and that, at the moment, we cannot develop new and stable concepts to replace the traditional and obviously outmoded ones. Fifth, that however good the researcher, he only sees what he wants to: he is totally confined by his own training and experience.

Two final thoughts occur. If I continue to live at Whittlesford, what else will I find? And will it make any more sense than the knowledge I have already? For only two hours before I penned these words in early August 1987, another quantity of medieval pottery emerged from new road works at Middle Moor.

PART III

Excavation

13

The Excavation of Dispersed Settlement in Medieval Britain

DAVID AUSTIN

INTRODUCTION

When Maurice Beresford and John Hurst began their work on deserted medieval villages, they started a unique and accessible archive based on their visits to sites throughout the length and breadth of England which now has thousands of individual entries all fully accredited to their own exacting standards. Housed currently in the National Monument Record of the Royal Commission on Historic Monuments in England and computerized for even easier access, the information will remain as a cornerstone for the archaeological and historical study of desertion and settlement for many years to come.[1] Dealing principally with nucleated sites, the archive has nevertheless made some attempt also to take account of the minor hamlets and individual farms which form the extensive small change of medieval settlement, and the recent amalgamation of the MVRG with the Moated Sites Research Group has now also brought the records of moated farmsteads and manors within the same organization. It is to be hoped that the two sets of data can ultimately be fully integrated, because the information they contain has much to tell us of where and to what extent the agricultural economy of the middle ages underwent significant change.

As with all archives of this sort, the question must be: what do we do next? The decision has been taken to close it as a record of research by two pioneering scholars, largely because the criteria used in verifying and accepting sites are unique to them and cannot be completely replicated. Yet there is another

---

[1] J. G. Hurst, 'The work of the Medieval Village Research Group 1952–1986', *MSRG Annual Report*, 1 (1986), pp. 8–13.

The programme of consultation and research needed to provide the background for this paper was generously funded by the British Academy. I have also benefited from discussions with several groups, units and individuals who have been, I am glad to say, as interested as I am in finding the way forward.

reason: both at a national and local level, comprehensive monument records are being assembled to serve the needs of both archaeological management and research. The national records, based essentially on the work of the Royal Commissions and the former Archaeology Division of the Ordnance Survey and supplemented from the fieldwork of other organizations and individuals, are being constructed to fit a series of universally applicable criteria of what might or might not represent an archaeological site. These are embodied in terminology and codification which define site and monument types by the use of specifically glossed keywords, which are increasingly designed to suit our computer age, and as such they are fast becoming essential tools for reviewing the present state of knowledge. In particular, the printouts of the National Archaeological Record remove much of the pain from the search for published and unpublished excavations in the field of medieval settlement. Even the most obscure references are to be found there.

Yet it must be asked whether these archives are tools for developing our knowledge or merely for encapsulating, perhaps even restricting, it. One of the important achievements of the Beresford and Hurst record was its organic growth, its capacity to absorb new types of site and evidence, but also its flexibility to allow these new forms of information to adjust the nature and shape of the archive and, more importantly, the academic criteria on which it was based. This, of course, leads to imperfections, especially those of inconsistency where one part of the record is not founded on exactly the same criteria as another. This may be construed as a problem, but it has had a dynamic vital to the development of the subject.

For this reason it is important to recognize that the local archives, however fraught with administrative and financial problems, have some element of that dynamic within them and are, therefore, a proper complement to the national record. One of the truisms, for example, of studying medieval settlement is its regional nature, particularly the variations through the spectrum from areas of major, almost urban, nucleations to those of dispersed farms and cottages, well exemplified on the zonal maps produced by Thirsk and Roberts.[2] This regionalism produces differences not just in the proportions of each type through that spectrum, but also in the character of the forms. For the county-based Sites & Monuments Records this inevitably means that judgements about the valid archaeology will be based on information and criteria different in each region or sub-region. These judgements must also, incidentally, be fitted to meet the requirements of local planning and development. The result is regional views of research, management and conservation strategies which will lay different stresses on similar archaeological phenomena, because something

---

[2] J. Thirsk, 'The farming regions of England', in *The Agrarian History of England and Wales Vol. IV 1500–1640*, ed. J. Thirsk (Cambridge, 1967), pp. 1–112, esp. fig. 1, p. 4; B. K. Roberts, *The Making of the English Village* (London, 1987), fig. 10.10, pp. 212–14.

that is important in Northamptonshire may well be marginal or peripheral in Devon or Cornwall. For example, nucleated villages and open fields in the east midlands were almost exclusively dominant in the high middle ages and an understanding of them through archaeology lies at the heart of the academic objectives of the region; in the south-west, by contrast, they are less frequent, indeed they are arguably peripheral to our knowledge of how these landscapes worked and may be more properly studied in connection with the origin and development of urbanism, which is another aspect of the archaeological strategy of that region.

Comparison of one local record with another is a salutary and essential experience and a useful and constant reminder that we cannot be complacent about the objectives or credibility of our national overviews from both an academic and administrative standpoint. Nowhere is this more apparent than in those parts of the country where dispersed farms with hamlets formed the dominant settlement pattern of the middle ages and on into the modern period. As the Beresford and Hurst archive reflects, the problems in studying and recording their archaeology are more intractable than those of village England. There is one immediately obvious reason for this. A village may encompass almost all the settlement and habitation activity of any one community and is, therefore, readily available, in a compact block, for study and excavation. It is relatively straightforward to move across the landscape or a map, with documents or air photographs in hand, to define, survey and even excavate where necessary, the often very visible and extensive abandoned elements of medieval settlement. The more scattered the habitation of a former community, the more difficult this task becomes. These problems centre on small size, extent of renewal, the fragmentary nature of visible field traces and poor documentation. These will be examined in detail later, but the overall effect on the national archive, on the national syntheses and on the national strategies for archaeology has been a comparatively comprehensive coverage of the phenomenon of the deserted, relocated or shrunken medieval village, but only intermittent and partial reference to the hamlet or farmstead, as can be seen on conventional distribution maps.[3] At local level, however, monument record compilers and administrators alike have been establishing new methodologies and criteria for assessment, based, for example, on more speculative use of place names and documentary references. In Cornwall, comprehensive lists for every parish derived from place-name studies target thousands of farms and small hamlets, most still existing, as potential archaeological sites, although the conventional indicators such as earthworks are otherwise missing. This technique has also been used to great effect in Devon, notably on the Roadford project. In Somerset Aston has shown how surnames in the lay subsidy of 1327

---

[3] M. W. Beresford, J. G. Hurst and J. Sheail, 'MVRG: the first thirty years', *MVRG Annual Report*, 28 (1980), pp. 36–8, esp. fig. 20.

can indicate potential sites which are now on the county's monument record, and in Yorkshire Moorhouse has drawn from the rich detail of the manor court rolls to identify a complex landscape of dispersed settlement.[4]

This contrast between the national and the local record is also reflected in both the nature and the use made of the evidence from excavations on rural sites in medieval Britain with a clear imbalance in favour of the village. In this chapter I want briefly to explore some of the issues involved, but primarily to examine how we have reached this situation and perhaps point to ways forward.

BACKGROUND AND DEVELOPMENT

It must first be recognized that the study of the dispersed settlement forms of our landscape have until recently pursued some very narrow objectives. At times, when reviewing the welter of minor excavations, the notices and reports of which litter the pages of our national and local journals, it is difficult to avoid the impression that some excavators have little other strategy than simply to find what is there. This may be justified as a product of scientific and positivist curiosity, but in designing the trenches and explaining the meaning of what has been found, this would seem to leave too much to chance and has clearly made it almost impossible for the results to be assimilated as part of the general synthesis, whether at a regional or a national level. This may seem unduly harsh as a judgement and it would be unfair to dismiss all excavation in this field as an exercise in futility because, in the past and very recently, there have been, and are, some clear targets. There are two main problems: first, it has happened, over the last decade or so, that our academic objectives for settlement excavation have radically altered from site-specific to contextual questions; and, second, the appropriate methodologies required to answer our questions about medieval communities have been easier to find for villages than they have for dispersed settlements. Consequently we are now coming to the end of a generation of effort, dominated by the names of Beresford and Hurst, in which we have seen field archaeology make major contributions, through a number of important excavations, to our knowledge of how villages were created, how they functioned and how they died, but with little real archaeological understanding of the dynamics of contemporary communities operating within regions of

---

[4] Cornish Archaeological Unit Sites & Monuments Record: I am grateful to the staff of the unit for sight of these records; see also A. Preston-Jones and P. Rose, 'Medieval Cornwall', *Cornish Archaeology*, 25 (1986), pp. 135–85; S. Timms, 'The Roadford Reservoir archaeological project, west Devon', *Devon Archaeological Society Newsletter*, 39 (1988), pp. 8–9; M. Aston, 'Deserted farmsteads on Exmoor and the lay subsidy of 1327 in west Somerset', *Somerset Archaeology and Natural History*, 127 (1983), pp. 71–104; S. A. Moorhouse, 'The township organisation: settlements', in *West Yorkshire: An Archaeological Survey to AD 1500, Vol. III The Rural Medieval Landscape*, ed. M. L. Faull and S. A. Moorhouse (Wakefield, 1981), pp. 585–613.

scattered farms and hamlets, except, perhaps, as we shall see, at their upland margins.

Before examining these methodological problems it is worth reviewing briefly what we have already sought to achieve and what information excavations have provided. At first the targets were straightforward and were the same as those for the village: a chronology for desertion was required, and information was needed about the medieval peasant's quality of life. Archaeology was asked to provide a view of both from the standpoint of material culture that could be set alongside those derived from documentary sources which were, in the 1950s and 1960s, being revised from marxist and other perspectives.[5] So it was that buildings and their contents became a primary focus of research, and they still remain an important element of our work.[6]

Perhaps the most outstanding example of this approach in relation to dispersed landscapes centred on the Welsh law codes and the indications in later, post-Edwardian, texts of ancient systems of tenure, inheritance and status. A whole literature has been generated about kin structures, systems of land holding and use, settlements and the activities which bind communities together.[7] The debate almost from the start involved archaeologists and architectural historians, especially Peate with his anthropological tendencies and Fox with his interest in the geographical determination of culture.[8] Indeed, the early surveys and excavations of the Foxes at Gelligaer Common and elsewhere drew attention to an important component in the field archaeology of dispersion, that is the margin at the interface of upland and lowland agriculture within the Highland Zone.[9] Here the survival of earthwork monuments, readily identified as belonging to the middle ages and the early modern period, provided an easily accessible body of archaeological information which could be related to documented farming practices such as, for example, the hafod/hendre system of short-distance transhumance.[10] In Wales these themes were continued

[5] E.g. R. H. Hilton, *A Medieval Society* (London, 1966); M. M. Postan, 'Medieval agrarian society in its prime: England', in M. M. Postan, *Cambridge Economic History of Europe*, vol. I, 2nd edn (Cambridge, 1966), pp. 548–632; M. W. Beresford, 'An historian's appraisal of archaeological research', in *Deserted Medieval Villages*, ed. M. W. Beresford and J. G. Hurst (London, 1971), pp. 169–81.

[6] See S. Wrathmell, ch. 14 in this volume, for an example of recent work in this field.

[7] F. Seebohm, *The Tribal System in Wales* (London, 1895); T. Jones-Pierce, 'Aspects of the tribal system in medieval Wales', *Géographie et Histoire Agraires, Annales de l'Est,* Mémoire no. 21 (1959); G. R. J. Jones, 'Post-Roman Wales', in *The Agrarian History of England and Wales Volume 1.ii AD43–1042*, ed. H. P. R. Finberg (Cambridge, 1972), pp. 283–382; W. Davies, *Wales in the Early Middle Ages* (Leicester, 1982).

[8] See, for a recent review of the subject, L. A. S. Butler, 'Domestic buildings in Wales and the Welsh Laws', *Medieval Archaeology*, 31 (1987), pp. 47–58; I. C. Peate, 'The Welsh house', *Y Cymrodor* 47 (1940); Sir C. Fox and Lord Raglan, *Monmouthshire Houses Part 1 Medieval* (Cardiff, 1951).

[9] A. Fox, 'Early Welsh farmsteads on Gelligaer Common, Glamorgan: excavations in 1938', *Archaeologia Cambrensis*, 44 (1939), pp. 163–99; C. and A. Fox, 'Forts and farms on Margam Mountain, Glamorgan', *Antiquity*, 8 (1934), pp. 395–413, esp. pp. 402–13.

[10] R. U. Sayce, 'The old summer pastures I: a comparative study', *Montgomery Collections*, 54 (1956),

in the work of the Royal Commission on Ancient and Historical Monuments in their post-war inventories, most notably Caernarvon.[11] The superb surveys generated for these publications were supplemented by limited programmes of excavation by the Commission's investigators with the purpose of providing some evidence to support tentative conclusions about date and function.[12] The momentum of survey on the Welsh upland has been continued both inside and outside the Commission, but the responsibility for excavation, however limited, has fallen to the archaeological trusts and other organizations.[13]

The early work in Wales, coupled with the growing awareness of the extent of late medieval settlement desertion, largely as a result of Maurice Beresford's work,[14] stimulated interest in similar environments in England, notably the south-west. In 1956, Lady Fox, after her move to Exeter, excavated a small upland farmstead on Dartmoor at Dean Moor.[15] Although she almost certainly mistook the remains of a classic longhouse for a barn and those of an outbuilding for a house, she drew the immediate parallel with the platform houses of Gelligaer and the southern Welsh uplands and the excavations clearly identified an earthwork type as belonging to the thirteenth and fourteenth centuries, as they did in Wales. The next stage was further fieldwork, and in 1966, Linehan published a seminal distribution map and sketch surveys which showed a pattern of sites around the periphery of Dartmoor and just above the limits of modern cultivation.[16] Further west similar sites were identified on Bodmin Moor and the north coast of Cornwall,[17] although here there had been a longer tradition of recognizing and, indeed, excavating this monument

pp. 117–45; idem, 'The old summer pastures II: life at the hafodydd', *Montgomery Collections*, 55 (1957), pp. 37–86; M. Richards, 'Hafod and hafoty in Welsh place names', *Montgomery Collections*, 56 (1959), pp. 13–20; E. Davies, 'Hafod, hafoty and lluest: their distribution, features and purpose', *Ceredigion*, 9 (1980), pp. 1–41.

[11] Royal Commission on Ancient Monuments in Wales and Monmouthshire, *Caernarvonshire*, vol. III, *West* (London, 1964), esp. clxxviii, fig. 107; L. A. S. Butler, 'The study of deserted medieval settlements (to 1968)', in *Deserted Medieval Villages*, ed. Beresford and Hurst, pp. 249–76.

[12] A. H. A. Hogg, 'A fourteenth-century house-site at Cefn-y-fan, near Dolbenmaen, Caernarvonshire', *Transactions of the Caernarvonshire Historical Society*, 15 (1954), pp. 1–7; L. A. S. Butler, 'A long hut group in the Aber Valley', ibid., 23 (1962), pp. 25–36; L. A. S. Butler, 'The excavation of a long hut at Bwlch-yr-hendre', *Ceredigion*, 4 (1963), pp. 450–7.

[13] R. S. Kelly, 'A medieval farmstead at Cefn craenog', *Bulletin of the Board of Celtic Studies*, 29 (1982), pp. 859–908; D. Austin, 'Excavations and survey at Bryn Cysegrfan, Llanfair Clydogau, Dyfed, 1979', *Medieval Archaeology*, 32 (1988), pp. 130–65.

[14] M. W. Beresford, *The Lost Villages of England* (London, 1954).

[15] A. Fox, 'A monastic homestead on Dean Moor, south Devon', *Medieval Archaeology*, 2 (1958), pp. 141–57.

[16] C. D. Linehan, 'Deserted sites and rabbit-warrens on Dartmoor, Devon', *Medieval Archaeology*, 10 (1966), pp. 113–44.

[17] M. W. Beresford and J. K. S. St Joseph, *Medieval England: An Aerial Survey*, 2nd edn (Cambridge, 1979), pp. 97–9; A. C. Thomas, *Gwithian: Ten Years' Work, 1949–1958* (West Cornwall Field Club, 1958); R. L. S. Bruce-Mitford, 'A dark-age settlement at Mawgan Porth, Cornwall', in *Recent Archaeological Excavations in Britain*, ed. R. L. S. Bruce-Mitford (London, 1956), pp. 167–96.

type.[18] From the 1960s, and this early fieldwork, onwards, there has been a steady stream of excavation, notably on Dartmoor at Houndtor, Hutholes, Dinna Clerks and Okehampton Park,[19] on Bodmin Moor at Garrow Tor and Bunnings Park,[20] and in north Cornwall at Crane Godrevy, Treworld and Tresmorn, as well as at Lanyon on West Penwith.[21] The results have confirmed a remarkably consistent material culture through the farmsteads of the region, especially in terms of house type and ceramics,[22] but there is continuing debate about the early chronology.[23] It is clear, however, from this work[24] and more recent intensive and analytical survey,[25] that a widespread pattern had been established on the south-western uplands by the early thirteenth century, consisting of individual farms and small hamlet clusters, linked to extensive arable field systems in a mixed agricultural economy. Arable production lasted only until the crises of the fourteenth century, but in the reversion to an essentially pastoral economy basic settlement patterns survived surprisingly intact and there are relatively small numbers of total desertion in the archaeological record. By contrast, there are clear signs of adjustment in the organization of farms and tenure recorded in the documents of the later middle ages and ultimately consequent changes in the buildings and settlement morphology. What is clear from recent work is the dissimilarity in the

[18] S. Baring-Gould, 'An ancient settlement on Trewortha Marsh', *Journal of the Royal Institution of Cornwall*, 11 (1892–3), pp. 57–70 and 289–90; P. M. Christie and P. Rose, 'Davidstow Moor, Cornwall: the medieval and later sites', *Cornish Archaeology*, 26 (1987), pp. 163–94.

[19] G. Beresford, 'Three deserted medieval settlements on Dartmoor', *Medieval Archaeology*, 23 (1979), pp. 98–158; D. Austin, 'Excavations in Okehampton Deer Park, Devon, 1976–1978', *Devon Archaeology Society Proceedings*, 36 (1978), pp. 191–239.

[20] D. Dudley and E. M. Minter, 'The medieval village at Garrow Tor, Bodmin Moor, Cornwall', *Medieval Archaeology*, 6–7 (1962–3), pp. 272–94; D. Austin, G. A. M. Gerrard and T. A. P. Greeves, 'Tin and agriculture: excavation and fieldwork in St. Neot's parish, Cornwall', *Cornish Archaeology*, 27 (1988), forthcoming.

[21] A. C. Thomas, 'Excavations at Crane Godrevy, Gwithian, 1969 interim report', *Cornish Archaeology*, 8 (1969), pp. 84–8; D. Dudley and E. M. Minter, 'The excavation of a medieval settlement at Treworld, Lesnewth, 1963', *Cornish Archaeology*, 5 (1966), pp. 34–58; G. Beresford, 'Tresmorn, St. Gennys', *Cornish Archaeology*, 10 (1971), pp. 55–73; E. M. Minter, 'Lanyon in Madron: interim report on the Society's 1964 excavation', *Cornish Archaeology*, 4 (1965), pp. 44–5, and plan in *Medieval Archaeology*, 9 (1965), fig. 46.

[22] D. Austin, 'Dartmoor and the upland village of the south-west of England', in *Medieval Villages: A Review of Current Work*, ed. D. Hooke (Oxford University Committee for Archaeology, monograph no. 5, Oxford, 1985), pp. 71–9. For ceramics, see various excavation reports cited here, since no full review of the evidence has yet been published.

[23] Austin, 'Dartmoor and the upland village'; G. Beresford, 'Three deserted medieval settlements on Dartmoor: a comment on David Austin's reinterpretations' *Medieval Archaeology*, 32 (1988), pp. 175–83.

[24] See a recent review: Preston-Jones and Rose, 'Medieval Cornwall', esp. pp. 139–53.

[25] RCHM (England), *Bodmin Moor: The Prehistoric and Historic Landscape* (forthcoming); P. C. Herring, 'Prehistory and History of Land-Use and Settlement on North-West Bodmin Moor, Cornwall' (unpublished M.Phil. thesis, University of Sheffield, 1986); D. Maguire, N. Ralph and A. Fleming, 'Early land use on Dartmoor – palaeobotanical and pedological investigations on Holne Moor', in *Integrating the Subsistence Economy*, ed. M. Jones (BAR, International ser. 181, 1983), pp. 57–105; D. Austin, R. H. Daggett and M. J. C. Walker, 'Farms and fields in Okehampton Park, Devon: the problems of studying medieval landscapes', *Landscape History*, 2 (1980), pp. 39–58.

sequences and treatment of the uplands of Wales and the south-west, despite the apparent similarities in house type and settlement monuments which so struck Lady Fox. In Wales there was no extensive expansion of the arable resource, particularly in those regions beyond English control, until the later thirteenth century.

This difference in the events affecting the medieval upland in Britain is all the more striking when other areas are considered. A comprehensive review of our knowledge in this area is long overdue, but this is not the place for it. Areas for a broad comparison are Exmoor, Mendip, the Cotswolds, parts of the Wessex chalk downlands, the Weald, the southern Pennines, the Yorkshire and Durham Dales, the Lake District, the northern Pennines with the southern Scottish uplands, the Grampians and the Scottish Isles. Excavation and fieldwork in these areas have produced a variety of different forms, sequences and explanations, enough to suggest that the medieval reaction to the upland was not a single phenomenon nor easily explicable in terms of monocausal explanations such as climate or population. Indeed, in these areas the archaeology among upland dispersed settlements has proved singularly fugitive and potentially complex. Deserted sites do exist, but not always in quantity or quality, and where they have been surveyed or examined archaeologically, they are difficult to interpret coherently. In the north Tyne area, for example, encroachment onto the pastoral upland from the valley floor was largely post-medieval,[26] while excavations at Alnhamsheles, a small deserted hamlet not far away in the Cheviots, has revealed a high medieval advance onto former shieling grounds, connected with extensive traces of arable production, all in serious decline by 1500.[27] The extent of abandoned ploughing on Cheviot is matched by the large areas noted by Parry on the Lammermuirs to the north,[28] but here there has been no excavation to provide dates and no pattern of related settlements established, although there are strong documentary indications to suggest that most of the activity can be related to the demesne policies of the Border abbeys. Elsewhere in Scotland, the Royal Commission has, since 1981, as reported by Corser and others, been very active in providing survey evidence of permanent farms and shielings throughout the upland areas, but there has been no excavation and little detailed documentary work to give them a context or a date.[29] This, in fact, brings us to the nub of the problem; we have now reached a phase in the archaeological study of the upland where neither excavation nor survey in isolation can hope to provide sufficient information for

[26] B. Harbottle and T. G. Newman, 'Excavation and survey on the Starsley Burn, North Tynedale, 1972', *Archaeologia Aeliana*, 5th ser., 1 (1973), pp. 137–75.

[27] P. Dixon, various interim notes: *MVRG Annual Reports*, 27 (1979), pp. 18–19; 28 (1980), pp. 13–14; 29 (1981), pp. 18–19; 30 (1982), pp. 15–16; 31 (1983), p. 16.

[28] M. L. Parry, 'Secular climatic change and marginal agriculture', *Transactions of the Institute of British Geographers*, 64 (1975), pp. 1–13.

[29] P. Corser, for RCAHM (Scotland), various interim notes: *MVRG Annual Reports*, 29 (1981), pp. 14–15; 30 (1982), pp. 12–13; 31 (1983), pp. 13–14; 32 (1984), p. 12; 33 (1985), p. 15.

the needs of analysing this use of the landscape. This is no new realization, since it has been creeping up on us for nearly a decade, but before examining this we need to take some account of the situation in the lowlands of England.

Here, the work on the dispersed settlements is fragmentary and difficult to characterize. There have, in fact, been several divergent streams of research which are difficult to reconcile in the space of a short summary. Most excavations have been small-scale, and few have raised themselves into the consciousness of the national debate on medieval settlement. In four recent syntheses of medieval archaeology which dealt with rural settlement it was noticeable that in very rare references to excavations on dispersed sites they mentioned only moated enclosures or a handful of those on the upland.[30] Indeed, the bitter truth is that the results from excavation on all forms of medieval settlement were used anecdotally or descriptively to illustrate historical arguments and conclusions. This is a desperate situation for the academic subject of archaeology and nowhere more so than in this field of dispersed settlement. Indeed, as with the upland sites, the principal emphasis from the start has been on the vernacular architecture and the general level of material culture, although the latter has actually received little serious attention outside of excavation reports. The understanding of the vernacular tradition has been immense and is well documented,[31] and individual sites such as Beere in Devon have contributed useful information from time to time.[32] Yet perhaps the single group of dispersed settlements in the lowlands to have received most attention has been the moated site, partly because it is archaeologically so distinctive, but partly also because it can be related to classes of architecture, above the vernacular threshold, which still survive in the rural landscape.[33] Archaeology has done much, in fact, to demonstrate the layout of seignorial establishments on such sites as Berry Court, Wintringham, East Haddlesey, Chalgrove, Milton, Hambleton, Writtle and a number of others.[34] Other

[30] J. M. Steane, *The Archaeology of Medieval England and Wales* (London, 1985), esp. pp. 143–9; H. Clarke, *The Archaeology of Medieval England* (London, 1984), esp. pp. 15–62; C. C. Taylor, *Village and Farmstead: A History of Rural Settlement in England* (London, 1983); J. G. Hurst, 'The medieval countryside', in *Archaeology in Britain since 1945*, ed. I. Longworth and J. Cherry (London, 1986), pp. 197–236.

[31] For example, R. W. Brunskill, *Illustrated Handbook of Vernacular Architecture* (London, 1971).

[32] E. M. Jope and R. I. Threlfall, 'Excavation of a medieval settlement at Beere, North Tawton, Devon', *Medieval Archaeology*, 2 (1958), pp. 112–40.

[33] See the *Annual Reports of the Moated Sites Research Group*; A. Aberg (ed.), *Medieval Moated Sites* (CBA Research Report no. 17, 1978); Clarke, *Archaeology of Medieval England*, pp. 47–62.

[34] G. Beresford, 'The medieval manor of Penhallam, Jacobstow, Cornwall', *Medieval Archaeology*, 18 (1974), pp. 90–145, idem, 'Excavation of a moated house at Wintringham in Huntingdonshire', *Archaeological Journal*, 134 (1977), pp. 194–286; H. E. J. Le Patourel, *The Moated Sites of Yorkshire* (Society for Medieval Archaeology, monograph no. 5, 1983); L. E. Webster and J. Cherry, 'Medieval Britain in 1978', *Medieval Archaeology*, 23 (1972), pp. 270–1, fig. 11; D. G. and J. G. Hurst, 'Excavation of two moated sites: Milton, Hampshire and Ashwell, Hertfordshire', *Journal of the British Archaeological Association*, 3rd ser., 30 (1967), pp. 48–86; L. A. S. Butler, 'Hambleton Moat, Scredington, Lincolnshire', *Journal of the British Archaeological Association*, 3rd ser., 26 (1963), pp. 51–78; P. A. Rahtz,

types of contemporary moated enclosure, most notably those identified by Roberts and others as the tenements of substantial freeholding farmers, for example colonists in the Arden of Warwickshire,[35] have not been so well served by excavation and their relationship to other contemporary farms of the period cannot be properly demonstrated.

Outside of vernacular architecture and moated sites, excavation of dispersed sites in the lowlands has contributed little to the national picture of medieval society and economy. Yet they have clearly had an importance in local and regional studies, especially in an attempt to give some account of the past patterns of farming where villages had been less prominent. Thus the excavation of a site at Pickwick Farm by Barton provides key evidence for the operation of landscapes south of Bath in Somerset during the middle ages.[36]

GENERAL HYPOTHESES

In this sketchy review of the past pattern of work in this field whether in the upland or the lowlands, a certain limitation in the objectives has been suggested, but in the years since John Hurst and Maurice Beresford edited *Deserted Medieval Villages* there has been a fundamental shift in ideas and methodology which, I shall suggest, has left the study of dispersed settlements somewhat stranded. When the excavation of medieval settlements began in earnest during the 1950s, the study was still dogged by the prevailing hypothesis that a major disjunction in the organization of society and culture occurred in the generation or so which saw the departure of the Romans. It was accepted that this profound change affected the material culture not just in the artefact assemblages, but also in the systems of agriculture and rural habitation. Such had been the success, in fact, of the historians following the tradition of Maitland and Round that archaeologists were bound to accept the dominant image of the Germanic free farmer who had brought with him the village and the open field as the primary institutions of his democratic way of life. Within this hypothesis the myth of the Anglo-Saxon's strong right arm and his steady progress was fostered, in which the vast tracts of lowland wildwood were said to have fallen beneath his heavy plough and the population in villages to have grown. This progress, it was represented, was modified by the feudalization of England in the wake of the Norman Conquest, but not stopped until the disasters of the Black Death. Within this hypothesis the occurrence of dispersed

Excavations at King John's Hunting Lodge, Writtle, Essex, 1955–7 (Society for Medieval Archaeology, monograph no. 3, 1969).

[35] B. K. Roberts, 'Moated sites in midland England', *Transactions of the Birmingham Archaeological Society*, 80 (1965), pp. 26–36.

[36] K. J. Barton, 'Pickwick Farm, Dundry, Somerset', *Proceedings of the University of Bristol Spelaeological Society*, 12 (1969), pp. 99–112.

settlements in the village landscapes of England were explained as assarts, usually late in the sequence, entrepreneurial colonization at the periphery cutting into remnant woodland or pushing out into newly drained marshlands or creeping up the flanks of the upland pastures. It would not be unfair to say that when Beresford and Hurst, between 1968 and 1971, wrote essays for their classic book *Deserted Medieval Villages*, this hypothesis was still substantially unchallenged by archaeologists. Even as late as 1976, Wharram Percy was still being explained in terms of gradual expansion from an Anglo-Saxon core near the church, and in a classic study the development of Whiteparish in Wiltshire was seen by Taylor as a steady accretion of new land on the edge of woods, curiously complete just before detailed documents began.[37] The hypothesis has failed to stand the test of more hesitant and questioning times and is now in tatters, although we still cling to elements such as the supposed steady rise in population through the Anglo-Saxon period for which there is actually no convincing evidence. Much to their credit, the excavators at Wharram and the fieldworkers such as Taylor have done a great deal, with others, in the intervening years to deconstruct the hypothesis and begin to put in place a new one with its own accumulating mythology.

This in broad terms states that there was essentially a continuum of the settled and agricultural landscape out of the Roman period into the Anglo-Saxon. Primarily this was a dispersed hamlet and farm system, although there may have been elements of nucleation which survived from the Romano-British or were introduced by migrant populations. These existed among enclosed arable fields and other managed resources, such as woodland and traditional pastures, which were at least as extensive, if not more so, as in the high middle ages. This situation survived until the end of the middle Saxon period in the late seventh or eighth century, when, along with other parts of western Europe, England started, or rather re-started, the process of centralization of powers which led to the establishment of the medieval states. Within the English landscape this was coupled with a fundamental shift towards the intensification of agriculture in the form of the nucleated village and the open field as well as the rebirth of towns associated with the money economy and centralized trade. The key agent at work in the countryside was the rural seigneur who relocated an increasingly demoted peasantry in villages next to his manor houses and changed the basis of tenure to accommodate a system of subdivided arable fields and rotation to provide pasture. This process of manorialization and nucleation was most intense in the Anglo-Danish midlands, but was still being implemented in the north and south as late as the eleventh and twelfth centuries. Within the new hypothesis, therefore, dispersed settlement patterns hidden among the

---

[37] M. W. Beresford and J. G. Hurst, 'Wharram Percy: a case study in microtopography', in *Medieval Settlement: Continuity and Change*, ed. P. H. Sawyer (London, 1976), pp. 114–51, esp. fig. 11.11; C. C. Taylor, 'Whiteparish, a study of the development of a forest edge parish', *Wiltshire Archaeological Magazine*, 62 (1967), 79–101; but for a recantation see Taylor, *Village and Farmstead*, p. 192.

otherwise nucleated landscapes were just as likely to be survivals of the ancient agricultural system as elements of new landtaking. As a corollary it could also be assumed that the areas of mixed dispersed and nucleated landscapes further west represented greater elements of survival, becoming noticeably more inclined towards hamlets and farms the further from the centralized core in the south and east one travelled. In this hypothesis the extensive failure of the village in the later middle ages onwards could be explained as the collapse of a somewhat aberrant system and reversion to the underlying dispersed character of the English landscape.

Inevitably this is a gross over-simplification and it undoubtedly represents a more hard-edged and unsophisticated statement than has hitherto been expressed,[38] but it does come to the heart of the matter and will help to isolate certain trends in settlement studies which have come together to substitute one hypothesis for another. One, perhaps the most, powerful motor in this change has been the drive towards classification of settlement and field forms through morphology. Captured within this, often in a very confused and confusing way, have been notions of hierarchy, progressive sequences and social structures. In a seminal article Uhlig, an historical geographer with considerable experience of British and north European data and representing a school of German thinking, proposed that language as a cultural and regional artefact through its terminology for settlement and field types acted as a barrier to a common understanding of their origins and development.[39] This early exercise in Europeanism progressed through international committees to an attempt to produce a universal classification which has not, however, found favour or use in this country.[40] In the same article, however, Uhlig suggested that the fundamental system in northern Europe, neither specifically Germanic nor Celtic, was the dispersed hamlet and farm with infield/outfield arable agriculture which could be linked to kinship-group structures of tenure, in other words tribal rather than state-organized. Some of the detail of this can now be questioned, but it did establish certain premises: the meaningful distinction between the two forms, the temporal and sociological primacy of one over the other, and the importance of classification through morphology as a basic instrument of debate. None of these premises, admirably propounded by Roberts and other historical geographers, have been overthrown or even seriously challenged.[41] Yet they have been applied by English archaeologists (including myself) with characteristic lack of rigour and much muddled thinking. I will expand on this theme elsewhere,[42] but one aspect is central to

[38] ibid. for fuller explanation, esp. pp. 109–50.

[39] H. Uhlig, 'Old hamlets with infield and outfield systems in western and central Europe', *Geografiska Annaler*, 43 (1961), pp. 285–307.

[40] idem (ed.), *Die Siedlungen des Landlichen Raumes* (Giessen, 1972).

[41] Roberts, *Making of the English Village*.

[42] D. Austin, *The Archaeology of the Medieval Landscape*, in preparation.

the subject here. Regular morphologies for both settlements and subdivided field systems have been taken to demonstrate the presence of planning,[43] and there has been a tendency to attribute this to lordship, although at least one historian has reminded us of the collective power of the vill in this context.[44] Within this tendency is another which assumes that the changes from dispersed to nucleated landscapes were sudden and comprehensive rather than gradually evolving. The archaeology of early Anglo-Saxon settlements has tended to confirm this, with the majority of abandoned units excavated being farms or unstructured minor clusters we can call hamlets,[45] and there is some evidence to suggest that manor houses provided the key elements of continuity from the previous system.[46] Fieldwalking in areas of well-developed ceramic sequences has also suggested that neighbouring small settlements finished at the same time, to be replaced by the strips of the open field and villages,[47] although there has been little effort to confirm the nature of what are principally pottery spreads in ploughed fields. There has been little work also on the dispersed settlements which, it is postulated, survived these major changes, such as in the west midlands or Kent. A few sites, however, such as Rivenhall in Essex, have provided some evidence for their continuity, although in this instance also it has come from a manorial context.[48]

The second influence on the recent shifts in thinking has been a strong interest in inductive models, derived from documentary sources, of how territory was structured and the processes, involving settlements, which functioned within it. The reconstruction of Anglo-Saxon estates through charters and discussions of their antiquity and continuity has been one strand in this,[49] but far more potent for the archaeologist has been the image of the pre-

[43] B. K. Roberts, 'Village plans in County Durham: a preliminary statement', *Medieval Archaeology*, 16 (1972), pp. 33–56; J. A. Sheppard, 'Medieval village planning in northern England: some evidence from Yorkshire', *Journal of Historical Geography*, 2 (1976), pp. 3–20; M. Harvey, 'Planned field systems in eastern Yorkshire: some thoughts on their origin', *Agricultural History Review*, 31 (1983), pp. 91–103; D. Hall, *Medieval Fields* (Aylesbury, 1983).

[44] C. Dyer, 'Power and conflict in the medieval English village', in *Medieval Villages*, ed. Hooke, pp. 27–32.

[45] T. Champion, 'Chalton', *Current Archaeology*, 59 (1977), pp. 364–9; M. Millett and S. James, 'Excavations at Cowdery's Down, Basingstoke, Hampshire', *Archaeological Journal*, 140 (1983), pp. 151–279; S. Losco-Bradley and H. Wheeler, 'Anglo-Saxon settlement in the Trent valley: some aspects', in *Studies in Late Anglo-Saxon Settlement*, ed. M. L. Faull (Oxford, 1984), pp. 102–14; S. E. West, *West Stow: The Anglo-Saxon Village* (East Anglian Archaeology Report no. 24, 1985).

[46] For example, D. Austin, 'Fieldwork and excavation at Hart, Co. Durham, 1965–75', *Archaeologia Aeliana*, 5th ser., 4 (1976), pp. 69–132; G. Beresford, *Goltho: The Development of an Early Medieval Manor c.850–1150* (London, 1987); G. E. Cadman, 'Raunds 1977–1983: an excavation summary', *Medieval Archaeology*, 27 (1983), pp. 107–22; J. R. Fairbrother, 'Faccombe, Netherton: Archaeological and Historical Research' (unpublished Ph.D. thesis, University of Southampton, 1984).

[47] In a summarized form see Taylor, *Village and Farmstead*, fig. 39, p. 113.

[48] W. J. and K. A. Rodwell, *Rivenhall: Investigations of a Villa, Church and Village 1950–1977* (CBA Research Report no. 55, 1986).

[49] P. J. Fowler, 'Continuity in the Landscape', in *Recent Work in Rural Archaeology*, ed. P. J. Fowler (Bradford on Avon, 1975), pp. 121–36; D. Hooke, *Anglo-Saxon Landscapes of the West Midlands: The Charter Evidence* (BAR, British ser., 95, 1981).

manorial territories which were the immediate tribal antecedents. Based on earlier ideas of institutional historians,[50] Glanville Jones and others have proposed, on analogy with units described in the Welsh law codes and the extents and surveys of crown land in north Wales, that multiple estates, or 'shires' in the English terminology, could explain early relationships of settlements to each other and their hierarchies.[51] The attraction of this for the archaeologist was that it could provide an instant contextual framework which operated beyond the narrow confines of the trench edge and the individual settlement being studied. Thus lines could be drawn on maps which defined integral units useful in establishing the strategies of research or explaining the processes of change in the landscape.[52] Again, however, there is an important aspect to this which can be linked to the morphological debate on dispersed settlement. The territorial models are derived in essence from systems of land use dependent primarily on kin-based tenure of arable, transhumant commons of pasture and short-distance tribute: in short, the dispersed landscapes of Uhlig's basic north European type. In archaeological terms, however, this has never been examined even in the heartlands of the multiple estate theory, in Gwynedd.

The third element in the readjustment of hypotheses arises from both the previous ones, but has also an honourable pedigree of its own: landscape history and archaeology. With its roots in local history of the Hoskins and Finberg type, there have been added important archaeological elements of theory, particularly an increased stress on contextual studies, and methodology, notably the growing emphasis on the kinds of evidence to be offered by the environmental sciences.[53] One strand in this has been the reconstruction of past landscapes and the human settlements within them, in the realization that only holistic studies of this nature are going to take us beyond the sterility of intra-site data which tend to tell us much about individual behaviour, but little about communities. Yet the more we have probed into the methodology and objectives of landscape archaeology in the middle ages the greater the range of potential information there is and the more unwieldy it has become, especially if excavation is a major component. We are only beginning now to realize the extent of the undertaking and the problems it raises, and no more so than in the dispersed landscapes of Britain where neither the objectives nor the methodology have been clearly defined.

[50] For example, J. E. A. Jolliffe, 'Northumbrian institutions', *English Historical Review*, 41 (1926), pp. 1–42.

[51] For example, G. R. J. Jones, 'Multiple estates and early settlement', in *Medieval Settlement*, ed. Sawyer, pp. 15–40; G. W. S. Barrow, *The Kingdom of the Scots* (London, 1973), esp. ch. 1.

[52] G. E. Cadman and G. Foard, 'Rounds, manorial and village origins', in *Late Anglo-Saxon Settlement*, ed. Faull, pp. 81–100; D. Austin, 'Central place theory and the middle ages', *Central Places, Archaeology and History*, ed. E. Grant (Sheffield, 1986), pp. 95–103.

[53] See Hodges, ch. 16 in this volume; Bell, ch. 15 in this volume.

CONCLUSION: SOME PROBLEMS FOR THE FUTURE

This then is the point we have reached in the late 1980s: the rural archaeology of the middle ages has become a morphologically driven exercise in understanding how individuals organized themselves within communities to use the resources of the landscapes within their control. Whether consciously or unconsciously, we have opted to study communities and blocks of landscape with the ultimate intention of comparing them so that we may draw conclusions about general trends. Our overall objective, therefore, seems to be a series of analytical but narrative accounts of a range of different landscapes within different cultural contexts. Of necessity these should be project-based with major cooperation between scholars in a number of different disciplines, and they will need major public resources. We have stumbled into a number of important projects of this nature, but usually without any clear strategy or understanding of the scale of what we are undertaking, and usually also in spite of, not because of, the outmoded rescue paradigm which controls the bulk of the finances at the disposal of British archaeology. Undoubtedly the best and most creative project is Wharram Percy, and indeed it has been vital in establishing a methodology for landscape archaeology, but this was achieved through the dedication of John Hurst, Maurice Beresford and a host of other individuals all contributing to an organic research programme with, latterly, major state *research* funding. Elsewhere, notably at West Heslerton, North Yorkshire, and Raunds, Northamptonshire, circumstances have enabled rescue funds to be used in landscape projects with sound research credentials.[54] This is, however, by chance and there are substantial aspects of the research in each of these projects which need to be done to achieve the account of the communities as I have described, but which lie outside the rescue remit and will, therefore, never be done, thus causing permanent harm to the validity of the research objectives.

If this is a dilemma, then we should recognize a crisis when we realize that none of these projects is dealing with communities in dispersed landscapes, for the same simple reason that had its effect on the Beresford and Hurst archive: in villages the settlement areas of the community are compact, readily defined and visible, but this also means that individual threats to their archaeological record can offer the potential at least for financing work on their core elements. By comparison and by definition, dispersed settlements are scattered in small pockets through the landscape, are often invisible to conventional fieldwork, and even when they are visible are often unspectacular and easily dismissed as unimportant by the administrative archaeologist. Critically, also, when individual threats come they are on isolated elements of communities and,

---

[54] D. Powlesland, 'Excavations at Heslerton, North Yorkshire 1978–82', *Archaeological Journal*, 143 (1986), pp. 53–173; Cadman, 'Raunds 1977–83'.

except in the upland, detached also from obvious traces of their contemporary landscape. In other words, rescue archaeology is ill suited to providing funds to help us understand the key factor in medieval rural settlement as defined by the prevailing hypothesis: the origins and context of dispersed farms and hamlets. It is no coincidence that it is precisely these types of site which need to be examined in the village landscape projects also, but which are not being funded. It is a final irony, therefore, that British academic archaeologists are going elsewhere in Europe to find the scope and types of funding which will allow them to undertake real landscape projects, and that it is in Brittany or the Volturno valley that the methodological and theoretical advances are being made.[55]

This is not to say, however, that worthwhile projects and research programmes have not been begun in Britain within dispersed landscapes. Currently it is possible to mention, for example, Hanbury in Worcestershire, Roystone Grange in Derbyshire, Caer Cadwgan in Dyfed, Woolcombe in Dorset, Roadford in Devon, Winchester's study of Cumbria or Aston's of Somerset.[56] Not all of these have involved excavation and, where they have, only Roadford has had access to central government resources, albeit limited. For this reason among others, there has been a marked reluctance to contemplate the scale of commitment and the level of cooperation needed to conduct a long-term interdisciplinary project. Yet we also have the problem of needing to develop new techniques to locate and excavate the minor settlements and to reconstruct their surrounding environments. These also require time, money and commitment. In order, therefore, to carry the study of medieval settlements forward we need to apply to some selected dispersed landscapes the kinds of co-operation, flexibility and endurance which Maurice Beresford and John Hurst have shown in nearly forty years both at Wharram Percy and in building their archive.

[55] G. Astill and W. Davies, 'Fieldwalking in East Brittany, 1982', *Cambridge Medieval Celtic Studies*, 4 (1982), pp. 19–32; and Hodges, ch. 16 in this volume.

[56] Unpublished interim reports of the Hanbury Survey, S. R. Bassett and C. Dyer, 1979–1982; S. R. Bassett, *Wootton Wawen Project, Interim Reports* (Birmingham, 1983–7). Hodges, ch. 16 in this volume; D. Austin, M. G. Bell, B. C. Burnham, R. Young, *Caer Cadwgan Interim Reports*, vols. 1–3 (Lampeter, 1984–6); A. M. Hunt, 'Woolcombe Farm', *Proceedings of the Dorset Natural History and Archaeology Society*, 106 (1984), pp. 155–9, and 107 (1985), pp. 172–3; Timms, 'Roadford'; A. J. L. Winchester, *Landscape and Society in Medieval Cumbria* (Edinburgh, 1987); Aston, 'Deserted farmsteads on Exmoor'.

14

Peasant Houses, Farmsteads and Villages in North-East England

STUART WRATHMELL

INTRODUCTION

Over the past thirty years north-east England has seen some of the most extensive and informative village excavations (figure 14.1). Wharram Percy, North Yorkshire, is unquestionably the richest rural settlement excavation, in terms of the structural and artefactual evidence recovered from relatively modest amounts of digging. It is also one of Maurice Beresford's and John Hurst's most significant contributions to the study of medieval archaeology. Thrislington (County Durham) and West Whelpington (Northumberland) have both been extensively excavated; more than 14,000 m sq. of the latter site were examined, amounting to about 20 per cent of its total area. For purposes of comparison and contrast 'the north-east' has been extended southwards into Lincolnshire and Derbyshire, to include the important excavations at Goltho and Barton Blount.

This chapter is concerned primarily with the peasant buildings and farmsteads in these and other villages. At a time when research interests are increasingly focused upon the wider aspects of settlement history, upon the broad shifts in settlement patterns and the circumstances in which villages were founded, on the rural landscape rather than the settlement site, the choice of these topics may seem perverse. It has been made in order to emphasize that the change of focus does not signify the fulfilment of earlier objectives. In fact, few of the questions addressed to medieval villages in the 1950s and 1960s have been adequately answered, mainly because of the failure of techniques and resources to cope with extensive earthwork sites, often in the face of deadlines set by contractors and developers. The West Whelpington and Thrislington excavations had both to be abandoned, the former because a quarry which had

I am very grateful to Chris Philo for producing the drawings which accompany this discussion, and to J. D. Hedges for allowing me to use reprographic facilities of the West Yorkshire Archaeology Service.

been destroying the site closed down, the latter because a quarry moved too quickly. The current phase of work on Wharram Percy village is scheduled to end in 1990. The immediate prospects for major village excavation in the north-east look rather bleak; it is, therefore, a suitable time for reassessment.

PEASANT BUILDING CONSTRUCTION IN THE LATER MIDDLE AGES

The past few years have seen a remarkable transformation in our ideas about peasant house construction, specifically about the durability of fourteenth- and fifteenth-century dwellings. The process is not complete; there may be numerous changes of direction and emphasis before a generally acceptable conclusion is achieved. Nevertheless, it is already clear that the concept of 'impermanent' late medieval houses, of houses built to last for decades rather than centuries, of houses entirely different in structural technique from surviving buildings, is no longer tenable. The challenge to established views has come not from archaeologists but from historians. It is one which archaeologists should take up at the earliest opportunity.

The perception in 1968, after almost two decades of village excavation, was that peasant houses, even when furnished with stone sills or walls, were not made to last. Walls were constantly rebuilt, buildings frequently realigned and repositioned.[1] Archaeological interpretation accorded with the views of architectural historians. For it was apparent that no medieval peasant houses had survived into recent times. The earliest dwellings which remained to signify ordinary tenant farmers could generally be dated no earlier than the sixteenth century. They were the product of the Great Rebuilding which, at varying times in different regions, saw the replacement of impermanent by permanent houses. The division was so clear-cut, the pattern so consistent, that it could not be the result of casual demolition: if medieval peasant houses had been built to last indefinitely, some would remain. It marked instead the 'vernacular threshold', the point at which ordinary farmhouses, those constructed of local materials in accordance with regional building traditions, began to be built as permanent structures and entered the record of surviving buildings.[2] The earliest remaining poor quality houses, such as the single-storey lofted buildings with thatched roofs supported by pairs of light cruck timbers, were still 'superior to those peasant houses which are known from excavation'.[3] Reconstruction drawings of medieval peasant farmhouses show

---

[1] M. W. Beresford and J. G. Hurst (eds), *Deserted Medieval Villages* (London, 1971), pp. 96–7 and 122–3.

[2] R. Brunskill, *Illustrated Handbook of Vernacular Architecture* 3rd edn (London, 1987), p. 27.

[3] E. Mercer, *English Vernacular Houses* (London, 1975), p. 23.

stone or clay walls supporting rafters which are merely uncarpentered poles; there are no major timbers to sustain the weight of the thatched roofs.[4]

There is, however, a strand of evidence which conflicts with such reconstructions. A study of Worcestershire manorial records, published over twenty years ago, provided references to the use of major timbers in late medieval peasant houses: to pairs of crucks, or forks, set at bay intervals as supports for the roof timbers; in fact to the kinds of structure employed in surviving buildings.[5] Recently this theme has been amplified and extended to other west midland counties and beyond.[6] For north-eastern England a few documented examples of medieval peasant cruck buildings are recorded in figure 14.1. One of them is derived from the accounts of the vicar of Kirkby Malham in the Yorkshire Dales. In 1454 the vicar paid carpenters for 'basyng' one of his tenants' houses – for laying great stones under the feet of the crucks.[7] Around Northallerton the use of crucks in tenant buildings is recorded in a fifteenth-century schedule of repairs.[8] Further north, County Durham offers several similar references: at Fulwell a pair of 'siles' (crucks) was needed for repairing a tenant's barn in 1371; and in 1459 a tenant at Billingham needed seven 'couples of syles' for a new granary.[9] Northumberland, a county in which only a handful of crucks survived into recent times,[10] offers considerable evidence of their use in medieval peasant buildings. The Percy estate baliff's rolls of 1471–2 refer to more than a hundred pairs of crucks in townships around Alnwick.[11] The references are all the more impressive in view of the limited duration of the record, and the fact that it was concerned only with repairs and rebuildings. The status of the buildings provided with these crucks is made clear in expenditure entries like one for South Charlton: 'Et in edificacione xiij copularum siles super tenementa diversorum tenencium domini ibidem.'[12]

It might be argued that the 'forks' and 'siles' recorded in these documents were different from the substantial timbers used in surviving cruck buildings. It is clear, however, that they could support substantial loads. Stone slates

---

[4] ibid.; I. Longworth and J. Cherry (eds), *Archaeology in Britain since 1945* (London, 1986), p. 224.

[5] R. K. Field, 'Worcestershire peasant buildings, household goods and farming equipment', *Medieval Archaeology*, 9 (1965), pp. 110–12 and 127.

[6] C. Dyer, 'English peasant buildings in the later middle ages', *Medieval Archaeology*, 30 (1986), pp. 22–31.

[7] J. W. Morkill, *Kirkby Malhamdale, Yorkshire* (Gloucester, 1933), p. 239.

[8] B. Harrison and B. Hutton, *Vernacular Houses in North Yorkshire and Cleveland* (Edinburgh, 1984), p. 6.

[9] J. Booth (ed.), *Halmota Prioratus Dunelmensis*, vol. II (Surtees Society, 82, 1889), p. 111; J. T. Fowler (ed.), *Extracts from the Account Rolls of the Abbey of Durham*, vol III (Surtees Society, 103, 1901), p. 638.

[10] N. W. Alcock (ed.), *Cruck Construction: An Introduction and Catalogue* (CBA Research Report no. 42, 1981), p. 134.

[11] J. C. Hodgson (ed.), *Percy Bailiff's Rolls of the Fifteenth Century* (Surtees Society, 134, 1921), pp. 24–43.

[12] Ibid., p. 43.

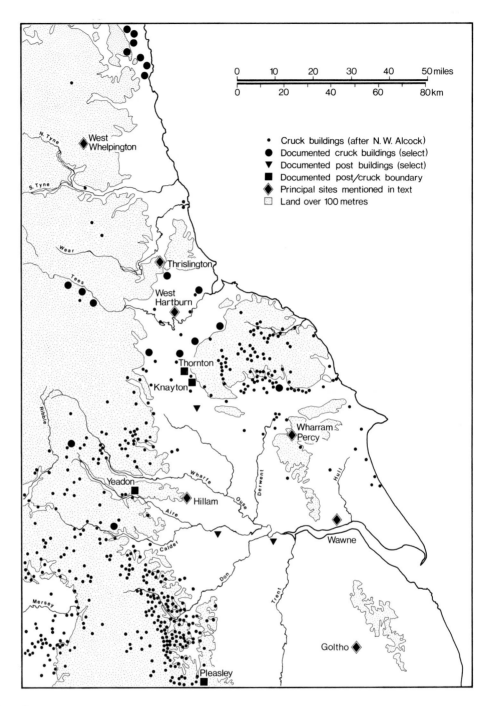

FIGURE 14.1 *Standing and documented buildings, and village excavations: Lincolnshire to Northumberland.*

('sclatston') as well as thatch were used to cover tenant barns in west Yorkshire,[13] and there is similar evidence for north Yorkshire.[14] Furthermore, there are references to tenants' buildings being moved and re-erected;[15] their portability an indication, not of impermanence, but of substantial timbers which were worth transporting and which could be dismantled easily.[16]

The final and most compelling evidence for regarding medieval peasant buildings as substantial structures is also shown in figure 14.1. The distribution of surviving cruck buildings indicates a clear boundary running from the Derbyshire–Nottinghamshire border northwards, through the middle of west Yorkshire.[17] The boundary skirts the Vale of York and returns south to enclose the North York Moors and the Yorkshire wolds. In the Vale, and to the east and south of this boundary, timber buildings are based not upon crucks but on upright posts supporting separate roof trusses.

Recent documentary research has shown that this boundary already existed in the later middle ages and that it can be related to peasant buildings. The southernmost reference on the map is to Pleasley in Derbyshire, where in 1373 a lessee of demesne land was to build eight houses in eight plots, each having three pairs of posts or crucks. This could suggest that in a boundary area either form of construction might be appropriate.[18] Further north, at Yeadon in west Yorkshire, a tenant was required in 1380 to build a new barn 'de sex postes vel sex crokkes'.[19] At the northern end of the Vale of York the boundary has been shown to have existed in the fifteenth century, in properties held by the Bishop of Durham's tenants: two settlements on the boundary, Knayton and Thornton, contained both cruck and post buildings.[20]

In view of the accumulating evidence for medieval peasant buildings of known vernacular construction it is appropriate, indeed necessary, to apply a 'vernacular' model, based on documents and standing buildings, to excavated peasant houses of the later middle ages, to attempt to interpret excavated buildings in a way which conforms to this model. The idea that somehow the excavated evidence can be left to 'speak for itself' is illusory.

Over most of north-eastern England the appropriate model is the cruck structure. The positions of crucks may be indicated by padstones, the 'basyng' stones of Kirkby Malham, substantial blocks of stone either set within the

---

[13] As at Thorner: Leeds City Archives, Thorner Accounts; I am grateful to J. Marriott and R. E. Yarwood for this information.

[14] Harrison and Hutton, *Vernacular Houses*, p. 5.

[15] For example, M. L. Faull and S. A. Moorhouse (eds), *West Yorkshire: An Archaeological Survey to AD 1500* (Wakefield, 1981), p. 808.

[16] Dyer, 'English peasant buildings', p. 29.

[17] Alcock, *Cruck Construction*, p. 77.

[18] J. Blair, 'Posts or crucks? Building on the north-eastern cruck boundary in 1373', *Vernacular Architecture*, 15 (1984), p. 39.

[19] C. Giles, *Rural Houses of West Yorkshire, 1400–1830* (London, 1986), p. 37.

[20] Harrison and Hutton, *Vernacular Houses*, p. 6.

thickness of the wall foundation or placed on the floor against the inner face of the wall; both positions might be found in a single building.[21] The excavator cannot, however, equate an absence of padstones with an absence of crucks, for timbers are known to have been placed also directly on the ground or in post-holes.[22] In other cases crucks were seated higher up, in slots in the inner faces of the walls.[23] The alignments of the pairs of crucks – the trusses – might well vary considerably, especially where the structure has been extended or partly rebuilt. The spacing of trusses need not be uniform, and there might be shorter bays at the ends of the building: there are documented examples of 'endforks' or 'gavelforks', single cruck blades rising from the centre of the end wall to support a roof hip (see figure 14.2a).[24]

Archaeologically, the most important aspect of this model is its significance for the interpretation of wall foundations. Walls were of minimal structural significance; the cruck truss and padstones (if any) took the full weight of the roof. The order of building was: first, rearing the cruck trusses; second, linking them with longitudinal timbers (the ridge pole, purlins and wall plates). Then came the walls, later in the sequence because they were simply screens, bearing none of the roof's weight. This applied even to the gable walls when endforks were used. The walls could thus be repaired, dismantled and replaced, in part or as a whole, without affecting the main timbers and roof covering. Walling materials varied according to what was available locally: in some parts of the region it was stone, at least for foundations;[25] there is also much evidence of wattle and daub, with or without a stone foundation.[26] Full stone walls seem gradually to have replaced wattle-and-daub panels.[27] It is the misfortune of archaeologists that excavated structural remains are almost entirely related to walls and wall foundations, to what were the least important and *least permanent* features of these buildings.

Most of these comments are also applicable to the non-cruck areas of north-east England, where peasant houses were recorded in terms of numbers of posts rather than crucks.[28] There are similar references for counties further south.[29] The posts were paired and formed trusses which divided the building into bays (see figure 14.3b). During construction the posts seem to have been 'reared' in

---

[21] J. Walton, *Early Timbered Buildings of the Huddersfield District* (Huddersfield, 1955), p. 18.

[22] ibid., p. 13; C. F. Innocent, *The Development of English Building Construction* (Cambridge, 1916), p. 65; J. Musty and D. Algar, 'Excavations at the deserted medieval village of Gomeldon, near Salisbury', *Wiltshire Archaeological Magazine*, 80 (1986), p. 147.

[23] S. Wrathmell, 'The vernacular threshold of northern peasant houses', *Vernacular Architecture*, 15 (1984), p. 30.

[24] Alcock, *Cruck Construction*, pp. 34–6; Harrison and Hutton, *Vernacular Houses*, pp. 6–7.

[25] For example, at Thorner, West Yorkshire: see n. 13 above.

[26] Harrison and Hutton, *Vernacular Houses*, p. 4.

[27] Walton, *Early Timbered Buildings*, p. 20; in other regions, wattle-and-daub screens were replaced by framed timbers: ibid., p. 19.

[28] Harrison and Hutton, *Vernacular Houses*, pp. 6–7.

[29] Dyer, 'English peasant buildings', pp. 31–2.

the same manner as crucks;[30] the trusses were fabricated on the ground, then raised and tied together by wall plates. Comparable buildings survived into recent times in the Lincolnshire Fens.[31] They were regularly dismantled and re-erected: in 1973 one 'was dismantled and re-erected in fifteen hours, excepting the roof of modern pantile and the wall-cladding'.[32] Post-truss buildings are in many ways closer in construction to crucks than to 'timber-framed' buildings, in which the structural members are interlocked.[33]

Having argued a general case for applying vernacular models to medieval peasant buildings, the next stage is to test the application in specific cases: to see whether particular excavated remains can be interpreted in terms of cruck and post trusses, set at bay intervals of around 3 to 4.5 m. Three have been chosen to provide a wide geographical spread: a barn at West Whelpington, a house at Wharram Percy, and a house at Goltho (figures 14.2 and 14.3).

West Whelpington is within the region of cruck construction, and it is a village which has produced evidence consistent with the use of crucks in buildings of the fifteenth to seventeenth centuries.[34] The barn shown in figure 14.2b was unquestionably standing before about 1320, when a small hoard of silver coins was secreted in its south-east corner.[35] The walls were represented by rough stone foundations, with various interruptions and changes in alignment. Three of the corners were distinctly rounded, probably indicating that the ends of the building were hipped, and were not full gable walls supporting purlins.[36] There was a wide, paved threshold, perhaps for a cart entrance, in the north wall, and the remains of a raised paved platform occupied the south-east corner. The ground plan shown here has been marked out with endforks supporting the hips and two full bays between. Although no obvious padstones were noted during excavation, it will be seen that some of the suggested truss positions, which are of course only approximate, coincide with changes in walling. The south end of the west truss, for example, falls at a break in the stonework. The south end of the centre truss lies at the junction of two distinct wall alignments.

The Wharram example is Building 1 in Area 6. The first definitive publication of this area was concerned with the overall development of the toft; for reasons of space much of the detailed evidence of individual structures was

[30] Harrison and Hutton, *Vernacular Houses*, p. 5.

[31] D. L. Roberts, 'The persistence of archaic framing techniques in Lincolnshire. Part II', *Vernacular Architecture*, 6 (1975), pp. 33–8.

[32] ibid., p. 37.

[33] F. W. B. Charles, 'Post-construction and the rafter roof', *Vernacular Architecture*, 12 (1981), pp. 15–16.

[34] Wrathmell, 'The vernacular threshold', pp. 30–1.

[35] D. H. Evans and M. G. Jarrett, 'The deserted village of West Whelpington, Northumberland: third report, part 1', *Archaeologia Aeliana*, 5th ser., 15 (1987), p. 237.

[36] See Alcock, *Cruck Construction*, p. 36.

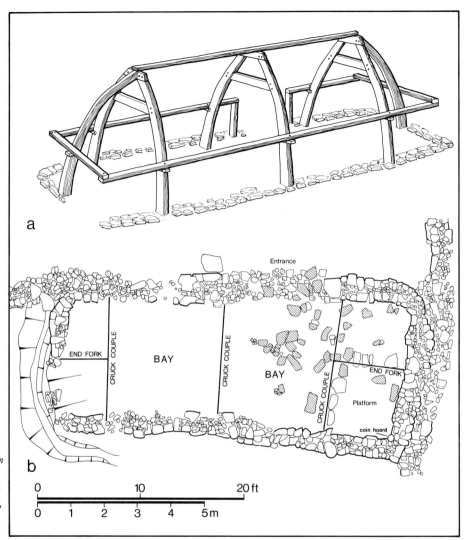

FIGURE 14.2 *(a) The skeleton of a cruck barn with endforks, based on b; (b) The foundations of a barn at West Whelpington, Northumberland (Site 14), marked out for cruck trusses.*

omitted.[37] Yet, as will be clear from earlier published accounts,[38] the signs of frequent rebuilding were unmistakable. A full discussion will be published shortly.[39] For the present there is an outline plan of the walls (figure 14.3a) with the different stretches of stonework marked by various types of shading. The overall picture of Building 1 is of a structure formed by discrete lengths of

[37] D. D. Andrews and G. Milne, *Wharram: A Study of Settlement on the Yorkshire Wolds, vol. I. Domestic Settlement, I* (Society for Medieval Archaeology, monograph, no. 8, London, 1979), pp. 51–4.

[38] For example, M. W. Beresford and J. G. Hurst, 'Wharram Percy: a case study in microtopography', in *Medieval Settlement: Continuity and Change*, ed. P. H. Sawyer (London, 1976), fig. 11.7.

[39] S. Wrathmell, *Wharram: A Study of Settlement on the Yorkshire Wolds, vol. VI. Domestic Settlement, 2* (York University Archaeological Publication, forthcoming).

foundation, reflecting the re-walling of individual bays. Their intervals have been combined with the positions of a few flat slabs, possible padstones, and with a few empty patches where padstones may once have been located, to suggest a cruck-truss building of six or seven bays. The east end seems to have been shortened at some time, and the west end extended; a post-hole with a stone base in the centre of the west wall may mark the position of an endfork. In general terms, this interpretation is very similar to one offered by John Hurst in 1971, when he wrote that the roof of this building was 'perhaps properly carpentered so that the repairs to walls were carried out in sections, leaving the roof intact'.[40] This suggestion merely lacked the appropriate cruck model.

Goltho, on the other hand, is within the post-truss region. It was a village on clay where building stone of any sort was scarce. The later medieval peasant buildings were in consequence marked, not by wall foundations, but by isolated slabs, padstones supporting the timber uprights. Clay walls or wattle-and-daub panels had presumably filled the gaps between the uprights. The excavator cited local vernacular buildings in his discussion of possible superstructures, but his reconstruction drawing differs from them in several ways.[41] House 18, Croft C (figure 14.3b), was used for this reconstruction. The padstones which marked its side walls did not form straight lines, but they seemed by and large to be paired across the building. To account for these characteristics the construction technique known as reversed assembly was invoked: each transverse pair of posts was connected at the top by a horizontal tie beam, and the wall plates were seated on the ends of the tie beams rather than along the tops of the misaligned wall posts. Such a reconstruction involves, in effect, no less than eighteen post trusses forming seventeen exceptionally narrow bays. It is not, however, the only possibility. Though the lines of padstones are on the whole irregular, they are composed of shorter straight lengths. By the addition of a few missing padstones the building can be divided into four bays, much more in keeping with the documentary references to post-built peasant houses (figure 14.3c), and much closer to the local post-built structures recorded in recent years.[42] Two of the suggested truss positions, on either side of the heated room, coincide with partition walls.

The results of these reinterpretations are promising, if not conclusive. A more effective test would require the excavation of further peasant houses, perhaps at Wharram Percy where the chalk walling, which demanded constant repair and replacement, is a sensitive indicator of change. Meanwhile, the Great Rebuilding no longer seems such a formidable barrier between medieval and post-medieval farmhouses. Its place in the history of housing, if it has one,

---

[40] Beresford and Hurst (eds), *Deserted Medieval Villages*, p. 122.

[41] G. Beresford, *The Medieval Clay-land Village: Excavations at Goltho and Barton Blount* (Society for Medieval Archaeology, monograph no. 6, London, 1975), p. 41; compare ibid., fig. 19, and Roberts, 'The persistence of archaic framing techniques', fig. 1.

[42] Dyer, 'English peasant buildings', pp. 31–2.

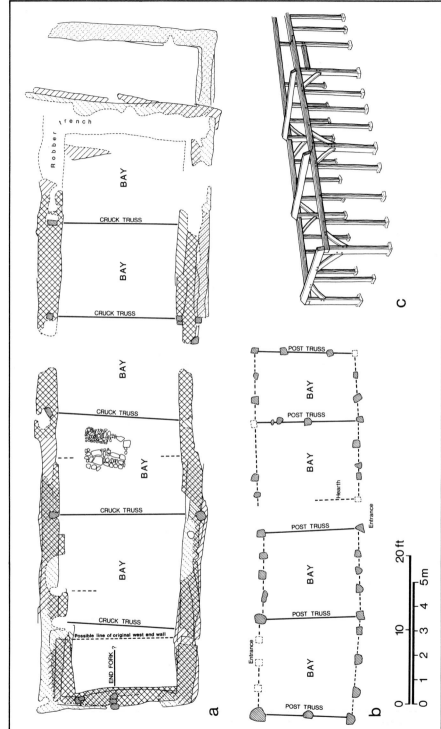

FIGURE 14.3   (a) Phase plan of Wharram Percy Area 6, Building 1, marked out for cruck trusses; (b) Plan of Goltho Croft C, House 18, marked out for post trusses; (c) The skeleton of a post-built house (without rafters), based on b.

is not at the 'threshold of survival', but at a later threshold: at the point where low-cost buildings, requiring a high degree of maintenance and repair, were replaced by high-cost, low-maintenance structures;[43] the point where single-storey cruck- and post-built dwellings were replaced by substantial two-storey farmhouses of masonry, of fully-framed timber or of brick.

We should not, on the other hand, assume that fourteenth-century cruck houses were identical to seventeenth-century examples. There were undoubtedly changes and developments, both major and minor. The gradual replacement of wattle-and-daub by stone has already been noted; and the use of dressed stonework for openings seems, in the north-east, to originate in the sixteenth and seventeenth centuries. At Wharram, the window glass and lead cames were probably introduced in the fifteenth century,[44] but there is no sign of stone-mullioned windows in the peasant houses. Glazing seems to have reached West Whelpington in the fifteenth or sixteenth century, but again window frames and door surrounds continued to be made of wood until desertion, in this case until the early eighteenth century.[45] The successor farmsteads at Whelpington were, in contrast, furnished with dressed stone jambs and lintels.

The later middle ages were also a formative time for vernacular house plan types, for in this period a shift in hearth position can be detected. It is seen, for example, at West Whelpington, where an early fourteenth-century longhouse (House 13) had a central hearth in its living room.[46] The late fifteenth- and sixteenth-century longhouses had hearths set against the partition wall which divided the living room from the entrance passage.[47] A 'central-hearth plan' was thereby replaced by what is known in vernacular architecture as a 'hearth-passage plan'.[48] At West Hartburn, a change of hearth position occurred during the life of a single house (House A): a central hearth was replaced, probably in the fifteenth century, by one set against the partition wall.[49] Fireplaces were presumably moved to facilitate the construction of firehoods. At Goltho and Barton Blount hearth-passage plan houses were already in use in the fourteenth century, and there was evidence from both villages of firehoods.[50] The introduction of hoods could, in turn, have been a response to the need for more loft space; just as, in higher status houses, the open hearth was banished from the hall to permit the insertion of upper rooms.

In sum, archaeological excavation offers the possibility of clarifying the

[43] Brunskill, *Illustrated Handbook*, p. 237.

[44] Andrews and Milne, *Wharram, vol I*, pp. 73, 115, 130.

[45] Evans and Jarrett, 'West Whelpington, part I', pp. 296–7.

[46] ibid., p. 235.

[47] Wrathmell, 'The vernacular threshold', fig. 1.

[48] For the latter see Harrison and Hutton, *Vernacular Houses*, pp. 42–73.

[49] L. Still and A. Pallister, 'The excavation of one house site in the deserted village of West Hartburn, Co. Durham', *Archaeologia Aeliana*, 4th ser., 42 (1964), figs 3 and 4: the entrance position is not clear, but the change may have resulted in a lobby-entry plan.

[50] G. Beresford, *The Medieval Clay-land Village*, pp. 26–8.

origins and early development of vernacular plan forms. Present evidence is tantalizingly vague, but a carefully targeted research strategy would do much to improve matters.

PEASANT BUILDING CONSTRUCTION IN THE TWELFTH AND THIRTEENTH CENTURIES

If a case can be made for placing later medieval peasant buildings in known vernacular traditions, what about earlier houses? One of the most consistent findings of village excavation has been a shift from earthfast construction to the kinds of wall foundations and padstones discussed above. Buildings marked either by separate post-holes, or by trenches for closely-set uprights, were generally replaced during the late twelfth and thirteenth centuries by buildings which relied entirely upon jointing for their stability. It has been claimed that the changeover was a response to deteriorating climatic conditions, a measure to waterproof houses more effectively.[51] The transition seems, however, to occur too early in some places to be associated with such a deterioration,[52] and may be instead a sign of greater need to conserve timber.

The forms of excavated walling associated with late medieval buildings go back to the thirteenth century; therefore, it has been argued, the cruck and post traditions go back only this far: the use of stone to inhibit rotting originated when crucks first began to be employed in peasant buildings.[53] It is an attractive hypothesis, but one which should not be accepted without question. We have seen that archaeological remains can be unrepresentative of building superstructures: for example, walls might come and go, and might display numerous archaeological 'phases' without affecting the main structural elements. Could the very clear archaeological division between earthfast and non-earthfast types of wall-formation be misleading?

The use of post-holes did not cease entirely when stone wall foundations were introduced. They are known in both cruck and post buildings which survived into recent times.[54] In the American colonies, there is evidence of substantial but earthfast buildings being underpinned and converted into above-ground structures with sills;[55] and architectural historians have been studying similar cases of reconditioning among standing buildings in this country.[56] In view of

---

[51] ibid., pp. 50–2.

[52] See dates suggested in G. Beresford, 'Three deserted medieval settlements on Dartmoor: a report on the late E. Marie Minter's excavations', *Medieval Archaeology*, 23 (1979), p. 127.

[53] Discussed fully in Dyer, 'English peasant buildings', pp. 35–7.

[54] T. Edmondson, *History of Fimber* (Malton, 1857), p. 5; J. Le Patourel, *The Moated Sites of Yorkshire* (Society for Medieval Archaeology, monograph no. 5, London, 1973), pl. IX.

[55] C. Carson, N. F. Barka, W. M. Kelso, G. W. Stone and D. Upton, 'Impermanent architecture in the Southern American Colonies', *Winterthur Portfolio*, 16, nos 2–3 (1981), pp. 147, 156–8.

[56] Information from R. A. Meeson.

this, it may be unwise to assume a sharp break in construction techniques on the basis of a change in the excavated evidence. We might see, for example, the post-holes of House 1, Period 1 at Goltho as the equivalent of the padstones in the later houses of that village.[57] The test of the hypothesis would be whether an individual building could be seen to undergo this transition: whether a set of wall foundations had been superimposed so precisely on a set of post-holes that it could not signify the demolition of one building and its replacement by another; rather, that it must be the result of underpinning a building, or cutting off the earthfast ends of the main posts and supporting them with stones while the superstructure remained intact. The possibility is one which has rarely been explored by archaeologists, but it is probably the explanation of pairs of post-holes underlying stone walls at Okehampton Park, Devon and at Hangleton, Sussex.[58] It deserves further investigation.

PEASANT FARMSTEADS: COMPOSITION AND FUNCTION

In 1971 John Hurst published a typology of peasant houses: it consisted of the 'peasant cot', the 'longhouse' and the 'farm'.[59] Since then, both excavation and documentary research have increased enormously the available data and have led inevitably to modifications of the typology.

The peasant cots are the dwellings of those who, in north-east England, are recorded as cottagers: the lowest documented stratum of peasant society. They had little, if any arable land in the open fields, but possessed grazing rights on the commons. West Whelpington has produced a number of small dwellings which it is tempting to ascribe to cottagers (figure 14.4c). Of the 13 possible examples, 9 had remains of low, semi-circular or rectangular platforms of stone at one end: these have been interpreted as hayrick bases. Six of these buildings had definite evidence of hearths. The most notable characteristic was that they were located, not in the 'private' spaces of the village, but on the edge of, or within the village green, without associated enclosures.[60] We should, however, beware of attributing tenurial status to particular kinds of buildings and farm groups. Documentary evidence suggests that tenants of 'cottager' status might well occupy groups of buildings as large as those of some tenants who had extensive lands in the open fields.[61] The differences between individuals within a tenurial grade might be archaeologically more apparent.

---

[57] G. Beresford, *The Medieval Clay-land Village*, p. 32, fig. 14.1.

[58] D. Austin, 'Excavations in Okehampton Park, Devon, 1976–78', *Proceedings of the Devon Archaeological Society*, 36 (1978), pp. 201–2; E. W. Holden, 'Excavations at the deserted medieval village of Hangleton, pt. 1', *Sussex Archaeological Collections*, 101 (1963), pp. 86–8.

[59] Beresford and Hurst (eds), *Deserted Medieval Villages*, pp. 104–12.

[60] Evans and Jarrett, 'West Whelpington, part 1', pp. 297–8.

[61] Dyer, 'English peasant buildings', p. 25.

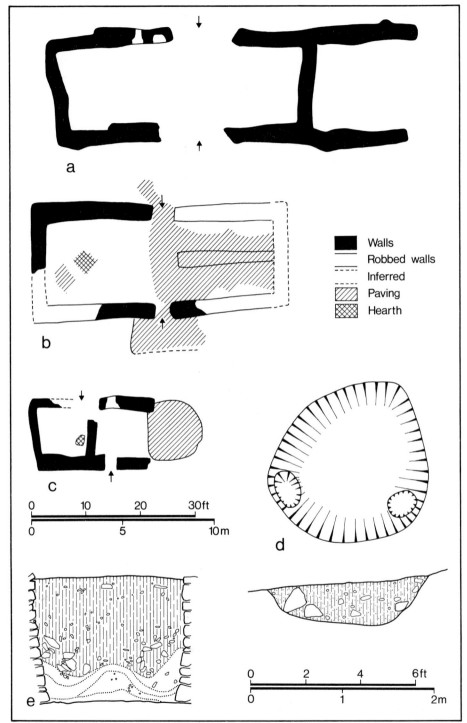

a

b

Walls
Robbed walls
Inferred
Paving
Hearth

c

d

| 0 | 10 | 20 | 30ft |
| 0 | 5 | | 10m |

e

| 0 | 2 | 4 | 6ft |
| 0 | 1 | | 2m |

FIGURE 14.4 *Barn 5a, West Whelpington, Northumberland; (b) House 8, West Whelpington; (c) House 16b, West Whelpington; (d) Latrine at Hillam, West Yorkshire; (e) Storage pit at Thrislington, County Durham.*

Turning to the larger holdings, the distinction between 'longhouse' and 'farm' seems less valid in the light of recent work. Documentation indicates that, in this region as elsewhere,[62] the peasant farmstead or *messuagium* comprised a number of substantial permanent structures, which might or might not include 'longhouse' types. The buildings of a 2-bovate holding at Nun Stainton, County Durham, were described in a lease of 1392. The term was two hundred years, and during that time it was incumbent upon the lessees to 'sustain' and 'maintain' the buildings. These comprised a house called 'le Firehouse' containing five couples of crucks ('syles') and two gavelforks; a barn (*grangea*) of three couples of crucks and two gavelforks; a barn (*grangea*) of one couple of crucks and two gavelforks, and a small house (*parva domus*) on the west side of the firehouse containing three couples of crucks and two gavelforks.[63] The firehouse was the dwelling – the house with the domestic fire. In view of the number of trusses it may have been 18 to 21 m long, and may therefore have incorporated non-domestic functions. The two barns together would have provided much the same amount of roofed space as the firehouse, presumably for the storage of agricultural produce. The small house may have been simply an outbuilding, or a subsidiary dwelling, or a former dwelling demoted to agricultural use. The fact that all the buildings had gavelforks at both ends indicates that they were free-standing structures, not parts of longer ranges of buildings.

Documents such as the manorial records for Methley and Thorner, west Yorkshire,[64] indicate that archaeologists can usually expect to find barns as well as houses in the peasant tofts of north-east England. This expectation has been realized at West Whelpington, which produced considerable numbers of outbuildings, usually in the toft areas immediately behind the houses, but sometimes at the far ends of the crofts, with access from back lanes rather than from the village green.[65] The early fourteenth-century barn shown above (figure 14.2) probably had a cart-width entrance, and some later barns had evidence of opposed cart entrances, perhaps with a threshing floor between (figure 14.4a).[66] Smaller outbuildings with single, narrower entrances were also found; some may have been stables. At West Hartburn, County Durham, a two-roomed building in the toft behind House A could have included a stable or fodder store, judging by the ironwork found beneath destruction material on its floor. A hearth below its latest flooring material seems to indicate an earlier domestic function.[67] Bakehouses, kilns and kitchens are occasionally recorded

[62] ibid., p. 26.

[63] W. Greenwell (ed.), *Feodarium Prioratus Dunelmensis* (Surtees Society, 58, 1872), p. 167.

[64] Information from J. Marriott and R. E. Yarwood.

[65] M. G. Jarrett and S. Wrathmell, 'Sixteenth- and seventeenth-century farmsteads: West Whelpington, Northumberland', *Agricultural History Review*, 25 (1977), figs 3–4.

[66] Evans and Jarrett, 'West Whelpington, part I', p. 300.

[67] L. Still and A. Pallister, 'West Hartburn 1965. Site "C"', *Archaeologia Aeliana*, 4th ser., 45 (1967), pp. 141–7.

as separate structures in the peasant messuage;[68] it cannot be assumed that every hearth and oven in a toft signifies a separate dwelling. On the other hand the conversion of a house to a barn is a well-documented process, especially at higher social levels, and there are even examples of peasant barns being converted into houses.[69] As was pointed out some years ago, archaeological remains are not always amenable to classification by function;[70] the definition of form is usually much easier and more reliable. Nowhere is this more apparent than in the lengthy and largely sterile debate on the identification of 'longhouses'.[71] The definition required by architectural historians involves the housing of cattle in part of the dwelling, but excavation may well fail to determine either the presence *or the absence* of cattle in the low end of the farmhouse.

Some of the clearest medieval longhouses (by this definition) are those from West Whelpington. They were in existence by the late thirteenth century and continued to be used and built throughout the middle ages. The byres were marked by wide stone drains which ran down the centre of the room.[72] The sumps collected manure from the cattle positioned on the (sometimes paved) standings at either side (figure 14.4b). House A at West Hartburn probably had similar arrangements in the western room, although the evidence is rather confusing.[73] Wawne, Humberside, produced a house (C7) containing a room with a sump edged by boulders; it was dated to the fifteenth and sixteenth centuries.[74] Wharram has failed to provide evidence of stone byre sumps, but this is to be expected on a site where the only building stone readily available was that which could be pillaged from the church or the manor houses. The peasant house Building 1, Area 6, was over 24 m long (figure 14.3a). It is an ideal candidate for a dual purpose house. The extent to which the chalk surfacing had been eroded throughout the length of the building suggests that the low end had some purpose other than storage.[75]

The houses at Goltho and Barton Blount were also probably dual purpose, the secondary usage being agricultural. The possibility that they were true

---

[68] Dyer, 'English peasant buildings', pp. 25 and 34; Faull and Moorhouse (eds), *West Yorkshire*, pp. 835–6; but 'kitchens' may signify bakehouses and brewhouses, rather than separate structures used for cooking daily meals: see E. Wiliam, 'Yr aelwyd: the architectural development of the hearth in Wales', *Folk Life*, 16 (1978), p. 97.

[69] Dyer, 'English peasant buildings', p. 26.

[70] G. Meirion-Jones, 'The long-house: a definition', *Medieval Archaeology*, 17 (1973), p. 136.

[71] Sterile because of the failure to achieve a generally acceptable definition: compare the definitions in Jarrett and Wrathmell, 'Sixteenth- and seventeenth-century farmsteads', p. 115 n; G. Beresford, 'Three deserted medieval settlements', p. 124; Andrews and Milne, *Wharram, vol. I*, pp. 68–9; N. W. Alcock and P. Smith, 'The long-house: a plea for clarity', *Medieval Archaeology*, 16 (1972), pp. 145–6.

[72] M. G. Jarrett, 'The deserted village of West Whelpington, Northumberland: second report', *Archaeologia Aeliana*, 4th ser., 48 (1970), pl. xxvi, 1 and pl xxviii, 1 and fig. 23.

[73] Still and Pallister, 'The excavation of one house site', pp. 194–5.

[74] C. Hayfield, 'Wawne, East Riding of Yorkshire: a case study in settlement morphology', *Landscape History*, 6 (1984), pp. 47–9.

[75] Beresford and Hurst, 'Wharram Percy: a case study', pl. 11.7.

longhouses was rejected in the excavation report, partly because of the lack of wear on the low-end floors,[76] partly on the basis that traditional farming practices in the region have involved the overwintering of cattle in yards, not in byres.[77] In this case there is, however, a problem in using 'vernacular' farming methods as a model for medieval practice. Documentary evidence indicates that longhouses were once much more widespread than their present distribution indicates. They seem to have been obsolescent in some parts of England in the thirteenth century,[78] but in the sixteenth century they still apparently existed in the Vale of York, an area in which there is now little sign of such a tradition.[79] Therefore we cannot assume that a region which is now without longhouses never had them. Nor can we expect that excavation will provide unequivocal evidence of their past distribution. In many instances the archaeologist will be able to determine only those elements which will allow plan-form classification: the position of the principal hearth, its relationship to entrances, the number of rooms etc. The use of unheated rooms may be impossible to establish.

The problems of determining function among the principal farmstead buildings may seem considerable, but they are overshadowed by the difficulty of identifying the more ephemeral structures, often marked only by fragments of footings, edgings or post-holes. Several ancillary post-hole structures and pits were recorded at Hillam, West Yorkshire.[80] These included a setting of four post-holes which was interpreted as the substructure of a raised-floor granary, and a two-post setting associated with a shallow, oval scoop interpreted as a 'garderobe' (figure 14.4d). Similar two-post settings were recorded at Goltho and Barton Blount and were again identified as garderobes.[81] These latrines were perhaps simple earth closets, the scooped depressions presumably the result of clearing manure heaps. It is difficult to imagine that peasant farmers would have troubled to dig proper cess-pits.

Deep pits are, nevertheless, a common feature of villages in the region; they were presumably used for storage. A structure at Hillam combined two rectangular pits: one of them had corner postholes; both had sharp, vertical sides which indicated that they had been lined, and had then been filled up rapidly at disuse.[82] Goltho and Barton Blount produced examples which have been interpreted as water containers, and a clay-lined pit in Building 9, Area 6

---

[76] But there was wear on the floor of House 3, Croft A at Goltho: G. Beresford, *The Medieval Clay-land Village*, p. 23.

[77] ibid., pp. 12–13.

[78] Dyer, 'English peasant buildings', pp. 24–5 and 40–1.

[79] Harrison and Hutton, *Vernacular Houses*, p. 12.

[80] S. A. Moorhouse and A. M. Slowikowski, 'Excavations at Hillam Burchard 1980', in *Medieval Settlement in West Yorkshire*, ed. S. A. Moorhouse (West Yorkshire Archaeology Service, forthcoming). I am grateful to J. D. Hedges and S. A. Moorhouse for permission to make use of this report in advance of its publication.

[81] G. Beresford, *The Medieval Clay-land Village*, p. 44 and fig. 21.

[82] Pits 75 and 78.

at Wharram was probably a liquid store.[83] West Hartburn House A also contained a circular-plan pit with a 'black mud' fill.[84] Further north, a toft at West Whelpington contained two pits, each about 1 m sq. and 0.5 m deep, cut into the bedrock.[85] Several rather more impressive rectangular pits were found at Thrislington, including the one illustrated here (figure 14.4e), which was stone-lined with an additional lining of plastic clay at the base. It may have been contained within a building.[86]

Some of these pits offer additional though incidental evidence of the domestic economy of the peasant farmstead. Once their original function ceased they seem to have been filled up immediately with raw rubbish which at Wharram, Hillam, Thrislington and perhaps West Hartburn included almost complete pottery vessels, mainly coarsewares. The vessels had possibly been thrown away as whole but redundant pots; it has been suggested that they were dairying vessels which had become contaminated.[87] Whatever the reason for their deposition, they provide a valuable indication of the forms in use together at the various farmsteads in the thirteenth century.[88] If they were indeed used for the same purposes on all these sites, they also show local variations in the shapes of particular types of vessels. Figure 14.5 shows the range of near-complete forms discarded at Hillam, Thrislington and Wharram.

By and large, the artefact assemblages published in village excavation reports provide little more than broad background information on agricultural and domestic economy, domestic and personal equipment and building fittings. This level of evidence should not be underestimated. At West Whelpington, for example, the absence of ceramic dripping pans from the assemblage as a whole confirms the expectation that, throughout the life of the village, roast meat was not the normal fare;[89] the diet consisted mainly of porridge and bannocks. Nevertheless, an absence of significant stratification, and a tendency for the later periods of farmstead occupation to erode the earlier, make it difficult to link particular artefact remains to particular phases of activity. This means that pit groups such as those described above have a special importance and are worthy of detailed treatment. At Thrislington, the contents of the

---

[83] G. Beresford, *The Medieval Clay-land Village*, p. 44; Andrews and Milne, *Wharram, vol. I*, p. 48.

[84] Still and Pallister, 'The excavation of one house site', p. 195.

[85] Jarrett, 'West Whelpington . . . second report', p. 221.

[86] D. Austin, *The Deserted Medieval Village of Thrislington, County Durham: Excavations 1973–4* (Society for Medieval Archaeology, monograph, forthcoming). I am grateful to David Austin for permission to use information from this report in advance of publication.

[87] Information from S. A. Moorhouse.

[88] The Wharram Percy group (pit J2) is dated to the later thirteenth century: Andrews and Milne, *Wharram, vol. I*, p. 135; Thrislington (pit NF 134) and Hillam (pits 75 and 78) are dated to the thirteenth and twelfth–thirteenth centuries respectively.

[89] Evans and Jarrett, 'West Whelpington, part 1', p. 255. No manorial homestead was found in the excavations.

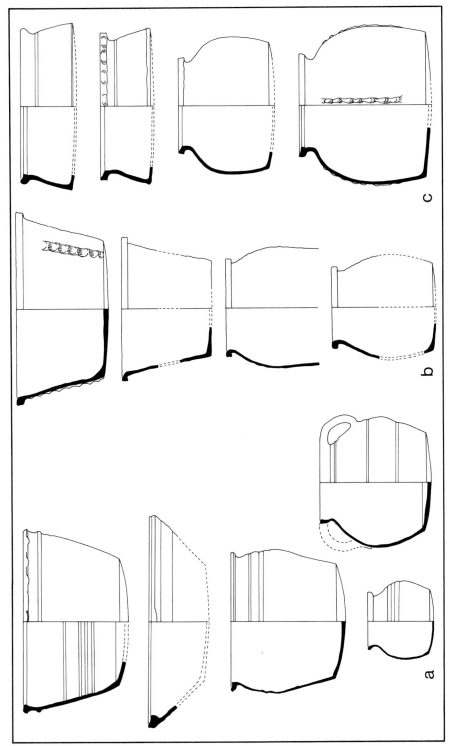

FIGURE 14.5 *Near-complete pottery vessels from pits at (a) Thrislington; (b) Hillam; and (c) Wharram Percy. Scale* 1/8

peasant toft pits have been compared with pit groups from the manorial enclosure.[90]

Outside such contexts, it is often only the final phase of occupation which offers the possibility of relatively undistrubed structures and associated artefacts. At West Whelpington the information on thirteenth- and fourteenth-century farmsteads was very fragmentary in those parts of the village which continued in occupation into post-medieval times; but in the south-west corner of the settlement a farmstead had been abandoned in the early fourteenth century and not reoccupied. There, a house and associated barn survived well, along with a trackway and the farmstead midden. A useful range of artefacts was associated with that phase of activity.[91] At Goltho and Barton Blount the final phases revealed worn yard surfaces, drains, middens, boundaries and buildings, the principal elements required for the interpretation of spatial organization in the farmstead.[92] A very detailed (and therefore time-consuming) record of artefact and bone distributions within a toft could provide invaluable information about function and farming routine, given a suitable site and appropriate conditions of excavation. All too often circumstances have not been appropriate. The kind of site worth treating in this fashion is exemplified by West Hartburn, where significant artefact groups were recovered from debris on the floors of buildings abandoned in the sixteenth century.[93] For earlier periods, the best opportunities would be afforded by settlements abandoned at earlier dates, rather than by the excavation of earlier levels in late-deserted villages.

CONCLUSIONS AND PROSPECTS

Most of the farmsteads excavated in this region are or were located in deserted villages. Unfortunately the amount of work achieved at any single village site has usually been too limited to give more than a fragmentary picture of the history and organization of the settlement as a whole. Even very restricted excavation will provide some information at this level: the artefact assemblage, for example, will indicate the minimum chronological range of occupation; but a fuller understanding of spatial organization and development requires large-scale excavation.

The scale of operations needed to achieve such an understanding can be seen at West Whelpington, where in the final seasons entire blocks of crofts and large parts of the village green were uncovered. This work enabled the

---

[90] The faunal remains from these pits are particularly important.

[91] In the house, a hole-set pottery vessel *in situ*; in the barn, a chest padlock and the coin hoard; in the midden and on the trackway, large quantities of pottery.

[92] G. Beresford, *The Medieval Clay-land Village*, pp. 16–17, figs 6–7.

[93] Still and Pallister, 'The excavation of one house site', pp. 196–200; idem, 'West Hartburn 1965', pp. 146–7.

excavators to draw conclusions relating to the settlement as a whole rather than to its components. For example, it was possible to show that the toft areas on one side of the village green had been cultivated as a single unit in the thirteenth century, before division into smaller plots: this accounted for the disproportionately large quantity of potsherds, and the recovery of joining sherds from different crofts; it also accounted for ploughmarks on the bedrock. Again, extensive work on the village green indicated that the west end of the settlement had been abandoned in the early fourteenth century, and that a new western boundary bank had been established to delimit the smaller settlement area.[94] This sort of information, at village level, is certainly no less significant than equivalent data at farmstead level. The problem is that village-wide questions cost far more to answer by excavation than farmstead-wide questions.

In these circumstances, it may be more realistic to employ 'village' excavation in a limited role: to use it to test hypotheses derived from field survey or documentary research. In the north-east, for example, it has been claimed on the basis of written and cartographic evidence that many villages were laid out (or restructured) with regular plans in the twelfth century, and that the plans then remained largely unchanged into post-medieval times.[95] The first part of this hypothesis has a measure of support from the main excavated sites: from West Whelpington, which seems to have been founded on a new site with a two-row plan in the late eleventh or twelfth century; from Wharram Percy, which may have acquired a regular layout of tofts and crofts in the twelfth century, and from Thrislington, where the regular rows of tofts were also probably laid out in the twelfth or early thirteenth century.[96] It could, however, be evaluated much more precisely if a site were chosen and an excavation designed specifically for this purpose. In the present circumstances, when the funding required for major village excavations is scarce, it is all the more important to define exactly the objectives, whether at peasant building, peasant messuage or village-wide level. The MSRG will, I hope, play a valuable role in the formulation of these objectives, in building upon the foundations laid by Maurice Beresford and John Hurst.

---

[94] Evans and Jarrett, 'West Whelpington, part 1', pp. 251 and 228.

[95] The hypothesis was originally presented in B. K. Roberts, 'Village plans in County Durham: a preliminary statement', *Medieval Archaeology*, 16 (1972), pp. 33–56; further discussion will appear in Austin, *The Deserted Medieval Village of Thrislington*.

[96] D. H. Evans, M. G. Jarrett and S. Wrathmell, 'The deserted village of West Whelpington, Northumberland, third report, part 2', *Archaeologia Aeliana*, 5th ser., 16, forthcoming; P. Stamper (ed.), *Wharram Research Project: Interim Report on 37th Season* (1986), p. 1; J. G. Hurst, 'The Wharram research project: results to 1983', *Medieval Archaeology*, 28 (1984), pp. 83–5; Austin, *The Deserted Medieval Village of Thrislington*.

15

Environmental Archaeology as an Index of Continuity and Change in the Medieval Landscape

MARTIN BELL

INTRODUCTION

Continuity and change are among the most important and intractable issues facing medieval archaeologists. A vast literature examines these processes from such varied perspectives as those of artefact typology, art history, settlement morphology, place names and historical sources. Such studies of rural settlement were, until recently, greatly hampered by the temporal and spatial frames of reference which archaeologists set for themselves. Projects were formulated within the straightjacket imposed by traditional archaeological periods and the emphasis was usually on the fortunes of individual 'sites' rather than the broader trends in landscape development as a whole. Today the emphasis has shifted towards multi-period landscape studies in which environmental archaeology has an important role to play because it provides us with additional sources of information against which we can test ideas derived from more traditional archaeological and historical sources.

Where sequences of environmental evidence are preserved in non-site contexts, such as lakes, peat and colluvial deposits, they can provide a much longer perspective on landscape evolution than we can generally obtain from individual excavated sites. Such sequences provide information about landscape utilization which is independent of the vicissitudes of individual failed settlements and may be a more effective way of measuring continuity and change. As Sawyer has pointed out, 'continuity of occupation can never be *proved* archaeologically'.[1] Yet a more critical question, especially in the context

---

[1] P. H. Sawyer, 'Medieval English settlement: new interpretations', in *English Medieval Settlement*, ed. P. H. Sawyer (London, 1979), pp. 1–8.

I should like to acknowledge the helpfulness of correspondents who have provided information about current work or sent copies of unpublished papers, in particular Grenville Astill, Tony Brown, Camilla Dickson, Joy Eide, Annie Grant, Julie Jones, Peter Murphy, Mark Robinson and David Windell. I am grateful to Michael Aston and David Austin for discussing these themes with me and to the latter for his percipient comments on an earlier draft.

269

of the shifting polyfocal settlement pattern envisaged by Taylor for much of England before the later Saxon period,[2] is whether there was continuity of activity. Here the tendency in the past has been to adopt a rather extreme position of assuming discontinuity of *land use* as well as settlement whenever the limited resolution of the evidence permitted.

In stressing the potential of non-site-based environmental sequences for medieval archaeology we should not lose sight of the importance of site-based evidence such as plant macrofossils and animal bones which give a particularly palaeoeconomic perspective to the problem of continuity and change.

This chapter will explore these issues in the period between *c*.410 and 1500 with particular emphasis on two aspects. The first is the comparison of traditional archaeological sequences and environmental evidence in the immediately post-Roman 'dark ages'. The second is the role of environmental archaeology in the study of deserted rural settlements of the later medieval period. The emphasis is not primarily palaeoeconomic and no attempt is made to summarize the animal bone or seed evidence available from medieval rural settlements. Such evidence is noted only where it provides examples pertinent to the main theme of continuity and change.

What role we see for environmental archaeology depends partly on how we define it as a discipline. Some see the objective as reconstructing the environment round archaeological sites. This in a sense provides a backcloth against which the historically and archaeologically attested action takes place. The idea that we are talking about background information finds its natural (if greatly exaggerated) expression in specialist contributions tucked away at the end of reports, or more recently hidden in microfiche, neither appearing to bear any relationship to the main objectives or conclusions of the project. A broader definition is the scientific study of man's past ecological relationships. Here the emphasis is very much on the interactive nature of man/environment changes through time. The stance is an explicitly ecological one as proposed by Dimbleby and Butzer.[3] Adoption of an ecological approach to past human communities means that study of settlement patterns or economic change cannot be divorced from work on their landscape interactions. The converse is equally true and many natural historians have come to appreciate that in order to understand the present character of many environment types we must look at the past history of human activity. Taylor has suggested that 'the history of settlement in England is more a reflection of man than his environment'.[4] It may, however, be more profitable to look at the interactions between these two factors than to try to measure their relative importance.

---

[2] C. C. Taylor, *Village and Farmstead: A History of Rural Settlement in England* (London, 1983).

[3] G. W. Dimbleby, *Ecology and Archaeology* (London, 1977); K. Butzer, *Archaeology as Human Ecology* (Cambridge, 1982).

[4] Taylor, *Village and Farmstead*, p. 108.

ENVIRONMENTAL ARCHAEOLOGY IN THE MEDIEVAL PERIOD

For more than a decade many prehistorians have incorporated major environmental programmes in their projects and the importance of this evidence has been emphasized by the Prehistoric Society in its 'Priorities for the future'.[5] Work on medieval sites has been more limited, perhaps because of the wider range of sources, particularly historical information, in this period. This is reflected by some of the general texts on environmental archaeology which give particular emphasis to bronze age and earlier events and less consideration to the emergence of a man-made agricultural landscape in later prehistory and the historic period.[6] Particular attention was, however, focused on man/environment relationships in the iron age to Anglo-Saxon period in a volume edited by Jones and Dimbleby; more recently Jones has examined the whole question of landscape evolution before Domesday and has done much to demonstrate the importance of the prehistoric settlement and landscape legacy to the archaeology of medieval England.[7]

In recent regional surveys of environmental archaeology author after author stressed the extreme paucity of evidence from post-Roman rural environments.[8] Publications on medieval rural sites often contain, at most, small-scale reports on biota. Sieving programmes do not appear to have been commonly employed. Where they have been carried out, however, valuable plant macrofossil evidence has been forthcoming, as for instance in East Anglia and in Wessex, where Green has demonstrated the value of comparing the biological evidence with documentary sources.[9] This point has also been made very effectively by Grant in a survey of the animal bone evidence from medieval sites.[10]

The most conspicuous achievements of post-Roman environmental archaeology have been in an urban context and are exemplified by the work at York.[11] In

[5] Prehistoric Society, 'Prehistory, priorities and society: the way forward', *Proceedings of the Prehistoric Society*, 50 (1984), pp. 437–43.

[6] J. G. Evans, *The Environment of Early Man in the British Isles* (London, 1975); I. Simmons and M. Tooley (eds), *The Environment in British Prehistory* (London, 1981).

[7] M. Jones and G. W. Dimbleby (eds), *The Environment of Man: The Iron Age to the Anglo-Saxon Period* (BAR, British ser., 87, 1981); M. Jones, *England Before Domesday* (London, 1986).

[8] H. C. M. Keeley (ed.), *Environmental Archaeology: A Regional Review* (2 vols, London, 1984, 1987).

[9] P. Murphy, 'Iron Age to late Saxon land-use in the Breckland', in *Integrating the Subsistence Economy*, ed. M. Jones (BAR, International ser., 181, 1983), pp. 177–209; F. J. Green, 'Iron Age, Roman and Saxon crops: evidence from Wessex', in *The Environment of Man*, ed. Jones and Dimbleby, pp. 129–54; F. J. Green, 'The archaeological and documentary evidence for plants from the medieval period in England', in *Plants and Ancient Man*, ed. W. Van Zeist and W. A. Casparie (Rotterdam, 1984), pp. 99–114.

[10] A. Grant, 'Animal resources', in *The Countryside of Medieval England*, ed. G. Astill and A. Grant (Oxford, 1988), pp. 149–87.

[11] A. R. Hall and H. K. Kenward (eds), *Environmental Archaeology in the Urban Context* (CBA Research Report no. 43, 1982); T. P. O'Connor, A. R. Hall, A. K. G. Jones and H. K. Kenward, 'Ten years of environmental archaeology at York', in *Archaeological Papers from York Presented to M. W. Barley*, ed. P. V. Addyman and V. E. Black (York, 1984), pp. 166–72.

urban situations, and in some other extreme forms of man-made environment such as castles and probably monasteries, which produce comparable biological assemblages, much of the evidence reached the sampling site as a direct consequence of human activity. The information is not so much about the environment around the site as about the pattern of past human activity, the quality of urban life and palaeoeconomy. Many scholars (for example, in the context of bones)[12] have lamented the paucity of contemporary rural data which makes it impossible fully to examine interactions between town and country. One example can be quoted which, though in a sense urban, is very pertinent to the theme of this chapter. Micromorphological examination by Macphail of post-Roman dark earths showed that some of them were deliberately deposited soils for the cultivation of crops within the urban area.[13] This accords with the archaeological evidence for largely depopulated towns, some of which continued as royal or ecclesiastical centres.[14]

Turning away from settlement-based studies to work on landscape, there have been some very major advances since the early 1960s. Of cardinal importance is the work of Turner who, as early as 1964, demonstrated to botanists the significance of anthropogenic factors and showed medieval archaeologists and historians the potential of comparing their data with the independent palaeobotanical record,[15] a theme subsequently developed by Bartley and well illustrated by Moffatt's recent comparison of historical and palynological sources on Battle Abbey estates.[16] A further source of evidence, which is not so readily applicable to earlier periods, is the use of present-day plant communities to help reconstruct earlier landscapes. Thus Hooper has demonstrated that the number of tree species in a hedgerow gives an indication of its age and that some hedgerows extend back at least as far as the Saxon period.[17] Of even greater significance has been Rackham's use of a wide range of evidence, particularly botanical composition and historical sources, to show the extent to which ancient woodland survives; in some instances a woodland history back to the Saxon period can be demonstrated and Rackham argues that the presence of some plant species implies a direct link back to the wildwood. Such areas may have survived not as waste but as a continually husbanded

[12] M. Maltby, *The Animal Bones from Exeter 1971–5* (Sheffield, 1979); J. Coy and M. Maltby, 'Archaeozoology in Wessex', in *Environmental Archaeology*, ed. Keeley, vol. II, pp. 204–49.

[13] R. Macphail, 'Soil and botanical studies of the dark earth', in *The Environment of Man*, ed. Jones and Dimbleby, pp. 309–31.

[14] M. Biddle, 'Towns', in *The Archaeology of Anglo-Saxon England*, ed. D. M. Wilson (Cambridge, 1976), pp. 99–150.

[15] J. Turner, 'Anthropogenic factors in vegetation history', *New Phytologist*, 63 (1964), pp. 73–89.

[16] D. D. Bartley, 'Palaeobotanical evidence', in *English Medieval Settlement*, ed. Sawyer, pp. 133–42; B. Moffat, 'The environment of Battle Abbey estates (East Sussex) in medieval times: a re-evaluation using analysis of pollen and sediments', *Landscape History*, 8 (1986), pp. 77–93.

[17] E. Pollard, M. D. Hooper and N. W. Moore, *Hedges* (London, 1974).

resource since woodland management was not a medieval innovation but extends at least back to the neolithic.[18]

For several years medieval environmental work has been on a convergent course with the developments in historical geography and local history which were stimulated by the work of W. G. Hoskins. Gradually there has been a welcome erosion of the barriers between academic disciplines and one manifestation of this has been the development of landscape archaeology. Only rarely, so far, has a range of sources of evidence been applied to a major investigation within a single study area, as for instance in Smith's retrogressive analysis of landscape in Staffordshire.[19] An example of what can be achieved comes from Steensberg's project at Borup, Denmark, where Mikkelsen has compared a pollen sequence adjacent to Viking and medieval settlement with the archaeological, historical and post-medieval cartographic record.[20]

THE PRE-SAXON LANDSCAPE LEGACY

A traditional view was expressed by Hoskins: 'Though most English villages had made their appearance by the time of the Norman Conquest vast areas remained in their natural state awaiting the sound of a human voice. In many regions like the extensive forest of Andredesweald or the great midland forest, the primeval woods were still shedding and renewing their leaves with no eye to notice and no human heart to regret or welcome the change.'[21] Subsequent work has dramatically changed this picture. We now know that by the Anglo-Saxon period the country was largely cleared of woodland and the landscape was already fully settled and utilized.[22] The extent to which views have changed is illustrated by work in the two parts of the country specifically noted by Hoskins. Andredesweald – the Weald of south-east England – was considered to be primary woodland until Saxon and medieval clearance; the evidence consisted of the limited prehistoric finds, place names, historical evidence for assarts and the belief that dependent settlements attested in the charters and later documentary sources must necessarily be late foundations. These issues have

[18] O. Rackham, *Trees and Woodland in the British Landscape* (London, 1976); idem, *Ancient Woodland: Its History, Vegetation and Use in England* (London, 1980); idem, *The History of the Countryside* (London, 1986); idem, 'Neolithic woodland management in the Somerset levels: Garvin's, Walton Heath and Rowland's tracks', *Somerset Levels Papers*, 3 (1977), pp. 65–71.

[19] C. Smith, 'Ancient landscapes in south eastern Staffordshire: a study in field archaeology and historical topography in the parishes of Alrewas, Fisherwick and Whittington' (unpublished Ph.D. thesis, University of Nottingham, 1977); idem, 'The historical development of the landscape in the parishes of Alrewas, Fisherwick and Whittington: a retrogressive analysis', *South Staffordshire Archaeological and Historical Society Transactions*, 20 (1980), pp. 1–14.

[20] V. M. Mikkelsen, *Borup: Man and Vegetation* (Copenhagen, 1986).

[21] W. G. Hoskins, *The Making of the English Landscape* (Harmondsworth, 1955), p. 76.

[22] Rackham, *Ancient Woodland*, p. 131; Taylor, *Village and Farmstead*; Jones, *England before Domesday*.

been critically discussed from the perspective of historical geography by Brandon, whilst subsequent work on the Battle Abbey estate by Moffat has demonstrated that there is no precise correlation between the historical and ecological sequences.[23] The pollen suggests dense woodland until about 1400; the historically documented assarts of the eleventh and twelfth centuries do not register because, as Moffat argues, they were small-scale and separated by woodland. Furthermore, a major clearance about 1400 occurs at all four pollen study sites and was accompanied by erosion but cannot, however, be correlated with historical records. It is accepted that the Weald was the largest concentration of woodland in medieval England and was perhaps 70 per cent tree-covered at the time of Domesday.[24] The critical question, however, is to what extent that woodland was primary or secondary. Pollen analysis of riverine silts at Sharpsbridge and Chiddingly show long histories of clearance and activity which, though not supported by radiocarbon dates, certainly go back well into prehistory.[25] Likewise Amberley, on the southern edge of the Weald, was open by the bronze age.[26] Accumulating evidence of early activity in the Weald lends support to the idea recently expressed by Sawyer and Taylor that the dependent territories are not necessarily late and could in fact reflect pre-Saxon modes of land use.[27] Elsewhere Roberts and others have drawn on pollen evidence to hint at possible pre-Saxon origins for shielings in Weardale, County Durham.[28]

The second area specifically noted by Hoskins was the midlands, where Smith has shown that the density of iron age sites, together with environmental evidence from sites like Fisherwick, indicates that substantial areas had been cleared of primary woodland by the end of the first millennium BC.[29] One area with very little pre-medieval archaeological evidence is the Arrow valley where Hooke suggests that extensive woodland remained for clearance in early medieval times; even here, however, the environmental record shows a very major episode of clearance and soil erosion from arable land during the first millennium BC.[30]

[23] P. Brandon, 'The South Saxon Andredesweald', in *The South Saxons*, ed. P. Brandon (Chichester, 1978), pp. 138–59; Moffat, 'Battle Abbey estates'.

[24] Rackham, *Ancient Woodland*, p. 124.

[25] R. G. Scaife and P. J. Burrin, 'Floodplain development in the vegetational history of the Sussex High Weald and some archaeological implications', *Sussex Archaeological Collections*, 121 (1983), pp. 1–10; R. G. Scaife and P. J. Burrin, 'The environmental impact of prehistoric man as recorded in the Upper Cuckmere Valley at Stream Farm, Chiddingly', *Sussex Archaeological Collections*, 123 (1985), pp. 27–34.

[26] P. V. Waton, 'Man's impact on the chalklands: some new pollen evidence', in *Archaeological Aspects of Woodland Ecology*, ed. M. Bell and S. Limbrey (BAR, International ser., 146, 1982), pp. 75–91.

[27] Sawyer, 'Medieval English settlement', p. 6; Taylor, *Village and Farmstead*, p. 182.

[28] B. K. Roberts, J. Turner and P. F. Ward, 'Recent forest history and land-use in Weardale, Northern England', in *Quaternary Plant Ecology*, ed. H. J. B. Birks and R. G. West (Oxford, 1973), p. 220.

[29] Smith, 'Ancient landscapes in south eastern Staffordshire'.

[30] D. Hooke, *The Arrow Valley, Warwickshire: An Archaeological and Landscape Survey* (Birmingham University Department of Geography, Working Paper 12, 1981); F. W. Shotton, 'Archaeological inferences from the study of alluvium in the Lower Severn-Avon valleys', in *The Effect of Man on the*

DARK AGE REGENERATION

Many authors have assumed that following the end of the Roman period large-scale woodland regeneration occurred. This assumption has even been used to date regenerations for which no radiocarbon date is available.[31] Consideration of the extent to which this traditional view is substantiated by the environmental record will begin with pollen sites not directly associated with settlement excavations.

Certainly there are many sites with evidence for a reduction in agricultural activity associated with regeneration between about the fifth and tenth centuries. Turner lists eleven widely distributed radiocarbon-dated sites, four in the north-east, two in the north-west, two in Scotland, and individual sites in Yorkshire, Derbyshire and Exmoor; to these the chalkland sites of Amberley (Sussex) and Snelsmoor (Berkshire) may be added.[32] An important aspect of some of the sites is that regeneration did not occur immediately following the Roman period but, in two sites in the north-east, as late as the seventh century.[33] Indeed two other north-eastern sites, Thorpe Bulmer and Steward Shield Meadow, show continued agricultural activity through the Anglo-Saxon period, and at the former site there was clear evidence of continuous hemp cultivation from 114 BC to AD 1098.[34] Similarly at Leash Farm (Derbyshire) there is little evidence of a decline in agricultural activity between the Roman and Norse episodes, and at Winnell Moors high levels of cultivars are found between 1000 BC and AD 1000 just north of Winchester.[35] The pollen diagrams at Hockham Mere show no post-Roman regeneration but some signs of a shift to pastoralism at the expense of cereals in the late Roman/early Saxon period.[36] Murphy reports macrofossil evidence from valley sediments at Chelmsford indicating continuous crop growing, including the cultivation of spelt (*Triticum spelta*) from late Roman to late Saxon times.[37] On the Somerset Levels the major peak of palynologically attested agricultural activity, which

---

Landscape: The Lowland Zone, ed. S. Limbrey and J. G. Evans (CBA Research Report, no. 21, 1978), pp. 27–32.

[31] P. D. Moore, 'Human influence upon vegetational history in North Cardiganshire', *Nature*, 217 (1968), pp. 1006–9.

[32] J. Turner, 'The vegetation', in *The Environment of Man*, ed. Jones and Dimbleby, pp. 67–74; Waton, 'Man's impact on the chalklands'.

[33] J. Turner, 'The environment of north-east England during Roman times as shown by pollen analysis', *Journal of Archaeological Science*, 6 (1979), pp. 285–90.

[34] D. D. Bartley, C. Chambers and B. Hart-Jones, 'The vegetational history of parts of south and east Durham', *New Phytologist*, 77 (1976), pp. 437–68.

[35] Leash Farm: Bartley, 'Palaeobotanical evidence'; Winnell Moors: Waton, 'Man's impact on the Chalklands'.

[36] R. E. Sims, 'Man and vegetation in Norfolk', in *The Effect of Man on the Landscape*, ed. Limbrey and Evans, pp. 57–62.

[37] P. Murphy, 'Plant macrofossils from two sections through river valley sediments on the Chelmsford by-pass, Essex', *Ancient Monuments Laboratory Report*, 120/87 (1987), pp. 1–13.

began at the time of the 'lake villages' *c.*250 BC, continued uninterrupted into the Romano-British period and well beyond at Meare Heath.[38] This fits very well with the cemetery and settlement record for Somerset which shows a major concentration of sub-Roman activity in an area which was probably not conquered by the Saxons until the seventh century. Being the only area of rich agricultural lowland to maintain its independence for so long, Somerset represents an important laboratory for investigation of the continuity question. Environmental evidence may help to establish whether agricultural activity on the Somerset clay levels continued and whether, as Rahtz has hypothesized, the distinctive society that emerged during this 300-year period owed more to indigenous pre-Roman society than to the wreckage of Roman Britain.[39]

Central Wales is also of special interest because the Romano-British period seems to have made so little impact on native economy and settlement, and the area was not significantly affected by dark age migrations. Turner's pollen diagram from Tregaron Bog shows an iron age pattern of largely pastoral activity continuing without interruption until the twelfth century.[40] Further pollen evidence from central Wales or the south-west would certainly be an effective way of helping to quantify the degree of continuity and facilitating comparison with other areas in the west of the British Isles. For instance, Pennington's Lake District work has identified a 'Brigantian' clearance episode which is late and post-Roman.[41] One possible cause might be population movements associated with the collapse of the Roman frontier. Further useful comparisons are with the situation in Ireland where Mitchell and Lynch have pollen evidence for a very marked expansion of agricultural activity in the early Christian period.[42] All thirteen of the horizontal mills, for which dendro-chronological dates have recently been obtained, were constructed between 630 and 926,[43] which confirms a high level of arable activity in the period when we know from archaeological evidence that a large proportion of raths and crannogs were occupied.

Though there are sites with evidence of dark age regeneration it seems that the environmental picture as a whole provides a significant element of support for the prevailing archaeological view that there was a substantial element of continuity in the post-Roman rural landscape.[44] Clearly the evidence of

[38] S. C. Beckett and F. A. Hibbert, 'The influence of man on the vegetation of the Somerset Levels – a summary', *Somerset Levels Papers*, 4 (1978), pp. 86–90.

[39] P. Rahtz and P. Fowler, 'Somerset AD 400–700', in *Archaeology and the Landscape*, ed. P. Fowler (London, 1972), pp. 187–221; P. Rahtz, 'Celtic society in Somerset AD 400–700', *Bulletin of the Board of Celtic Studies*, 30 (1983), pp. 176–201.

[40] Turner, 'Anthropogenic factors'.

[41] W. Pennington, 'Vegetational history in the north-west of England: a regional synthesis', in *Studies in the Vegetational History of the British Isles*, ed. D. Walker and R. G. West (Cambridge, 1970), pp. 41–79.

[42] F. Mitchell, *The Irish Landscape* (London, 1976), pp. 135–7; A. Lynch, *Man and Environment in South West Ireland* (BAR, British ser., 85, 1981).

[43] M. G. L. Baillie, *Tree Ring Dating and Archaeology* (London, 1982), p. 192.

[44] P. J. Fowler, 'Agriculture and rural settlement', in *The Archaeology of Anglo-Saxon England*, ed. D. M.

continuity is not confined to the west of the country and some of the sites are within the lowland villa zone of Roman Britain. Furthermore it must be stressed that our environmental, particularly pollen, evidence, in common with our archaeological evidence for relict landscapes, tends to be biased away from the best agricultural land where, it could be argued, the greatest degree of continuity of activity is to be expected. Environmental evidence, in tandem with radiocarbon dates, will be particularly important for investigations of the continuity question in parts of the country which were effectively aceramic at this time and where it is consequently very difficult to identify and date post-Roman activity.

DARK AGE SETTLEMENTS

Few Romano-British sites have been examined for environmental evidence pertinent to the continuity question. Archaeological evidence is more common, for instance at Shakenoak where, however, a largely speculative account of the site's vegetational history published by Woodell in 1972 followed traditional lines in suggesting that much of the land fell into disuse at the end of the Roman period. The limited biological evidence published in a subsequent Shakenoak volume includes nothing to support this argument; indeed, there are hints of largely open conditions in post-Roman times.[45] At Barton Court Farm the archaeology shows continued settlement by Anglo-Saxons close to the villa.[46] There was no evidence for a significant increase in woodland at this time and continued cultivation of flax (*Linum usitatissimum*) can be inferred from the presence of seeds associated with an unusual weed of flax crops (*Camelina alyssum*) in both Romano-British and Anglo-Saxon contexts.[47] Despite the fact that there is arguably more evidence of continuity between Romano-British and Anglo-Saxon than between the two Romano-British phases in the site's development, significant changes did take place during the early fifth century. The Romano-British buildings and agricultural installations were abandoned and the environmental evidence suggests less intensive settlement and agriculture exemplified particularly by the abandonment of cultivation on low-lying ground which presumably required the maintenance of drainage. Well to the north on moorland at Fortress Dyke camp, radiocarbon and pollen evidence

Wilson (Cambridge, 1976); Taylor, *Village and Farmstead*; J. G. Hurst, 'The medieval countryside', in *Archaeology in Britain since 1945*, ed. I. G. Longworth and J. Cherry (London, 1986), pp. 197–236.

[45] S. A. J. Woodell, 'Changes in vegetation at Shakenoak', in A. C. Brodribb, A. R. Hands and D. R. Walker, *Excavations at Shakenoak Farm, Nr. Wilcote, Oxfordshire*, vol. III (Oxford, 1972), p. 156; vol. V (Oxford, 1978), pp. 161–8.

[46] D. Miles, *Archaeology at Barton Court Farm, Abingdon, Oxon* (CBA Research Report no. 50, 1984).

[47] M. Robinson and B. Wilson, 'A survey of environmental archaeology in the south midlands', in *Environmental Archaeology*, ed. Keeley, vol. II, p. 59, and M. Robinson, pers. comm.

suggest that cereal growing associated with an agricultural settlement continued into the seventh century.[48] Such evidence should also perhaps prompt us to re-evaluate the date of the enclosure itself, which has hitherto been seen as Romano-British.

Environmental data from dark age settlements themselves is often fairly limited but is supplemented by evidence of the field relationships between Romano-British and dark age features. The settlements at Cowdery's Down, Chalton, Bishopstone, Heslerton, West Stow and Mucking were all in landscapes cleared and exploited long before the dark ages. None of these sites produced any sign of regeneration between Romano-British and dark age phases. However at Brandon (Suffolk) there is a clear landscape change associated with the foundation of a middle Saxon settlement when a valley peat sequence shows that heath vegetation was burnt.[49] At Cowdery's Down late Roman field boundaries preceded the settlement and these produced molluscan evidence of a change from arable to pasture.[50] At Bishopstone Romano-British occupation lasted until at least the end of the fourth century but Anglo-Saxon buildings spread over the lynchets of earlier Celtic fields which the Mollusca suggest then reverted to pasture until post-medieval times.[51] The Chalton Anglo-Saxon settlement was in an area of Romano-British pasture surrounded by arable (figure 15.1).[52]

Though several of these sites have evidence of Romano-British activity and sometimes settlement, none is associated with a major focus of settlement. This is most clearly illustrated by West Stow in the Lark valley, an area intensively occupied in the Roman period when the foci of settlement were on the fen edge. West notes, however, that Saxon settlements are all on the gravel terraces and hypothesizes a shift from the fen edge occasioned by climatic or sea level change.[53] The coincidence of that change with the Anglo-Saxon occupation is perhaps more explicable in terms of the suggestion that the Saxon settlement was slotted into an unused heathland corner of a still flourishing Romano-British estate.[54] Certainly Murphy's environmental work shows that the site was heathland of low grazing potential.[55] The possibility of continuous crop growing somewhere within the site's catchment is suggested by the continuance

---

[48] H. M. Tinsley and R. T. Smith, 'Ecological investigations at a Romano-British earthwork in the Yorkshire Pennines', *Yorkshire Archaeological Journal*, 46 (1974), pp. 23–33.

[49] Murphy, 'Land-use in the Breckland'.

[50] M. Millett and S. James, 'Excavations at Cowdery's Down, Basingstoke, Hants, 1978–81', *Archaeological Journal*, 140 (1983), pp. 151–279.

[51] M. Bell, 'Excavations at Bishopstone', *Sussex Archaeological Collections*, 115 (1977), pp. 1–299.

[52] B. W. Cunliffe, 'Chalton, Hants: the evolution of a landscape', *Antiquaries Journal*, 53 (1973), pp. 173–90.

[53] S. West, *West Stow: The Anglo-Saxon Village* (East Anglian Archaeology, 24, 1985), vols I and II, pp. 159–63.

[54] Taylor, *Village and Farmstead*, p. 119.

[55] P. Murphy, 'The cereals and crop weeds', in West, *West Stow*, pp. 100–9.

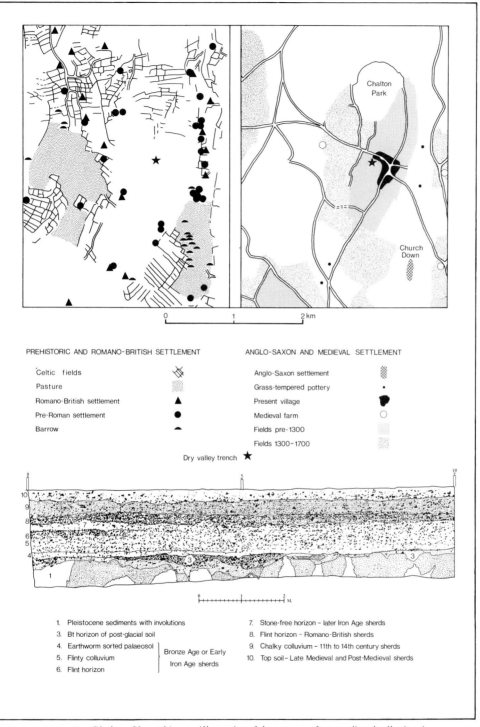

PREHISTORIC AND ROMANO-BRITISH SETTLEMENT

Celtic fields

Pasture

Romano-British settlement ▲

Pre-Roman settlement ●

Barrow ⌒

ANGLO-SAXON AND MEDIEVAL SETTLEMENT

Anglo-Saxon settlement

Grass-tempered pottery ·

Present village

Medieval farm ○

Fields pre-1300

Fields 1300–1700

Dry valley trench ★

1. Pleistocene sediments with involutions

3. Bt horizon of post-glacial soil

4. Earthworm sorted palaeosol ⎤
5. Flinty colluvium ⎬ Bronze Age or Early
6. Flint horizon ⎦ Iron Age sherds

7. Stone-free horizon – later Iron Age sherds

8. Flint horizon – Romano-British sherds

9. Chalky colluvium – 11th to 14th century sherds

10. Top soil – Late Medieval and Post-Medieval sherds

FIGURE 15.1 *Chalton, Hampshire: an illustration of the presence of pre-medieval colluvium in an area covered by medieval fields, which otherwise lacks evidence of earlier settlements and cultivation.*

of spelt as the main crop from the Romano-British into the early phase of the Saxon settlement and some continued exploitation of the heavier clay soils is evidenced by the finding of *Anthemis cotula* among the weed species. Hints of continuity of activity also come from Heslerton where one of the field boundaries associated with the Anglian settlement perpetuated a major landscape boundary first established *c.*1000 BC. At both Heslerton and West Stow the fragile and somewhat marginal nature of the ecosystems settled is emphasized by evidence for aeolean sand deposition, though at West Stow this is dated to the thirteenth century.[56] The marginal or hilltop nature of all of the sites suggests that they may have been established within landscapes which were already fully utilized. Eventual abandonment of these sites, often after relatively short occupations, could have as much to do with declining agricultural returns as with more widespread settlement pattern changes.

So much depends on what was going on in the valleys and vales where traditionally archaeologists have believed settlement shifted in the Anglo-Saxon period with desertion of the uplands. It now appears that the evidence of earlier activity in these areas is buried by medieval colluvium or obscured by the very intensity of later land use.[57] At Heslerton in North Yorkshire the use of the landscape transect concept illustrates that the Vale of Pickering was at least as intensively settled as the archaeologically better known, partially relict landscape of the Yorkshire Wolds.[58] Chalton (Hampshire) provides a case study (figure 15.1). The valley floor area of medieval arable was largely empty of prehistoric and Romano-British sites on Cunliffe's distribution maps.[59] Investigation of dry valley sediments within the medieval fields next to the present village revealed a long history of agriculture stretching back to the bronze age or early iron age.[60] The Mollusca and sediments indicate open, dry, probably arable conditions since prehistory. No evidence was found of early/middle Saxon sherd scatters which might have related to a settlement established directly after abandonment of the hilltop site on Church Down, although Cunliffe reports grass-tempered pottery elsewhere in the parish.[61] Intensive land use as represented by sherd scatters probably from manuring seems to have begun as late as the eleventh century and to have reached a very definite peak in the thirteenth and fourteenth centuries.

[56] Murphy, 'Land-use in the Breckland'.

[57] M. Bell, 'Valley sediments as evidence of prehistoric land-use on the South Downs', *Proceedings of the Prehistoric Society*, 49 (1983), pp. 119–50.

[58] D. Powlesland, 'Excavations at Heslerton, North Yorkshire 1978–82', *Archaeological Journal*, 143 (1986), pp. 53–173, esp. fig. 4.

[59] Cunliffe, 'Chalton, Hants'.

[60] M. Bell, 'Valley sediments as evidence of prehistoric land-use: a study based on dry valleys in south-east England' (unpublished Ph.D. thesis, University of London, 1981), p. 387.

[61] B. W. Cunliffe, 'Saxon and medieval settlement pattern in the region of Chalton, Hampshire', *Medieval Archaeology*, 16 (1972), pp. 1–12.

LATER MEDIEVAL SETTLEMENT

The shifting settlement pattern exemplified by the early Saxon settlements is seen by Taylor as the norm for England since prehistory.[62] The trend towards apparent stability, the nucleation of settlement, the formation of villages and the establishment of the open-field system he regards as a largely late Saxon and medieval process. Perhaps the eleventh-century date for the onset of intensive cultivation round Chalton should be seen in this context, though it is some two centuries later than the date originally put forward by Cunliffe.[63] Elsewhere environmental evidence of intensification occurs at a variety of dates and its causes are often unclear. For instance at Hockham Mere cereal growing increased greatly between AD 650 and 850, and it has been suggested that this was a result of the introduction of new crops (for example, rye, *Secale cereale*) which were less susceptible to drought,[64] of more favourable climatic conditions,[65] or of settlement pattern changes. There is certainly environmental evidence for intensification at the time of the archaeologically and historically attested agricultural peak in the twelfth to fourteenth centuries. This is as true of the lowland zone, for example Rimsmoor and sites in the Upper Thames Valley,[66] as it is of moorland sites. The relationship of these changes to the process of settlement nucleation remains, however, to be investigated.

The most detailed picture of the relationship of deserted medieval settlement to the continuum of landscape development comes from Wharram Percy, Yorkshire. Here the first twenty-five years of the project emphasized its medieval aspects and suggested discontinuity with the limited evidence of Romano-British activity. Since the mid-1970s it has become clear that part of the plan of the medieval village was determined by the layout of the Romano-British fields and there is considerable evidence of Anglo-Saxon activity. So far environmental work has been relatively small-scale considering the archaeological importance of the project. The first report includes accounts of bones and small groups of charcoals, charred seeds and molluscs.[67] More recently medieval millpond deposits have produced good assemblages of pollen, cereals and weed seeds which suggest a landscape largely devoid of woodland with much evidence of crop growing.[68] Prehistoric to medieval colluvial deposits in

[62] Taylor, *Village and Farmstead*.

[63] Cunliffe, 'Chalton, Hants.', p. 187.

[64] Sims, 'Man and vegetation in Norfolk'.

[65] Murphy, 'Land-use in the Breckland'.

[66] Waton, 'Man's impact on the chalklands'; Robinson and Wilson, 'Environmental archaeology in the south midlands'.

[67] D. D. Andrews and G. Milne, *Wharram: A Study of Settlement on the Yorkshire Wolds* (Society for Medieval Archaeology, monograph no. 8, London, 1979), vol. I.

[68] G. Hillman, 'Wharram Percy: cereal remains from the thirteenth century dam' (unpublished report); M. Bush, 'Report on the palynology of the samples from the ponds at Wharram Percy' (unpublished report, Department of Geography, Hull University, 1981); J. Jones, 'Wharram Percy, Site 71 Graveyard boundary SE' (unpublished report on plant macrofossils).

a glacial hollow may help to establish the origins of this landscape. The long-lived boundaries and lynchets are also of potential interest because molluscan and artefact studies could show whether there was continued or interrupted land use.[69] It is ironic that British archaeologists working on the Brittany survey have made intensive investigations of lynchet deposits, whereas in the British Isles such work has been very limited since the studies of Wood and Whittington which were designed to date strip lynchets rather than specifically to confront the continuity question.[70] Environmental work would also show what landscape changes, if any, were associated with the progression envisaged by Beresford and Hurst from a number of separate settlements in Romano-British and Anglo-Saxon times to the emergence of the nucleated polyfocal settlement in the medieval period.[71]

Issues of this kind are currently being confronted by another multi-period landscape project at Raunds (Northamptonshire), where there is potential for an environmental sequence from post-Roman times to c.fifteenth century, in particular from a palaeochannel associated with the West Cotton deserted medieval hamlet.[72] Plant macrofossil evidence from West Cotton points to medieval cultivation of the heavy claylands and valley floors and it will be interesting to see whether this precedes establishment of the hamlet in about the ninth century. Another facet of the problem concerns the crops grown; at present Romano-British contexts produce mostly spelt (*Triticum spelta*) whilst in medieval contexts the main crop was rivet wheat (*Triticum turgidum*).

SETTLEMENT OF UPLAND AND OTHER 'MARGINAL' AREAS FOR ARABLE

In these areas the potential for good associated environmental sequences is greater, particularly where pollen is preserved, but perhaps there is less inherent likelihood of continuity of land use. A lowland zone example is the medieval farmstead established in the late twelfth century at Kiln Combe (East Sussex) as a result of agricultural expansion onto a block of dry downland which appears to have been devoid of settlement since the fourth century.[73] The farmstead lasted until the sixteenth century and palaeo-environmental evidence

[69] Bell, 'Excavations at Bishopstone', pp. 251–66; P. L. Drewett, *The Archaeology of Bullock Down, Eastbourne, East Sussex: The Development of a Landscape* (Sussex Archaeological Society, monograph I, 1982), pp. 17–21, 99–104, 130–2.

[70] G. Astill and W. Davies, 'Fieldwalking in East Brittany, 1982', *Cambridge Medieval Celtic Studies*, 41 (1982), pp. 19–31; P. Wood and G. Whittington, 'Further excavation of strip lynchets north of the Vale of Pewsey in 1958', *Wiltshire Archaeological and Natural History Magazine*, 57 (1959), pp. 322–38.

[71] M. W. Beresford and J. G. Hurst, 'Wharram Percy: a case study in microtopography', in *English Medieval Settlement*, ed. Sawyer, pp. 52–85.

[72] J. Eide and A. Brown, pers. comm.

[73] Drewett, *The Archaeology of Bullock Down*, p. 143.

suggests that sheep and crop growing were the basis of the economy and that crops were represented in comparable proportions to those suggested by late medieval documentation for elsewhere in the region. Arable activity of an intensive nature is indicated by the existence, adjacent to the settlement, of deep colluvial deposits (figure 15.2) containing large quantities of medieval pottery.[74] These sediments sealed and masked evidence for Romano-British, iron age and beaker activity on the valley floor and the sediments and molluscs between them suggest open conditions since prehistory. There was, however, no certain evidence for cultivation or pottery scatters between the fourth and twelfth centuries.

Cefn Graeanog (Gwynedd) is a comparable farmstead with a significantly different history.[75] Its life was relatively brief in the twelfth and thirteenth centuries but this area too had evidence of agriculture extending back to the bronze age. A Romano-British enclosed hut group continued in use into the sixth century and, though no settlement has been excavated between then and the establishment of the medieval farmstead, it is clear that arable activity continued, as demonstrated by Chambers's pollen analysis of a colluvial deposit.[76] Charred macrofossils from the medieval farmstead show that oats (*Avena* sp.) were the main crop confirming historical evidence from the area.[77] On the Romano-British site spelt and six-row barley were the main crops, but an element of continuity is suggested by the continued growing of some spelt in the medieval period.

Environmental evidence has played an important part in demonstrating medieval expansion of agriculture onto Dartmoor. Pollen diagrams at Holne Moor, Okehampton Park and Houndtor[78] show cereal growing, which on some sites is radiocarbon-dated between the twelfth and fourteenth centuries. Sometimes the episode was very brief, as at Shaugh Moor where there were only occasional cereal grains in basically pastoral spectra.[79] Elsewhere, however, as in the Holne Moor lobes, cultivation seems to have been longer-term. The radiocarbon dates at both Houndtor and Okehampton Park could

---

[74] Bell, 'Valley sediments as evidence of prehistoric land-use', p. 143.

[75] R. Kelly, 'The excavation of a medieval farmstead at Cefn Graeanog, Clynnog, Gwynedd', *Bulletin of the Board of Celtic Studies*, 29 (1982), pp. 859–908.

[76] F. Chambers, 'New applications of palaeoecological techniques: integrating evidence of arable activity in pollen peat and soil stratigraphies, Cefn Graeanog, North Wales', in *Integrating the Subsistence Economy*, ed. M. Jones (BAR, International ser., 181, 1983), pp. 107–22.

[77] Hillman, in Kelly, 'Cefn Graeanog', p. 901.

[78] D. Maguire, N. Ralph and A. Fleming, 'Early land use on Dartmoor – palaeobotanical and pedological investigations on Holne Moor', in *Integrating the Subsistence Economy*, ed. Jones, pp. 57–106; D. Austin, R. H. Daggett and M. J. C. Walker, 'Farms and fields in Okehampton Park, Devon: the problems of studying medieval landscape', *Landscape History*, 2 (1980), pp. 39–57; D. Austin and M. J. C. Walker, 'A new landscape context for Houndtor, Devon', *Medieval Archaeology*, 29 (1985), pp. 147–52.

[79] S. C. Beckett, 'Pollen analysis of the peat deposits', in K. Smith, J. Coppen, G. J. Wainwright and S. Beckett, 'The Shaugh Moor Project 3rd report', *Proceedings of the Prehistoric Society*, 47 (1981), pp. 245–66.

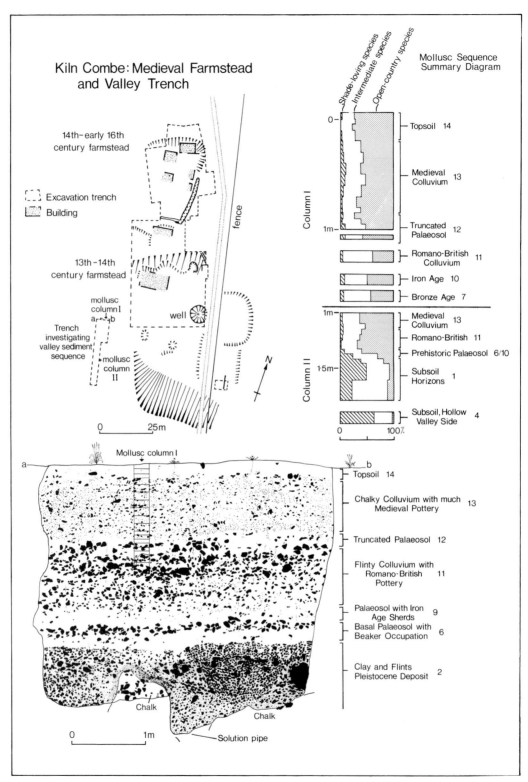

FIGURE 15.2 *Kiln Combe, East Sussex: an illustration of the time depth of activity in valley sediments adjoining the medieval farmstead.*

also suggest relatively long-term cereal growing. As for the origins of the associated field systems, Saxon precursors have been argued for the Holne Moor lobes and Beresford sought a Saxon origin for Houndtor, though here Austin favours much later foundation which may have helped to trigger peat inception at the pollen site during the earlier thirteenth century.[80] Only at Okehampton does the pollen sequence extend back into the Anglo-Saxon period and in largely pastoral spectra there is very little cereal pollen until post-Saxon times.

Desertion of upland medieval settlements has often been associated with the Little Ice Age, a climatic change well attested by early instrumental records (in its latter phases) and by a wide range of proxy sources.[81] Parry has investigated the effect of these changes on medieval upland settlement.[82] He has demonstrated that in the Lammermuir Hills of south-east Scotland, at the limits of cultivation 300 m OD, a decline in annual temperature of as little as 0.3°C could lead to a doubling of the frequency of harvest failure.[83] Climatic change is thus a possible cause of the clear retreat of settlement from this upland area between 1300 and 1600. Guy Beresford has argued that climatic change was an important factor, not only in the abandonment of Houndtor,[84] but also the clayland settlement at Goltho (Lincolnshire), where he suggested that architectural styles reflected increasing wetness.[85] This argument seems to put too great an emphasis on climatic determinism to the exclusion of other possible factors. Kelly has more cautiously suggested that the abandonment of Cefn Graeanog, archaeomagnetically dated *c.*1240, might also have been climatically caused.[86] This is not, however, substantiated by Chambers's subsequent work on peat humification which showed a correlation between humification (often taken to indicate a drier, more favourable climate) and *reduced* agricultural activity.[87] He concluded that in this instance peat humification reflected land use rather than climatic factors. Parry has urged a cautious approach, arguing that 'space time coincidences between climatic change and economic change do not necessarily indicate a causal connection.'[88] Ladurie is equally circumspect

[80] G. Beresford, 'Three deserted medieval settlements on Dartmoor: a report on the late E. Marie Minter's excavations', *Medieval Archaeology*, 23 (1979), pp. 98–158; D. Austin, 'Dartmoor and the upland village in the south-west of England', in *Medieval Villages*, ed. D. Hooke (Oxford University Committee for Archaeology, monograph no. 5, Oxford, 1985), pp. 71–9.

[81] E. Le Roy Ladurie, *Times of Feast, Times of Famine: A History of Climate Since the year 1000* (London, 1972).

[82] M. L. Parry, *Climate Change, Agriculture and Settlement* (Folkestone, 1978).

[83] M. L. Parry, 'Evaluating the impact of climatic change', in *Consequences of Climate Change*, ed. C. Delano-Smith and M. Parry (Department of Geography, Nottingham University, 1981), pp. 3–16.

[84] G. Beresford, 'Climatic change and its effects upon the settlement and the desertion of medieval villages in Britain', in *Consequences of Climate Change*, ed. Delano-Smith and Parry, pp. 30–9.

[85] G. Beresford, *The Medieval Clay-land Village: Excavations at Goltho and Barton Blount* (Society for Medieval Archaeology, monograph no. 6, London, 1975).

[86] Kelly, 'Cefn Graeanog'.

[87] Chambers, 'New applications of palaeoecological techniques'.

[88] Parry, 'Evaluating the impact of climatic change'.

and argues that future work on climatic history should be based on comparative analyses of various sources.[89] Desertion has been a major preoccupying theme of medieval rural studies and the relative importance of plague, climatic, social and economic factors have been debated many times. A review of the evidence in the context of settlement ecology and specific site-based studies is long overdue.

CONCLUSIONS AND THE FUTURE

The environmental evidence reviewed in the first part of this chapter suggests a significant element of continuity in landscape exploitation from Roman into post-Roman Britain, rather more so perhaps than is suggested by the historical sources, place names and by individual excavated settlements. Regeneration, though it occurred, was not universal and the number of sites showing continued activity after c.410 is growing; on some of them there was continuity in the growing of specific crops. The second part of this chapter has tended to put more emphasis on discontinuity, perhaps because the later evidence comes particularly from upland and moorland areas. The lowland valleys and vales are perhaps inherently more likely to have been continuously cultivated and we need more information about their land use history in dark age and medieval times. Pollen analyses of localized peats and alluvial sequences, together with mollusc work on colluvial deposits and more extensive sieving and sampling programmes, will all help. Such studies are also pertinent to an understanding of the landscape context of nucleation and desertion and could profitably be used to investigate the vegetation history of specific areas of surviving ancient woodland in order to establish whether they have an unbroken history back to the wildwood.

Medieval archaeologists need to give a higher profile to environmental work in their research designs. A proportion of the new generation of projects should be specifically selected close to suitable environments of deposition where the environmental and cultural sequences can be closely correlated. Specialists need to be involved with the planning of projects and on a regular basis during excavation. All this demands a concentration of specialists and resources on certain key projects. Only then will we have sufficient comparative data fully to test archaeologically and historically derived ideas against the environmental record.

[89] Ladurie, *Times of Feast, Times of Famine*, p. 308.

16

Parachutists and Truffle-hunters: At the Frontiers of Archaeology and History

RICHARD HODGES

INTRODUCTION

Emmanuel Le Roy Ladurie commented wryly that there are two kinds of historians: parachutists and truffle-hunters. The former observe the past from afar, slowly floating down to earth. The latter, transfixed by the discovery of buried treasures, keep their noses close to the ground. Not unnaturally, these two kinds of historian find it difficult to work together. The archaeological community has a slightly different constituency. Truffle-hunters abound, of course, but the parachutists are really sky-divers. They depend upon teamwork and have exhibitionist tendencies. Nonetheless, after the showmanship they must pull the ripcord and float gently to earth. Once there, if they have any sense, they cannot overlook the truffles.

Le Roy Ladurie, it has to be admitted, exaggerates the polarization of history. Few historians can avoid studying truffles, even if – as in the case of Ladurie – their vision is global. As they float earthwards, it is their early training in truffling that makes it possible to interpret the past. Even the practitioners of the 'isms', as Lawrence Stone caustically describes them,[1] have

[1] L. Stone, 'The revival of narrative; reflections on a New Old History', *Past and Present*, 85 (1979), pp. 3–24.

The San Vincenzo project has been a collaboration between the Soprintendenza Archaeologica del Molise and the University of Sheffield, funded by the Soprintendenza, the British School at Rome, the British Academy, the Craven Fund and the Society of Antiquaries; the Montarrenti project was a collaborative investigation between the universities of Sheffield and Siena, funded by them and by the Provincia di Siena; the Roystone Grange project is a Sheffield University first-year undergraduate training school funded by the university, the Peak Park Planning Board and Sheffield City Museum.

I had the opportunity to write this paper while Visiting Professor in the University of Copenhagen, supported by a grant from the Danish Research Council. In writing it I appreciate the debt that I owe to Peter Hayes and Chris Wickham at San Vincenzo, to Riccardo Francovich at Montarrenti and to Graeme Barker, Robin Torrence and Martin Wildgoose at Roystone Grange. Truffling with these parachutists has been enormously stimulating! Finally, I am grateful to David Austin for making some valuable comments on a first draft.

some training in truffle-hunting. But the archaeology of the historic periods is at first sight a deviant 'ism' wherein trufflers focus upon habitat, or the sky-divers make sweeping sketches of the panorama while descending too rapidly to focus on anything in particular. Finding common ground amongst archaeologists meriting the attention of historians has proved a challenge.

In this essay I wish to consider how this challenge might be met to the profit of such a diverse academic community. First, we must take stock of who we are, as Eleanor Searle has recently pointed out.[2] Searle argues that some of us are naturally either parachutists or truffle-hunters in everyday life: we approach the past, therefore, charged with our experiences of the present. This is no great revelation, but Searle's cautionary views are nonetheless instructive. Archaeology has long been populated with those who claim it is impossible to reconstruct the past,[3] just as it has had some who counter that they can bring to life the attitudes of past peoples.[4] The reality is more complex, as I hope to show.

Secondly, we must be prepared to define the past as closely as we can. Historical archaeologists have been singularly unhappy about doing this. To set up a model of 'how it was' (to quote Lewis R. Binford)[5] undeniably begs many questions. Nevertheless, the model is not a definition of truth; it is simply a hypothesis and one model may be substituted for another. The alternative which has predominated in historical archaeology is to *assume* that features of the present existed in some rudimentary guise in the past. Marx described such an approach as vulgar history,[6] that is a history framed to sustain the ideology of the prevailing *status quo*. For example, any student of the middle ages needs to appreciate that the concepts of modern marketing are an inappropriate guide to interpreting this period.[7] Similarly, modern social concepts are most inappropriate models with which to interpret medieval society. Likewise, the environment and climate varied considerably during the middle ages and cannot be assumed to have been static. In a nutshell, models of the middle ages devised over the past century are being superseded by those worked out in recent decades, invariably by interdisciplinary scholarship. Even so, our models are inevitably shaped by historiography. Shaping and reshaping these models will continue until all the attributes of the past can be satisfactorily simulated. As a result a symbiotic relationship will continue to connect truffle-hunters, who analyse the data in detail, and parachutists, who invariably devise the models. This process in the case of medieval Europe is being much enlarged by archaeologists. Their trufflers are shedding light from unexpected

---

[2] E. Searle, 'Possible history', *Speculum*, 61 (1986), pp. 779–86.

[3] J. Hawkes, 'The proper study of mankind', *Antiquity*, 42 (1968), pp. 255–62.

[4] I. Hodder, *Symbols in Action* (Cambridge, 1982).

[5] L. Binford, *In Pursuit of the Past* (London, 1983).

[6] M. Leone, 'Some opinions about recovering mind', *American Antiquity*, 47 (1982), pp. 742–60.

[7] R. Hodges, *Primitive and Peasant Markets* (Oxford, 1988).

sources on this period, while the sky-divers, because of the highly developed interdisciplinary basis of the subject, are finding new ways of interpreting the information.[8]

Thirdly, and arising from the last point, we need to be clear about what archaeology and history are. Archaeology concerns the study of material culture. At an antiquarian level this may amount to no more than stamp-collecting, but modern archaeology has sought to serve the human sciences. It involves studying the past in such a way as to reveal human behaviour. Thus, through the archaeological study of settlement systems in a geographical or spatial way, past regions, communities and household units within those communities are illuminated. The material attributes of these systems, in addition, permit archaeologists to illustrate production, distribution and consumption patterns, as well as the ways in which, across space and time, people chose to express themselves. In this respect written documents are archaeological objects. Hence archaeologists must be attentive to the expression of views in them, but recognize also that invariably they are cultural expressions of an elite, and to assume that these adequately reveal society as a whole would be a fallacy. The principal goal of the archaeologist must be to reconstruct the behaviour not only of those who made history (from the architects of our cathedrals to the kings of England), but of those, the majority, denied history. This appears to be all the more important in medieval Europe wherein the marxist picture of a feudal elite and a passive peasantry is rapidly being superseded by a more complex appreciation of evolving socio-economic relations between classes, paving the way for the inception of capitalism.[9] For instance, George Dalton has rightly distinguished the traditional peasant marketing system of medieval western Europe from those systems practised in other early modern and pre-industrial societies as well as those practised in colonies.[10] These bald distinctions have been fiercely criticized by Eric R. Wolf,[11] but nonetheless they serve to make a point which calls attention to our historical poverty as far as peasantries, those denied history, are concerned.

History, as Braudel defines it, lies beyond the scope of the documentary analyst. History in his view involves three systemic levels of interaction: first, *la longue durée*, man's timeless interaction with his environment; second, social process in which the behaviour of peoples is observed; and third, the short-lived intervention of individuals and events.[12] The written sources are simply

[8] R. Hodges, 'Spatial models, anthropology and archaeology', in *Landscape and Culture*, ed. J. M. Wagstaff (Oxford, 1987), pp. 118–33; see K. Randsborg, *First Millennium: From Roman Empire to Medieval Society* (Cambridge, forthcoming).

[9] J. A. Hall, *Powers and Liberties. The Causes and Consequences of the Rise of the West* (Harmondsworth, 1986).

[10] G. Dalton, 'Peasantries in anthropology and history', *Current Anthropology*, 13 (1973), pp. 385–415.

[11] E. R. Wolf, 'Comments, on Dalton's *Peasantries in Anthropology and History*', *Current Anthropology*, 13 (1973), pp. 410–11.

[12] F. Braudel, *On History* (London, 1980).

not good enough to write a history of pre-modern times in this way. The sample of documents is difficult to assess and patchy in its coverage and, above all, it dwells upon the lifeways of the elite, the minority. Inevitably, the archaeologist, with a great diversity of data at his disposal derived from both the elite and the peasantry and with an increasingly scientific methodology, must find common ground to work with the documentary historian.

One of the real problems with archaeology, however, is that excavated material taken from any cultural system is far too small a sample to allow adequate evaluation. Archaeologists have been guilty of sustaining biases in their approaches to the past, such as concentrating upon certain landscapes and neglecting others, or certain categories of sites, or those parts of sites which are materially rich in débris. To take account of this problem, archaeologists in recent years have followed geographers and historians in focusing upon regional units of socio-economic interaction. Binford, in particular, has drawn attention to the immensely complicated behavioural patterns fossilized in past landscapes,[13] while Robert Foley introduced the term 'off-site archaeology' to describe those patterns where significant non-sedentary activities occurred.[14] Prehistorians are now beginning to appreciate what medieval archaeologists have long since recognized:[15] no part of the landscape may have been inaccessible to humans.[16] Yet at best the archaeologist is a parachutist trying to make sense of the complex and ever-changing use of the landscape in the past. Indeed, to be a truffle-hunter, content to concentrate on only the pitifully small parts of the past uncovered in excavations, is to eschew any understanding of this complexity.

The key to making some sense of this complexity lies in the sampling strategy that the archaeologist adopts. Sampling horrifies truffle-hunters, as Kent Flannery illustrated most amusingly,[17] and as medieval archaeologists in dinosaur-like mood confirm at annual meetings of the Society for Medieval Archaeology.[18] But, in the words of Lewis Binford (writing more than a decade ago), 'the days of argument about whether sampling is appropriate in archaeology are over, and those engaged in such discussion are . . . fossils of a past era.'[19] Sampling strategies depend upon defining research goals. Any

[13] Binford, *In Pursuit of the Past*, p. 110.

[14] R. Foley, 'Incorporating sampling into initial research design: some aspects of spatial archaeology', in *Sampling in Contemporary British Archaeology*, ed. J. F. Cherry, C. S. Gamble and S. Shennan (BAR, British ser., 50, 1978), pp. 49–66.

[15] C. C. Taylor, *Fieldwork in Medieval Archaeology* (London, 1974).

[16] H. M. Wobst, 'We can't see the forest for the trees: sampling and the shapes of archaeological distributions', in *Archaeological Hammers and Theories*, ed. J. A. Moore and A. S. Keene (London, 1983), pp. 37–85.

[17] K. Flannery, *The Early Mesoamerican Village* (London, 1976).

[18] ibid.; D. Hinton, 'Introduction', in *25 Years of Medieval Archaeology*, ed. D. Hinton (Sheffield, 1983), pp. 3–11.

[19] L. Binford, 'Sampling, judgement and the archaeological record', in *Sampling in Archaeology*, ed. J. W. Mueller (Tucson, Arizona, 1975), pp. 251–7.

archaeologist who wishes to understand past cultural systems cannot expect to excavate entire regions or even entire communities. The research strategy instead must be explicit, taking account of field resources, the present conditions in the landscape and the existing information about the fossilized past. The archaeological record poses problems because there are so many unknowns, quite unlike, for example, the problems faced by ecological sampling where the surface outlines, at least, are transparently clear already. Indeed, it is not an exaggeration to claim that the existence of the often enigmatic and inestimable character of the archaeological record has been a major constraint upon archaeological investigation, inhibiting the scientific exploration of historical problems.

In the illustrations which follow, I hope to demonstrate how sampling techniques permit parachutists to come to terms with truffling. The three projects described here examine aspects of medieval history from the standpoint of the peasant. Each endeavours to forswear the divide that separates archaeology and history, aiming instead to reveal patterns in the past that will serve as significant contributions, new models, for rewriting the history of those who made Europe.

DETECTING UNKNOWN SITES

The San Vincenzo Project, Molise, Italy

This project was designed to examine the early medieval monastery of San Vincenzo al Volturno and its relation with other settlements in its *terra*. Initially, it was intended to define only the broad outlines of the monastery, notably its size and its general topographical features over the course of its long history. It seemed unreasonable, as actually happened, to suppose that something approaching the St Gall Plan[20] might be literally excavated, let alone a palimpsest of plans on one spot.[21] At the outset also, a well-dated crypt on the site was already known, containing paintings in which a historical figure was depicted as being alive. This meant that a key chronological point existed to which excavated stratigraphy could be linked, and from which one might then hope to devise a tight chronology for the kinds of low-value artefacts that occur not only at an elite centre like a monastery, but at rural sites as well. Potsherds, in particular, might then be used to identify elusive peasant habitations.

With this knowledge, therefore, an extensive (50 km sq.) survey of the *terra* of San Vincenzo was undertaken. This territory extends from the mountains of

[20] W. Horn and E. Born, *The Plan of St. Gall* (Berkeley, Cal., 1979).

[21] R. Hodges (ed.), *San Vincenzo al Volturno: Excavations and Surveys 1980–86* (British School at Rome, London, forthcoming).

the Mainarde at 2000 m to the valleys around the old Roman towns of Isernia and Venafro (figure 16.1). In ecological terms this is marginal hill country which in recent years has been the scene of marked agrarian poverty. The San Vincenzo survey was limited to the ploughed zones within each of the transects spread out across the region; it was impossible, for example, to examine the wooded hillsides, hilltops and the areas covered by modern settlements. Nevertheless, the survey conclusively revealed that early medieval potsherds of the type encountered at the monastery in well-dated levels did not occur on first- to fifth-century sites. In fact, no diagnostically early medieval potsherds were found in the field survey. Any early medieval sites, it could be safely concluded, must lie outside the bounds of the survey.[22]

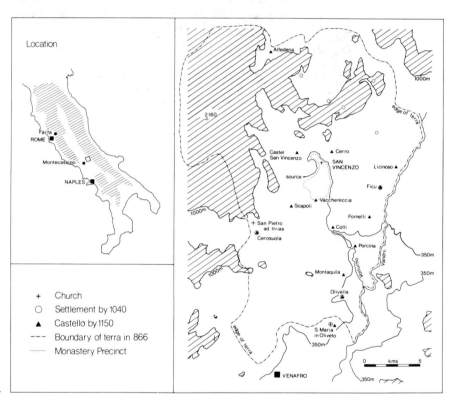

FIGURE 16.1 *Location of Italian sites mentioned in the text.*

As a result, using the historical sources as a guide, each of the medieval villages in the *terra* was identified and visited. Several of these are still villages, but seven are deserted medieval villages, occupying hilltop situations. Two of these, Colle Castellano (*Olivella*) and Vacchereccia (*Baccaricia*) (plate 16.1), at either end of the *terra*, were selected for further investigation. The village of

[22] ibid.

PLATE 16.1 *A view of Vacchereccia from Rocchetta al Volturno looking southwards down the Volturno valley. The twelfth-century village of Vacchereccia was discovered on the summit of the hill. The test-pitting took place on the hidden (south-facing) side of the hill (see figure 16.2).*

Olivella on the hill now known as Colle Castellano could be examined with trial-trenches in a straightforward manner.[23] Vacchereccia, however, posed problems. The historical sources suggest that the community might have begun as a *conduma* (a small farm owned by a tenant or slave) as early as the seventh or eighth centuries AD. Its charter, issued by San Vincenzo, attested to six households in 985.[24] The archaeology, however, offered a different view of this hill's past. A later Roman villa occupied the red, calcareous, well-textured soils at the base of the hill, while remains of a deserted later medieval village were located on the top of the hill. In 1981 a line of shovel pits (each ½ m × ½ m) were dug at 10 m intervals up the south-facing slope of the hill from its base (close to the Roman village) to the village on the top. This was no mean feat as it required cutting – that is, axing – a path through the thick, steep woodland that had grown over the twelve terraces which exist along this face of the hill.[25]

The pits on the summit of the hill produced typical later medieval (twelfth- to fifteenth-century) sherds, but those on terraces 3, 4 and 5 produced characteristic eighth- to eleventh-century sherds of a type well known at San Vincenzo, 4 km away (figure 16.2). In 1981 a trial trench within the downslope garden areas of the village on the summit confirmed that only later

---

[23] S. Coccia et al., 'Excavations at Colle Castellano (Province of Isernia): an early medieval village in the territory of San Vincenzo al Volturno', *Archeologia Medievale*, 15 (1988), forthcoming.

[24] R. Hodges et al, 'Excavations at Vacchereccia (Rocchetta Nuova)', *Papers of the British School at Rome*, 52 (1984), pp. 148–93.

[25] ibid.

medieval material was to be found here. As a result, in 1982, our attention turned to the mid-slope terraces. Here we excavated about sixty 1 × ½ m pits in an attempt to define the precise location of the settlement nucleus. This was eventually identified, centring on an earthen bank (F) separating terraces 4 and 5. After this we set out a trial trench to determine the extent and chronological range of the site, which was then followed by a small, open-area excavation and associated trenches which helped us to form an impression of the character of the settlement in some detail.

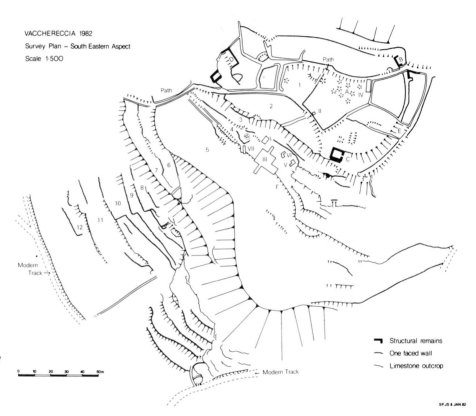

VACCHERECCIA 1982
Survey Plan – South Eastern Aspect
Scale 1:500

Structural remains
One faced wall
Limestone outcrop

FIGURE 16.2 *Map of Vacchereccia showing the terracing on the hill, the deserted medieval village on the hilltop and the trenches in which the early medieval site was located.*

This investigation, rough and ready though it was, permitted us to make an historical breakthrough of considerable importance, since it identified an early medieval settlement which experienced significant changes in the tenth century and again in the twelfth, close to the monastery of San Vincenzo. The developmental sequence involving settlement form, production, distribution, consumption and cultural expression, is similar in many ways to those discovered at Colle Castellano, the other village that was investigated in the *terra*, but altogether different from the pattern of development identified in the coastal region beyond the mountains where we also carried out surveys and excavations.[26] Two types of village development, therefore, appear to exist in the two broad ecological zones in this region. In addition, of course, the material culture of Vacchereccia (and Colle Castellano) can be tellingly compared to the staggering record discovered in the excavations of the monastery itself. This is not the place to describe this information, but our sample, while in many ways being no more than an archaeological glimpse comparable with the documentary glimpses, nonetheless permits us to begin the process of rewriting history. In this case the parachutist, who began with a grand problem of European significance, was forced after excavating half a hectare of San Vincenzo al Volturno and fieldwalking 50 km sq. of landscape, to pinpoint places for detailed investigation, and there, while shovel-pitting, he was regularly mistaken by surprised locals for . . . well . . . a mushroom-hunter!

SAMPLING MEDIEVAL COMMUNITIES

The Montarrenti Project

The sampling of regions to identify the location of sites has an inherent logic which has won approval from most archaeologists. But the archaeological sampling of communities tends to generate a good deal of debate, if not anger. The traditional archaeologist (and here I invent a genial character) assumes that the sampling of communities necessarily involves the laying out of trenches in an arrangement decided by some mathematical criteria. Quite clearly, random or probabilistic sampling has a place in archaeology. Charles L. Redman successfully illustrated its merits in his innovative excavations of the small late medieval town at Qsar es-Seghir, Morocco.[27] Likewise Grenville Astill and Susan Lobb[28] employed this technique to obtain palaeoeconomic data from the threatened middle Saxon rural site at Wraysbury (Berkshire). But Redman, the celebrated exponent of sampling in archaeology, has urged that 'judgement sampling', founded upon a logical ranking of questions, is no less an important technique for investigating sites where some information already exists. Redman demonstrates how he employed these two types of sampling at Qsar es-Seghir, and illustrates their relative merits. Perhaps the most impressive illustration of judgement sampling is to be found in operation at Ipswich

[26] R. Hodges, G. Barker and K. Wade, 'Excavations at D85 (Santa Maria in Civitá)', *Papers of the British School at Rome*, 48 (1980), pp. 70–125; R. Hodges and C. Wickham, 'Incastellamento and after: the evolution of hilltop villages in Molise', in *A Mediterranean Valley*, ed. G. Barker (Cambridge, forthcoming).

[27] C. L. Redman, *Qsar es-Seghir: An Archaeological View of Medieval Life* (London, 1986).

[28] G. Astill and S. Lobb, 'Sampling a Saxon settlement site: Wraysbury, Berks', *Medieval Archaeology*, 26 (1982), pp. 138–42.

(Suffolk). Here, under the direction of Keith Wade,[29] the middle Saxon emporium sealed beneath the modern city centre has been explored in a three-stage programme of rescue investigations: first, using watching briefs to define the extent of the Anglian settlement; second, a campaign of small excavations to ascertain variations across the 40 ha site; and finally, judiciously chosen large-scale excavations to provide detailed information about housing, rubbish disposal and so on. This is a remarkable enterprise because the sampling has had to be based upon the incidence of rescue threats, rebuilding and development. Yet already a picture is emerging of the settlement as a definable entity, as opposed to a picture resting upon some presently indeterminate fraction. Those excavations which offer only inestimable glimpses of the past are regarded by Redman as unscientific grab samples. Little use is made of extant information to construct a multi-stage investigatory strategy. Such excavations do not serve the historian well.

Nonetheless, exponents of sampling theory have seldom, if ever, had to investigate medieval villages which exist as earthwork sites. The sampling of communities is simpler if nothing can be identified on the surface, as was the case at Qsar es-Seghir, and as is the situation in Ipswich. Wharram Percy, for example, poses very different problems.[30] The outlines of the latest phase of many deserted dwellings can be clearly discerned on the surface, though the palimpsest of earlier phases extending back over half a millennium remain, as at Ipswich, concealed from the archaeologist.

Similar problems were encountered by Riccardo Francovich and myself at the comparable deserted medieval village of Montarrenti in the province of Siena (figure 16.3). Like Wharram, the outlines of many of the late medieval dwellings could be distinguished on the horseshoe-shaped shelf on the side of the lone hill it occupied. Unlike Wharram, though, two tower-houses and the stump of a third, forming the greater part of the medieval manorial complex, have survived to this day. Indeed, tower A is still partly inhabited by one household, while tower B was occupied by a family up until 1980. Montarrenti, therefore, comprises two parts:

1   The hilltop which was the seignorial sector of the settlement.
2   The horseshoe-shaped lower *bourg* extending from the shaded (north) side of the hill, around to a point on the sunny (south) side where two, much modified, medieval dwellings were occupied until the nineteenth century.

---

[29] K. Wade, 'Sampling at Ipswich: the origins and growth of the Anglo-Saxon town', in *Sampling in Contemporary British Archaeology*, ed. Cherry, Gamble and Shennan, pp. 279–84; K. Wade, 'Ipswich', in *The Rebirth of Towns in the West, AD 700–1050*, ed. R. Hodges and B. Hobley (CBA, 1988), pp. 93–100.

[30] J. G. Hurst, 'The Wharram research project: results to 1983', *Medieval Archaeology*, 28 (1984), pp. 77–111.

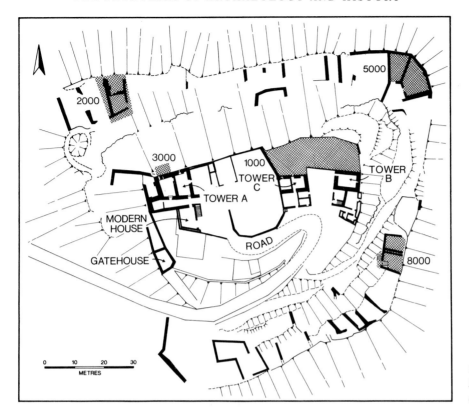

FIGURE 16.3 *Map of Montarrenti showing the excavated areas.*

The investigation of medieval villages in Tuscany is still in its infancy, so the project at Montarrenti was designed to examine critical historical questions. The following questions were posed at the beginning of the project in 1982:

1 At what date was the first hilltop village settled here?
2 What form did this village take; was it a small nucleus concentrated in one spot, or was it scattered across the hill?
3 At what date did the creation of the sectors within the village occur, bringing into existence the two separate parts and the seemingly planned arrangement of dwellings within the lower *bourg*?
4 Were the two sectors distinguished by different patterns of wealth in terms of their material culture?

The excavations spanned eighteen weeks over five seasons terminating in 1987, and involved a team of up to seventy undergraduates from Sheffield and Siena universities.[31] The samples were selected in order to answer these

[31] R. Francovich and R. Hodges (eds), 'Scavi nel villaggio abbandonato di Montarrenti (SI). Relazione preliminare 1982', *Archeologia Medievale* 10 (1983), pp. 317–32; R. Francovich and R. Hodges (eds), 'Il progetto Montarrenti (SI). Relazione preliminare, 1983', *Archeologia Medievale*, 11 (1984), pp. 255–95; R. Francovich and R. Hodges (eds), 'Il progetto Montarrenti (SI). Relazione preliminare, 1984',

questions. Area 1000 (about 10 m × 30 m) was excavated beside tower B on the hilltop where we expected to obtain the garden and rubbish deposits associated with this seignorial building, and underneath which we hoped to expose any pre-tower structures and levels relating to the earliest occupation of Montarrenti. In addition, the archaeology of the seignorial complex was investigated by Roberto Parenti, an architectural historian, who was able to phase and interpret each of the three towers. In the lower *bourg* three sample areas were selected. Area 2000 (10 m × 15 m) was a house-plot on the shaded, north side of the hill; area 5000, a trapezoidal area beside the eastern gate, lay in the apex of the horseshoe, and area 8000 (10 m × 7 m) is situated on the southern, sunny side of the hill. In all, about 5 per cent of the hilltop and three out of a total of approximately twenty-six house-plots were excavated.

As the excavations have so recently finished, any conclusions are bound to be only of a preliminary nature. Nonetheless, as a result of the sampling strategy, despite its rudimentary formulation, some general aspects of the community as a whole are clear. First, traces of early medieval dwellings cut into the rock were discovered on the hilltop (in area 1000), and making use of natural ledges in areas 2000, 5000 and 8000. On the hilltop (in area 1000) these buildings had been superseded by large post-built structures on the same alignment which were either burnt down or associated with a fire close by. Two radiocarbon dates for these structures suggest that they were destroyed about 950–1050 (this date is consistent with the pottery associated with these structures). The initial rock-cut buildings, therefore, belong to the later ninth or tenth century. Montarrenti, in other words, has been a hilltop village for just over a millennium, and is a typical example of what Italian historians term *incastellamento*. Of course, it is quite possible, because of the restricted size of our sample, that elsewhere on the hill there lies undetected an even earlier phase of settlement belonging to the wholly obscure period between the demise of classical dispersed farmsteads in the fourth century and the tenth century (cf. Vaccchereccia above).

The answer to our second question, however, differed from that which we had anticipated. We expected that the first village would have been concentrated on the hilltop. In fact, traces of rock-cut structures were discovered in each of the excavated samples. The structures in the lower *bourg*, however, ran along the contours, unlike the subsequent medieval dwellings whose long axes were aligned across the contours. Hence, although we might postulate that the village covered much the same area in the tenth century as it did three centuries later, it nevertheless included fewer buildings and thus, presumably, a smaller population. The size of the tenth-century settlement is most perplexing. Was it a new site, or, since we are restricted by the archaeological chronology for this

Archeologia Medievale, 12 (1985), pp. 403–45; R. Francovich and R. Hodges (eds), 'Il progetto Montarrenti (SI). Relazione preliminare, 1985', *Archeologia Medievale*, 13 (1986), pp. 257–320.

phase, are we observing the remains of a rapid demographic expansion of a small, long-running settlement within the space of one or two generations?

The sampling strategy has also boldly illuminated the sequence of changes to the village morphology over the millennium. The hill top sector was ambitiously altered in the early to mid-twelfth century when the tower-houses were constructed. These appear to have replaced long timber buildings that ran alongside the upper enclosure wall in area 1000. The tower-houses were plainly modelled on urban structures such as those still to be seen in Pisa, San Gimignano and Siena. Like their urban counterparts, it appears that those at Montarrenti incorporated the rooms, which had once been spread out across the hill, into multi-storied towers. This left plenty of space for a terraced garden alongside the enclosure wall.

At the same time the lower village was replanned. The first-phase dwellings running along the contours were replaced by slightly larger buildings placed in a line at right angles to the contours. Using the slope in this way provided sufficient space for two storeys in the downslope half of the dwelling. This pattern, like the narrow alleys which separate each house, are characteristic of Tuscan (and most traditional Italian) villages up until recent times. The new village was splendidly built in fine stone and displayed grandiose urban pretensions. Like similar villages investigated by Riccardo Francovich in Tuscany (at Rocca San Silvestro and Scarlino), Montarrenti is a vivid illustration of the great surge of wealth experienced in the countryside as the west Mediterranean economy regained momentum after seven centuries of slumber.[32]

For these reasons the patterns of wealth within the settlement are most interesting. A preliminary study shows that a higher proportion of poly-chrome–glazed thirteenth-century pottery occurs in area 1000 than within the dwellings in the lower *bourg*. Certainly, glassware occurs frequently within the garden levels on the hilltop, but is absent from the dwellings in areas 2000, 5000 and 8000. A preliminary analysis of the animal bone assemblages tends to confirm this picture. Finer cuts of meat were being discarded by the inhabitants of the hilltop than by their counterparts living below. None of this is too surprising, of course. After all, Sienese frescoes graced the walls of tower A in the fourteenth century, leaving us in no doubt of the social standing of the lords of Montarrenti on the eve of the Renaissance. Yet the deep middens of pottery, as well as the ironwork, coins and miscellaneous objects of late medieval date associated with the lower *bourg*, indicate that the peasantry of Montarrenti had ample opportunity to participate in the burgeoning markets of this region.

The picture of Montarrenti derived from this sample can hardly be described as scientifically acceptable. Ideally, twice the sample size is required

---

[32] R. Hodges, 'Anglo-Saxon England and the origins of the modern world system', in *Anglo-Saxon Settlements*, ed. D. Hooke (Oxford, 1988), pp. 191–207.

to be assured of the conclusions drawn here. Yet it is an hypothesis that offers a portrait of the community through time, and depicts many themes in such a way that they are of value for the history of medieval Italy as well as for the study of medieval archaeology.

SAMPLING OFF-SITE ARCHAEOLOGY

The Roystone Grange Project

Landscape archaeology has involved a shift away from traditional settlement-oriented investigation, putting pre-industrial communities into an appropriate agrarian context. However, landscape archaeology has been concerned with the recording of fossilized remains of agricultural activities (field systems, pens etc.) which, like the earthworks of deserted settlements, reflect the ultimate behaviour and not the sequence of activities. Robert Foley, in his studies of early hominids, urged archaeologists to step beyond the edge of their excavations to sample the 'off-site' archaeology of the landscape around: 'Most field archaeologists can predict intuitively the areas that contain the most material, and will gravitate towards them. If spatial information pertaining to human behaviour is to be extracted, then this temptation must be resisted, and the archaeologist must learn to spend more time in "poor" archaeological areas.'[33] In the valley of Roystone Grange, Derbyshire, 300 m up in the White Peak, Sheffield University has attempted an exercise in landscape archaeology that employs the experience of Wharram and heeds Foley's advice.

The Roystone Grange Project covers an area of about 4 km (north–south) by 3 km (east–west) of a valley and the plateau flanking it.[34] The project was designed to examine activity of all periods in the area, with a view to treating it as a microcosm of the White Peak plateau as a whole, and providing the first illustration within the Peak District National Park of the long-running antiquity of a present hill farm. The barrow cemetery in the valley is comparatively well known as a result of Thomas Bateman's antiquarian activities.[35] The Romano-British village, however, was unknown when we began, as were the extensive remains of the Cistercian grange. In the course of ten seasons (1978–87), therefore, a grid of test-pits (½ m × 1 m) has been excavated across the landscape to reveal the patterns of prehistoric 'off-site' archaeology (figure 16.4). In addition, a prehistoric stockpen was partially excavated. At the same time there has been a programme of excavations on the

---

[33] Foley, 'Incorporating sampling into initial research design', p. 52.

[34] R. Hodges and M. Wildgoose, 'Roman or native in the White Peak', *Derbyshire Archaeological Journal*, 101 (1981), pp. 42–58.

[35] R. Hodges, J. Thomas and M. Wildgoose, 'The barrow cemetery at Roystone Grange', *Derbyshire Archaeological Journal*, 109 (1989), forthcoming.

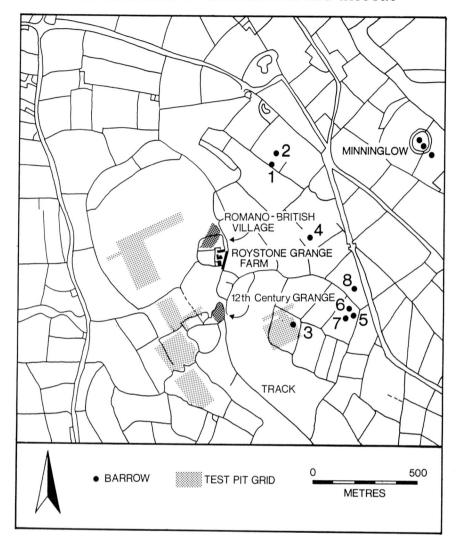

FIGURE 16.4 *Map showing the areas test-pitted at Roystone Grange, Derbyshire.*

Roman, medieval and post-medieval settlements. One Romano-British dwelling was entirely excavated, as was the yard of another, while samples of two further farms were also investigated.[36] Two of the principal buildings of the twelfth- to thirteenth-century grange have been excavated, while a full survey has been made of all the other earthworks.[37] Several of the post-medieval buildings have been fully surveyed, and one large area within the nineteenth-century

[36] Hodges and Wildgoose, 'Roman or native in the White Peak, Derbyshire'.

[37] R. Hodges, M. Poulter and M. Wildgoose, 'The medieval grange at Roystone Grange', *Derbyshire Archaeological Journal*, 102 (1982), pp. 88–100; R. Hodges and M. Wildgoose, 'The Cistercian grange at Roystone', *Derbyshire Archaeological Journal*, 109 (1989), forthcoming.

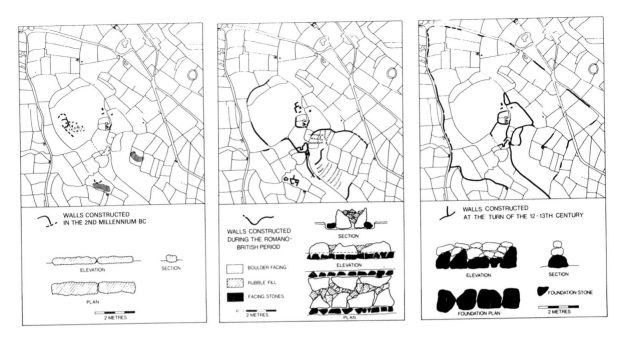

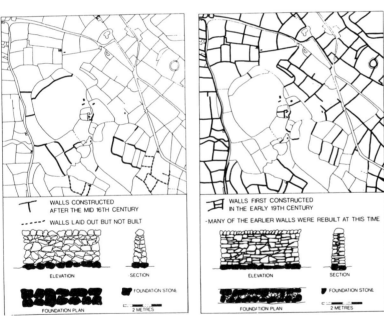

FIGURE 16.5 *Five millennia of field walls at Roystone Grange.*

brickworks has been excavated. Added to this, the 72 km of field walls and all the features in every field have been systematically surveyed (figure 16.5).[38]

In fact, Martin Wildgoose's survey of the field walls has made it possible to trace the evolution of the farm as an agrarian community since prehistoric times, while the test-pitting reveals the level of 'off-site' activity in this landscape over the same five millennia. Like Montarrenti, we are still at the stage of assembling and processing these data. Nonetheless, some patterns for the historic periods are already apparent.

Romano-British community   The pattern of walls and farms suggests that the valley was colonized in the early second century. Two large, walled enclosures, each about 26 ha in area, were constructed, embracing the hills either side of the settlement. The western enclosure is on poor ground, within which the test-pitting produced negligible quantities of Romano-British pottery. By contrast in the eastern enclosure, not only were small numbers of sherds found but also traces of fossilized Romano-British field systems. Evidently the community manured extensively, cultivating the high marginal ground, especially in later Roman times as the stress of the third-century crisis began to take its toll.

Cistercian grange community   The grange was owned by Garendon Abbey (Leicestershire) from the late twelfth century, one of three Peakland estates in their possession. Excavations of the sequence of twelfth- to thirteenth-century farmhouses indicates that this was a modestly affluent community, which to judge from the pattern of field walls, maintained an estate of about 150 ha. Within this, small garden plots lay close to the farm itself, and a tight inner ring of fields was disposed around the valley bottom, leaving large open areas divided by driving walls terminating in sheep pens on the hills above. Not only the assemblage of medieval pottery, mostly from the midlands, but the pattern of fields attests an economy based upon cash-cropping sheep. Foodstuffs were produced in modest measure, and manuring, if the pottery is a reliable index of this activity, only occurred in the garden plots. No sherds of medieval pottery were found elsewhere in the test-pits.

The late medieval to early post-medieval farm   The initial site of the grange was deserted by *c.* 1300 in favour of drier ground in the valley to the north. Here a linear arrangement of earthworks survives. It is likely that the grange remained here until the shift to the present site in the eighteenth century. During this period, in the sixteenth century, Roystone engaged in litigation with a neighbouring farm, Ballidon, about intervening common land. The walls enclosing this disputed land have provided us with a historically attested wall-type which can be used to illustrate a different usage of the valley at Roystone.

---

[38] M. Wildgoose, 'Roystone Grange', *Current Archaeology*, 105 (1987), pp. 206–8.

In particular, the number of fields in the valley was increased, while the pasture on the hilltops was divided into large paddocks. Test-pitting has produced small numbers of seventeenth- to eighteenth-century manganese-glazed wares only in the valley bottom; if these are associated with manuring, it shows how limited it was at this date. It seems that although the farm is recorded as running 600 sheep in the sixteenth century, and although parts of the landscape are scarred with lead-workings of this date, Roystone nevertheless shifted towards a greater emphasis on a mixed agrarian regime than had existed since later Roman times.

The agricultural revolution Just as the impact of the Emperor Augustus's imperial aspirations ultimately left an imprint upon these margins of iron age Britain, so the industrial revolution altered its complexion. According to local legend, Napoleonic prisoners-of-war constructed the miles of field walls and the many stone-lined field drains which are an outstanding feature of this valley and all parts of the White Peak today. The farm, a little before this, had moved to the site it occupies today, and the ensemble of the nineteenth-century farm buildings attests to the mixture of agrarian activities which took place here. The entire area had been divided into a mosaic of fields involving an immense investment of labour. The pattern suggests the intention, well known from other parts of England,[39] to intensify a mixed output of farm produce. The presence of lime-kilns for making fertilizers, for example, appears to confirm this impression of a quantum leap in agricultural activity that was as important as that better documented in our industrial towns. Interestingly, the test-pits seem to reveal that the integration of town and country described by Adam Smith, and recently analysed by Anthony Wrigley, can be traced even in an upland landscape.[40] The landscape contains notable amounts of broken plates, cider jars, drinking-cups and, less commonly, glassware belonging to the nineteenth century. Many of the objects may indicate intensification of manuring, but others surely reflect incidental farm work in the fields and also, perhaps, the changing attitudes to materialism generally.[41] In short, the wall-builders, wall-repairers, shepherds, farmhands as well as Roystone's household could afford to be as careless with their material culture as the inhabitants of Montarrenti had been five centuries before.

This brief description of some of the results of the Roystone Grange project aims to illustrate the kinds of historical themes which the archaeologists can examine by treating the past community as an entity that extends beyond the

[39] For example, S. Wade-Martins, *A Great Estate at Work: Holkham Estate and its Workers in the Nineteenth Century* (Cambridge, 1984).

[40] A. Wrigley, 'Urban growth and agricultural change: England and the continent in the early modern period', *Journal of Interdisciplinary History*, 15 (1985), pp. 683–728.

[41] K. Hart, 'On commoditization', in *From Craft to Industry*, ed. E. N. Goody (Cambridge, 1983), pp. 38–49.

edges of the dwellings. The 'off-site' archaeology, like the landscape itself, can be sampled with valuable results.

CONCLUSION

Each of these projects has yet to be fully published, whereupon historians ranging from parachutists to trufflers will be able to assess not only the results but also the manner in which these have been obtained. Each of these projects, however, has boldly attempted to serve greater ends with one singular model in mind: Wharram Percy. It is no idle act of homage to record that the frontier separating archaeology and history as well as the frontiers separating parachutists and trufflers would not be assailable were it not for the pioneering work of Maurice Beresford and John Hurst at Wharram Percy. This great project serves to illustrate to historians how fast archaeologists have come to terms with the need to understand those denied history. It also illustrates beyond any doubt that the integration of the human sciences, using the many methodologies at our disposal, will make us all the richer as far as understanding our past is concerned and will inform us more clearly of the role of our history in the making of the modern world.

List of Contributors

MICHAEL ASTON is Staff Tutor in Archaeology in the Extra-Mural Department of Bristol University. He is interested in all aspects of rural settlement, of all periods. He is author of *Interpreting the Landscape* (London, 1985) and editor of *Medieval Fish, Fisheries and Fishponds in England* (Oxford, 1988).

DAVID AUSTIN is Senior Lecturer in Medieval Archaeology at Saint David's University College, Lampeter, and Chairman of the Society for Landscape Studies. He applies a landscape approach to medieval settlement. His most recent work is *Thrislington, Co. Durham: Excavation of a Deserted Medieval Village 1973–4* (monograph, Society for Medieval Archaeology, 1989).

DAVID BAKER is Principal Conservation and Archaeology Officer in Bedfordshire County Planning Department and past Chairman of the Association of County Archaeological Officers. A medievalist when local government duties permit, he has written generally about the conservation of the historic environment in *Living with the Past* (Bletsoe, Bedford, 1983).

MARTIN BELL is Lecturer in Archaeology at Saint David's University College, Lampeter. He is an environmental archaeologist who excavated the Anglo-Saxon settlement at Bishopstone, Sussex, and is currently preparing monographs on two Bronze Age sites.

C. J. BOND, after seventeen years in county museum services in Worcestershire and Oxfordshire, now works freelance as a landscape historian and field archaeologist. He has written a number of articles and books on aspects of the medieval and post-medieval landscapes of the midlands and south of England.

CHRISTOPHER DYER is Reader in Medieval History at the University of Birmingham, and Secretary of the Medieval Settlement Research Group. He approaches rural settlements as a social and economic historian. His most recent work is *Standards of Living in the Later Middle Ages* (Cambridge, 1989).

H. S. A. FOX, Senior Lecturer in English Topography in the Department of English Local History at the University of Leicester, approaches social and economic history as a topographer. His interests lie in the south-western counties of England, from the fifth century to the fifteenth.

DAVID HALL is Fenland Survey Officer for the Cambridgeshire Archaeological Committee, based at the Department of Archaeology, University of Cambridge. He studies field systems and settlements using both fieldwork and historical sources. His *Fenland Landscapes and Settlement between Peterborough and March* was published in the East Anglian Archaeology series in 1987.

P. D. A. HARVEY is Emeritus Professor of Medieval History at the University of Durham. He works on medieval English social and economic history, and on the history of cartography, and publishes in both fields.

RICHARD HODGES is an archaeologist and Director of the British School at Rome. His recent publications include *Primitive and Peasant Markets* (Oxford, 1988) and *The Anglo-Saxon Achievement* (London, 1989).

DELLA HOOKE is a Research Fellow in the School of Geography, University of Birmingham, with interests in the evolution and conservation of the rural landscape. Recent works include *The Anglo-Saxon Landscape: The Kingdom of the Hwicce* (Manchester, 1985) and she has edited *Anglo-Saxon Settlements* (Oxford, 1988).

BRIAN K. ROBERTS, Senior Lecturer in Geography at the University of Durham, is concerned with using landscape evidence as a source for historical settlement studies. His most recent work is *The Making of the English Village* (London, 1987).

C. C. TAYLOR is a landscape historian, Investigator for the Royal Commission on the Historical Monuments of England and President of the Medieval Settlement Research Group. He is the author of *Village and Farmstead* (London, 1983).

PETER WADE-MARTINS is County Field Archaeologist for Norfolk and Assistant Director of the Norfolk Museums Service. In the 1960s he excavated and field-walked Anglo-Saxon and medieval settlement sites, and he has since then been running the Norfolk Archaeological Unit.

D. R. WILSON is Curator in Aerial Photography at the University of Cambridge. He has been engaged in air photography for academic research of all kinds, but is essentially a field archaeologist. He is the author of *Air Photo Interpretation for Archaeologists* (London, 1982).

STUART WRATHMELL is an archaeologist with the West Yorkshire Archaeology Service, and joint General Editor (with John Hurst) of the Wharram Research Project reports. He is the author of a forthcoming volume on the medieval peasant farmsteads at Wharram Percy.

Acknowledgements

Permission to reproduce the photographs in the volume, and sources for material referred to in the figures and tables, are gratefully acknowledged as follows:

PLATES

6.1 M. Aston A/P 18436; 6.2 Roy Canham, Wiltshire County Council, Library and Museum Service, AER 1635; 8.1 Cambridge University Collection of Air Photographs, AMT98; 8.2 Cambridge University Collection of Air Photographs, AQS45; 8.3 Cambridge University Collection of Air Photographs, AEX10; 8.4 Cambridge University Collection of Air Photographs, CHZ16; 8.5 Cambridge University Collection of Air Photographs, AAQ68; 8.6 Cambridge University Collection of Air Photographs, AAQ64; 8.7 Cambridge University Collection of Air Photographs, ARB6; 8.8 Cambridge University Collection of Air Photographs, AAQ60; 8.9 Norfolk Archaeological Unit, TF9819/ALU/AXZ5, copyright reserved; 9.1 Photograph by David Baker; 10.1 Cambridge University Collection of Air Photographs, BLD 23; 10.2 Cambridge University Collection of Air Photographs, ATU 47; 10.3 Cambridge University Collection of Air Photographs, ANW 78; 10.4 Cambridge University Collection of Air Photographs, BLD 15; 10.5 Cambridge University Collection of Air Photographs, BLC 25; 11.1 Photograph by David Hall; 16.1 Photograph by Richard Hodges.

FIGURES

4.3 Source: Ordnance Survey 6″ to 1 mile maps, First Edition 1856–65; 4.4 Sources: A. M. Armstrong, A. Mawer, F. M. Stenton and B. Dickens, *The Place-Names of Cumberland* (Cambridge University Press, 1950); and A. H. Smith, *The Place-Names of Westmorland* (2 vols, Cambridge University Press, 1967); 4.5 Source: Ordnance Survey 6″ to 1 mile maps, First Edition sheet 40 (1860) and Second Edition sheets XL SE (1898) XLI SW (1898), and V SW (1900). The analysis of structural characteristics is based on B. K. Roberts, *The Making of the English Village* (Longman, 1987) figs. 3.11 and 3.12; 6.3 Somerset County Record Office, DD/MI c/186, reproduced with permission; 6.4 Reproduced with permission from John Hunt, James Russell and the Bristol and Avon Archaeological Research Group; 9.1 Map transcript S. Coleman; © Bedfordshire County Council Planning Department; 14.1 Distribution of cruck

309

ACKNOWLEDGEMENTS

buildings after N. W. Alcock (ed.), *Cruck Construction: An Introduction and Catalogue* (Council for British Archaeology Research Report 42, 1981); 15.1 Survey plans after B. W. Cunliffe, 'Chalton, Hants: the evolution of a landscape', *Antiquaries Journal*, 53 (1973), pp. 173–90, and 'Saxon and medieval settlement pattern in the region of Chalton, Hampshire', *Medieval Archaeology*, 16 (1972), pp. 1–12; 15.2 Settlement plan after P. L. Drewett, *The Archaeology of Bullock Down, Eastbourne, East Sussex: the development of a landscape* (Sussex Archaeological Society Monograph I, 1982).

Index

Note: References in italics indicate plates, figures or tables

Index by A. R. Crook